The Four Horsemen of the Apocalypse

This book offers a new and exciting interpretation of early modern European history. Cunningham and Grell's point of departure, and a prism through which events of the period are interpreted, is Dürer's famous woodcut of the Four Horsemen of the Apocalpyse. This image came to characterise the outlook and expectations of most early modern Europeans, who experienced a dramatic rise in population, leading to repeated episodes of war, epidemics and famine. These were seen as indicating the imminent end of the world. The book is lavishly illustrated with fascinating contemporary images which, like many texts of the period, are preoccupied with apocalypticism and eschatological expectations. Lucidly written and carefully organised, it brings together religious, social, military and medical history in one survey, giving a unique insight into why the early modern world linked all the crises of the age to the Day of Judgement.

ANDREW CUNNINGHAM is a Wellcome Trust Senior Research Fellow in the Department of History and Philosophy of Science, University of Cambridge.

OLE PETER GRELL is a Lecturer in Early Modern History at the Open University.

They are general editors of the series 'History of Medicine in Context' published by Ashgate. Their numerous publications in early modern history include *Medicine and the Reformation* (edited by Grell and Cunningham, 1993); *Calvinist Exiles in Tudor and Stuart England* (by Grell, 1996); *The Anatomical Renaissance* (Cunningham, 1997); and *Health Care and Poor Relief in Counter-Reformation Europe* (by Grell and Cunningham, 1999).

The Four Horsemen of the Apocalypse

RELIGION, WAR,
FAMINE AND DEATH IN
REFORMATION EUROPE

Andrew Cunningham

Wellcome Trust Senior Research Fellow,
University of Cambridge

AND

Ole Peter Grell

Lecturer in Early Modern History,
Department of History,
the Open University

CAMBRIDGE
UNIVERSITY PRESS

PUBLISHED BY THE PRESS SYNDICATE OF THE UNIVERSITY OF CAMBRIDGE
The Pitt Building, Trumpington Street, Cambridge, United Kingdom

CAMBRIDGE UNIVERSITY PRESS
The Edinburgh Building, Cambridge CB2 2RU, UK
40 West 20th Street, New York, NY 10011-4211, USA
10 Stamford Road, Oakleigh, VIC 3166, Australia
Ruiz de Alarcón 13, 28014 Madrid, Spain
Dock House, The Waterfront, Cape Town 8001, South Africa

http://www.cambridge.org

First published 2000

Printed in the United Kingdom at the University Press, Cambridge

Typeface Quadraat, 10/14.25pt   *System* QuarkXPress™   [SE]

A catalogue record for this book is available from the British Library

ISBN 0 521 46135 9 hardback
ISBN 0 521 46701 2 paperback

Contents

Preface

The gestation of this book has been somewhat longer than we anticipated some eight years ago when we first discussed the subject. Unfortunately other duties and obligations had to take priority along the way. Considering our title and topic we are obviously relieved to have been able to finish it before the Millennium, even if we still have to rely on Cambridge University Press to publish it after that significant date!

Bearing in mind the broad coverage we intended, covering a considerable number of historical fields over more than a century and a half, and the geographical spread needed, our Four Horses(men) had to begin life in a less developed form, as foals so to speak, in a course of lectures in the Department of History and Philosophy of Science at the University of Cambridge, only to be expanded, modified and changed and then presented to students in the History Faculty in the same University. This provided us with an invaluable forum in which to test and develop our ideas, while the often enthusiastic response with which the lectures were received convinced us that we had got certain things right while other aspects had not yet been fully developed or thought through.

Considering the magnitude of the task before us we have gratefully relied on a number of collegues at home and abroad to provide us with information, assistance and encouragement. Our thanks go especially to the late Professor Bob Scribner of the University of Harvard, USA, and to Professor Michael Müller, Martin-Luther University, Halle-Wittenberg, Germany, Professor Robert Jütte, Institut für Geschichte der Medizin der Robert Bosch Stiftung, Stuttgart, Germany, Professor Christopher R. Friedrichs, University of British Columbia, Canada, Professor Ernestine van der Wall, University of Leiden, The Netherlands, Professor Mark Greengrass, University of Sheffield, and Dr Sachiko Kusukawa, University of Cambridge, not to forget a number of constructive anonymous readers for the Press. The responsibility for the final product, however, remains ours alone.

We should like to thank Cambridge University Press and Richard Fisher in particular for taking on this project at an early stage and offering patient and helpful advice at several key stages in the process. We are also grateful to the many libraries and museums which have provided us with photographs of the broadsheets and illustrations used in this work.

ANDREW CUNNINGHAM

Cambridge, The Feast of St Michael and All Angels, 1999   OLE PETER GRELL

And there appeared another wonder in heaven and behold a great
    red dragon, having seven heads and ten horns, and seven
    crowns upon his heads. . . .
And there was war in heaven: Michael and his angels fought
    against the dragon; and the dragon fought and his angels, and
    prevailed not.

(*Revelation* 12:3 *and* 7–8)

Illustrations

FIGURE

TABLES

1 Introduction: An Apocalyptic Age

More than any other period of European history the sixteenth and early seventeenth centuries were characterised by apocalyptic expectations, eschatological speculations and millenarian dreams. To contemporaries it felt as though they were living through the Last Days. This preoccupation with the end of the world, the end of time, and the arrival of the thousand-year kingdom of Christ, was rooted in the deep religious, social, political, economic and – above all – the demographic crises of the time. The year 1500, being a half-millennium, was greeted as a year of special apocalyptic significance. Even the Roman curia, which actively discouraged apocalyptic speculation, had announced 1500 as a special Jubilee year, a holy year, where pilgrimage would be particularly rewarded. The increase in apocalyptic preaching, claiming that the arrival of Antichrist was imminent, in fact obliged the Fifth Lateran Council in 1513 to forbid preaching about such matters.

Historians have long recognised the period 1490 to 1648 as an age of crises in Europe. There was crisis in religion: Eastern Christianity, with the fall of Constantinople in 1453, had come under the control of the Turkish Muslims, who continued to threaten Western Christianity throughout the period, while Western Christianity itself, for so long controlled by the Roman curia, broke up after 1517 with Luther's 95 theses being pinned to the door of the Castle Church in Wittenberg, and the religious upheavals which followed. There was crisis in the social structure: feudal society was in the process of breaking up, with peasants in rebellion in Germany from the 1520s, in Scandinavia from the 1530s, in England in 1536, in France in the later sixteenth century. There was crisis in the political realm: as the medieval feudal states became obsolete, so war became endemic across Europe as new dynastic and territorial states were brought into existence. There was crisis in the economy: a money economy came to replace the feudal economy of services and exchange of goods, and inflation, until then relatively unknown to contemporaries, brought untold hardship and starvation to many. There was crisis in demography: for the first time since before the Black Death of 1348, towards the end of the fifteenth century the European population began to expand inexorably, and people began moving in great numbers from the countryside to the towns and cities. Thus what had been a stable society, where the majority could expect to continue the life of their forefathers in the locality where they were born, became a dynamic society, characterised by migration from country to town and by enforced mass emigration across Europe. The Jews were expelled from Spain in 1492, more than 100,000 Reformed fled the southern Netherlands from 1567 onwards as a consequence of the Spanish reconquest by the Duke of Alva, and thousands of Huguenots fled France after the St Bartholomew Day massacre in 1572, and these were only some of the major crises of dislocation.

Finally, there was a crisis in world-view, moving from the known to the unknown: the voyages of Christopher Columbus from 1492 first revealed parts of the world hitherto unknown to Europeans, especially the so-called 'new world' of America, while the mental voyage of Nicolaus Copernicus, *On the Revolutions of the Heavenly Spheres*, published in 1543, revealed that the earth was not the centre of the universe, but revolved around the sun as a mere planet, an observation so radical that it took nearly a hundred years to gain full acceptance. Indeed, 'crisis' has been one of the main categories of research and explanation among early modern historians over the last twenty years.[1]

What these crises had in common for contemporaries, was that they were all interpreted in religious and biblical terms, and especially that they were interpreted apocalyptically: as evidence of the approaching Day of Judgement and the return of Christ. The tendency of modern historiography to divide and to develop subdisciplines such as demographic history, military history, Reformation history, medical history, agricultural history and social history (to mention just a few) has certainly enhanced our knowledge of different areas of the early modern past. But in the process it has unwittingly sacrificed much of the contemporary world-view. Our book is an attempt to recapture something of contemporary religious and apocalyptic interpretations of the crises of the early modern period, on the one hand, while, on the other, using some of the insights offered by modern specialised historiography in order to understand why an apocalyptic interpretation of events and crises in early modern life made sense to a Christian society under stress.

One of the distinctive features of the Reformation was the emphasis on the Bible, especially the Gospel, as the basis for Christian faith and life. For the first time, through the benefits of the recently invented art of printing, the Bible, whole or in part, became widely available, not only to the learned world in Latin, or to the common people who themselves could read it in the affordable vernacular translations, but also to those who could not read at all, through illustrated editions and through other people reading the text aloud.[2] Appearing as it did in an apocalyptic climate of fear and anxiety,[3] the Bible came to be closely read, especially in the growing evangelical circles, for evidence that the many crises of war, famine, disease and faith that people were experiencing, were indeed signs of the End and the Coming of Christ. Thus the growing availability of biblical texts in turn served to enhance the apocalyptic mood of the age.

Christ's own prophecy of what would happen in the Last Days, before His return, was frequently quoted and used in sermons. There are two accounts of it in the Bible, one by Matthew (24: 3–13), and the other by Luke (21: 5–32). According to Matthew, Jesus foretold His own return like this:

> many shall come in my name, saying, I am Christ; and shall deceive many.
> And ye shall hear of wars and rumours of wars: see that ye be not troubled: for all these things must come to pass, but the end is not yet.
> For nation shall rise against nation, and kingdom against kingdom: and there shall be famines, and pestilences, and earthquakes, in divers places.
> All these are the beginning of sorrows.
> Then shall they deliver you up to be afflicted, and shall kill you: and ye shall be hated of all nations for my name's sake.
> And then shall many be offended, and shall betray one another, and shall hate one another.
> And many false prophets shall rise, and shall deceive many.
> And because iniquity shall abound, the love of many shall wax cold.
> But he that shall endure unto the end, the same shall be saved.
> And this gospel of the kingdom shall be preached in all the world for a witness unto all nations; and then shall the end come.

False Christs, wars and rumours of wars, famines and pestilences, Christians persecuted and killed, false prophets, the dominance of evil and the decline of mutual love, and finally the preaching of the true Word again: all these things could be seen to be happening in this period. In the account by Luke, Christ also spoke of portents in the sky, such as eclipses and comets: 'And there shall be signs in the sun, and in the moon, and in the stars; and upon the earth distress of nations, with perplexity; the sea and the waves roaring.' It was quite clear to people at the time that prophecy was being fulfilled and that the End was near.

It was Antichrist who, more than any other figure or event, heralded the imminence of the Apocalypse. 'Little children', the apostle John had warned the early Christians, 'it is the last time: and as ye have heard that antichrist shall come, even now are there many antichrists; whereby we know that it is the last time' (1 John 2: 18). The arrival and identification of Antichrist was essential to Protestants in particular, and helped convince them that they were indeed living through the Latter Days. Early on, Luther and the other reformers identified Antichrist as the pope. Antichrist provided the basis for one of the most successful works of visual propaganda in the early Reformation, Lucas Cranach's *Passional Christi und Antichristi* (1521).[4] To speak of Antichrist was to speak of the Last Days. Thus, it has to be remembered that whenever people of the early modern period spoke of Antichrist they were in fact talking in apocalyptic terms.

Christ's prophecies of what was to happen around the Day of Judgement seemed to be expounded at length in the Book of Revelation, or Apocalypse, the vision of John. Thus this, the most visionary document of all the books of the Bible, naturally became the most frequently printed, and also the most frequently illustrated. Between 1498 and 1650, at least 750 separate editions of the Book of Revelation, and commentaries on it, were published, many of them in convenient and cheap editions.[5] Considering that this figure does not include the many reprints of these editions, or the many editions of the Bible in which it was included – sometimes as the only illustrated part – it is clear that the impact of this text on popular perception and culture was colossal.

Of all the illustrations of the Book of Revelation, none became more influential than those made by Albrecht Dürer for an edition produced in both a Latin and a German version, published in Nuremberg in 1498. For Dürer's edition seems to have reached an exceptionally large audience, according to modern research.[6] And of the fifteen illustrations Dürer produced for this edition, the one that became the most celebrated and familiar was that of the Four Horsemen of the Apocalypse (Plate 1.1). This is undoubtedly also the image which most potently encapsulates the anxieties and preoccupations of the age.

The text which it is illustrating is as follows:

Plate 1.1 (opposite) Albrecht Dürer, *Four Horsemen of the Apocalypse* (1498)

And I saw when the Lamb opened one of the seals, and I heard, as it were
    the noise of thunder, one of the four beasts saying, Come and see.
And I saw, and behold a white horse: and he that sat on him had a bow; and
    a crown was given unto him: and he went forth conquering, and to conquer.

And when he had opened the second seal, I heard the second beast say,
  Come and see.
And there went out another horse that was red: and power was given to him
  that sat thereon to take peace from the earth, and that they should kill one
  another: and there was given unto him a great sword.
And when he had opened the third seal, I heard the third beast say, Come
  and see. And I beheld, and lo a black horse; and he that sat on him had a
  pair of balances in his hand.
And I heard a voice in the midst of the four beasts say, A measure of wheat
  for a penny, and three measures of barley for a penny; and see thou hurt not
  the oil and the wine.
And when he had opened the fourth seal, I heard the voice of the fourth beast
  say, Come and see.
And I looked, and behold a pale horse: and his name that sat on him was
  Death, and Hell followed with him. And power was given unto them over the
  fourth part of the earth, to kill with sword, and with hunger, and with death,
  and with the beasts of the earth.

Previous illustrations of the Four Horsemen in late medieval block-books and paintings had all, in accordance with the text, portrayed them separately, arriving one at a time with their curses of war, famine, disease and death. Most of these pictures were relatively anodyne and undramatic in their portrayal of the disasters prophesied in the text.[7] This is particularly evident in the Dutch block-books of the Apocalypse – thin, hand-made, picture books of the late fifteenth century[8] (Plate 1.2). By contrast, Dürer's newly invented modelling system, which Erwin Panofsky has termed 'dynamic calligraphy', enabled Dürer to enlarge the format and present the Four Horsemen together, and to do so with great dramatic force.[9]

Dürer's image of the Four Horsemen riding across the sky, with the archangel hovering above them, conquering and slaying everything before them, while the monster of Hell devours the mighty of this world, is vivid and haunting, and it came to affect generations of artists. For instance, when Lucas Cranach, the court painter of Luther's patron the Elector of Saxony, provided the illustrations for Luther's German New Testament of 1522, he took it as his model[10] (Plate 1.3). The only part of this New Testament to be illustrated was the Book of Revelation, and it was Luther who insisted on this, despite the doubts he then had about its authenticity and value. Thus, as this picture appeared in the first Protestant vernacular edition of the New Testament, it set the agenda not only for subsequent illustrated editions of the Bible, but also for Protestant and Reformed interpretations of the Apocalypse. A century later, the leading German illustrator, engraver and publisher, the Frankfurt-based Mattheus Merian, was still being similarly inspired in the engravings he produced for the illustrated Bibles he published between 1625 and 1630. The Merian Bible became the most widely circulated family Bible in southern Germany and Switzerland[11] (Plate 1.4). Merian elaborated Dürer's concept. While the Four Horsemen still charge together across the sky, Merian also includes in the same pictorial space the prophecies which concern the opening of the fifth and sixth seals in the Book of Revelation, chapter 6. Thus we see how 'the stars of heaven fell unto the earth', and how a great earthquake was followed by the sun becoming black as sackcloth of hair, 'and the moon became as blood'. And in the top left-hand corner of the engraving, we see under the altar 'the souls of them that were slain for the word of God' being redeemed.[12]

Not only was Dürer's image of the Four Horsemen innovative artistically, but his edition of the Book of Revelation was also innovative in textual terms, for this was the first time that the full text appeared in an illustrated edition. The Dutch block-books, by comparison, had only offered brief inscriptions, cut in relief into the woodblock of the picture itself. The popular impact of bringing the two together – text and illustration – in an age preoccupied with these themes, cannot be overestimated.[13]

Ours, of course, is far from being the first modern book on apocalyptic expectations in the early modern period. Out of what has become a considerable literature, a few works need to be mentioned. Norman Cohn's celebrated book *The Pursuit of the Millenium, Revolutionary Millenarians and Mystical Anarchists of the Middle Ages* (New York, 1961), takes the apocalyptic story well into the sixteenth century. His main concern is with millenarian thought and where it led to outbreaks of social radicalism and revolution. Robert Lerner, by contrast, in a series of studies, has demonstrated that millenarianism was a widespread and constant phenomenon in European history by the end of the middle ages.[14] Katherine Firth, Bryan Ball and Paul Christianson have all shown that apocalyptic expectations were pervasive in late sixteenth- and early seventeenth-century England, while Charles Webster has shown the impact on social thinking and planning of such expectations amongst English Puritans in the period 1626–40.[15] Robert Barnes has done the same for Germany and German Lutheranism.[16] Jean Delumeau, the French *Annales* historian, has explored the pervasiveness of sin and fear in Europe in our period and beyond (1400–1800), emphasising their apocalyptic roots.[17] In the light of so many recent studies on the theme, it is clear that there was an extraordinary diffusion of apocalyptic expectations in the period.[18]

Plate 1.2 Dutch block-
book, *Four Horsemen of the
Apocalypse* (c. 1470)

Our book differs from all these in two major ways. First, with respect to chronology, we limit our study to the period from the 1490s to 1648, which we consider to be the apocalyptic period par excellence. Dürer's famous woodcut of the Four Horsemen, which so neatly encapsulated the apocalyptic mood of the age, was of course published in 1498, shortly after the brief millenarian reign of the friar Savonarola in Florence. Throughout the century and a half we deal with here, the apocalyptic vision and eschatological speculations can be found across Europe, but especially within the Protestant world. Not only did it affect theologians and the learned, but it shaped the world-view of common people, as can be seen from sermons and from some of the most widely diffused popular literature, such as almanacs and astrological forecasts. The ongoing conflict between Protestantism in all its forms, and Counter-Reformation Catholicism, ensured that the apocalyptic mood would continue throughout the sixteenth century, with the Wars of Religion in France and the war of independence in the Netherlands. In the first decades of the seventeenth century the apocalyptic and millenarian temperature rose considerably, not least through the formation of the Protestant Union and the Catholic League in Germany, and of course the outbreak of the Thirty Years War. By 1648, and the end of the Thirty Years War, this mood had largely evaporated in most of Europe, not least because the confrontation between Protestantism and Catholicism – between Christ and Antichrist, according to Protestant terminology – was resolved by the victories of the great Protestant 'saviour', Gustavus Adolphus of Sweden, and the intervention of France on the Protestant side in the 1630s. Only in England were the apocalyptic and millenarian expectations given an extra lease of life through the confrontations between 'Arminians' and Puritans in the 1630s, the Civil Wars and Interregnum. If the age of confessionalism came to an end around the middle of the seventeenth century, so too did most of the social, political and material crises of the age which had underpinned the apocalyptic vision. Demographic growth began to level out around 1650, and peacetime famine became less common. The 'military revolution' petered out in mid-century. Plague virtually disappeared from Europe.

Second, our book differs from others on apocalyptic themes with respect to interpretation, for we take literally the preoccupation that people of the period had with the mental image of the Four Horsemen in the Book of Revelation.[19] This image brought together war, famine, disease and faith, leading people to interpret social, political and religious problems in apocalyptic terms, as indications of the imminence of the Last

Plate 1.3 Lucas Cranach, *Four Horsemen of the Apocalypse* (1522)

Plate 1.4 Mattheus Merian, *Four Horsemen of the Apocalypse* (1630)

Days. Many works and sermons were published during the period, which interpreted contemporary sufferings as God's visitations, either in the persons of the Four Horsemen, or as the three scourges of God's anger: war, famine and disease.

The figure on the White Horse, whom we treat first, had since the later middle ages come to be identified with the Second Coming of Christ the Conqueror and the time leading up to the Day of Judgement.[20] Not surprisingly, Luther's appearance on the scene as a religious reformer and recoverer of the Gospel, came to be seen in a prophetic and eschatological light. Luther was repeatedly referred to as a prophet of the Last Days, in particular as the second Elijah, sent to expose Antichrist and announce the Second Coming of Christ. As has been lucidly stated by Bob Scribner:

> The contemporary usage of *reformatio* was laden with overtones of popular belief. It would occur through a decisive intervention of God in human history, bringing about a 'great change' in the state of the world. This 'great change' had utopian and apocalyptic features, for it would inaugurate either a new age of the world, an 'age of the spirit', or even perhaps the Last Days themselves, as foretold in the *Book of Revelation*. It would be announced by a *reformator*, a holy man or prophet sent by God as the instrument of this change. Luther's central role in the movements of religious reform that arose after 1520 can be traced in great part to the fact that he was identified with this figure.[21]

Not only did Luther and his contemporaries consider Luther as part of the unfolding eschatological drama, but the view that they were living through the Last Days was shared by virtually all the reformers. The imminence of the Second Coming accounts for the urgency with which the reformers preached the Gospel and pressed forward the Reformation.

The Protestant Reformation can indeed be seen as a response to the demands and stresses of these apocalyptic expectations. As such, it also helped generate and amplify them. Thus Luther's challenge to papal authority, the questioning of received dogma, the emphasis on Scripture, faith and grace, and the ambition to take the Church back to its apostolic roots, were all responses to the religious and social anxieties of the age. It might even be claimed that the facts of late fifteenth- and early sixteenth-century life, namely the perceived increase in war, famine and disease, created the particular eschatological atmosphere in which the Reformation emerged.

Such expectations were confirmed by the stars. Comets, new stars, great conjunctions, all seemed to confirm that the Last Days were imminent. Natural and supernatural events similarly indicated that the Day of

Judgement was near and that the world in its old age was turned upside down. The sky and Nature were continuously scanned for evidence of the Second Coming: natural disasters (disaster literally meaning 'negative star') such as floods, storms, monstrous births and beings, and a great increase in witchcraft and demonic activity, were all part of a host of extraordinary phenomena which foretold the End of Time.

The second Horseman is on the Red Horse, the horse of war. War was generated by the collapse of the traditional feudal structures, and by the princes trying to establish absolutist and dynastically oriented states. On the one hand the princes fought their noble subjects, and on the other hand, as was the case in Germany and the Netherlands, they fought their imperial overlord. This increase in warfare not only led to a growth of armies but also to an improvement of military hardware and tactics, which in turn caused greater devastation, injury and death. These larger armies made greater organisational, financial and economic demands on society, they often devastated the countryside and cities they marched through, bringing in their wake famine, disease and death to the civilian population. The period came to be characterised by large-scale sieges, mercenary armies, and increasingly powerful instruments of destruction, such as guns and cannons. Large-scale conflicts took place over many areas, such as the Peasants' Wars of the 1520s, the Schmalkaldic Wars of the 1540s, the Wars of Religion in France from the 1560s to the 1590s, the Eighty Years War between Spain and the United Provinces, and the Thirty Years War which involved most of the European powers. The two last wars were both finally concluded in 1648. Thus the core of this section on the Red Horse treats the military revolution, the growth of armies, the improvement of weaponry and tactics, the spoliation necessary to provision the military machine, and especially the consequences of this new type of warfare on society: the fear it generated and the apocalyptic context in which it was interpreted. We also discuss the development of military surgery and medicine to cope with new kinds of wounds (especially from gunshot and shrapnel), diseases associated with armies, and the creation of a new type of surgeon to tend the military machine.

The third Horseman is on the Black Horse, the horse of famine. The population level of Europe had seen a steady decline after the Black Death of 1348. It did not start to recover until the late fifteenth century, and did not reach its pre-1348 level again until 1500. But then the rate of increase of the European population continued at a high level until the mid-seventeenth century, and only then did it begin to stabilise. While the

Figure 1.1 Population changes in Europe, AD 1000–1900. From David Grigg, *Population Growth and Agrarian Change. An Historical Perspective*, Cambridge 1980, p. 52.

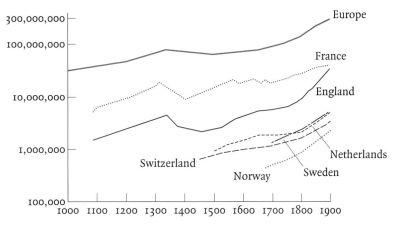

absolute population either of Europe as a whole or of any particular country, cannot be known with certainty, yet the evidence that the population increased markedly is overwhelming. In fact the population probably doubled in these 150 years[22] (Figure 1.1). Accordingly, this period witnessed a radical transformation of the demographic trend, moving for the first time for well over a century from a static or contracting population towards an expanding population and economy. Contemporaries were very aware of the population increase and the transformation of cultivation that followed on from it. They felt that the countryside was full and the towns were filled to bursting-point. A chronicler writing in 1550 about the people of Swabia, for instance, said they had increased in recent times to such an extent that 'they started to plough the fields and stock the meadows once more, and the place where a village had stood years before began to look like a village again . . . never in the memory of man has the land been so much opened up. No corner, even in the densest forest or highest hills, but is ploughed and inhabited.'[23] Indeed, this demographic change, this population pressure, underlay all the crises of the age: it can be said to have created the crisis mentality which made the 'Four Horsemen of the Apocalypse' the popular image of the age.

The population growth put stresses on the food supply, and made crop failures more critical, causing intense famines which were perceived to be more catastrophic than before, and which had major social impact. For instance the harvest failures in the years 1490–4, 1500–4 and 1515–19 caused severe famine in Germany, and have been seen as a major cause of the Peasants' Wars of the 1520s.[24] For France it has been estimated that general famine was a serious problem on seven occasions in the fifteenth century, on thirteen occasions in the sixteenth century, and on eleven occasions in the seventeenth.[25] Crises in the agrarian economy, caused by vulnerable systems of cultivation, bad weather and the effects of human conflict, meant that a general crisis of agrarian production was always an imminent risk. The history of food production and supply in the period is therefore explored in this section on the Black Horse, together with its effects on the functioning of society, on public perceptions of crisis and on communal responses as in the creation of poor laws. The marginal existence of the majority of the population is in contrast to the access of the upper classes to luxury items, such as spices and other specialities, including the conspicuous consumption at grand feasts.

The fourth and last Horseman is mounted on the Pale Horse, the harbinger of disease and death. Here we cover the incidence of the major epidemic diseases of the age, their nature and their effects. Plague and pox were the most scary of the epidemics, and constantly present. Average life expectancy was about thirty-five years, and disease was a constant threat. The population pressure put under great stress the traditional ways of coping with disease, epidemics and death, especially in the growing towns. This led to the creation of a body of health regulations, medical policing, the foundation of hospitals and a gradual expansion of medical provision, most of which served a double purpose: Christian charity and social control. The increase of war, trade, travel and social interchange all facilitated the rapid spread of epidemic disease. This in turn helped emphasise the ephemeral nature of early modern life, and guaranteed a continuation of the late medieval fascination with death, dying and decay.

In taking our point of departure from Dürer's image of the Four Horsemen of the Apocalypse, we have in the course of writing this book been greatly concerned with the importance and impact of mass-produced illustrations such as woodcuts and engravings in the sixteenth and early seventeenth centuries. This was of course the period where affordable printed books for the first time became available to ordinary people who could read. The invention of printing was considered, even by Catholic church officials, to be a gift from God.[26] By the early sixteenth century the invention of print had acquired eschatological significance. This was acknowledged by Jean Albertin, a priest from the Valais in southern Switzerland, who in 1524 wrote that before the End of the World 'books will be revealed in the face of the firmament, and everyone will see them at the same time. The books for the most part will be revealed by the art of printing, through which the infinite number of books which were lost will come to light.'[27] It was, however, the Reformers who made real use of the potential of the printing press as a mass medium.[28] Luther himself described printing as 'God's highest and extremest act of grace, by which the business of the Gospel is driven forward', and he also considered it to be 'the last flame before the extinction of the world'.[29] Similarly John Foxe, the English Protestant author of *The Book of Martyrs*, stated that 'God has opened the press to preach, whose voice the Pope is never able to stop with all the puissance of his triple crown'.[30] The Reformation led to a publication explosion. At the beginning of the sixteenth century some forty new editions of works in German were being published each year; by 1519 this had reached 110; four years later the presses produced nearly 500 new titles, of which more than 400 were generated by the Reformation.[31]

This period was also the first time in history when illustrative material became widely available at prices most people could afford. Most of these illustrations appeared as single-leaf broadsheets, sometimes including an explanatory text in prose or verse. We often talk about an 'information revolution' taking place towards the end of the twentieth century. How much more apt is this description for what happened from the beginning of the sixteenth century, when books small and large, and illustrated broadsheets were suddenly everywhere. Being a hybrid form of image and print, and given the nature of reading in this period, when texts were often read aloud, the broadsheet encompassed image, text and oral communication, and was aimed at the literate as well as the illiterate mass market. It was a hugely efficient mode of propaganda for Protestants, which was aimed at both the committed and the uncommitted. Germany can be considered to have been backward in terms of painting and sculpture, especially compared to Italy, at the beginning of the sixteenth century, but this was not the case with respect to the woodcut, which through the collaboration of painters, draughtsmen, woodblock cutters, and printers, both technically and artistically came to surpass other forms of images and was soon the dominant form of visual communication. It was not only in the hands of masters such as Albrecht Dürer and Lucas Cranach that this medium became so influential, but also through their lesser-known pupils such as Hans Sebald Beham and Erhard Schoen. By the end of the sixteenth century the woodcut was gradually replaced by the engraving, which further extended the artistic possibilities. The 'low status and ephemerality' of print and the printed image meant that they were available for the expression of popular issues, which were unlikely to be addressed in another medium.[32] Luther himself recognised the instructive value of printed images and illustrations 'above all for the sake of children and the simple folk, who are more easily moved by pictures and images to recall divine history, than through mere words or doctrines'.[33] Early modern historians have come to appreciate the role and significance of the printed word in the sixteenth and early seventeenth centuries; but we should not forget how important images and illustrations were in the creation and dissemination of ideas. It has been estimated that popular broadsheets appeared in editions of only about 350. This, however, seems a serious underestimation of the print runs, especially as we know that on occasion local authorities were able to seize up to 1,500 copies of a single broadsheet from a printer.[34]

Accordingly our own book is a marriage of text and image, especially in the parts concerned with religion, war and disease, because these issues were the ones which the people of the time themselves chose to use printed images and text for, in order to inform, persuade, ridicule and warn. Of course, on occasion we also use images in a more conventional way, to illustrate particular points.

For obvious reasons we have had to be selective in this book. In describing the impact of the Four Horsemen of the Apocalypse, we have often been impressionistic. Because the apocalyptic mood was widespread and pervasive across Europe, especially in the areas which became Protestant, we have tried to achieve as great a geographical coverage as possible, and across the whole timescale. Often we have preferred to use less well-known examples in order to illustrate our points, rather than concentrate on the rich and often familiar material from the English Civil War in particular. Our debts to other scholars are considerable. We have, however, also included fresh material and, we believe, some new interpretations.

2 The White Horse: Religion, Revelation and Reformation

> And I saw when the Lamb opened one of the seals, and I heard, as it were the noise of thunder, one of the four beasts saying, Come and see. And I saw, and behold a white horse: and he that sat on him had a bow; and a crown was given unto him: and he went forth conquering, and to conquer. (Revelation 6: 1–2)

LUTHER, THE REFORMATION AND THE LAST DAYS

By the second decade of the sixteenth century a growing number of people had come to identify the conqueror on the white horse with the Second Coming of Christ, and the time leading up to the Day of Judgement when the godly would be saved and the ungodly punished. This view was closely related to the break-up of Western Christianity which had commenced with Luther's 95 theses being pinned to the door of the Castle Church in Wittenberg on 31 October 1517 and the rapid growth of the evangelical movement with its renewed emphasis on the Gospel which followed during the 1520s.

There was, of course, ample biblical evidence for such an interpretation; white was the colour associated with purity, sinlessness and God's appearance, while the arrows represented God's wrath and punishment, and the bow was seen as a symbol of God's covenant with his elect people.[1] Furthermore, this was an interpretation which was easily facilitated by Dürer's famous illustration of the four horsemen. In this context Luther's claim to have retrieved the Gospel and the true church from human corruption and manipulation proved particularly cataclysmic and served to encourage the popular view of him as an apocalyptic prophet and forerunner of the imminent return of Christ.

Thus the Reformation came to be seen as evidence of an unfolding eschatological drama and a sign of the impending Day of Judgement not only by contemporaries, but also by Luther and most, if not all, the evangelical Reformers. Without this important aspect, and the sense of urgency attached to it, the impact of Protestantism would undoubtedly have proved far less rapid and significant. The fact that the Reformers were able to appropriate the apocalyptic mood of the age for their own propaganda purposes proved crucial. The value of being able to claim that they were the godly troops of Christ fighting the ungodly soldiers of the papacy – Antichrist in Rome – in the last eschatological battle portrayed in the books of Daniel and Revelation can, as we shall see, hardly be overestimated.

Albrecht Dürer with his roots in the humanistic milieu of Nuremberg became an early follower of Martin Luther. In a letter written at the beginning of the year 1520 to Georg Spalatin, secretary to the Elector Frederick the Wise of Saxony, Dürer asked Spalatin to beg the Elector to protect Luther 'for the sake of Christian truth' which matters more 'than all the riches and power of this world'.[2] While later in mid-May 1521, during his journey through the Netherlands, rumours reached Dürer in Antwerp that the Imperial safe conduct granted Luther in order that he appear at the Diet of Worms (April 1521) had been broken and Luther, 'a man enlightened by the Holy Gost, a follower of Christ', as Dürer put it, 'treacherously' taken prisoner. The rumour was only correct in giving the place of Luther's imprisonment as being near Eisenach. Luther, however, had not been arrested by the Emperor, but had, in fact, been 'kidnapped' by agents of Frederick the Wise who wanted to provide him with protection within the walls of Wartburg Castle. Undoubtedly the thinking of Dürer, as well as that of Frederick the Wise, was influenced by the fate of Johan Hus, the Bohemian martyr, who had been granted safe conduct by Emperor Sigismund a century earlier to appear at the Council of Constance, only to be arrested and burnt at the stake as a heretic.

The rumours made it impossible for Dürer to find out whether or not Luther had been killed, but even so, he was convinced that Luther had suffered for the sake of Christian truth and because he had done battle 'with the un-Christlike papacy'. For Dürer there was no doubt that this was an event of apocalyptic proportions, and he discussed it in great detail in his diary:

> But, Lord, Thou willest, ere Thou judgest, that as Thy Son Jesus Christ was constrained to die by the hands of the priests and rise from the dead and after to ascend to heaven, that so too, in like manner, it should be with Thy follower, Martin Luther, whose life the pope compasses, with money, treacherously towards God, him, Thou wilt quicken again. And as Thou, Lord, ordainedst that Jerusalem should be destroyed, so wilt Thou also destroy this selfassumed authority of the Roman chair. O Lord, give us thereafter the new beautified Jerusalem, which descends from heaven, whereof the Apocalypse writes, the holy pure gospel which is not darkened by human doctrine.

The fact that Luther, God's prophet, once more had made the unadulterated Gospel available to Man, could only mean that the Second Coming of Christ, and the end of the world, as indicated in the Book of Revelation, was near:

> Oh, ye Christian men, pray God for help, for his judgement draws near and His justice shall appear. Then shall we behold the innocent blood which the pope, priests, bishops, and monks have shed, judged and condemned. Apocalypse: 'These are the slain who lie beneath the altar of God and cry for vengeance, to whom the voice of God answers, Await the full number of the innocent slain, then will I judge'.[3]

Dürer was far from unique among early evangelicals in viewing Luther as an apocalyptic prophet who had appeared to preach the Gospel while simultaneously announcing that the final period of the world had commenced and the eschatological end-game was in place. This view of Luther and the Reformation as representing the final eschatological events before the return of Christ was reinforced by a wealth of medieval popular prophecies, which were widely circulated and printed by the beginning of the sixteenth century. Hildegard of Bingen (d. 1179), whose prophecy that the world would sink into deep corruption before the true Church would be recovered shortly before the End, was seen as further proof of the apocalyptic urgency and relevance of the evangelical message and as such it was published by the Lutheran pastor, Andreas Osiander, in Nuremberg in 1527.[4] Similarly, the so-called Magdeburg prophecy, which forecast woe and danger to the Church, the rise of Antichrist, famines, plagues, while the whole world would be conquered by the 'beast of the West' and the 'lion of the East', was seen as confirmation that tremendous and apocalyptic changes were at hand. These forecasts achieved lasting influence during our period not least because they were included in the influential and often reprinted *Carion's Chronicle*, first published in 1532 with the assistance of Luther's friend and collaborator Philip Melanchthon.[5] However, by far the most significant of these prophecies were those of the fifteenth-century Franciscan monk, Johann Hilten, who had predicted the rise of a great reformer who in 1516 would initiate a reformation of the Church. No clearer proof could be given for Luther's prophetic consequence, and even the Reformer himself accepted this prophecy.[6]

Another Observant Franciscan, Johann Eberlin von Günzburg, who became one of Luther's early followers after having read his famous pamphlets from 1520, *Address to the Christian Nobility of the German Nation*, *The Babylonian Captivity of the Church* and *The Freedom of the Christian*, and whose writings and sermons proved particularly popular with the laity, published a pamphlet in 1524 entitled, *A friendly Warning to all pious Christians in Augsburg, where it will be shown that Dr. Martin Luther was sent from God*, which portrayed Luther as a latter-day prophet.[7]

It is somewhat paradoxical, considering Luther's deep hostility to the mendicant orders, that members of one of them especially, the Franciscans, indirectly and directly should contribute so much to the success of the Reformation in general, and its eschatological appeal in particular. This was, not least, due to the fact that they and their founder Francis of Assisi had become the main heirs to the prophecies and interpretation of the Book of Revelation by the Calabrian abbot Joachim of Fiore (1131–1202), by far the most original and influential prophetic thinker of the medieval period. As opposed to other medieval theologians who all interpreted the Book of Revelation as an allegorical document, Joachim introduced a literal and historical interpretation which underlined the fulfilment of prophecy throughout the history of the Church. Using the Bible as his key Joachim divided the history of Man into three stages, each presided over by a person of the Trinity. First had been the age of the Father, where man lived in fear under the Law; second followed the age of the Son, an age of faith and teaching in which Joachim himself lived. This would soon be followed by a third and final age, that of the Spirit, which would be characterised by Christian love and spirituality, which was just around the corner by 1200, and would, according to Joachim, last for a few generations before the Final Judgement. Despite its positive connotations the age of the Spirit was by no means seen as an age of perfection by Joachim. However, many of his readers interpreted it differently. Thus it served to encourage millenarianism and Joachim's writings led others to see them as proof of an earthly millennium to come.[8] Joachim's work became increasingly popular among Protestants during the sixteenth century. Even if his Trinitarian division of history was never accepted, Joachim's views, despite being both complicated and deeply obscure, proved influential in establishing a historical interpretation of the Book of Revelation among Protestants, who came to see and use it as a key to the continuous history of the Church in what was then perceived to be its Last Days.

Accordingly we should not be surprised to discover that the first two Protestant commentaries on the Book of Revelation were published by two former Franciscans, Francis Lambert and Sebastian Meyer, whose works appeared in 1528 and 1539 respectively. Lambert, who originated from Avignon, had arrived in Zurich in 1522 where he had been strongly influenced by Zwingli. From there he had gone to Wittenberg where Luther had supported him, but before he arrived in Marburg to reorganise the church in Hesse for Landgrave Philip, Lambert had spent time in Strassburg where he had heard the Spiritualist, 'Strassburg Prophets'. As can be expected his commentary portrayed the papacy and the Turks as the embodiment of Antichrist, but more surprisingly he proved himself to be an early mainstream, Protestant chiliast, expecting a brief period of peace on earth after the fall of Antichrist which he equated with the millenial age in Revelation 20. Evidently his sojourn in Strassburg had radicalised his ideas. Sebatian Meyer became a minister in Bern where he took a leading role in the reformation of the city after the religious disputation in 1528. His commentary, even if it is hostile to the Catholic Church in general and the papacy in particular, is a far more cautious text than Lambert's; however, had the planned illustrated edition from the 1540s been published with Matthias Gerung's forceful woodcuts and their pertinent identification of the papacy with Antichrist, its significance might have been considerably greater.[9]

In 1522 Michael Stifel, a former Augustinian monk like Luther, published his first evangelical work, entitled *Von der christförmigen Lehre Luthers ein überaus schön künstlich Lied samt seiner Nebenauslegung* (an extremely beautifully artful song about Luther's teaching shaped by Christ including its explanation), which went further than just portraying Luther as a prophet by identifying him with the angel in Revelation 14: 6f.:

> Then I saw another angel flying in midheaven, with an eternal gospel to proclaim to those who dwell on earth, to every nation and tribe and tongue and people; and he said with a loud voice, 'Fear God and give him glory, for the hour of his judgement has come.'

Considering Stifel's lifelong preoccupation with eschatology it is not surprising to learn that it was in 1520, through his reading of the Book of Revelation, that he reached his evangelical faith and realised that Pope Leo X was Antichrist.[10]

Stifel's apocalyptic identification of Luther with the angel caught on, not only in the general sense as a messenger from God, but also as an angel sent to overthrow the papacy, the Babylonian whore, as can be seen from pamphlets published during the early 1520s.[11]

Luther, however, was also portrayed as a New Testament apostle, as can be seen from a pamphlet published by 'the student Laux Gemigger' in 1520, but predominantly he was seen as a prophet, in particular as a second

Elijah, who was identified with one of the two witnesses mentioned in Revelation 11:3–13, sent to expose Antichrist's identity.[12] The first reference to Luther as a second Elijah appears to have materialised as early as January 1520, and surprisingly not from one of his immediate followers, but from the Swiss Reformer Huldrych Zwingli.[13] The following year the evangelical preacher, Johannes Mathesius, claimed in a pamphlet that Luther was God's instrument, Elijah sent out of Paradise, finally to reveal the underhand actions of Antichrist and his helpers. This identification of Luther with the prophet Elijah became and remained common throughout the Reformation period, and Luther was constantly referred to as the 'Elijah of this most ruinous and last age' or 'Elijah of the last times, who restores all things', while some evangelical converts gripped by the apocalyptic fervour of the age began dating their letters from this 'Elijah's appearance'.[14] More than anyone else it was Melanchthon who promoted this apocalyptic vision of Luther. Like Luther, Melanchthon was convinced that the world was in a deep crisis: the Turkish threat and the precarious state of Christendom confirmed that they were living in the Last Days. Now more than at any other time a proper and careful understanding of the Bible was needed. In a couple of letters to Georg Spalatin written in the early 1520s Melanchthon described Luther as being imbued with the spirit of Elijah. While referring directly to the commentary on the Apocalypse by Joachim of Fiore, he emphasised Joachim's identification of Antichrist with the papacy and pointed to Luther as 'the Elijah' of the Latter Days.[15]

This view of Luther had a broad, popular and lay base as can be seen from the writings of the Nuremberg shoemaker Hans Sachs. In his poem, *The Wittenberg Nightingale*, published in 1523, Sachs lauded Luther as the great prophet of the new age, by implication associating him with the eschatological prophet who was expected to come from the East at the end of time. Like another lay evangelical pamphleteer from Nuremberg, the painter Hans Greiffenberger, Sachs defended Luther because he considered him to be an apocalyptic prophet, who, having retrieved the Gospel, signalled the end of the world.[16] In his pamphlet, *About the far sounding Name of Luther: What he means and how he is misinterpreted*, published in Augsburg in 1523, the Imperial soldier and paymaster Haugh Marschalck voiced similar views and pointed to Luther as an eschatological prophet, either a second Enoch or Elijah, sent to overthrow the Roman Antichrist and to renew Christendom.[17] Such views of Luther remained popular among the German laity even after 1525 and the damage to Luther's image caused by the Peasants' Wars.

Even if Luther appears to have discouraged the specific view of himself as the second Elijah sent to proclaim the return of Christ, he clearly considered himself and his message to be of prophetic significance.[18] Thus he had not the least doubt that Hilten's prophecy referred to him personally, and he was convinced that the prediction by Johan Hus, allegedly made shortly before he was executed, that he himself might be a weak goose (in Czech *Hus* means goose), but stronger and more far-sighted birds such as falcons and eagles would follow him, applied to him too. Luther himself, who increasingly identified Hus as a forerunner for his reformation, or someone close to him, eventually combined Hus's statement with another by Jerome of Prague, who together with Hus had been condemned to the stake, and who had declared that he wished he could see what would be made of his conviction a hundred years later:

> Holy Johannes Hus prophesyed about me when he wrote from his Bohemian prison that they might now be roasting a goose (for Hus means goose), but in a hundred years they will hear a swan sing, which they will not be able to silence.[19]

The pervasiveness of the view of Luther as a latter-day prophet was far from being limited to Protestant countries, as can be seen from the way he was characterised by many popular writers in Catholic Italy. Here his apocalyptic significance was reversed and he was portrayed as a pseudo-prophet, or one of the false prophets who Christ had stated would appear shortly before the End.[20]

Linked to these apocalyptic expectations that a great prophet would appear, was another medieval prophecy, the so-called Sibylline Oracles, about the advent of a Last Emperor, who would reform both State and Church before the Last Judgement. This prophecy occasionally carried with it arguments for social and political reforms as can be seen from writings such as the *Reformation of the Emperor Sigismund* (c. 1438). It often took the form of a prediction of the coming of a third Emperor Frederick, a successor to Frederick II Barbarossa (1194–1250), who would emulate his predecessor by taking on the papacy and renew Christianity, thus preparing the way for Christ's return. Many pamphleteers, including Luther himself, identified this Frederick with Luther's protector Frederick the Wise of Saxony.[21] The other great anti-authoritarian figure of the early sixteenth century, the so-called 'Luther of medicine', Paracelsus, later elaborated this prophecy. According to Paracelsus, Emperor Frederick Barbarossa, whose emperorship had in fact turned increasingly messianic and eschatological, had discovered an image of a monk over whose head was the inscription *Lutherus* in a monastery in Carinthia, thereby foretelling the name of the future Reformer.[22]

Parallel with Luther's tacit acceptance of the role of 'divinely-ordained prophet' promoted in the popular literature, ran what can best be described as an iconographic campaign which sought to portray Luther as a holy man, a Protestant saint, chosen by God to fulfil his great apocalyptic scheme for the world. Clearly this was a pictorial representation of him which was not unacceptable to Luther since he never voiced any doubts about it. Among the earliest portraits of the reformer we find him depicted with a dove, symbolising the Holy Spirit, hovering over his head. Such pictorial symbolism had until then been reserved for the great fathers of the Church, such as saints Ambrose, Augustine and Gregory. The message was simple: like theirs, Luther's teaching was divine. Later in 1521 a halo of sainthood was added to the dove which served to enhance the image of Luther's godliness further.[23] Thus the image of Luther as a divinely inspired prophet was promoted in texts as well as pictures.

Luther undoubtedly saw all mortal life engulfed in the never-ending conflict between God and the Devil from which there was no escape, as pointed out by Heiko Oberman. His fear of the Devil caused his deep pessimism towards this world, from which he only found relief in faith through God's grace.[24] He was convinced that he himself lived in the Last Days and that the Gospel of St Matthew fully applied to his own time. Thus by 1514 he was convinced that 'the Gospel of St Matthew counts such perversions as the sale of indulgences among the signs of the Last Days'.[25] Some years later, in 1522, he chose as his subject for an Advent sermon the signs of Christ's coming and the Last Days:

> I would compel no man to believe me, and yet in this matter I will not yield up my Judgement to any other, namely, that the Last Day is not farr off . . . Let us not therefore be wanting to ourselves, disregarding the most diligent premonition and prophecie of Christ our Saviour; but seeing in our Age the Signs foretold by him, do often come to pass, let us not think that the coming of Christ is far off.[26]

Like most people in this period Luther awaited the apocalyptic moment with some anxiety, vacillating between fear and hope, depending on whether or not the Final Judgement or the salvation of the faithful was at the forefront of his thoughts. If anything Luther grew more convinced throughout his life that the End was near. A year before his death in 1546 he wrote that he and his followers were 'the last trumphet' who preceded Christ's Second Coming. Adding that even if they were weak and insignificant and were hardly heard in this world, they would 'sound greatly in the assembly of the heavenly angels who will follow us and our horn and thus make the end'.[27]

For his understanding of his own age Luther depended on Scripture and in matters concerning prophecy he initially relied on the Book of Daniel. It was from Daniel that Luther found confirmation for a view which had become increasingly popular towards the end of the middle ages – that of historical degeneration – a notion which implied that the world would eventually wither away, dying of old age. The world had witnessed a gradual decay since the time of the patriarchs; not only human civilisation, but nature, morality and faith showed signs of degeneration. From the outset Luther was preoccupied with establishing correlations between the prophecies in Daniel and particular historical events. He had no doubt that most of these prophecies had already been fulfilled, and that Daniel's visions of the End applied to his own age. He ended his introduction to the Book of Daniel by emphasising that he was convinced that the Day of Judgement was near. Luther added that it mattered little that the precise date of the End was unknown – it might eventually be discovered – but what mattered was the certainty that the Last Days were at hand.[28]

Initially Luther, like Erasmus of Rotterdam, and other mainstream Reformers such as Zwingli and Calvin, doubted the canonical authenticity of the Book of Revelation. Despite their doubts, it should be emphasised that both Zwingli and Calvin were convinced that they were living in the Last Days, as we have already seen from Zwingli's identification of the second Elijah with Luther, and as can be seen from some of Calvin's sermons:

> True it is, that according to our fleshy senses, it cannot sinke into our heades
> that the comming of our lord Iesus Christ is at hand . . . And though our flesh be
> not able to reach unto it, yet we must beholde it with the eyes of faith . . . let us
> love this comming of the Sonne of God.[29]

In the preface to his translation of the New Testament published in 1522, Luther wrote of the Book of Revelation that 'my spirit cannot make its way into this book'. Still, this was the one book he insisted on having illustrated in the early editions of his New Testament. Evidently Luther recognised the power of the prophetic images in the Book of Revelation and the importance of having them properly interpreted. Together with Melanchthon he oversaw Lucas Cranach's design of the illustrations with their strong anti-papal polemic, which in particular served to identify Antichrist, the Babylonian whore of the Apocalypse, with the pope and the papacy in contemporary popular culture from 1522 onwards.[30]

Luther's identification of the papacy in Rome with Antichrist undoubtedly proved the most significant of all his biblical, prophetic discoveries and by far the most consequential for the apocalyptic mood of the age. The appearance of Antichrist was, according to both the Bible and Christian tradition, intimately linked to the Last Days. The ambivalence of the figure of Antichrist only served to add to its legendary qualities as did the vague scheme of eschatological events attached to his defeat. Thus earlier critics of the Church such as Hus and Savonarola had already identified him with the pope. But whereas their claims had been founded on moral grounds, the worldliness and depravity of the pope and his cardinals in particular, Luther's indictment, as has been pointed out by a number of Reformation historians, was one of doctrine and principle. Thus for Luther reforming the Church was not about improving its ethics, but about the fundamental and urgent need to salvage the Gospel from the agents of the Devil before it was too late.[31] Luther had made this discovery as early as 1518, but did not flesh it out in detail until his major publications in 1520.

However, the full propaganda value of this argument was first utilised by Luther's friend, the Saxon court painter, Lucas Cranach, in a small illustrated pamphlet, containing twenty-six woodcuts, each with a brief comment by Philip Melanchthon, *Passional Christi und Antichrist*, published in 1521. As pointed out by Bob Scribner, the colossal impact of this work which simply juxtaposed the life and actions of Antichrist with those of Christ in a series of forceful illustrations with simple explanatory texts, can hardly be exaggerated. In a few years alone it ran through no fewer than one Latin and ten German editions. Moreover, it also came to shape and influence the form and direction of evangelical, anti-papal propaganda for decades to come, giving it a strongly apocalyptic flavour, underlining the moral, spiritual and, not least, theological opposition of Antichrist to Christ and the Gospel.

Numerous broadsheets appeared which promoted the identification of Antichrist and the Devil with the Catholic Church and the pope. A broadsheet from 1551 entitled *About the Origin of the Monks. About the Origin of Antichrist* (*De Origine Monachorum. De Origine Antichrist*), is typical of how this motif was repeatedly treated in Protestant propaganda (Plate 2.1). Combining natural birth with defecation, thereby demeaning this particularly important event and turning it upside down, the woodcut shows pregnant devils walking up a latrine and giving birth/defecating monks. Other devils then place the monks in a large mortar where they are mashed up for

Plate 2.1 Anon., About the Origin of Monks. About the Origin of Antichrist (1551)

the chief devil to create the papal Antichrist, easily recognisable with his papal tiara.[32]

A somewhat more urbane treatment of the same theme can be seen from a Dutch/French broadsheet from 1599 entitled: *The Papal Pyramide* (*Piramide papistique*) (Plate 2.2). This engraving shows an obelisk consisting of one large serpent, wearing the papal tiara on its head and holding its own tail and the host in its mouth. Intertwined with its body are several smaller serpents wearing a variety of Catholic, clerical headgear, such as a bishop's mitre and the flat hat of the Jesuits. However, the serpent is threatened by lightnings and fire in the form of the Word of God coming from the sky. Underneath the obelisk rest a variety of objects associated with the Catholic faith and rejected by Protestants as un-Christian, such as letters of indulgence, pictures of saints and rosaries. The French verses underneath, and their Dutch translation, inform the reader–viewer that this bundle of serpents is the offspring of Hell which is intended to plague Man with their false teachings while spilling their poison across the earth. In the last couple of lines the hope, however, is expressed that God will soon curtail these unholy activities of Antichrist. If the engraving was not immediately recognisable to contemporaries these lines would have jogged their memories and showed them that this serpent was identical with Satan, who in this form had caused the Fall of Man, and who was clearly identified in the Book of Revelation (12:9 and 20:2). Furthermore, the association between the pope and Antichrist is enhanced by the quotations from the Bible in and around the border of the engraving.[33]

This motif undoubtedly found its most forceful expression in 1522 with Cranach's illustrations to Luther's translation of the New Testament, especially, of course, those relating to the Book of Revelation. If woodcuts had already appeared showing the pope as the seven-headed beast of the Apocalypse, Cranach here proved innovative by equating the whore of Babylon of Revelation 17 with the papacy, an image which was to prove so significant in subsequent evangelical propaganda. Later in 1534 with the Wittenberg edition of the complete Bible, Luther and his collaborators demonstrated their acceptance and sensitivity to the popular prophecies which assigned strong apocalyptic significance to the Turkish invasions, especially after their siege of Vienna in 1529. Thus the illustration in the Wittenberg Bible of Revelation 20:9 showing the armies of Gog and Magog besieging 'the beloved city' depicts the Turks laying siege to Vienna.[34]

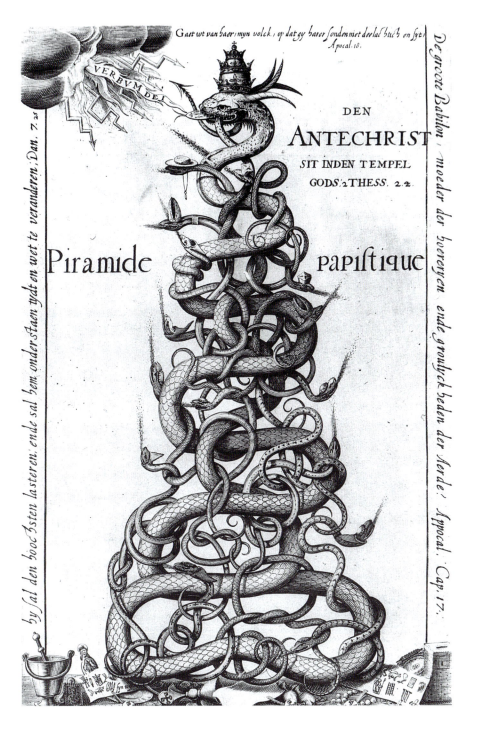

Plate 2.2 Anon., The
Papal Pyramide (1599)

THE MILLENNIUM AND RADICAL CHILIASM

The social upheavals and the Peasants' War of the mid-1520s, which were closely associated with the chiliasm and millenarianism of radical Reformers, such as Thomas Müntzer, only added to Luther's doubts about the acceptability of the Book of Revelation. However, having seen off the radical challenge to his Reformation, Luther towards the end of the decade eventually accepted the Apocalypse as a genuine and important prophecy, which not only complemented Daniel, but also served as an important tool for understanding God's plan for His Church. More than anything else it appears to have been the Turkish threat which had become particularly menacing by 1529 when Ottoman forces besieged Vienna, which convinced Luther that the Book of Revelation was an important part of the Bible with exceptional significance for his own age.[35]

But before Luther had reached such conclusions the Book of Revelation and significant aspects of the eschatological expectations attached to the evangelical movement had been appropriated by the rapidly emerging radical, Spiritualist wing of the Reformation who added their own distinct chiliastic and millenarian interpretation to these anticipations. Their militant views were quickly denounced by both Luther and Zwingli, but riding on the crest of the major social and economic dissatisfaction which eventually resulted in the Peasants' Wars in 1524–5, the Spiritualists succeeded in adding their chiliasm to the peasants' cause.[36] The most prominent of the Spiritualist evangelicals was undoubtedly Thomas Müntzer (c. 1490–1525), not least because of the violent chiliasm he expressed and his direct involvement in the Peasants' Wars. Not only did Müntzer believe that he had a prophetic ministry – he saw himself at different times as either a new Jeremiah, a new Elijah, a new Daniel, or even a new John the Baptist – but throughout he believed that the End of the world was imminent and that the actions of the Saints, the true Christians, God's elect, would help accelerate its arrival.

Initially, Müntzer had envisioned that such action should be taken under the guidance and leadership of the Christian princes but, increasingly disappointed with civil authority, he began to emphasise that if they failed in their duty their place should be taken by the common man. In his 'Sermon to the Princes', preached before Duke John of Saxony and his son, Müntzer presented himself as a new Daniel who could expound apocalyptic history and interpret visions and dreams. He was convinced that God's kingdom was about to break through and that it was imperative that the evangelical princes should now wield the sword against all those who opposed the

Gospel. If they failed in their God-given task, the peasants, who perceived the evangelical truth much more clearly, would take their place.[37] This call to violent action in order to hasten the End and bring about a just kingdom of God spectacularly failed to appeal to the German evangelical princes, but it gained considerable support and popularity among the rebellious peasants of southern Germany, many of whom found further justification for their cause in Müntzer's chiliastic interpretation of the Gospel. Shortly before the outbreak of the Peasants' Wars in the spring of 1524 Müntzer stated his position in a letter to his followers at Eisenach. Quoting Daniel 7 – 'And the kingdom and the dominion and the greatness of the kingdoms under the whole heaven shall be given to the people of the saints of the Most High; their kingdom shall be an everlasting kingdom, and all dominions shall serve and obey them'– Müntzer argued that power was now passing to the common man and that this 'everlasting' kingdom will become Christ's at his Second Coming. Here at the End God's prophet, Thomas Müntzer, confronted his followers with a simple choice: they could either opt for or against the kingdom of God which was to arrive shortly; significantly Müntzer signed this and a number of his last letters 'Thomas Müntzer with the sword of Gideon'. Thus, it was in order to help bring about this millenarian kingdom of God that Müntzer, as a second Gideon, together with his followers took up arms and joined the rebellious peasants in the battle at Frankenhausen in May 1525 only to be defeated by Landgrave Philip of Hesse, and in the case of Müntzer and a number of his supporters only to be captured and later beheaded.[38]

One of the few of Müntzer's followers who managed to escape from the battlefield was the bookseller and bookbinder Hans Hut (c. 1490–1527) who was to inherit and modify Müntzer's mantle. After the peasants' defeat Hut appears to have identified the 'true' godly with the pacifist Anabaptists gathered round the former Nuremberg minister Hans Denck who re-baptized Hut in May 1526 in Augsburg. Like his former mentor, Müntzer, Hut believed in the imminent arrival of the kingdom of Christ. Müntzer's execution and the defeat at Frankenhausen do not appear to have turned him into a true pacifist; it seems only to have caused him to rework the apocalyptic timetable in the light of his recent experiences. Consequently Hut anticipated the Second Coming would take place in the summer of 1528 when he expected the elect to assist Christ in his cleansing of the world and to help in the judgement of sinners. First, however, there would according to Hut be a period of serious tribulation when the Turks would cause havoc in Europe. They would act as God's instrument and bring death and destruction to his enemies (mainly the Catholics and mainstream evangelicals). Only at this stage would the elect take up arms to conclude this purification of the world before the millennium could be inaugurated. Hut, however, together with a number of his followers, was arrested by the Augsburg authorities in August 1527 in connection with the so-called 'Martyrs' Synod' (a meeting of Anabaptists in Augsburg). During an escape attempt in December 1527 Hut died, thus avoiding the disappointment of seeing his apocalyptic visions and timetable failing to materialise in 1528.[39]

Meanwhile many of Hut's disciples had sought refuge in Strassburg due to the increasing persecution they faced from the civic leaders in Augsburg, and here they awaited the expected sign from Christ ready to join in the Last Battle with the ungodly before the millennium. By the start of the Peasants' Wars most city councils had become wary of millenarian ideas which were increasingly perceived as providing ideological ammunition and justification for rebellion against lay authority. City council records across Germany show plenty of complaints about the danger of common people being lead astray by their reading. Thus, during the great apocalyptic scare of 1524 – the year witnessing the first peasants' rebellions and having been forecast as one of horrifying floods and natural disasters by evangelical theologians and a deluge of almanacs and *Prognostica* – the magistracy of Ulm forbade conventicles of common people in private houses where they were reported to be reading and discussing the Bible.[40]

While toleration of the Spiritualists and Anabaptists was rapidly disappearing within the urban centres in most of Germany, not least due to the experiences of the Peasants' Wars, which served to link social rebellion to the active or perceived active apocalypticism of the Spiritualists, Strassburg and its leaders proved particularly receptive and tolerant of such groups from the mid- to late 1520s. Consequently a flood of Spiritualist refugees arrived in the wake of the Peasants' Wars. Not surprisingly nearly all the radical evangelicals active in Strassburg, until the clampdown by the city council in 1533, were refugees, such as Hans Denck, Caspar Schwenckfeld, Sebastian Franck, Michael Servetus and Melchior Hoffman, just to mention a few of the major figures. The Spiritualists appear, however, to have appealed to a substantial group among the lower middle classes in Strassburg in particular, and they inspired local, lay preachers such as Clemens Ziegler and evangelical prophets such as Lienhard and Ursula Jost. The city became a virtual hive of apocalyptic expectations, and since censorship was lax local printers were more than keen to print the eschatological tracts written by the Spiritualists, not least because of the considerable demand for such works. The result was that Strassburg became the centre for the dissemination of radical evangelical propaganda for over a decade until the city abandoned its tolerant policy in 1533–4.[41]

Melchior Hoffman (c. 1495–1543/4), the itinerant furrier and lay preacher, like many of the radical Spiritualists had begun his career as a follower of Luther. Throughout his life, however, Hoffman retained and enhanced a strong apocalyptic expectation, and wherever he travelled and preached in the Baltic and Scandinavia he invariably fell out with more cautious evangelical leaders and local authorities. Shortly before he arrived in Strassburg in June 1529 Hoffman had been expelled from Schleswig and Holstein after a public disputation initiated by Duke Christian and his father, King Frederik I of Denmark and Norway, who according to Hoffman had originally offered him his protection and given him permission to preach in all Holstein in 1527.[42] By 1526 when he published his pamphlet on Daniel 12, it is evident that Hoffman was deeply engulfed in apocalyptic speculation. He was convinced that the Last Days had begun. The return of Christ was imminent since the unmasking of falsehood had already taken place and Hoffman expected the Second Coming to be only seven years away.

None of the leading Strassburg theologians such as Martin Bucer and Wolfgang Capito wanted to add their blessing to Hoffman's ministry and he therefore decided to reach out to the common people in Strassburg instead. According to him such folk were deserving and starving in spirit, and he emphasised that he would rather 'sit with God's prophets and prophetesses in filth and disgrace than to possess a full maggot-ridden belly with the blind leaders of the Lutherans and Zwinglians'.[43] Hoffman appears to have been particularly comfortable with the Anabaptist 'prophetesses' in Strassburg, especially Ursula Jost and later Barbara Rebstock whose chiliastic prophecies inspired and guided him. They all belonged to a much larger group of lower middle-class citizens of Strassburg who, under the name the 'Strassburg Prophets', came to constitute the core of Hoffman's following in the city. These prophets served to confirm Hoffman in his conviction that the Last Days had definitely arrived. In 1530 Hoffman edited and published a volume of Ursula and her husband Lienhard's visions. With this publication Hoffman not only wanted to draw attention to the apocalyptic nature of the age, but he also wished to draw his readers away from their ungodly obsession with 'stargazers, nature-worshippers and magicians' and instead encourage them to listen to God's true prophets.

Ursula Jost's visions appear to have been of a hallucinatory nature. She would either be confronted or woken by a bright light as if she was very close to the sun and the images which appeared before her filled her with deep fear. Despite being unable to explain or interpret most of the images she had no doubt that it was God who was revealing Himself to her. Most of her visions were concerned with the wrath of God and His punishment of His sinful people in the Last Days: such as God shooting burning arrows at the world, or cosmic disasters with rivers of blood which filled the sky, or water, fire, pitch and brimstone raining down from heaven burning people and leaving the earth in chaos; or visions of the destruction of a great city (i.e. Strassburg). War and soldiers also played a significant part in Ursula Jost's visions, and from 1529, when the Turks first laid siege to Vienna, they began to appear too, evidently, as they had done for Müntzer and Hut, serving as God's tool in bringing His punishment upon an ungodly world at the End of Time. However, according to Ursula Jost the main targets for God's wrath were the Catholic prelates and the pope, whom she identified with Antichrist. Her husband, Lienhard, expanded that analogy to include the Lutherans and the Reformers of Strassburg whom he considered 'the most cruel of Antichrists'.[44]

Lienhard Jost also prophesyed that Strassburg was to be the New Jerusalem from where the 144,000 'apostolic messengers' referred to in the Book of Revelation were to emerge to spread the true knowledge about Christ and give birth to a new covenant between God and His chosen people through the baptism of believers. However, before this could happen, the Emperor, identified with the dragon mentioned in the Book of Revelation, would lay siege to Strassburg and only through this severe military trial of the city and its population would the new apostles appear.

In Strassburg, as so often was the case, we also find Franciscan inspiration and encouragement for the growing apocalyptic mood and expectations among many of the citizens. In this case it was an Italian and former Franciscan Spiritualist monk, Venturinus, who through his prophecies in 1530 confirmed the 'Strassburg Prophets' in their views. He informed the citizens that God was again speaking directly to his people as He had in Old Testament times. They needed to repent urgently and call on Luther in particular to complete the Reformation he had started. God would use the Turks to demolish His enemies and the unrepentant. They would take Emperor Charles V captive and kill King Ferdinand while destroying the pope, 'the prince of Satan' and his servants of priests and monks. After this punishment an 'angelic pastor' would appear who would convert the whole world, including the Muslims, and prepare the way for the millennium. The significance of Venturinus can be seen from the fact that the Strassburg prophetess Barbara Rebstock later referred to his prophecies in her visions.

Neither the Strassburg prophets nor Hoffman wanted their followers to help bring about the millennium by force. As opposed to Müntzer and Hut they forbade their co-religionists to carry weapons and their 'apostles' to use the sword, and Hoffman considered Müntzer a false prophet who had been inspired by the Devil. Considering the setbacks and persecution he had encountered since 1526 and the publication of his commentary on the Book of Daniel it is surprising that Hoffman's eschatology remained unchanged and politically conservative until 1530. Despite his expulsion from the duchies of Schleswig and Holstein Hoffman still retained his faith in Frederik I of Denmark and Norway as a godly man – one of the kings who would defend the true Christians against the beast (the Emperor) during the final persecutions. Accordingly, in 1530, he dedicated his second major work, a commentary on the Book of Revelation, to the king.[45] Gradually, however, after his arrival in Strassburg and under the influence of the writings of Hans Denck and the prophecies of Lienhard Jost in particular, Hoffman radicalised his eschatology. Not least due to the adoration he enjoyed among the 'Strassburg Prophets' he came to believe that he himself was the second Elijah who had come to announce the Last Days. More significantly, Hoffman accepted the potentially revolutionary idea that a godly interregnum on earth would have to be established to prepare the way for Christ's Second Coming. Where previously he had talked about a 'spiritual Jerusalem' the new Jerusalem was now going to be the city of Strassburg. It therefore became an obligation of the magistracy of the city to create a theocracy, root out the ungodly, and arm the city in preparation for the Final Battle with the apocalyptic 'dragon' (the Emperor). Hoffman's followers among the Anabaptists would assist the godly magistracy, not by taking up arms, but by digging trenches and taking on guard duties, thus helping the city to defeat the besieging imperial forces of Antichrist – the rest of the Imperial cities would then follow Strassburg's example and go through the same purifying process of siege, suffering and glorious victory. Following this victory 144,000 apostles (Revelation 14), who would be invulnerable, would pour out of the city and preach the unadulterated Gospel to the rest of the world. Even if Hoffman still managed to retain a pacifist apocalypticism, his eschatology had moved from a passive expectation of the Last Days where human actions meant nothing, to a voluntarism where human activity was essential to bring about the Second Coming. That his followers in Münster, in Westphalia and the Netherlands were to take his views to their natural consequence and take up arms as God's warriors in order to prepare Christ's Second Coming, can hardly surprise.[46]

The growth of the apocalyptic/Anabaptist movement in southern and central Germany was, not surprisingly, closely linked to the severe social, economic and political disruptions of the 1520s and early 1530s. Such social crisis lay behind the Peasants' Wars in 1524–5, while the dreadful famines which hit the region between 1528 and 1534 gave the movement a new lease of life and militancy.[47] More surprising, however, is the fact that the Strassburg Prophets' visions appear to have been closely related to these social crises. Thus of the seventy-seven reported prophecies by Ursula Jost, fifty-eight occurred during the Peasants' Wars, while the Strassburg Prophetess had only one vision over the following three years of relative peace. Not until the harvest failures which commenced in 1528 and the persecution of Anabaptists which intensified after the Imperial mandate of 1528 (accepted by the Second Diet of Speyer in 1529) ordering the summary execution of all adult Anabaptists, did Ursula again have a significant number of visions – no less than eighteen during 1529.[48]

In this situation, characterised by increasing hardship and starvation, to which was added vicious persecution by most local authorities – the number of executions of Anabaptists rocketed and increased four-fold during 1528 alone, and it has been calculated that 80 per cent of Anabaptists executed between 1525 and 1618 were killed between 1527 and 1533[49] – Strassburg proved a safe haven for displaced Anabaptists, many of whom were granted citizens' rights. The city's tolerant attitude to fellow evangelicals was considerable, even if its policy of banishment against some of the moderate leaders of the Anabaptist refugees with hindsight only served to add to the apocalyptic fury among the expanding number of Anabaptists within its walls. Likewise Strassburg was well placed to assist the starving refugees who sought assistance in the city, since it had the foresight to fill its municipal granaries thereby making it possible to sell corn to the poor well under market price. It is noteworthy that the city's resources for helping its poor were rapidly dwindling by 1533, which in turn served to generate a growing xenophobia and hostility towards the mainly refugee Anabaptists within the city among the native population.

This in turn led the Council to restrict those who could receive assistance to those who had held citizens' rights for a minimum of five years. It is hardly a coincidence that these moves coincided with the termination of the city's policy of toleration towards the apocalyptic Anabaptists. External as well as internal developments argued for an end to Strassburg's policy of toleration by then. The city, which until 1530 had pursued a predominantly Reformed policy in the religious domain, by then felt obliged to move closer to Lutheranism as a reaction against the looming alliance between the Elector of Saxony and Emperor Charles V. In May 1530 Andreas Karlstadt was banished from the city because his presence was considered harmful to Strassburg's relations with Lutheran Saxony. Internally, the presence of a growing, and increasingly vociferous, radical sectarian movement driven on by their active apocalypticism had led the evangelical leaders in the city, especially Bucer, to try to convince the authorities to take action against what they perceived to be a danger to the Gospel and public order. After a public disputation between the preachers and the Nonconformists staged by the Council in June 1533, Bucer, Capito and their fellow preachers won the day and religious conformity was introduced in the form of the so-called *Sixteen Articles* and *Confessio Tetrapolitana*, but not without a delay of nine months due to hesitation within the Council. Considering that 1533 was the year that Hoffman's followers expected Christ to return this proved a timely intervention. Hoffman, who had returned from East Frisia to Strassburg in March 1533, had been arrested on 20 May after one of his followers had accused him of planning a rebellion by the Anabaptists in the city. Despite Hoffman's denials of any revolutionary intent, his pacifist credentials, and the lack of any concrete evidence against him, the Strassburg Council was convinced that his doctrines were dangerous and could lead to civil disorder, and consequently he was to spend the rest of his life in prison (†1543) without ever being formally sentenced. By the turn of the year 1533–4, however, the apocalyptic mood in Strassburg had reached fever-heat. The Reformed preachers tirelessly tried to force the Council to introduce religious conformity based on *Tetrapolitana* and the *Sixteen Articles* with little success until events in Münster in Westphalia and the establishment of the so-called 'Anabaptist Kingdom' came to their aid and scared the Council into action. Consequently religious conformity was finally established and a series of measures were taken against the Anabaptists.[50]

Despite the fact that he himself remained a firm pacifist, Hoffman's activist eschatology undoubtedly proved the major inspiration for the militant apocalyptic uprising in Münster in 1534. During his travels and sojourns in the Low Countries in the early 1530s Hoffman's proselytising had found a particularly receptive audience among the urban middle and lower classes in the Dutch cities, not least because of the severe economic depression which in particular affected this sector of the population in the Netherlands between 1531 and 1537. Here Hoffman's ideas found the mass support they previously had proved unable to generate in Germany and the Baltic region. It was these Dutch militant followers of Hoffman who established the 'Anabaptist Kingdom' in Münster. That their New Jerusalem happened to be Münster was only due to the particular local circumstances of this Westphalian city which briefly became the centre for the apocalyptic upheaval which affected a considerable area stretching from Groningen to Maastricht in particular.

Münster, a city of around 15,000 people, which enjoyed a large measure of self-government under its territorial ruler, the Catholic Bishop of Münster, had already witnessed a reformation when the former priest and then follower of Luther, Bernt Rothmann, with the support of the cloth merchant Hermann Knipperdolling, a prominent member of the local magistracy, had defied the authority of the city Council and that of the Bishop, and with considerable popular support had taken over all the city's churches, except the cathedral, in August 1532. Shortly afterwards, however, Rothmann and his collaborators appear to have come under the influence of Anabaptist ideas in general and Hoffman's militant eschatology in particular. In early 1533, inspired by proselytes of Melchior Hoffman, they began to reject infant baptism and advocate believer's baptism. By the end of 1533 Rothmann and his now militant Anabaptist faction were in total control of Münster, finding their power base considerably enhanced by the arrival in the city of a rapidly expanding number of radical chiliasts from across Germany and the Low Countries.

Meanwhile, one of Hoffman's followers, Jan Matthijs of Haarlem, had taken over the leadership of the Melchiorites in the Low Countries (followers of Melchior Hoffman) and resumed adult baptism. Originally, back in 1531, Melchior Hoffman had decided to halt this practice until the time of Christ's return had come, due to the resulting persecution of the Anabaptists, who had seen a considerable number of their leaders being executed. However, by 1533 Matthijs claimed to have received a revelation from God which instructed him to restart adult baptism in order that God's chosen people could ready themselves for the coming Apocalypse. Among the first of his 'apostolic messengers' to receive adult baptism was his future collaborator and successor, Jan Beukels from Leiden, or John of Leiden, with whom he was to establish the 'Kingdom of Münster'. In January 1534 two of Matthijs's prophets arrived in Münster adding fuel to an already explosive situation, preaching that the Last Judgement was imminent and salvation was only open to those who repented and received believer's baptism. They proceeded to re-baptise the radical leadership in Münster, including Rothmann and Knipperdolling. A week later another two prophets, one of them John of Leiden, arrived informing the Münsterites that the second Enoch – which is who Matthijs claimed to be – taught that the godly were allowed to take up arms against a godless, secular authority. The seeds were being sown for a millennial kingdom to be established by force by the godly. The following month Matthijs himself arrived, declaring that all enemies of God and the New Jerusalem had to be destroyed by the faithful, if necessary by using the sword.

By then the radicals had taken over the city Council and the Bishop had commenced his siege of Münster. Consequently, the 'non-believers' in Münster, those who refused re-baptism, and who were therefore considered unreliable, either left or were expelled by the Anabaptists and more than 2,000 people left the city. Meanwhile, messages went out from the chiliastic leadership to their brethren in the Low Countries encouraging them to set out for Münster, the New Jerusalem, to help defend it against the forces of Antichrist. Hundreds of armed Anabaptists from Holland, Friesland and the Maas valley made their way to Münster eager to help bring about the Millennium, but significantly the much larger gatherings of between 14,000 and 16,000 Anabaptists, who had assembled in Holland, never made it to Münster and disbanded, while twenty-seven ships with more than 3,000 armed Anabaptists aboard were easily stopped and disarmed by a few hundred soldiers near Genemuiden. Likewise, the Anabaptists in Amsterdam proved unable to come to their assistance, despite having commissioned six ships and bought a considerable amount of weaponry.[51]

When the expected Second Coming did not take place over Easter 1534 as prophesyed, Jan Matthijs claimed to have received a new revelation, which convinced him that he himself with a small group of apocalyptic warriors was to initiate the great eschatological battle by defeating the besiegers. He was proved wrong when the sally failed and he himself was killed on 5 April 1534. However, the population of Münster was quickly rallied by John of Leiden who told them that this was all God's will and that He would send them another and significantly much greater prophet than

Jan Matthijs had been. Not surprisingly John himself turned out to be that 'higher prophet' and he immediately proceeded to establish a theocracy in Münster, the city Council was abolished and twelve elders were appointed in their place. This, together with the pressure from outside, caused by the prolonged siege, gradually led to a regime of terror within the walls of Münster, with rigorous conformity and summary executions of dissenters, while new social systems were created such as community of goods and polygamy, all justified with Old Testament precedents. The failure of the Bishop of Münster's forces to take the city by storm in May further under-pinned John of Leiden's position and his claims to being a special prophet. After further military successes against the besiegers John had himself crowned king. He saw himself as a new David chosen by God, who would head an eschatological kingdom, from the New Jerusalem of Münster, which was to bring vengeance on the godless. As king he would prepare the kingdom of Christ, by restoring the apostolic church of Christ, after the age of Antichrist and perversion of the Gospel had ended in 1533.[52] However, by the end of 1534 the tide had turned against the 'Anabaptist Kingdom'. The Bishop, together with new allies from within the Empire, strengthened his military position. By now totally blockaded, disease and starvation caused untold hardship within the city and on 24 July 1535 Münster was betrayed from within and taken by the Imperial forces. Around 4,000 Münsterites, among them Rothmann, who had been so instrumental in driving on the reformation, were slaughtered, while John of Leiden and Knipperdolling were imprisoned only to be executed six months later.

However, the memory of the 'Kingdom of Münster', especially its excesses, persisted as an example of a satanic regime of terror not only in Germany, but across Europe as a whole. Thus in Denmark, the Catholic humanist, Paulus Helie, included a detailed description in his chronicle under the year 1534 about events in Münster, emphasising the Lutheran origin of the 'madness and excesses' of the Anabaptists there.[53]

Even if the apocalyptically driven Dutch Anabaptists failed to relieve Münster in 1535 their militant eschatological activities had a direct impact in the Netherlands. Thus in March 1535 a group of 300 Frisian Anabaptists took over the Cistercian abbey of Oldeclooster, near Bolsward, where they established their New Jerusalem. Another band of Anabaptists from Groningen failed in their attempt to join them and only by using artillery was the local stadholder able to suppress this rebellion. Many of the Anabaptists were dead when the abbey finally fell while a significant number of those who survived were later executed. In Amsterdam on 10 May 1535 armed Anabaptists seized the town hall and were only dislodged by the magistracy after a fierce battle which left dozens of dead and dying in the streets. The collapse of the 'Anabaptist Kingdom' in the summer of 1535 undoubtedly killed off most of the chiliastic expectations among the Anabaptists, but some extremists continued to seek to bring about the hoped for millennium by military action. Most notorious were the groups which were led by Jan van Batenburg, son of a Dutch nobleman. They continued to raid monasteries and villages in western Westphalia and the northern Netherlands even after Batenburg himself had been caught and executed in 1537.[54]

PERSISTENT APOCALYPTICISM WITHIN EUROPEAN PROTESTANTISM

Surprisingly enough such chiliast excesses did little to diminish the apocalyptic expectations within mainstream Protestantism. Luther himself had certainly been hesitant about the value of the Book of Revelation in the mid-1520s not least due to his arguments with evangelical radicals, such as Müntzer and Karlstadt, and the social upheavals which resulted in the Peasants' Wars, but by 1530 he had come to accept it as a highly valuable part of the Gospel, something which the excesses in Münster did nothing to diminish; if anything Luther towards the end of his life became increasingly convinced that the Last Days were at hand. He claimed that Germany was a far more evil place than Sodom and Gomorrah had been. The Gospel would be driven underground while he expected the Devil to become even more active, inspiring murderous sects and heresies (such as the Anabaptist Kingdom of Münster), while famine, plague and war would devastate the countryside. Germany in particular would be singled out for the wrath of God because here the Gospel had shone the brightest and been least appreciated.[55] Increasingly he expected that the Last Days were close at hand. In 1532 he thought it might come before the end of that year, while later he was convinced that the world would come to an end in 1548.[56]

Luther's continued significance in sustaining the apocalyptic mood of the age, in particular among Protestants, can be seen from the many collections of his prophecies which began to be published less than a decade after his death in 1546. Initially they appeared in brief pamphlets such as the *Several Prophetic Statements of Doctor Martin Luther, the Third Elias*, published in 1552; later, by 1574, these collections had grown to include no less than 200 prophecies in books of more than 300 pages, while a wealth of

publications mixing Luther's prophecies with other apocalyptic statements aimed at a popular mass market were printed. The proliferation of
apocalyptic tracts in the decades after Luther's death would indicate that
rather than abating, the general conviction that the Last Days were imminent was, in fact, growing.[57] This was a feeling which was not restricted to
Germany alone, but affected most of Europe, especially those regions
where the new evangelical teachings had gained ground.

   In Denmark it made an impact via the considerable literary output of the
country's dominant Reformation superintendent, Peder Palladius, who
had spent six years at the University of Wittenberg following the lectures of
Luther and Melanchthon in particular.[58] In 1554 Palladius published his
most important work in Danish, entitled, *A Useful Book about St. Peter's Ship.
That is about the Holy Christian Church's Persecution in the Old, as well as, the New
Testament.* The title-page also carried a reference to Revelation 18 with the
added explanation: *The fall of the Roman Babylon.* Based on a series of
sermons he had preached the previous year in Copenhagen Palladius demonstrated how the Roman Antichrist, the great whore of Babylon, had
nearly destroyed the ship of St Peter (metaphor for the true Church), until
God had removed her hand from the rudder and handed it over to Luther to
guide the ship safely into harbour. In his introduction Palladius emphasised that despite the fact that the ship was tilting dangerously, as if it was
going to sink, it wouldn't, because ultimately God would look after His
faithful and steer His ship safely from place to place, from harbour to
harbour, as He had done 'from the beginning of the world and to this day,
and will continue to do until the Day of Judgement which is not far away
and soon reached. Because the ship is an ancient one in this six thousandth
year and can no longer cope with much.'[59] Thus Palladius had no doubt
that the Last Days were imminent and his reference to the six thousandth
years from the Creation to the end of time indicates his acceptance and
familiarity with the prophecy of Elias which via the Talmud and the rabbini-
cal literature had entered Lutheran eschatology, especially through *Carion's
Chronicle* which Melanchthon had been instrumental in having published in
1531, and which undoubtedly was Palladius's source.

   The image of the Church as a ship had become a central part of popular
devotion on the eve of the Reformation, as pointed out by Bob Scribner.
Thus it had already been ingeniously used by Sebastian Brant in his satircal
and hugely popular work, *The Ship of Fools* (1499), where St Peter's barque
(the true Church) had been compared with the ship of Antichrist (the false
church). It is therefore hardly surprising that it became regularly used in

Protestant propaganda, as can be seen from a repeatedly printed broadsheet, entitled *The Last Journey of the Papal Galley* (*Die letzte fart der Baptischen Galeieu*) from 1600 (Plate 2.3).[60] This engraving depicts the Catholic Church as the ship of Antichrist. The ship consists of an apocalyptic monster floating on its back while its six legs support a church with a steeple which also serves as mast for the sail. While winged demons/devils fan the sail and pull the boat, the pope is steering this monster-galley surrounded by Jesuits and bishops, which is being rowed by clergy and monks. The verses underneath indicate that this last journey of the ship of the papal Antichrist is going to Spain after the recent successes of Protestantism in France (possibly the recent Edict of Nantes in 1598) and the Netherlands (possibly the victory of the Dutch over the Spanish at Nieuwpoort in 1600).

Similarly, Palladius demonstated a detailed knowledge of Johann Hilten's prophecy and took the opportunity to remind his readers that they ought to take to heart the Word of God rather than being preoccupied with worldly affairs, and seriously consider how they would fare if Hilten's prophecies were shortly to be fulfilled and the Last Days to arrive.[61] A couple of years later Palladius returned in greater detail to Johann Hilten's prophecies in his introduction to a translation of the Lutheran, Andreas Musculus's work, *Vom Hosenteuffel* (1555) (About the Stocking Devil), which was a fierce attack on the loose morals and customs of the period. In his introduction to this work Palladius took the opportunity specifically to attack the immorality and ungodliness among his fellow Danes, detailing the punishments God had already visited on them for their sins, while warning them to mend their ways before it was too late. In this context he referred to Hilten who:

> prophesied great wretchedness in these times, part of which has already been fulfilled while another part still remains, like in the time he wrote a commentary on the *Book of Daniel*, he prophesied a great deal about the disturbance and destruction of the papacy, and likewise about the attack of the Turks on Germany and surrounding countries. And in accordance with what he wrote and prophesyed about the desolation of the papacy, that it should never be restored or recover, it is happening daily to an increasing extent and it began in the year 1516 after the birth of Christ, just at the same time Luther commenced his battle with the ungodly and tyrannical nature and false holyness etc. of the Roman popes.[62]

Therefore Hilten's prophecies for the future had to be taken seriously, in particular his prediction for 1600, when he had prophesyed that a gruesome ruler would govern the whole of Europe including Denmark, who

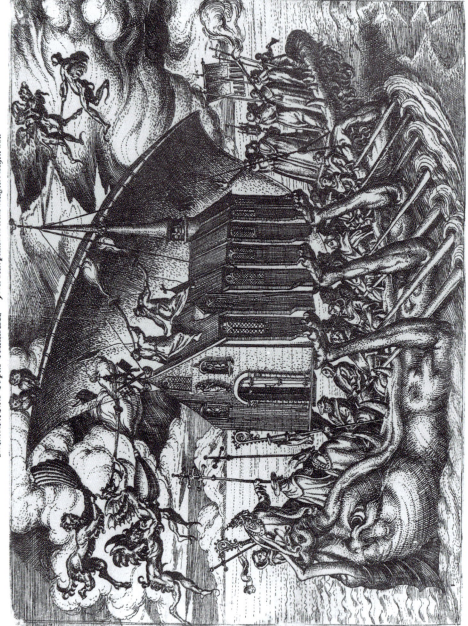

Die letzte farr der Bapstlichen Galeen.

Anmercket diese Bapstis Golenn wol/   Mit dem pfunent seine heilgen Knechte wol.

Plate 2.3 Anon., *The Last Journey of the Papal Galley* (1600)

was identified with the Turk, as was the predicted rule of Europe by Gog and Magog by 1606. Palladius called for immediate prayers and repentance in this 'the old age of the world' in order to avert the worse effects of these severe trials of the Last Days, referring his readers to the apocalyptic scenario of Matthew 24.[63] Palladius finished his edition and translation of Musculus's work by including a poem 'about the last and short time of this evil world'. Here once more the ungodliness and uncharitable nature of the age was pointed out, warning that God would punish the world with 'war and bloodshed, plague, hunger and dearth'. Either the Day of Judgement was just upon the world, or God was to visit it with ferocious destruction, great rebellion, and new government in many places. Salvation could only be hoped for by those who repented and turned to God in the short time left.[64]

Equally in Sweden, the country's leading Reformer Olaus Petri was convinced that he was living through the Last Days. Already in his book of sermons – Een lijten Postilla – published in 1530, Petri had stated that what could be read in the Bible about the Last Days was now being daily fulfilled, as everyone could observe for themselves. The world had become so wicked that things could hardly get worse. By now seven-year-old children demonstrated more wickedness than had previously been possible by evil old men; no longer did faith and love prevail, but hate and depravity ruled the world, a sure sign that the Day of Judgement was impending.[65]

In 1539 when Olaus Petri had fallen from royal favour in Sweden and stood accused of treason it is noteworthy that one of the central accusations against him was that in 1535 he had, against the wishes of King Gustav Vasa, given a series of sermons in Stockholm about the Apocalypse based on the Book of Revelation, thereby providing inspiration to the conspirators behind the Swedish gunpowder plot of 1536, which had been aimed at Gustav Vasa. Considering that Petri had collaborated with the supposed leading conspirator of this plot in having a painting made and hung in the city's main church of the multiple suns which had been seen over Stockholm in April 1535, it is more than likely that he had taken the opportunity to preach about this unusual astronomical event arguing that it was a sure sign of the Last Days. Like Luther and so many of the evangelical preachers of this period, this sign would undoubtedly have convinced Petri that the Second Coming was imminent and great disturbances and violent changes were at hand, something he felt obliged to share with the people of Stockholm who, since 1527 and the eschatological preaching of Melchior Hoffman, may well have been positively inclined towards such apocalyptic visions and interpretations.[66] That Olaus Petri may have used such eschatological sermons to criticise the political leaders of Sweden in general and King Gustav Vasa in particular can be seen from another of his published sermons which significantly appeared in 1539 – the year he was convicted for treason – where he stated that because the world had become such an evil place, the End was now close at hand as were horrific plagues and trials which God would send to match the dreadful sins of mankind which the authorities had done nothing to prevent.[67]

Like Luther, Petri appears to have been increasingly preoccupied with apocalyptic speculation towards the end of his life, clearly convinced that the Last Judgement was imminent. His last work, published in 1548, four years before his death, was a small eschatological pamphlet entitled *About the World's greatest Transformations and Age*, which proved popular and was to see several reprints during the period we are concerned with. Accepting the prophecy of Elias from the *Talmud*, Petri like so many evangelicals who had read *Carion's Chronicle* was convinced that the world from the Creation to the Last Day would last for a little less than 6,000 years. Of the last 2,000 years, the first belonged to Christ and the Church Fathers while the second was dominated by Antichrist and Satan whom God had let loose to punish a decayed and evil world. Considering that the year was now 1548 and that the reign of Antichrist was to be shortened by the Grace of God, Olaus had no doubt that 'the world was in its Last Days'.[68]

Now with the first generation of Protestants dead and the Second Coming still outstanding, it became imperative to find new prophetic evidence and information which could sustain the apocalyptic fervour and prove that the Day of Judgement was, indeed, at hand. History in particular, as a providential expression of God's will, and Nature, seen as a complementary 'book' to the Bible, were both increasingly studied for evidence of God's plan for the world and more significantly its End. Sweden was far from unique in witnessing a proliferation of apocalyptic writing in the second half of the sixteenth century, which more often than not was based on a deep historical pessimism.[69] Gone was the eschatological optimism of the early years of the Reformation when most evangelicals had expected the Second Coming to happen immediately and accordingly had felt no inclination to search for further proof of the Last Days. By the mid-sixteenth century a much greater and varied prophetic and apocalyptic literature became available than had been the case in the 1520s and 1530s, emanating from an increasing number of printing presses which were increasingly adept at catering to the interest of a growing mass market of readers. Even if Protestant clergy continued to dominate this market in apocalyptic pamphlets and books, it is noteworthy that other authors began to make a significant impact post-1550. In this age of increasing literacy there was evidently a growing demand for apocalyptic literature, which led to a bulging output of this type of literature. Thus supply and demand served to reinforce each other and fuel the eschatological expectations.[70] Such works ranged from the monumental and influential book by the Gnesio-Lutheran Matthias Flacius Illyricus, *Catalogus testium veritatis*, published in Basel in 1556, which was more concerned with prophetic legitimation of the Reformation than apocalyptic clarification as such, via the much more popular and apocalyptic work by another minister, Melchior Ambach, *On the End of the World and the Coming of Antichrist*, published in Frankfurt in 1550, to the wealth of popular pamphlets containing warnings and prophecies by otherwise unknown people about terrible punishments to come in the Last Days. In other words this period witnessed an impressive expansion and amplification of a prophetic and apocalyptic literature which emphasised the need for repentance before it was too late and the Day of Judgement had arrived.

Luther, whose apocalyptic understanding was firmly based in history, had increasingly towards the end of his life come to consider history a useful and God-given tool for the understanding and interpreting of the Gospel. However, it was Melanchthon who became the real promoter of the study of time and history among Protestants in general, and Lutherans in particular. For him history was the record of God's work; next to the Bible the study of history was the most beneficial to mankind, because here one could observe the manifestation of God's promises and prophecies.

That was Melanchthon's reason for editing Johann Carion's universal history, *Carion's Chronicle*, which became a standard work among Protestants. Between 1532 and 1564 it went through no less than fifteen German editions and when in 1537 it appeared in Latin it was quickly translated into a number of other European languages where it proved just as popular. As opposed to another famous Protestant historical work of the period, the *Magdeburg Centuries*, by Matthias Flacius and others, *Carion's Chronicle* was of a manageable size and presented a much more forceful apocalyptic interpretation, even if the *Centuries* proved inspirational in their attempt to prove that the Protestants were the true successors of the Apostles and the Ancient Church which had been corrupted by Rome. Even if *Carion's Chronicle* distinguished between sacred and profane history, its suggestion that the gift of prophecy to the Church served to unite these two domains unavoidably led to their fusion, thus creating a Protestant providential history which constantly sought and found biblical parallels to contemporary events, especially in the Old Testament. This again served to actualize biblical time, transporting it into the present, reinforcing the Protestant monopoly of righteousness and godliness. Johann Carion's work was, however, not unique, and a host of other, similar historical publications or chronologies were published across Protestant Europe during the sixteenth century. They all mirrored the same view on history, among the most influential of which was the Spiritualist Sebastian Franck's *Chronica* or *Geschichtbibel*, published in Strassburg in 1531, which was instrumental in popularising the idea of God's controlling hand in history while emphasising that the Last Days were imminent. Another important work was Johann Sleidan's short world chronicle which became widely used in schools. Based on the four monarchies in the Book of Daniel, it underlined that the last empire or monarchy was now approaching its final days.[71]

Accompanying this emphasis on providential history was a growing interest among Protestants in the second half of the sixteenth century in chronology. Since the awaited Second Coming seemed surprisingly slow in materialising it clearly proved essential to know roughly when it could be expected, even if most evangelicals agreed that no exact knowledge was possible. A wave of such speculative works were published in Germany and beyond, beginning with Andreas Osiander's influential work, *Conjectures on the Last Days and the End of the World*, published in Nuremberg in 1544, which predicted that Antichrist would fall in 1672, after which would follow a short period where the Gospel would be preached purely and unrestricted before the Second Coming would take place. This interest became closely linked within mainstream Protestantism to the idea, for which there was reasonable biblical evidence, that some form of limited Christian triumph on earth would follow the fall of Antichrist – some sort of full Reformation, concluding what Luther had begun, but not a Kingdom of God or a millennium, as promoted and expected by most Spiritualists and radicals.[72] If nothing else this served to add a somewhat positive perspective on what could otherwise have been a deeply depressing cultural outlook among Protestants of this period.

However, this eschatological obsession with chronology among Protestants did result in some rather surprising reactions. Thus, when the Gregorian calendar was introduced in 1582 to replace the Julian system, which was widely acknowledged as inexact, Protestants rejected it, because it had been ordered by the pope, who deliberately, as Antichrist, was seeking to bewilder and impair the godly. Lutherans in particular linked the new calendar to events at the time of the Council of Nicaea (325), when Antichrist, according to most Protestant students of history, had first appeared and when changes had been made in the traditional way of calculating the time of Easter. It resulted in a spate of apocalyptic speculations and publications which, based on what was perceived as attempts to manipulate time and chronology by Antichrist, offered new and precise dates for the Day of Judgement.[73] Thus the introduction of the Gregorian calendar served to add to the general anxiety among Protestants and enhance an already rampant apocalyptic mood, despite its obvious improvements on the Julian calendar.

Eschatological and apocalyptic expectations, however, were not the prerogative of Lutherans, nor did such ideas see their greatest flowering in Germany, or for that matter in England as many scholars of this particular branch of history have claimed.[74] Similarly it would not make sense to make millenarianism a purely Spiritualist or radical affair, or to see the spread of such ideas as affecting one or two geographical areas in particular. Such expectations undoubtedly characterised the outlook of the whole of Protestant Europe in general, but they also influenced Catholic views in places such as Italy and France, especially during the Wars of Religion. The sixteenth and early seventeenth centuries were in other words characterised by a general anxiety which found expression in, and was stimulated by, apocalyptic expectations and speculations, which at given times reached fever pitch within certain Protestant denominations or groups in particular geographical areas. They were often set off or intensified by a variety of natural, social, economic and military diasters, but it is important to bear in mind that such eschatological expectations formed a latent framework out of which most contemporaries deciphered and interpreted the world and events around them.

REFORMED PROTESTANTISM AND APOCALYPTICISM

Initially, the leading Reformed preachers such as Zwingli and Calvin had expressed reservations about the value of the Book of Revelation, despite the fact that most of them were convinced that they were living through the Last Days. It fell to Zwingli's successor in Zurich, Heinrich Bullinger, to highlight the value of this biblical text to the Reformed world and to make eschatological expectations and apocalypticism an essential part of Reformed thinking. Considering the prominence given to God's covenant with his elect people throughout history within Reformed theology, and the growing significance Reformed leaders attached to providential history as evidence of God's plans for His chosen flock, this can only be described as an organic and integral development. Well before he preached his hugely influential 100 sermons on the Apocalypse between 1555 and 1556 Bullinger had already been attracted to the Book of Revelation which he had often cited and considered not only canonical, but a work by the Apostle John. Similarly his eschatological focus was of a much earlier date. Thus in 1542 he had written a commentary on Matthew where he dealt extensively with the apocalyptic scenario in Matthew 24; by then he had no doubt that the Book of Revelation offered a key to the understanding of Church history and the future of the Church. Only a year after he had preached his 100 sermons they were published in Basle. They subsequently went through numerous editions and were quickly translated into a number of vernacular languages and, like most of what Bullinger wrote, proved highly influential within the Reformed world.

Bullinger dedicated his work to all the exiles 'for the name of Christ' in Germany and Switzerland, who had fled France, England, Italy and other nations in particular, and more generally to 'all the faithful where soever they be, abiding and looking for the coming of Christ our Lord and Judge'. Referring to the historical evidence for the doctrine that the pope is Antichrist, Bullinger not only mentioned Joachim of Fiore, but Savonarola, whom he considered particularly significant because of his 'holiness of life'. Instead of adding a list of further authorities for this interpretation Bullinger just referred his readers to the recently published *Catalogue of Witnesses of the Truth* by the Lutheran, Matthias Flacius Illyricus, where they could find a comprehensive list of all the godly who had named the bishop of Rome as 'that Antichrist which should come into the world'.[75]

Significantly Bullinger used the introduction to his sermons on the Book of Revelation to remind his readers why the 'Apocalypse in our time is not only profitable but necessary':

> For the Papistes omit nothyng, which may make for repayring of their king-dome, & for the pulling down of the kingdom of Christ. Therefore where as these fellowes spare neither paynes nor cost, so they may turne all thinges to oppresse the fayth of the Gospell, & to drive the simpler sorte to forsake it. We ought not to suffer that the Church & the simple people which are afflicted and tempted by them, should want that comfort, admonition, & doctrine which in tymes past the Lord Jesus himselfe by S. John, hath prepared for these hard cares and tymes by revealing his Apocalipse. And in deede these things here which are here revealed to us of God haue a singular force. Neither shall the aduersary and

enemy of Christ be ouerthrowen with any corporall weapons, saue onely with
the sword of Gods word. For now it is needeful that Antichrist should waxe bile
and perishe in the myndes of men, that Christ alone might liue agayne and be
glorified for euer.[76]

The Book of Revelation was, in other words, particularly useful for
Bullinger and his fellow Reformed because it helped to explain the social
and religious reality they were faced with, actively persecuted by a revived
Counter-Reformation Catholic Church, which had driven, and was
increasingly to drive, waves of Reformed believers into exile. In this situation its apocalyptic prophecies proved highly appropriate. It served to give
hope and guidance to those who considered themselves part of the new
Covenant and who had been forced into exodus for the sake of their faith.
The 'kingdom of Antichrist' might be growing daily, but such trials had to
be considered and endured within the context of the apocalyptic battle
which was raging and which would eventually see Christ and the godly win
through before the Day of Judgement which was rapidly approaching.[77]

In his sermon on Revelation 6 and the Four Horsemen, Bullinger
pointed out that horses of various colours were used in the Bible to signify
the bearing and state of God's chosen people, a label applicable to the
Protestant community in general, and the Reformed in particular. The
white colour indicated innocence, purity, victory and felicity. The white
horse therefore meant the 'prosperous preaching of the Gospel', while the
horseman's bow and arrows referred to his ability to strike his enemies far
off and triumph over them. Bullinger concluded: 'Through Christ therefore preceedeth the preaching of the word; he geueth strength to the
preachyng; he shaketh hys bent bow. What force so euer the Worde hath,
that same is whole due to the horseman.'[78]

Bullinger's work encouraged a host of Reformed commentaries and
writings on the Apocalypse during the late sixteenth and early seventeenth
centuries, among them the influential and chiliastic commentary by James
Brocard first published in Latin in 1580 and quickly translated into a
number of vernacular languages. Having served within both the French
and Dutch Reformed churches, where his apocalyptic interpretation of the
Bible had caused alarm, before finally settling among the Reformed in
Bremen, Brocard's work and life are intimately bound up with the age of
Philip II of Spain and the Eighty Years War between Spain and the United
Provinces. His commentary on Revelation 6 bears witness to that:

Lykewise when the Preaching was begun in the Lordes second comminge,
the first beast sheweth the Whyte horse, when in Luther, and other, Chryste

ouercommeth, and the Preachinge goeth forwarde. The seconde beaste sheweth the Red Horse when during the Preaching the Inquisition, and Tyrannes, kill the believers. The third Beast sheweth a Blacke Horse, whylest many are tryed by persecution, and some there are which revolte from their Life and doctryne; the Blacke man the Pope by the first Councell of Trent doth publish his owne deuises, for matters agreeable to the Gospel; the fourth beast sheweth the pale Horse, in whom the pale death of them is signified, to whom it is sayde; he that hath not believed shal be condemned.[79]

Thus it was also most fitting and somewhat prophetic that Brocard's English translator James Sandford dedicated the English edition of his commentary to the Calvinist Robert Dudley, Earl of Leicester, who three years later was to play a significant, if brief, role in the Spanish–Dutch conflict, as Governor-General of the United Provinces from 1585–87.[80] Here Sandford stated:

what greater deformity of the inward man hath there ben at any time then in these dayes, when all abroade there is such variety of opynions violently oppressing the truth, and such grievous conflicts for the truthes sake, that now truely may be sayd that Chryste commeth with Fyre, and Sword to reforme that which is amysse, to roote out wickednesse and to prepare the way for his king-dome. Chrystes Scepter of Iron, mentioned in the second Psalme of David, together wyth the whole Psalme and the yron Rod spoken of in Reuelation, is nowe to bee well wayghed, and considered.[81]

Bullinger's sermons on the Book of Revelation found a particularly recep-tive audience among the many Marian exiles from England, some of whom, like John Bale and John Foxe, who were by then already working on apocalyptic themes of crises and martyrdom in history in the neighbouring city of Basel, were to lay the foundations for the vigorous apocalypticism which came to characterise the Church of England from the 1560s until the mid-seventeenth century, especially its Calvinist/Puritan wing. The Marian exile of English Protestants and the execution of a number of leading English Protestant bishops provided Protestant propagandists with further proof that the Catholic Church was indeed the church of Antichrist. Some time between 1553 and 1555 a broadsheet appeared simultaneously in a Latin, a German and an English version entitled *The Lambe speaketh. Why do you crucifie me* (Plate 2.4).[82] It shows the Catholic bishop of Winchester, Stephen Gardiner, with a wolf's head biting the neck of the Christ-lamb in front of the altar, while to the right his fellow Catholic bishops and clerics, all wolf-headed, catch the lamb's spurting blood in their chalices. Above them hangs an apocalyptic, winged devil, who in an inscription expresses his approval of 'the prophets being slain'. In the German version, this devil

Plate 2.4 Anon., The
Lambe speaketh. Why do
you crucifie me (1553–5)

states that he is the pope, thereby identifying the papal Antichrist as the instigator of this horrible deed. Below the altar rest the already killed sheep of the English Protestant bishops, Thomas Cranmer, Nicholas Ridley, John Hooper, Hugh Latimer and others. To the left of the engraving a group of laymen, symbolising the common people are being pulled along by their noses by Stephen Gardiner, while a couple of noblemen in vain try to restrain the Catholic bishop. For contemporaries the message was clear: these wolves were the anti-christian enemies of the godly. Jesus had, after all, specifically warned his disciples that they would be 'as lambs in the midst of wolves' (Matthew 10:16 and Luke 10:3).

Bullinger's commentary, together with that of John Bale, in his work *The Image of bothe Churches* (1551), also found their way into the marginal notes on the Book of Revelation of the English Genevan Bible, despite this work's overall Genevan character.[83] Due to the Genevan Bible's considerable popularity, as can be seen from its numerous editions, which to a large extent is explained by its relatively low price, their historical and prophetic interpretation of this text proved hugely influential not only among readers, but also among the many who only attended the services and sermons in their parish churches. The Elizabethan bishop of Norwich, John Parkhurst, who as a refugee in Zurich in the late 1550s had himself listened to Bullinger's sermons, instructed the clergy in his diocese to buy a copy of Bullinger's commentary on the Apocalypse.[84]

Despite the contributions of other early English reformers such as William Tyndale and Robert Barnes, John Bale's works, especially his *The Image of bothe Churches*, came to shape the Protestant apocalyptic tradition in England more than any other work.[85] Together with John Foxe and his influential *Acts and Monuments* (1563), Bale accentuated the historical interpretation of the Book of Revelation, whereby biblical and historical time were seen as identical.[86] Thus persecuted and exiled, the Marian refugees fused their battle against the Catholic regime of Mary with their expectations for the Second Coming of Christ. This eschatological interpretation of their time and the Reformation also came to distinguish most of the Elizabethan bishops, such as Ridley, Aylmer and Sandys, who, of course, had all experienced the anxiety of exile, and all of whom emphasised the twin agencies of Antichrist to be found in the papacy and the Turks.[87] The impact of the apocalyptic writings of Bale and Foxe, however, was not restricted to Britain, but their works were read across Europe, even in Scandinavia where their views appear to have fed and inspired local apocalyticism.

In Sweden Bale's history of the papacy, *Acta Romanorum Pontificium usque ad Paulum IV*, provided the basis for an apocalyptic work by the Stockholm preacher and later dean of Uppsala, Olaus Petri Medelpadius. In accordance with Bale Medelpadius detailed the anti-Christian and apocalyptic nature of the papacy. Medelpadius's particular emphasis that Antichrist had also arrived in Sweden is an obvious reference to King Johan III's introduction of a new, more Catholic liturgy in Sweden in 1577 which saw leading Protestants within the Swedish Church confront the Crown and its Jesuit advisers in the battle for the soul of the Swedish Church. This conflict undoubtedly served to give Swedish Protestantism a deeply apocalyptic flavour in the last decades of the sixteenth century. Thus, the later archbishop, Abraham Angermannus, who attacked Rome as the seat of the Babylonian whore and considered the introduction of the Gregorian calendar as an attempt to smuggle Antichrist into the true Church, i.e. the Protestant churches, was convinced that the Day of Judgement was imminent and that the papal Antichrist was about to fall and all his followers to be condemned to eternal punishment.[88]

In Denmark where the Lutheran Reformation had been on a solid footing since 1536, such eschatological interests were more muted until the second decade of the seventeenth century when the growing confrontation in Europe between Catholics and Protestants leading up to the Thirty Years War appears to have caused a significant growth in apocalyptic interest. However, some Lutheran ministers clearly shared the apocalyptic expectations of their German colleagues before that date, as can be seen from a letter the minister Albert Meyer wrote to his friend in Schleswig, the rural dean, Johannes Pistorius, in January 1600. Here Meyer expressed his fears that the Spaniards would fullfil the prophecies of Johann Hilten and Luther for 1600. Accordingly he expressed his incomprehension of the carelessness and lack of concern demonstrated by the German princes, since he had no doubt that the Spaniards intended to destroy all of Germany and Protestantism.[89] This was a reference to Hilten's prophecy that a terrible tyrant – Gog and Magog – would rule Germany and Italy in 1600 while a gruesome persecution of the true Church would take place. For most of the sixteenth century this tyrant had been identified with the Turk, but since the beginning of the wars in the Netherlands and the Spanish Armada of 1588 it had increasingly come to be applied to Habsburg Spain.

By 1611, when the minister Niels Mikkelsen Aalborg published a commentary on the Book of Revelation which drew heavily on John Foxe's commentary on the Apocalypse (1587), heightened apocalyptic expectations had clearly begun to make an impact in Denmark.[90] Already in 1596 Mikkelsen had acquired a copy of the 1596 Geneva edition of Foxe's work in Copenhagen which he meticulously annotated throughout his life.[91] Not surprisingly Mikkelsen also proved deeply interested in chronology and predictions on the End, and in 1628 and 1629 he published two *Chronologia Sacra*, based on compilations from the Hamburg preacher Philipp Nicolai's influential *History of the kingdom of Christ*, first published in 1598. Considering that Nicolai had predicted that a final persecution of the true Church by the pope would commence in 1625, his prophetic qualities and calculations were self-evident by 1628/29, by which time the Protestant cause appeared lost due to defeats in the Thirty Years War and the issue of the recent Edict of Restitution (1629), which threatened the continued survival of Protestantism in Germany. This persecution was, according to Nicolai, the last of three final periods of trouble which would afflict the godly in the Last Days; the first had begun after the death of Luther in 1546 and had resulted in bewilderment and savage wars, while the second had begun in 1588 with the Spanish Armada and subsequent persecutions of Protestants by the Catholic Counter-Reformation Church.[92]

The general anxiety felt in Denmark due to the outbreak of the Thirty Years War and the Protestants' defeats in general and the country's disastrous entry into this war in 1626 in particular, resulted in a number of special days of prayer and repentance in the country's churches. In this context a series of litany sermons were given by the country's leading theologian, Bishop Hans Poulsen Resen, which clearly reflected the general mood of the time. In 1617 Resen pointed out that the Danes had shown a blatant disregard for the benefits God had brought them through the Reformation. God had therefore punished them with epidemics and high prices in the wake of the recent war with Sweden (1611–13). Similarly a surprising number of deaths among the country's leaders had occurred, not to mention the appearance of prodigies, fierce storms, floods, peculiar sea-monsters and monster births which all indicated the wrath of God. In 1619 Resen specifically referred to the divine warnings implied by the highly visible comet of 1618, while in 1626, having for years preached about God's punishing hand visible in the horrors of the Thirty Years War which had caused deaths, crop failures and epidemics, Resen emphasised that Luther's eschatological prophecies of the disasters which were to befall Germany in the Last Days were now happening.[93]

From the beginning of Elizabeth's reign English Protestants saw the Reformation as part of the general conflict which would engulf the world in

the Last Days. The idea that the Day of Judgement was at hand even pene-
trated the popular Elizabethan literature to such an extent that a group of
ballads were produced around this topic, such as the 'Bell-man for
England' ringing his warning bell to wake up people before the Second
Coming.[94] The works of Bullinger, Bale and Foxe did much to enhance
such a view, which remained ever present for the next century, even if it provided only a backdrop when things were going well from a Protestant perspective, as opposed to times of crisis or perceived national crises, such as
the Spanish Armada in 1588, the Gunpowder Plot in 1605 and the civil wars
which began in 1642, or major international crises such as the St
Bartholomew's Day Massacre of French Huguenots in 1572, or the outbreak of the Thirty Years War in 1618, when the apocalyptic significance of
the age would totally take over. The outbreak of civil war in England added
new poignance to such interpretations as can be seen from many of the fast
sermons preached before Parliament by Puritan ministers in the early
1640s. A prime example of this type is the sermon preached in January 1643
by John Arrowsmith from Kings Lynn:

> If we look to the flock of Christ before Popery, how hath the Sword beaten in
> pieces those seven golden Candlesticks in Asia meerly for their Covenant-
> breaking? If to Christian Churches since the happy time of Antichrist drooping
> it will be easie to observe that the Sword which hath of late been made fat with
> the flesh, and drunk with the blood of so many in Europe, for the space of more
> than twentie yeers, began to be unsheathed in Bohemia, which was the seat of
> the first open and authorized Reformation. That this should be the course of the
> Sword to come where the Gospel hath first been, and then opposed, is not
> obscurely prophecied of, *Revel. 6*, where upon invitation to come and see, John
> saw and beheld a white horse, and he that sate on him a bowe, and a Crowne was
> given unto him, and he went forth conquering and to conquer, vers 2. The white
> horse represents the Gospel of peace, on which the Lord Jesus rides with a bowe
> in his hand, shooting his arrows of conviction, those arrows spoken of, Psal. 45,
> which are so sharp in the hearts of the Kings enemies, conquering and convert-
> ing souls by his spirit and grace; yea, going on to conquer still more and more,
> his conquests being to have no end till the end of the world.[95]

John Foxe's works with their emphasis on providential history did much
to enhance the idea of England as playing a special role in this great eschatological drama, being a select nation, even if such aspects were only fully
argued in all their national fervour by the Bedfordshire clergyman,
Thomas Brightman, in his *Apocalypsis Apocalypseos*, first published in 1609,
and subsequently translated into English and Dutch and repeatedly
reprinted. Brightman's lengthy work came to shape the apocalyptic

outlook of English Puritanism for decades to come and helped give it a distinct millenarian tinge. Like James VI of Scotland, later to be James I of England, who had published *A fruitful meditation* in the Armada year of 1588, based upon Revelation 20: 7–10, and later wrote an interpretation of the Book of Revelation, Brightman had been inspired to write his exposition by the real or perceived threat to Protestantism of the Catholic Counter-Reformation in general, and the Jesuits in particular. It was similar concerns which caused James Ussher, the Archbishop of Armagh to take a lifelong interest in providential history and to believe that history and prophecy showed that the papacy was the Antichrist foretold in the Book of Revelation while the Church of England was the truest of the true churches. Ussher dedicated his work from 1613 on the continuity of the true Church to James I, who himself, as he pointed out, had identified the papacy with Antichrist, encouraging the King 'to apply strong medicine to the popish plague'.[96]

A couple of generations of English Puritans brought up on stories about the Spanish Armada and the Gunpowder Plot considered England's role as an elect nation absolutely central for success in the forthcoming apocalyptic battle against Antichrist. It influenced Puritan writers such as Alexander Leighton, Joseph Mede and William Prynne, just to mention a few of the most prominent, who all claimed that it was only true godliness which had preserved England when confronted by the 'powers of Hell' and Antichrist in the form of the Armada and the Gunpowder Plot.[97] Retrospectivly the defeat of the Armada had proved the validity of the widely circulated prophecy by the German astronomer Regiomontanus, issued some forty years earlier, that 1588 would be a year of special eschatological significance: 'Great happenings and wonders could be expected that year if the world did not come to an End.'[98] Retrospectively English Puritans came to interpret the Armada and the Gunpowder Plot as near apocalyptic events which confirmed England's status as elect nation. Thus in 1621 the Puritan preacher in Ipswich, Samuel Ward, designed a broadsheet depicting the two events together, which he had printed in Amsterdam with the title: *To God. In memorye of the double deliveraunce from the invincible Navie and the unmatcheable powder Treason* (Plate 2.5). It shows how England had been preserved from the anti-Christian machinations of the pope, his cardinals, the Devil, and the King of Spain, through God's grace. God watched over His flock and had blown and scattered the Spanish Armada, while His watchful eye had spotted and prevented the planned 'dark deeds' of the Gunpowder conspirators. The timing of Samuel

Plate 2.5 Samuel Ward, To God. In memorye of the double diliveraunce from the invincible Navie and the unmatcheable powder Treason (1621)

Ward's print with its Dutch and English texts, however, had as much to do with politics as religion. Not only did it appear when the Twelve Years Truce between Spain and the United Provinces had come to an end, but it also materialised at a time when the final negotiations about a Spanish marriage for Prince Charles were being conducted to the despair of most English Calvinists. Ward himself was to suffer imprisonment by the Privy Council for his audacity, not least because the Spanish ambassador to London, Gondomar, complained that the print was an insult to his master the King of Spain.[99]

That Regiomontanus's apocalyptic prophecy for 1588 also made an impact in the Netherlands can be seen from the chronicle of the Ommeland farmer Abel Eppens where it is reported among other signs of the Last Days.[100] From the outset the Dutch Revolt was fanned by a combination of anti-Spanish and anti-Catholic propaganda which portrayed both Habsburg Spain and the papacy as anti-Christian and more often than not in strongly apocalyptic terms. Such views were, of course, reinforced by the persecutions instigated by the Duke of Alva and his notorious Council of Blood or Trouble which sought to suppress heresy and stamp out sedition, thereby causing more than 100,000 people to flee the southern Netherlands between 1567 and 1573 for Germany, England and the northern Netherlands in particular.[101]

The Dutch Reformed were quick to promote the rebel cause by portraying it in chiliastic terms and a stream of pamphlets and prints to this effect were published. One of the most forceful from this period is an anonymous engraving from around 1568 with both Dutch and French text, entitled The Church of Christ (Plate 2.6). It shows the true Church, obviously the Reformed Church, being assaulted by the combined forces of Antichrist, commanded by the pope, the emperor, the Turk, and last but not least, the Duke of Alva, who personally fires one of the four large siege-guns against the godly, while another two are being fired by the Cardinal of Lorraine and Cardinal Granvelle and the fourth is being energetically reloaded by Satan himself. It is noteworthy that the canons of Alva and Satan have been given monster-heads, evidently indicating that their potential for evil and destruction was greater than that of the Cardinals' guns. The Children of God, the Reformed, can be seen fleeing their besieged City/Church naked in order to indicate both their innocence and suffering, while the buildings are on fire, being scaled by monks and pulled down by the Spanish Inquisition. The reference to the flood of Reformed refugees who had fled or were fleeing the southern Netherlands faced with persecution because

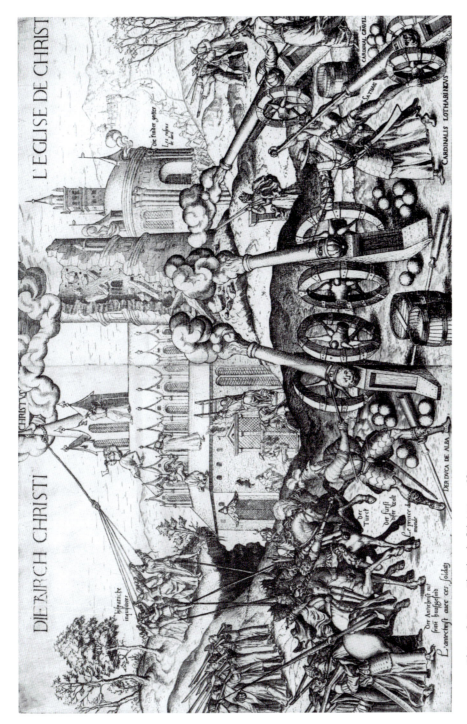

Plate 2.6 Anon., *The Church of Christ* (c. 1568)

of their faith is obvious. Clearly their sufferings had to be considered as part of the unfolding chiliastic drama which was now engulfing the world.[102]

A far more optimistic Protestant, eschatological scenario was portrayed in a broadsheet issued around 1615 in connection with the prolonged succession conflict over the strategically important duchies of Jülich-Cleves close to the border between Germany, France and the United Provinces. This Dutch engraving entitled The Display and Explanation of St. George of Cleves (Verthooninghe ende verclaringhe van den Cleefschen S. Joris) refers specifically to the Spanish and Dutch involvement in this crisis and the confrontation between Maurice of Nassau and Ambrosio Spinola in 1615 (Plate 2.7).[103] It demonstrates how the Dutch, fighting under the banner of Reformed Protestantism, appropriated the iconography of St George and the dragon for propaganda purposes. This motif had, of course, already been used to considerable effect by German Protestants since the middle of the sixteenth century.[104] In the foreground of the print St George (Maurice of Nassau/the Dutch) comes to the rescue of the virgin comforting the lamb (Christ/the true Church) who is under attack from the seven-headed apocalyptic monster which is ridden by a Spanish nobleman (Ambrosio Spinola). The monster is clearly the papal Antichrist wearing the papal tiara on its main head, while the other heads wear other clerical headgear, such as a Jesuit's hat and a bishop's mitre. Further association between the papacy and 'the whore of Babylon' is made by the building of the tower of Babel which is taking place in the background behind the monster and under papal supervision.

Apocalyptic concerns were also much in evidence among the first professors at the University of Leiden, the first university to be established in the United Provinces in 1575. Thus, the Geneva-educated Franciscus Junius, who became professor of theology in Leiden in 1592, provided the commentary on the Book of Revelation for the post-1560 editions of the influential Genevan Bible. Another Huguenot and Leiden professor, Joseph Scaliger, who was deeply engaged in a re-translation of an annotated edition of the New Testament which was not published until after his death in 1609, held similar views despite his mainly philological concerns, as among other things can be seen from his commentary on Revelation 17:5. Here he identifies the pope with Antichrist, pointing to the fact that the great whore of Babylon had the word 'Mysterium' written on her forehead and that the same word is inscribed on the papal tiara. Later, in 1627, another Reformed refugee-professor, Louis de Dieu, published an edition

Plate 2.7 Anon., *The Display and Explanation of St. George of Cleves* (c. 1615)

of the Book of Revelation based on a recently discovered Syriac manu-
script.[105]

Likewise one of the most influential Dutch Reformed theologians of the
early seventeenth century, Johannes Coccejus (1603–69), was convinced
that he lived in the Last Days and that the weakening of the power of
Antichrist (the pope) had begun with the Reformation, but that the forces
of Antichrist had once more been strengthened with the outbreak of the
Thirty Years War, while on the blast of the seventh trumpet mentioned in
the Book of Revelation Christ would return to establish his Kingdom.
Furthermore, there were plenty of heterodox chiliasts present in the
wealthy and dynamic cities of the United Provinces who vociferously promoted millenarian views, such as the deposed minister, Petrus Serrarius
(1600–69).[106]

The religious tolerance prevalent in Dutch cities such as Amsterdam,
Leiden, Rotterdam, Arnhem and Middelburg, just to mention a few, had by
the seventeenth century made them attractive places to settle for many
English, Puritan dissenters who found life increasingly difficult at home.
Consequently, a number of English Separatist and Reformed churches were
established. As a result English eschatological and millenarian thinking to
a significant extent came to be nourished and promoted by these immigrant
churches and their preachers. Thus, it was from the presses of Amsterdam
that the first English versions of Thomas Brightman's influential work on
the Apocalypse appeared. Likewise, Hugh Broughton, preacher to the
Merchant Adventurers in Middelburg from 1606 to 1611, started his apocalyptic preaching among the Puritan immigrants in the Netherlands. His *A
Revelation of the holy Apocalyps* was published in Amsterdam in 1610. Here
Broughton argued that Britain, as an elect nation, had been saved from the
machinations of Antichrist as demonstrated by the successful defeat of
the Spanish Armada and the detection of the Gunpowder Plot, but that the
country still remained in apocalyptic danger because it had not seen a full
Reformation, despite having thrown off the papal yoke.[107] Later Broughton
and Brightman's eschatology and millenarianism was taken over by the
minister to the English Reformed Church in Arnhem, Thomas Goodwin. In
his fast sermon preached in the Netherlands in 1641, *A Glimpse of Sions Glory*,
Goodwin sketched a scenario whereby the separatist undertakings were
portrayed as a necessary preparation for the Second Coming. According to
this, Christ's imminent return was to be expected in 1650 (also Brightman's
date) thanks to Independency, from when He would reign over the world for
1,000 years.[108]

These millenarian expectations within the English churches and other sects naturally caused deep worries among the leadership of the Dutch Reformed churches in the Netherlands. Such advocates were seen as dangerous not only to civil authority, but also to the weaker members of the Dutch Reformed churches. Such fears were undoubtedly also fed by the many Dutch translations of English chiliastic works which were printed in the Netherlands. Thomas Brightman's book was translated into Dutch in 1621 while the influential work of the Scotsman John Napier, *A plaine discovery of the whole Revelation of Saint John*, first published in 1593, was translated into Dutch in 1600 by the Middelburg minister Michiel Panneel. Like Brightman's translator, the minister Vincentius Meusevoet, who had spent his childhood in Norwich, Panneel also had roots in the Dutch communities in East Anglia, having served the Dutch churches in Ipswich and Norwich as a minister between 1571 and 1577. As a refugee from the southern Netherlands, having experienced the persecutions of Alva, Panneel considered himself to be living in the Last Days. Thus, writing to the consistory of the Dutch Church in London in November 1576, he saw the recent conquests of Maastricht and Antwerp by 'the Spanish bloodhounds' as being part of God's wrath as portrayed in Revelation 16. Accordingly he suggested that the Dutch churches in England should hold a day of fasting and prayer under the modified text from Revelation 6:10: 'O Lord, who is holy and true, how long before thou will judge and avenge our innocent blood on the bloodthirsty Spaniards?' Some time in the late 1590s Michiel Panneel had been commissioned to translate John Napier's work by the magistracy of Middelburg to whom he very judiciously dedicated his translation, pointing out that the Book of Revelation is 'full of sombre visions and prophecies which are daily being fullfilled'.[109]

Despite the activities of ministers such as Panneel and Meusevoet which clearly found considerable popular support and led to several editions and reprints of the eschatological works they translated, the Dutch Reformed Church never felt totally at ease with such apocalyptic undertakings which so easily might result in millenarianism and active chiliasm. Thus, the consistory in Amsterdam kept close tabs on the Spiritualist Englishmen Thomas Leamer and Humphrey Bromley, the former a merchant and the latter a chandler and bookseller who had already been suspended from Communion in the English Reformed Church in Amsterdam for being a follower of Paracelsus, not least because their millenarian publications caused a stir and they themselves attracted quite a following. In 1610, Leamer claimed that Antichrist was shortly to be overthrown and that

Christ would descend from heaven within the next twenty years in order to establish his millennial Kingdom.[110] The fact that Meusevoet, unusually for his many translations, refrained from adding an introduction of his own to his translation of Thomas Brightman's work on the Apocalypse is important. It is a clear indication of the growing sensitivity of such matters and the occasional need for caution among apocalyptically inclined ministers within the Dutch Reformed Church.[111]

The crisis which hit European Protestantism in the form of the Thirty Years War and the renewed Wars of Religion in France (1620–9), which saw the Huguenots struggle for survival, fuelled renewed and urgent eschatological expectations among Protestants across Europe. Among them was the influential Herborn professor Johann Heinrich Alsted whose writings on Daniel and the Book of Revelation were widely read by Protestants in general and Calvinists in particular, and who taught other apocalyptically inclined scholars of the age such as Jan Amos Comenius. Under the influence of the defeats suffered by the Protestant side in the Thirty Years War and the devastation caused to his home-town of Herborn by the Imperial armies and a subsequent outbreak of plague, Alsted moved from a fairly restrained apocalyptic outlook to a millenarian and chiliastic position by 1627 when he published his famous, *Diatribe de mille annis Apocalypticis*, which was quickly translated into a number of vernacular languages. For Alsted the suffering of the godly in Germany served to give meaning to the Book of Revelation and pointed to the imminent arrival of Christ and the millennium, which Alsted expected to begin in 1694.[112]

By the 1620s the eschatological temperature had been steadily rising for a couple of decades, not least due to the growing search for occult and prophetic wisdom among Protestants, generated in particular by what Hugh Trevor-Roper has labelled 'the Paracelsian Movement', which had its roots in the great scheme for the publication of Paracelsus's works which was already well under way by 1570.[113] Hopes for a great spiritual change or 'new reformation' grew after 1600. Joachimist ideas merged with the prophetic hopes of Paracelsus who had reinterpreted the old prophecy about a last Elijah, turning him into a great natural philospher and a wise man who would reveal all the secrets of nature – the *Elias artista* – who would fulfil what Christ had foretold in the Bible, namely, that all that had remained hidden should finally be revealed.[114] This apocalyptic anxiety was further enhanced by the growing confessional confrontation of the day where the perceived threat to Protestantism of a revived Counter-Reformation, Catholic Church was seen as greater than ever before by the Protestant side.

Thus, it was via Paracelsianism that French Calvinism became infused with apocalyptic expectations which in turn caused Huguenot statesmen such as Philippe du Plessis-Mornay to interpret contemporary events such as the succession crisis in the duchies of Jülich and Cleves in 1609 in a distinctly apocalyptic light. Mornay argued that King Henri IV's proposed military intervention in this crisis should be seen as a strike against Antichrist which would cause not only Babylon, i.e. Rome, to fall, but initiate a new age or millennium.[115]

The military successes of the Huguenot, King Henri IV, in the conflicts connected with the succession to the throne of France which saw him crowned in 1594, after having converted to Catholicism for political reasons, caused great optimism among Protestants in Europe. In Germany these successes were used for propaganda purposes in a broadsheet entitled *Ugh, Devil eats Priests shits Lansquenets* (*Pfuh Teufel friss Pfaffen scheiss Landtsknecht*), issued around 1590 (Plate 2.8).[116] Once again Protestant propaganda linked Catholicism, the Devil and defecation to great effect. This time it mocked French Catholics by suggesting that they might improve their military fortune if they could induce the Devil, the leader of their church, and here represented in Capuchin robes, to transform some of their superfluous clergy into soldiers. Accordingly the engraving shows the Devil in the process of eating three Jesuits while defecating lansquenets.

It was in this atmosphere of mystical apocalypticism and chiliasm that the first Rosicrucian manifestoes, the *Fama Fraternitatis* and *Confessio Fraternitatis*, were published in Kassel in 1614 and 1615 respectively. They added further to the growing eschatological expectations within European Protestantism, packed as they were with anti-papal and prophetic chiliasm. According to these works and the many which subsequently emulated them the fall of Antichrist – the pope – was imminent and a new and universal Reformation was to be expected. These hopes were similar to those already promoted by the leaders of the pre-Pietist movement within Lutheranism such as Johann Arndt, many of whom had been positively inclined towards Paracelsianism. The Rosicrucian excitement lasted less than a decade, and even if its political significance has been overemphasised, it undoubtedly proved significant in the ideological and religious sphere adding a feverish thrill to the growing eschatological expectations.[117]

One of the prophetic themes found in the *Confessio* was the Paracelsian prophecy of the Lion of the North who would come to save the godly. This

hope for a religious–political saviour who would fully reform both State and Church had, as we have already seen, been popular from the beginning of the Reformation period as demonstrated by the high hopes for the advent of a Last Emperor. In Luther's day he had been identified with Frederick the Wise of Saxony. Inspired by the new star of 1572 and the St Bartholomew's Day Massacre of French Hugenots in that year this apocalyptic prophecy was revived and transformed by the Stuttgart minister, Helisaeus Roeslin, and the visionary schoolmaster Paul Grebner from Lüneburg. They promoted a Leonine alliance of European Protestants to fight the final eschatological battles against the representatives of Antichrist, in their case the Austrian and Spanish Habsburgs. These battles would, according to them, precede the return of Christ and the election of the Elector of Saxony as Holy Roman Emperor. From then on this prophecy was variously applied to the royal houses of England and Denmark, and briefly to Frederick V of the Palatinate when he was elected King of Bohemia in 1617, but in particular to Gustavus Adolphus of Sweden, especially after his successful intervention in the Thirty Years War in 1630. Between 1631 and 1632 no less than fifteen German pamphlets were published which promoted the view that the apocalyptic Lion from the North was none other than the Swedish King Gustavus Adolphus. Thus, with the deliberate support of Gustavus Adolphus himself, he came to be identified with this Lion who miraculously would appear and save the godly in their darkest hour, as repeatedly prophesyed.[118]

APOCALYPTIC SIGNS AND PORTENTS IN THE SKY

These eschatological expectations of a great saviour, prophet, or conqueror coming from the North, gained further authority, as did so much of the apocalyptic excitement of our period, from astrological forecasts. Thus the prophecy of the Lion from the North found new support by the great conjunction of the planets in Leo in 1623, but already some twenty years earlier it had been applied to someone expected to come from Finland, then part of Sweden, by the Danish astronomer Tycho Brahe, who in his *Astronomia Instaurata* of 1602 had predicted that a new 'millenarian' age would arise through a conqueror coming from, or born in, southern Finland.

Throughout most of his adult life Tycho Brahe appears to have been convinced that he lived in the Last Days. In his publication about the new star of 1572, *De Stella Nova* (1573), Tycho summed up the significance of

Plate 2.8 Anon., *Ugh, Devil eats Priests shits Lansquenets* (c. 1590)

this unexpected celestial phenomenon by pointing out that neither theologians, philosophers nor mathematicians had any explanation for it:

> In the end we have to acknowlege that this spectacle from God, the Creator of
> the whole World, has to excite our devout admiration more than anything else in
> Nature, and that it was decided by Him in the Beginning and now finally shown
> to the world while it is approaching its evening.[119]

When in 1588 he published his observations of the comet of 1577 Tycho
Brahe included a lengthy section on its astrological significance, hardly
surprising since comets were then generally recognised to be particularly
powerful and miraculous signs from God. The comet of 1577 being much
larger than most comets was evidently of particular prophetic significance. Not only did it indicate that terrible wars were to be expected and
that dreadful epidemics and dearth would soon take effect, but above all
that major religious changes were at hand. Western Europe would be particularly badly affected according to Brahe. Catholic Spain would be
singled out for punishment by God, not least because of its inhuman persecution of many pious Christians in the Netherlands, but this would not
happen before the Spaniards had done much harm to the godly in Germany
and the Netherlands. More importantly, however, despite his declared
inability to indicate anything definite about the exact time of the Day of
Judgement, which he, as a good Lutheran, acknowledged was only known
to God, Brahe was convinced that the Last Days were imminent and that the
comet of 1577 together with the conjunction of 1584, the seventh great
conjunction, signified as much. Evidently Tycho Brahe subscribed to the
ancient and popular notion of a cosmic week. Mirroring the act of
Creation, where God had taken six days to create the world and rested on
the seventh, the world would come to an end after the seventh conjunction,
also known as the Sabbath conjunction, and as Brahe put it 'the eternal
sabbath of all beings is present in this conjunctio maxima'.[120]

It was, however, not only the astrological dimension of astronomy
which served to heighten the apocalyptic expectations in our period. The
fact that Nicolaus Copernicus (1473–1543) had shown that the earth is not
stationary and not at the centre of the universe, but rotates around its own
axis while orbiting the sun, as demonstrated in his *De Revolutionibus*, first
published in 1543, clearly added to the uncertainty and anxiety of the age.
What matters here, however, is the fact that at a time of general doubt and
anxiety when religious dogma was being questioned by the reformers
and material and social changes seemed to shatter the traditional existence
and outlook of many Europeans, the centrality of the earth and its role in

the universe was also queried. It signified the breakdown of an Aristotelian cosmology which had remained unquestioned for centuries and replaced the certainty of unchanging heavens with one of a changing and corruptible universe. To contemporaries it must have seemed that few if any certainties remained. Taken together this could only mean that the Second Coming was imminent.

Simultaneously Copernicus's discoveries served to stimulate the tremendous astronomical and astrological interest which came to characterise the sixteenth and early seventeenth centuries and which in turn did so much to fuel eschatological expectations.[121] While new stars and comets, the most notable being the stars of 1572 and 1604 and the comets in 1577, 1596, 1607 and 1618, undoubtably served to generate intense interest in astronomy among natural philosophers and the learned elite, and caused those involved to develop their observational and mathematical skills, these major celestial events were also widely recognised as portents or prophetic signs from God.[122] As such they played a significant part in the growing number of astronomical and astrological works which were published during the second half of the sixteenth century and most of which interpreted them as divine warnings and calls for repentence in order to avoid the threat of the impending terrible wars, famines and epidemics, all part of the imminent eschatological confrontation which was to precede the return of Christ.[123] The sixteenth century and the first decades of the seventeenth century became a golden age for astronomy and apocalyptic astrology.

Many of the early reformers, such as Luther and Calvin, were deeply sceptical if not downright negative about astrology and astrological prediction. Despite his doubts, however, Luther acknowledged that the well-known astrologer Johann Lichtenberger had got some forecasts right in his *Prognostica*, and Luther was clearly influenced in his own eschatology by his reading of Matthew 24:29 and Luke 21:25 which spoke of signs in the sun and the moon, eclipses and falling stars, as indications of the Last Days. In his advent sermon from 1522 about the signs of Christ's coming and the Day of Judgement Luther referred to the recent significant eclipses of the sun and moon.

> Besides, we have seen not a few Comets, having the form of the Cross, imprinted from heaven, both on the bodies and garments of men, new kind of diseases, as the French Pox, and some others. How many other signs also, and unusual impressions, have we seen in the Heavens, in the Sun, Moon, Stars, rain-bows and strange Apparitions in these last four years?[124]

Even if astrology did not become an integral part of Protestant apocalyptic expectations until the second half of the sixteenth century, when it came to be seen as a spiritual art which complemented biblical eschatology, many evangelical preachers had been quick to utilise it. Thus, as we have already seen, the Swedish reformer Olaus Petri considered the portent of multiple suns seen over Stockholm in 1535 important enough, not only to preach about it, but also to have it immortalised in a painting hung in the city's main church.

Undoubtedly Melanchthon's famous lectures on astrology, which were given and published after Luther's death, did much to facilitate this coming together of Protestant theology and astrology, basically papering over the inherent contradiction of human ability to comprehend and act as indicated by astrological forecasts, and human inability to affect and comprehend the preordained actions of God, which was a central tenet of Protestant theology. Despite this paradox astronomical prophecy developed into a kind of preaching which emphasised that the world was in its last, decrepit and old age. This in turn underlined the urgent need to discover God's hidden plan or to decipher the hidden prophetic message He had sunk into His Creation – Nature. By 1600 the idea that the best astrological forecasts were in perfect agreement with the prophecies in the Bible was widespread in Protestant Europe. The famous German, pre-Pietist Lutheran minister, Johann Arndt fully embraced the use of astrology as an apocalyptic tool. He claimed that the Lord himself had told of signs in the heavens, in the sun, moon and stars. Citing the Bible repeatedly, Arndt claimed that the heavens were a great mirror, in which a wise man could learn of future happenings on earth.

Arndt, who was positively inclined towards Paracelsianism and Neoplatonism, saw astrology as a way of understanding how the macrocosm – the universe – affected Man, the microcosm. For him the Book of Nature complemented God's other book – the Bible – both had to be studied and investigated in order to understand God's plan for the world, even if the Bible still took precedence for Arndt. The boundary between the heterodox mysticism of Paracelsus, packed as it was with apocalyptic themes, and the apocalypticism of mainstream Protestantism had by then become blurred. In the overheated religious climate which characterised the decades leading up to the Thirty Years War, however, it often seems to have disappeared altogether, as, for instance, in the case of the Rosicrucian writings. A good example of how apocalyptic, Protestant writers gradually were sucked away from a fairly orthodox position into a heterodox Paracelsian position, is the development of the Leipzig preacher Paul Nagel. When Nagel published his treatise on the new star of 1604 his interpretation was still within the Lutheran eschatological tradition: the star was a sign of God's wrath and the impending Last Judgement and a call for repentance. In his work about the great comet of 1618 Nagel, however, had become deeply influenced by Paracelsianism. He now believed that through the right observation of Nature the same lessons could be drawn as from the Book of Revelation, and that the two were not only complementary, but identical and to be revealed by the person with the right spiritual insight.[125]

More than anything else it was the spectacular and irregular astrological events such as eclipses and comets which were seen as signs of the Last Days, especially since they were considered to be occurring with alarming frequency in our period. This was emphasised by many contemporary writers such as the Wittenberg professor Johann Pfeffinger who claimed that they were particular apocalyptic signs to an old and decaying world. He claimed that these 'signs in the heavens' were accumulating around 1562 when he was writing. Besides all types of terrifying shapes and visions in the sky, blood-coloured clouds, eclipses of both sun and moon, they included an increasing number of meteors and comets.

Not surprisingly the spectacular new stars of 1572 and 1604 and the great comets of 1577, 1596, 1607 and 1618 generated a huge number of apocalyptic pamphlets and broadsheets dealing with them. On the eve of the Thirty Years War the alliance between prophetic Protestantism in particular and apocalyptic astrology had probably, as recently argued by Robin Barnes, reached its zenith. From then on Protestant church leaders increasingly began to associate astrology with magical and occult heresies and treat it with suspicion.[126]

By the late sixteenth century it had become routine for Protestant preachers to relate biblical texts such as Luke 21 and Matthew 24 in which Christ had spoken of the heavenly signs of the Last Days, to recent natural or 'supernatural' events. Thus the Rostock minister Simon Pauli in a sermon given around 1570 and drawing on Luke 21 pointed out that even if recent eclipses had natural causes they were nevertheless indications of great punishments to come. In particular he considered the two or three suns seen in 1566 as firm indications of approaching great sufferings and the Day of Judgement.

This phenomenon of multiple suns, generally in the trinitarian number of three, was increasingly reported across the whole of Europe during our period, from Sweden in the north, as we have seen, via Germany, to Italy in the south. Parhelia, as it is technically known, was generally considered to be an omen of horrible sufferings to come, such as bloody wars, epidemics and famine, all trials and punishments linked to the coming of Christ and the End. Occasionally, positive connotations could be linked to the phenomenon as in Bologna in 1531, where it was seen to announce a universal peace, a kind of millennium, before the return of Christ.[127] When Jan Matthijs, the Anabaptist prophet, launched his sally from besieged Münster in April 1534 which led to his death, it was said to have been inspired by the apocalyptic sight of three suns appearing in the sky over the city. Likewise the reported vision of three suns, of which the middle had a red cross, over Mecklenburg in March 1625 while the Thirty Years War raged in Saxony may well have served to encourage King Christian IV of Denmark to intervene in the war on the Protestant side the following year.[128]

It has been argued that this apocalyptic excitement might have been less pervasive than the considerable literature of the period would lead historians to believe, and that its effect might have been limited to a group of 'doomsday intellectuals' – obsessed theologians and natural philosophers – beyond whom few took little or no notice.[129] Considering the extent to which the apocalyptic mood of the age influenced popular print and illustrated broadsheets that can hardly have been the case. Thus apocalyptic expectations and interpretations dominated the most common and popular form of literature of the age: the vernacular almanacs or *practica*.

These mass-produced, cheap publications, consisting of sixteen leaves or less, providing astrological and prophetic predictions for the coming year, were widely available across Europe. In Germany alone it has been calculated that at least 3,000 were published between 1480 and 1630. This figure does not take into account the many larger *practica* or *prognostica* which contained forecasts for up to several decades and which included the most sensational astrological writings of the age by popular writers such as Johann Lichtenberger, Joseph Grünpeck and Johann Carion, the Brandenburg court astrologer who later wrote the famous *Chronicle*.

Like Carion, Paracelsus made his reputation in this genre too. Paracelsus's first published work, *Practica gemacht auf Europen 1530–1534*, appeared in Nuremberg in 1529 and was reprinted no less than five times within the first year of its appearance. Likewise, it is noteworthy that *practica* account for the majority of works published by Paracelsus during his lifetime – sixteen out of a total of twenty-three – and among them a number of annual *practica*.[130] By the middle of the sixteenth century collected editions of some of the more popular and prominent prophecies by Paracelsus, Lichtenberger, Grünpeck, Carion and others gained considerable popularity and an increasing number were published.

The fact that sixteenth-century apocalyptic astrology and preaching led to a number of major and widespread scares across Europe is further evidence of how pervasive the idea had become that the world was going through its last phase and that the Day of Judgement was imminent. The apocalyptic speculations in connection with the conjunction of planets in Pisces in February 1524 generated nearly 160 tracts, mainly almanacs and *practica*, written by some sixty authors, in the five years between 1519 to 1524. This vast literature made an immediate impact, and generated what can only be desribed as eschatological hysteria and collective panic in many places in Germany, Switzerland and Italy. Apart from fear of the typical disasters, such as war, famine and epidemics which would lead up to the End in 1524 or 1525, the main scare was about the expected Second Deluge, obviously encouraged by the conjunction in Pisces, but also inspired by Christ's reference to such an event in connection with his Second Coming in Matthew 24:37–9. In the first months of 1524 Vienna appears to have been particularly badly affected by widespread panic which caused many of its leading citizens and nobles to flee into the surrounding hills and mountains seeking shelter from the expected flood.[131]

Some astrologers, such as Johann Carion, set a precise day for the expected disaster – in his case 15 July 1525. How widespread and forceful this fear of a Second Deluge was by 1524 can also be seen from the apocalyptic dream Dürer had on 4 June 1524, when he dreamt that the earth was deluged by a colossal and shattering cloudburst. This experience disturbed him so much that afterwards he painted a watercolour of it and added a description of the nightmare underneath. Despite the fact that the deluge did not appear astrological prophecies maintained their hold over the popular imagination not least due to the fact that a number of *practica* apart from the deluge had also predicted uprisings by the peasants and that the common man would seek to institute a regime of social justice and equality. This forecast, of course, was with hindsight seen as vindicated by the social upheavals in connection with the Peasants' Wars in Germany.[132]

A similar scare in the 1580s made a particular impact in Elizabethan England where a stream of publications, sermons, popular tracts and almanacs added to the apocalyptic expectations which had been in evidence from Queen Elizabeth's accession. The author of a number of

English almanacs, John Securis, translated the prophecies of the famous Bohemian astrologer Cyprian Leowitz, which predicted the end of the world some time between the conjunction of Saturn and Jupiter in 1583 and the old forecast by Regiomontanus for 1588. These prophecies were republished in 1573 and resulted in a series of popular pamphlets which elaborated the motif, often adding sensational details. Local almanac-writers such as the brothers John and Richard Harvey predicted that at noon on 28 April 1583 a great storm would commence the scourges which would shortly lead to the Day of Judgement. That the conjunction passed without any of the many disasters forecast taking place clearly served to undermine popular faith in astrology in England, and the two Harvey brothers were openly mocked by Londoners. In the case of John Harvey it caused a total loss of apocalyptic belief as can be seen from his subsequent almanacs where he repudiated all such speculations.

Fortunately for apocalyptic astrology political events once more came to its assistance. This time it was in the form of Philip II and the Spanish Armada of 1588 which appeared to fulfil some of the prophecies while simultaneously showing God's mercy on a godly nation when it repented. As such the victory over the Armada was used by godly English ministers and astrologers until the Restoration in 1660, while the lack of repentance served the opposite purpose, explaining why disasters had hit godly Protestants. This was the way the astrologer William Lilly explained the disasters of the Thirty Years War and the English Civil War in the 1640s. First God's warning of 1572 – the new star – had remained unheeded, then his second warning – the comet of 1618 – had caused neither princes nor clergy to repent or mend their ways; the dire consequences of such persistent sinfulness had led to the Thirty Years War. The English, showing no concern for such lessons, then ignored a final warning, namely the conjunction of superior planets in 1642 and had now been punished with civil war.[133] In this respect Lilly was only reflecting the general apocalyptic mood which issued from many English pulpits, as can be seen from the fast sermons preached to Parliament in those years. These were days of shaking, trouble, rebuke and fear, as the minister John Wittaker put it in 1643:

> First, the judgements of God upon England: may wee not say who gave up England for a spoyle and Ireland unto Robbers? Hath not the Lord against whom wee have sinned? Therefore hath he powred upon us the fury of his anger, and the strength of the Battell, it hath set us on fire round about, yet we carry our selves as though we knew not, and though it burnes we lay it not to heart, and these shaking Judgements may the rather move us because this concussion is

universall, the disease is Epidemicall, this shaking began in the Palatinate Bohemia, but it hath spread itselfe over France, Spain and all over the Christian World.[134]

THE ESCHATOLOGICAL DECAY OF NATURE: THE WORLD TURNED UPSIDE-DOWN AND WITCHCRAFT

However, signs and portents of approaching apocalyptic disasters were not seen as restricted to the sky. Nature itself in its accelerating decay and old age was providing similar signs of the impending End. Furthermore, the world, as it had been known to contemporaries, was changing rapidly and drastically. Due to the great voyages of discovery a new world was being added to the old. Here again old certainties were dismantled and replaced with uncertainty and anxiety.

Some discoverers, such as Christopher Columbus, clearly saw their undertakings in an apocalyptic light, helping to fulfil God's plan for the world, making it possible to convert all the earth's people to Christianity before the Second Coming. Columbus considered his own mission to discover a new route to Asia as part of a divine plan whereby a Spanish king would conquer Jerusalem which, together with his discoveries, would initiate a golden age of universal conversion to Christianity which would precede the return of Christ and the End.[135] This eschatological dimension of the discoveries of new lands was echoed by many Protestants in our period, such as the Hamburg minister Philipp Nicolai, who claimed that it had been prophesyed in the Bible that before the Second Coming many new lands would be found.[136]

The world, or Nature, was in other words in a flux of transformation and it provided plenty of signs and portents to those who in growing numbers watched with anticipation and fear, that the End was close at hand. It was clearly being turned upside-down. The medieval Christian–Sibylline apocalyptic forecast of a great battle to take place in connection with Christ's return resurfaced in numerous prophecies in the sixteenth and early seventeenth centuries. In Sweden it was reiterated by the minister in Sveg in the 1560s who claimed that at the time of his twelfth successor a bloody battle would take place on the plain next to the church in Sveg. Not only would the blood of the many fallen warriors cover the whole plain, but it would constitute a deep pool, reaching well over the hoofs of the horses. Only one man would survive this eschatological battle, and he would ride away on a white or a black horse and spread the news of the result of this confrontation. It seems more than likely that this particular rider was meant to be none other than our White Horseman – Christ, the conqueror. The fact that St Birgitte of Sweden in the fourteenth century is supposed to have prophesyed a similar battle to take place near the monastery of Vadstena may well have provided the direct line of inspiration for the minister in Sveg.

More important than such prophecies, however, became visions in the sky of armies engaged in fierce battle. Thus among the many omens and portents reported by the Swedish minister Joen Petri Klint from 1568 until his death in 1608 is a vision that had been seen over Rome in 1580 – one army clearly dressed as Turks had fought and beaten an army of Christians. So bloody had the battle been that the Turkish horses eventually stood knee-deep in Christian blood. Similarly, the Swedish astrologer Sigfrid Aronius Forsius reported that in the late 1590s the inhabitants of a small town near Helsinki had seen a terrible battle in the sky and subsequently discovered much blood in the fields below.[137]

From the middle of the sixteenth century such visions in the sky began to be depicted in popular broadsheets. More often than not their message was distinctly apocalyptic, as can be seen from this German woodcut from 1566 entitled *True Description of a Vision . . . over Dessau* (*Warhafftige Beschreibunge des Gesichts . . . zu Dessau*) (Plate 2.9).[138] Surrounded by clouds and stars a horseman, a heavily armoured knight, gallops across the sky towards a half-moon surrounded by a halo, underneath which hangs a spread eagle. The text underneath the woodcut informs the reader that this vision prophesies great suffering for Germany in the days leading up to the return of Christ and the Day of Judgement. Furthermore the text indicates that this horseman is none other than the White Horseman – Christ, the Conqueror from the Book of Revelation. The eagle, on the other hand, may represent several things: it might refer to the author of the Apocalypse, being the symbol of John the Evangelist; it might be the eagle of woe 'to those who dwell on earth' from Revelation 8:13; and finally it might be the Habsburg eagle indicating the predicaments of the Holy Roman Empire then fighting the Ottoman Turks in Hungary.

In connection with the battle of Strångebro in September 1598 which saw the rightful claimant to the Swedish throne, the Catholic King Sigismund of Poland, defeated by his uncle Duke Karl, an event which finally secured a Protestant future for Sweden and closed the door on the Catholic Counter-Reformation, a number of portents were observed.

Plate 2.9 Anon., *True Description of a Vision . . . over Dessau* (1566)

Exactly a year prior to the battle two peasants from Strångebro had first heard a terrible noise and then seen two armies in the sky – one clearly Swedish, the other Polish – engaged in a fierce battle which eventually resulted in victory for the Swedes. Similar signs were reported during the first months of 1598 at Kalmar and Skälby respectively. They all illustrate the apocalyptic garb in which the political and religious confrontation with Poland and its Catholic ruler, King Sigismund, was perceived within a by then predominantly Protestant Sweden.[139]

Identical visions of armies involved in eschatological battles were repeatedly reported in most of Protestant Europe in our period and often illustrated in broadsheets, as can be seen from an example from 1616 entitled *Two true and terrible new visions* (*Zwo warfftige und erschröckliche Newe*

Zeitungen) (Plate 2.10).[140] This woodcut combines two visions, one in the sky, and another on the ground, which supplement each other. As proof of their authenticity the text underneath the picture claims that they were simultaneously seen in several places in Germany. A large blood-red sun surrounded by three bunches of brushwood separates two armies, one clearly Turkish the other European, about to attack each other. In the clouds underneath a white cross, signifying the return of Christ, as pointed out by Luther in 1522,[141] and a bier, serving as a *memento mori*, while the bunches of brushwood serve as signs of divine punishments to come. Underneath the sun a chariot of fire pulled by horses of fire unites the two visions. This chariot, similar to that which took the prophet Elijah up to heaven (2 Kings 2:11) signifies not only the return of the prophet, but also that the End is at hand. This interpretation is confirmed by the vision on the ground which depicts the return of Christ the Child announced by a cherub while a young girl is confronted by Death equipped with a bow and arrow. The vision is then authenticated by the four burghers in the lower right-hand corner of the woodcut.

Apart from the perceived growing frequency of major natural disasters such as storms, including hailstorms with hails as large as rocks, floods, and earthquakes, which were all seen as natural indications of the world's growing decay and corruption and taken as proof that the End was impending, supernatural events such as rain of sulphur and blood, the appearance of monsters and monster-births were widely reported. In his *Prognosticon* from 1609 the astrologer Sigfrid Aronus Forsius offers a typically apocalyptic and pessimistic view of nature. He thinks the world has become lame with age. Despite the fact that the sun, according to Forsius, by then had come much closer to the earth than it had been in classical times, it was unable to warm it properly, because its rays were losing their force. Likewise, the four Elements were weakened and had become impure, and together with the sun they were unable to nourish and maintain the number of plants, animals and fish as had hitherto been the case. Also the age of Man had much diminished, where our forefathers lived for hundreds of years, Forsius refers to the case of Methuselah who is supposed to have lived for 969 years, by 1609 you could exceptionally expect to reach only 70 or 80 years. Nothing lasted any longer, bricks, which had previously withstood time for 100 or 200 years, now lasted little more than three or four years, while old wood was much stronger than the new. This was to Forsius definite proof that the world was suffering from the infirmity of old age and it was rapidly coming to its End. According to Forsius's

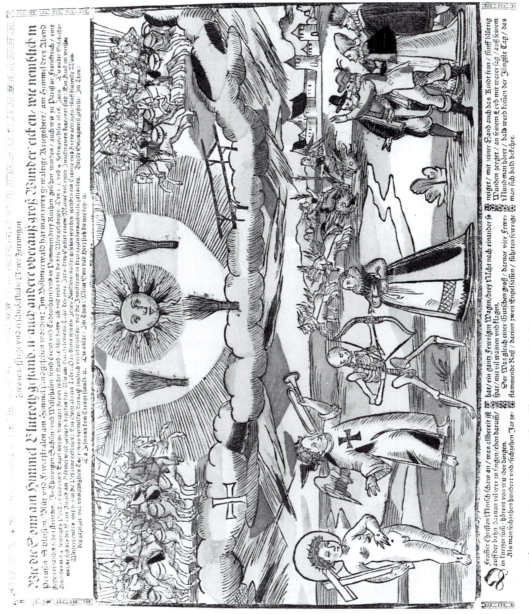

Plate 2.10 Anon., *Two true and terrible new visions* (1616)

Prognosticon for 1620 the End would most likely come in the form of a Second Deluge.[142]

In Lutheran areas in particular such omens and portents were often closely linked to the appearance of lay prophets who preached repentance and warned of the approaching Day of Judgement. It has been calculated that around 300 such prophets appeared in Germany and Scandinavia between 1550 and 1700.[143] As a rule such prophets would emerge in times of local or national, political and/or social crises, more often than not receiving their prophetic messages from angels. Some were 'genuine' such as the Lübeck citizen David Frese, who in 1629 encountered an old man dressed in white who gave him a message for the local authorities.[144] Others, however, were shown to be fraudulent after investigation by the relevant lay and ecclesiastical authorities. This was the case of the Württemberg vintner Hans Keil who claimed to have encountered an angel in a vineyard above his village in February 1648. According to Keil the angel had instructed him to inform the authorities about terrible punishments to come if the people of Württemberg in particular, and Germany in general, did not repent. When writing down his experience Keil made clear references to the sufferings of Germany and Württemberg during the Thirty Years War. He emphasised that if the prince and the authorities failed to make the people change their evil ways God would send terrible storms which would destroy no less than seven cities and kill many people and animals, while most of those who survived would starve to death. Finally, Keil added to his apocalyptic scenario by claiming that 'a fierce people will descend and will plunder the remaining places. The people will completely languish, for the Lord will call together all of the heathen and shall make an end to Christendom.'[145]

From his interrogations it is obvious that Hans Keil had decided to take up his prophetic activities after having been inspired by sermons as well as contemporary broadsheets and prints, some of which were found pinned to the walls of his bedroom and the back of his bedroom door.[146] Investigations of 'pseudo-prophets' such as Keil are particularly valuable to us because they document the way such apocalyptic prophetic activities spread via oral communication and the printed and illustrated popular literature.[147]

It is more than likely that another 'false' prophet who appeared in Viborg in Denmark in 1629 fetched his inspiration from similar sources to those of Keil. Peter Bruchner, the local hangman in Viborg, was a former German soldier who had remained in the town after the recent occupation of Jutland by Imperial forces. Bruchner claimed that on Easter Day 1629 a human spirit dressed in white with a red beard had appeared before him and instructed him to tell the local ministers to admonish the people to repent and mend their ways. When Bruchner had failed to do as instructed the spirit had returned three days later instructing him to encourage people to repent or God would punish them with plague and violent thunderstorms. During his third and final appearance the spirit informed Bruchner that if he failed in getting the ministers in Viborg to exhort the people to repent and refrain from selling their corn at prices which caused the poor to starve to death, God would burn up all the fields in Jutland. An omen in the form of a monster – half human, half calf – had recently been born near Viborg and was a further indication of punishments to come. If the people did not repent, God would send Tartars, Turks and other evil men of war into the country who would not spare even the unborn babies in their mothers' wombs.[148]

The corruption of nature was to be expected towards the End and monstrous births, like the one referred to by Bruchner, became a particular obsession in a wealth of popular and illustrated pamphlets, indicating the wrath of God and the punishments He meted out on His sinful people. Typically the French surgeon and natural philosopher Ambroise Paré in his work, *Des Monstres et Prodiges*, first published in 1573, claimed that monsters were things that appeared outside nature usually as a sign of some misfortune to come, while marvels happened completely against nature as an act of God to warn people of impending upheavals.[149]

The fact that many princes were willing to receive such self-appointed apocalyptic prophets in this period is further evidence of the intense anxiety and eschatological expectations which pervaded early modern life. In 1577 King Frederik II of Denmark received a peasant from the island of Samsø who claimed to have encountered a mermaid who had instructed him to inform the king that God would punish the country if the government and the Church did not prevent the growing immorality, lasciviousness, vice and sin and once more encourage 'traditional' frugality and piety. In this case the prophetic message of the peasant was somewhat spoiled by his simultaneous attempt to have his annual fee to the crown rescinded due to his old age.[150]

In Stockholm in 1585 at a time when several portents had already appeared such as rain of sulphur and fire, a prophet holding a sword in his hand began to preach penance in the city emphasising that all sorts of hellish plagues were imminent if the people did not repent. The effect of his preaching must have been considerable since King Johan III and his court came down to the castle entrance to hear his message. A month later Stockholm was hit by what must have been a particularly fierce thunderstorm which one Sunday morning placed the city in near total darkness apart from the occasional flash of lightning, while to those who were attending service in the main church it looked as if fire was coming down from heaven through the roof and vaults. It caused a great outcry and alarm among the churchgoers who not only feared that the church was about to collapse on top of them, but that the Day of Judgement had arrived.[151]

Fish, not suprisingly considering their significance in the Bible and their centrality for life along the North Sea and Baltic coastlines, were taken to be particularly important omens in their natural as well as supernatural form. In the Bible, Man's fate is likened to that of fish caught in a net, while in the early Church the fish was a symbol of Christianity: the Greek word for fish being an acronym of Jesus Christ, Son of God, Saviour. In 1587 extraordinary herrings were caught along the Norwegian and Swedish coasts which carried signs and inscriptions which were considered portents of the imminence of the Day of Judgement, while the Danish King Frederik II is reported to have considered them particularly ominous signs for himself. This was undoubtedly a tradition which retrospectively was encouraged by the King's sudden death in 1588. That year more wonder-fish were caught in the Baltic, close to the Danish coast and Greifswald. This time they were garfish equipped with all sorts of martial weaponry, all seen to prophecy the End of the world and bearing a remarkable resemblance to the large fish which was later caught off the coast of Holstein in 1615 and presented to Christian IV.[152]

In the United Provinces a number of stranded whales caused great uproar in several places. From prints, reports and pamphlets it would appear that contemporaries were of the opinion that an unusually high number of these large animals were stranded and perished during our period. These events were seen as just another proof that the world was becoming a less predictable and reliable place in its old age. More often than not they were seen as portents either of disasters to come or as signs of future victories for the United Provinces over Catholic Spain. Like fish, the whale, of course, carried biblical and prophetic significance with it, having swallowed Jonah and thus saved him from the tempest (Jonah 1:17).[153]

It is hardly a surprise that in a deeply apocalyptic age obsessed with signs and portents of the End a whole new literary genre established itself: the so-called wonder-books, which contained collections of divine signs and wonders in nature which were all explained as indications of the imminence of the Day of Judgement. The first appeared in Germany in 1532, one written by the prominent Lutheran Joachim Camerarius with a foreword by Melanchthon, but the genre witnessed an explosive growth in the decades after 1560 and remained popular well into the early seventeenth century. More than anything else it was the works of the Wittenberg professor Job Finckel which served to popularise this type of literature in Germany in particular. Finckel justified his works on wonders by arguing that apart from the prophecies in the Bible the most reliable proof of the rapidly approaching events associated with the Second Coming could be found in the increasing number of wonders which had appeared since 1517. Finckel was broadly representative of his age and most Protestants, including Calvinists, would have agreed with him. Thus Simon Goulart, Beza's successor in Geneva, told his readers to ponder such marvels in nature because it was the best way to know and revere God. His Lutheran colleague in Weissenfeld in Germany in 1595 had no doubt that the great number of recent wonders and portents signalled that the Last Day was at hand. Likewise the spectacularly monstrous child born in Cracow in 1543 is supposed to have provided the apocalyptic warning, 'Watch, your Lord and God cometh', before it died.[154]

It is also within this eschatological interpretation of a decaying world turned upside down during its Last Days that we should consider the great European witch hunt which culminated between 1580 and 1650 and which saw between 100,000 and 200,000 people prosecuted for witchcraft.[155] The vogue for portents and prodigies coincided chronologically with the burgeoning of interest in demonology. Demons and witches were considered to be further eschatological evidence that the End was near. Thus sermons, such as the one the German minister Leonard Breitkopf preached on Good Friday in 1591, were typical of the way witches were seen as eschatological portents:

> Nothing but dread and alarm, devils and spectres, sorcerers, witches, prodigies, earthquakes, fiery signs in the heavens, three-headed visions in the clouds, and numerous other signs of God's wrath . . . And these secrets, develish arts are

multitudinous, and the whole world is deceived with them, so that it is high time that the Day of Judgement came.[156]

The expectation that an increase in the manifestation of demons and witches was part of the apocalyptic scenario leading up to the Second Coming had, of course, a reasonable biblical basis. Apart from 1 Timothy 4:1 which spoke of those who towards the End would depart from the faith, 'giving heed to deceitful spirits, and doctrines of demons' there was, of course, the often quoted verse from the Book of Revelation (12:12) which referred to the Devil's arrival on earth, 'in great wrath, because he knows that his time is short'. Futhermore this had already been clearly stated in the original preface to the hugely influential work on witchcraft *Malleus maleficarum*, first published in 1486: 'And so in this twilight and evening of the world, when sin is flourishing on every side and in every place, when charity is growing cold, the evil of witches and their iniquities super-abound.'[157] Similar views were repeatedly voiced in the second half of the sixteenth and early seventeenth centuries by leading Lutherans, such as Andreas Musculus, not to mention prominent Calvinist ministers such as Pierre Viret and Lambert Danaeus; even a relatively hesitant eschatologist such as the English Calvinist William Perkins saw witchcraft as part of the overall apocalyptic picture, claiming that 'in this last age of the world and among us also, this sinne of Witchcraft ought as sharply to be punished as in former times'.[158]

When the Frankfurt printer Lazar Zetzner republished the *Malleus maleficarum* in 1588 he took the opportunity to add his own strongly apocalyptic preface to the text, connecting all forms of demonic activity and witchcraft with the rapidly approaching Day of Judgement. Similarly, it was undoubtedly Revelation 12:12 King James VI of Scotland had in mind in the conclusion to his *Daemonologie* (1597), where he pointed out that the reason for the huge increase in witchcraft was the fact that the Second Coming was at hand which caused Satan to accelerate and multiply his evil acts, in the knowledge that his demise was imminent.

Witches and demons were considered to be the henchmen of Antichrist by Catholics, as well as by Protestants. Thus the Catholic author of an anonymous Dutch tract from 1524 considered both Lutherans and Calvinists to be forerunners for Antichrist while simultaneously describing witches as Antichrist's assistants. Three-quarters of a century later the leaders of the Reformed Church in Amsterdam were promoting identical views when they condemned sorcerers as promoters of the Devil and Antichrist, even if they, of course, added the significant adjective 'Roman' to their Antichrist.[159] Such views were also widely articulated by English, Calvinist divines, such as Thomas Cooper who in his work on the secret doctrines of witchcraft from 1617 pointed out that witches were particular upholders of Antichrist's kingdom, and Thomas Brightman who considered the Catholic Church to be the real promoter of sorcery. Because the history of Antichrist was more often than not written in the 'language of demonology' witchcraft became one of Antichrist's important characteristics, as recently emphasised by Stuart Clark.[160]

Accordingly contemporaries were not left in doubt that the growing number of witches detected and burnt was proof that not only were all things turned upside down, but the End was near, as many commentators, such as Lambert Danaeaus, were at pains to emphasise. Or in the words of Bullinger's successor in Zurich, Rudolph Gualther, that Antichrist was strengthened by hordes of magicians and sorcerers who would initially instruct him during his early years in all the necessary 'abominable sciences' and devilish arts.[161] Likewise Catholics, such as the Frenchman Henri Boguet, were convinced that one of major indications of Antichrist's arrival was a dramatic intensification of witchcraft, while the Jesuit Martin Del Rio, who believed fervently in the reality of witches' sabbaths, considered such gatherings as proof of the imminent arrival of Antichrist.[162] The image of the the witches' sabbath was often reproduced in broadsheets by the early seventeenth century. This German etching from around 1625 entitled *See, how the devilish witches swarm* (*Sih, wie die Teüfflisch hexen rott*) (Plate 2.11) is typical of the genre, depicting a large number of devils, demons and witches involved in all sorts of nightly, magical and demoniacal activities in a mountain valley, while the text warns the reader of the dangers of such activities.[163]

Thus, what historians have labelled 'the great European witch-hunt' was very much a product of the general apocalyptic mood of our period. The alarming increase in the incidence of witchcraft together with what was perceived to be a stunning increment in the number of astrological signs and warnings from God, such as new stars and comets, not to mention the swelling of supernatural events and portents in a decaying, old world, all served to enhance the eschatological outlook of an age which embraced the Reformation and its retrieval of the Gospel as proof of the imminence of the Apocalypse. This was, indeed, an age when the arrival of Christ the

Plate 2.11 Anon., *See, how the devilish witches swarm* (1625)

Conqueror on his White Horse as prophesyed in the Book of Revelation was widely and intensely anticipated. The English poet George Wither put it forcefully in a poem written in 1644 while serving with the Parliamentary forces in the Civil War:

> I see as plainly as I see the Sun,
> He draweth near who on the white Horse rides;
> The Long expected Battel is begun.[164]

3   The Red Horse: War, Weapons and Wounds

> And when he had opened the second seal, I heard the second beast say, Come and see. And there went out another horse that was red: and power was given to him that sat thereon to take peace from the earth, and that they should kill one another; and there was given unto him a great sword. (Revelation 6:3–4)

WAR

The apocalyptic harbinger of war – the Red Horse – is in Albrecht Dürer's famous image of the Four Horsemen of the Apocalypse represented by a soldier wearing Turkish-inspired headgear, but swinging a straight, European sword. This part-association of the violent last days before the arrival of Christ or the millennium with the threat of the expanding Turkish or Ottoman empire to Western Christendom was to become an enduring image and metaphor in most of Europe during the next 150 years.[1]

The Ottoman empire by the sixteenth century comprised the Balkan Peninsula south of the Danube and the part of the Hungarian kingdom which lay between the Danube and Buda. Since their conquest of Constantinople in 1453 which had brought Eastern Christendom under Muslim control the 'Turkish threat' was perceived to be imminent to Western Christendom. Despite further Turkish conquests in east-central Europe and the Mediterranean the threat to Western Christendom may not have been serious, but it was perceived as such by contemporaries and proved invaluable in propaganda terms, remaining a catalyst for activating and uniting Christians, emphasising the dangers presented by the 'infidels'.[2] Not surprisingly the Turkish threat was portrayed in numerous, popular broadsheets. Hans Schäufelein's woodcut of a battle with the Turks from around 1532 is representative of this genre (Plate 3.1). Schäufelein, who had worked in Dürer's workshop in Nuremberg at the start of the sixteenth century, and who later joined another of this period's great artists, Hans Holbein the Elder, in Augsburg, shows the Ottoman army in retreat. In the background to the battle-scene are ruined buildings,

Plate 3.1 Hans Schäufelein, *Battle with the Turks* (c. 1532) (left half)

while in the ruins in the foreground some praying women have taken
shelter. The church in the middle of the picture has been torched by the
fleeing Muslim soldiers, while in the church tower a desperate civilian is
requesting help from the approaching Christian soldiers.[3] More often than
not, however, Turks were portrayed in the act of perpetrating far more
horrid acts or atrocities, especially against innocent Christian civilians
such as women and children. Not surprisingly the Muslim, Ottoman
empire became identified with the major apocalyptic figures of Gog and
Magog, or Antichrist, in a popular mythology which was increasingly
eschatologically preoccupied.

Obviously the expectations associated with the arrival of the half-
millennium of the year 1500 cannot but have encouraged eschatological
speculations and preoccupations as is so strongly in evidence in Dürer's
fifteen illustrations to the double edition of the Book of Revelation in
1498.[4] The significance of this moment had long been acknowledged by
the Catholic Church which had declared 1500 a special Jubilee Holy Year of
Indulgence.[5] It is noteworthy that around this time the papacy was constantly appealing for crusades against the 'infidel' Turks and that in 1502
the pope initiated the sale of indulgences in order to finance such a
crusade. Considering that it was the sale of indulgences which in the first
instance called Luther into action in 1517 and thus started what became the
Reformation, and that the later equation between papacy, Turk and
Antichrist became such a central image in Protestant anti-Catholic and
apocalyptic propaganda of this period, it is somewhat paradoxical to find
that two of these elements were already closely intertwined at the turn of
the fifteenth century.[6]

War, of course, was one of the three scourges of war, famine and disease
with which God, according to the Old Testament, repeatedly tested and
punished His chosen people. But few or no representations of individual
soldiers nor detailed military panoramas were produced before 1500 and
even if soldiers' cruelty to civilians had found representations in the
fifteenth century, they were few and rather unimpressive compared with
the cruelty portrayed in the mass of popular broadsheets produced in the
sixteenth and early seventeenth centuries.

As has been pointed out by John Hale, it is not surprising that northern
European art of the sixteenth century is full of associations between soldiers and death considering the popularity since the late middle ages of the
Dance of Death motif in this part of the world. Once again it is Dürer who
has produced some of the most forceful images of this association, best

represented by his haunting engraving entitled *The Knight, Death and the Devil* from 1513[7] (Plate 3.2). The image was widely used and we have a fair number of broadsheets with popular verses such as the *Death and Lansquenet* picture from 1504 by an unknown artist (Plate 3.3).[8] However, the relevance and popular resonance of this image was undoubtedly closely associated with the growing reality of war during this period when news of battles and sieges quickly reached most European urban centres via the new printing presses of northern Europe.

War had undoubtedly been an integral part of medieval life too, but before 1494 warfare in Western Europe had mainly consisted of minor wars characterised by brief and irregular campaigns, such as the Wars of the Roses in England (1455–85), the Hundred Years War between France and England (1337–1453) and the Swiss confederation fighting off the emperor in the 1490s. The sixteenth and seventeenth centuries proved unusually belligerent by comparison. The sixteenth century witnessed less than ten years of complete peace while there were less than a couple of years of peace in the first half of the seventeenth century. As emphasised by Geoffrey Parker, Spain and France were hardly at peace during the sixteenth century, while during the seventeenth century the Ottoman empire, the Austrian Habsburgs and Sweden found themselves at war for two years in every three, Spain for three in every four, Poland and Russia for four in every five.[9] To this can be added the many rebellions which plagued northern Europe during the first half of the sixteenth and early seventeenth centuries, not to mention the three major conflicts which dominated the age and which became closely interlinked, namely the Eighty Years War (the struggle of the United Provinces for independence from Spanish hegemony), the French Wars of Religion, 1562–1629, and the Thirty Years War. Even Britain, which appears to have been the exception to this picture, with only brief interludes of war, eventually succumbed to a decade of Civil War in the 1640s. The fact that warfare became such a dominant feature of early modern life post-1500 gives it a central role in the dramatic social and cultural changes which affected life in Western Europe in this period. Among the most significant changes was the growth in the size of armies of the sixteenth and seventeenth centuries. A conservative estimate would indicate that the number of men under arms grew ten- or twelvefold in this period. In the 1490s a large army would have consisted of less than 20,000 men, by the 1550s it would have been twice that, while towards the end of the Thirty Years War the leading European states would have fielded armies of close to 150,000 men. Nothing on this scale had ever been seen before, and

Plate 3.2 Albrecht
Dürer, *The Knight, Death
and the Devil* (1513)

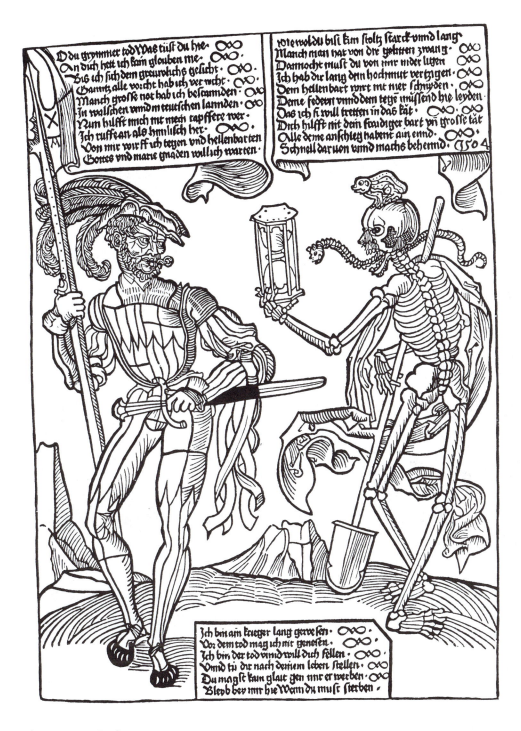

Plate 3.3 Anon., *Death
and Lansquenet* (1504)

whether or not this development initially reached a plateau around 1550, only to witness another round of significant expansion in connection with the Thirty Years War, as claimed by some historians, is of little consequence in this context where we are concerned with the impact of these developments, both real and perceived, on early modern society, and not the so-called military revolution *per se*.

The reasons for this increase in the incidence and scale of warfare should be sought in the breakdown of the traditional social structure of late medieval society. The stable feudal system which in particular had served the European aristocracy so well had come under considerable stress towards the end of the fifteenth century, as had the associated political structure, as a result of the pressures generated by the population growth. The positive effect of this population growth was economic growth, its negative result was rising prices and inflation which undermined social stability by causing greater poverty and migration. This weakening of feudal society provided the territorial rulers or princes with the chance to enhance and strengthen their personal power within increasingly absolutist territorial states. On the one hand they fought and repressed their noble subjects and rebellious peasants, while on the other, as was the case in Germany and the Netherlands, they fought their imperial overlord. Population growth within increasingly centralised and better administered states was not only what made more wars possible within Europe itself, but it also helps explain the 'external' Ottoman threat to Western Christianity in this period, which was itself rooted in Turkish demographic expansion.[10]

The great feudal landlords, who had been such a potent force both militarily and politically in the middle ages, were either disappearing or becoming less influential by the end of the fifteenth century. Not only was the acreage held by aristocrats shrinking, but simultaneously the number of royal fiefs available to them in return for military service was falling. Numerically, as well as economically, the aristocracy was losing out to the wealthy burghers, whose political and financial influence was expanding. The fully armoured, heavy cavalryman may still have been considered the most honourable form of military service by aristocrats, but his significance was already diminishing militarily before the lessons of the new weapons of pike and gun rendered him obsolete. Cost alone would have served to discourage increasingly impoverished aristocrats from finding the vast sums necessary for fielding such heavy cavalrymen, not to mention the number of retainers escorting them as infantrymen with crossbows and longbows. Aristocrats continued to serve as officers and commanders throughout our period, but as a rule they did not raise their own forces any longer. This radical change in how armies were raised was recognised by contemporaries. In his charge to the commission for almshouses in Maidstone in England in 1593 William Lambarde JP emphasised that 'not only in old time but also within the reach of our own memories' the nobility and gentry used to go to war bringing with them not only their wealthy neighbours, but also their tenants, and household servants, 'of the which three sorts, two were able at their return to live of their own, and the third was never forsaken of their lords and masters under whom they had adventured'. This sadly had now changed and instead prisons were emptied, and highways and streets swept to find soldiers. Lambarde was not surprised that such recruits on their return from the wars either resorted to begging or theft and ended up being hanged.[11]

The balance of power had swung decidedly towards the territorial prince. Increasingly rulers within powerful territorial states sought to protect or expand their lands. The expansion of states was as a rule based on dynastic and therefore 'legitimate' claims, often stated in terms of inheritance. Thus dynastic rivalry between the Valois and Habsburg families lay behind the wars in Italy, beginning in the 1490s – wars which expanded north of the Alps after 1530. However, it should be borne in mind that such claims were seldom made without strategic considerations.

A simple explanation of the increase in warfare in our period lies in the fact that early modern rulers found it so much easier than their medieval predecessors to start a conflict. They had much larger, and importantly, enlistable, populations, available internally as well as externally, from among the growing number of poor and displaced people. Growing economies provided them with larger revenues which their extended and improved bureaucracies proved more efficient in collecting. They also had access to much better and larger credit facilities from the expanding merchant/banking houses of northern Europe, while the new printing presses provided them with a significant source of propaganda.[12]

The evangelical movement which brought about the Reformation and the break-up of Western Christianity, guaranteed that religious antagonism came to play a significant part in the many conflicts of our period. Only when confronting the Ottoman threat could some unity between Protestants and Catholics occasionally be found. No conflicts, however, apart from the Anabaptist takeover of Münster and the city's siege in 1534–5 and Emperor Charles V's war against the German Protestant princes in 1546–7 – the Schmalkaldic war – can be understood in purely religious terms. Nevertheless, religion was a major component in all the major conflicts of the period, beginning with the German Peasants' Wars in the 1520s, the French Wars of Religion (1562–1629), via the Eighty Years War in the Netherlands (1567–48), and the Thirty Years War (1618–48), and ending with the English Civil War (1642–51).

Religious conflict fed popular tension, fear and expectations and provided the necessary backdrop for the simmering apocalypticism of the age. It provided fertile ground for propaganda and it often made the fighting especially bitter, thus indirectly proving the chiliastic interpretation of events so readily available in the popular and scholarly literature and contemporary preaching. Likewise religious antagonism may well have served to prolong conflicts and made them more difficult to resolve by negotiation.[13] But if motives and rationale among the main political actors of the age were mixed when waging war, for the common man the religious dimension with its latent apocalypticism was of paramount importance.

Three years before he posted his 95 theses on the church door in Wittenberg in 1517 Luther had already told his students that among the major signs of the Last Days clearly spelt out in Matthew 24, were wars and rumours about wars, and the fact 'that nation will rise against nation'. Such views were far from being restricted to learned circles as can be seen from the poem of 1545 by the Nuremberg shoemaker Hans Sachs, entitled The Gospel: The Last Judgement and Signs to Precede it, where Sachs wrote that great wars and rumours about them would intensify in preparation for the Last Days.[14]

Towards the end of the sixteenth century, when King James VI of Scotland, later James I of England, wrote his first meditations on the Book of Revelation, the religious wars on the continent constituted a major sign of the impending Day of Judgement. Similarly Thomas Brightman, the Bedfordshire clergyman, was convinced that the religious wars of the late sixteenth century signified the final battle between the hordes of Babylon and the godly warriors of Christ. According to Brightman the Turk and the pope were conspiring to destroy the true Church; the godly, however, would eventually prevail in battle and conquer Rome. After a final siege of Calvinist Geneva and a subsequent battle – which Brightman identified with the battle of Armageddon (Revelation 16:14–16) – the victory of the saints would be assured and Christ would return, while the converted Jews would destroy the Turks in the East.[15] Preaching to the House of Commons in January 1643 John Arrowsmith, preacher of King's Lynn, specifically referred to the Red Horse of the Book of Revelation when he stated that 'where the Gospel and Covenant take not place, there expect combustions and warre'. He then continued with direct reference to the English Civil War:

> Let me not incurre the cencure of curiositie if I note upon this occasion, that the late terrible battell betweene Kynton and Edgehill was fought in a place called, *The vale of the red horse*; as if God thereby had meant to say, I have now sent you the red horse to avange the quarrels of the white; intending to punish your contempt of my Gospel by the sword, even by your own.[16]

When in 1586 William Lambarde reflected on the growing conflict between England and Spain he looked back nostalgically to the 'long-enjoyed' peace of Elizabeth's earlier reign, even if he loyally supported the Queen's decision which was taken firstly for the 'Cause of God and His truth' and only secondly with regard to 'her own estate'. He then went on to warn of all the evils to be expected from this conflict. The world was to be turned upside down:

> For now such men as have more valor in their bodies than virtue in their minds will think that all the labor lieth on their hands and will therefore grow insolent and boldly adventure upon the breach of laws in hope that (for the necessity that we have of their service) they may not only escape punishment but pass without controlment for it. Now will your sons and servants strive to draw their necks out of the yoke of due obedience. Now will loiterers and idle persons think themselves warranted to walk at their wills. Now will beastly drunkards and blasphemers vaunt that they be valiant and serviceable men. Yea, now will thieves and robbers take upon them as if they were the only soldiers of the world.

This had all happened, as Lambarde explained, because 'we are fallen into the last age and times of the world, wherein, as our Saviour Christ hath promised, we see it truly come to pass that sin and wickedness doth mightily abound'.[17]

As a consequence of the increased incidence of war between much larger forces, armies acquired greater permanence during our period, while military campaigns became lengthier. No longer were they restricted to the spring and summer seasons solely, but more often than not they continued into autumn and winter. This increased need to be able to wage war at any given moment encouraged many states to retain large troops of professional soldiers in peacetime, which could serve as a core to which further and less experienced troops could be added at short notice. By the beginning of the seventeenth century a number of small- and medium-sized states were maintaining larger forces than before whether at peace or at war.[18]

Historians of the military revolution appear to agree that the increase in the size of armies was particularly marked initially in the first half of the sixteenth century and then again in the first half of the seventeenth century in connection with the Thirty Years War.

But who were these soldiers and how were they recruited? Apart from the Swedish and Finnish soldiers of Gustavus Adolphus's army in the Thirty Years War who were mainly recruited through a form of conscription, most of the men at war in our period were volunteers, raised internally by government-appointed captains, or recruited externally by military entrepreneurs. The latter was by far the most popular option because most governments in this period did not possess a suffient bureaucracy or adequate finances to be able to raise an army on their own. Armies raised this way became quasi-private institutions which often depended to a far greater extent on the contractor who raised and paid them, than the prince they fought for. This system reached its apogee during the Thirty Years War and undoubtedly found its most prominent exponent in the Bohemian nobleman and Imperial commander, Albrecht von Wallenstein, who twice raised and financed armies for Emperor Ferdinand II, in 1625–30 and again in 1632–4, until finally murdered by his distrustful employer.[19] Vast amounts of venture capital were deployed by networks of financiers, often through a complex web of subcontracting, in order to raise and equip such large forces. For such financiers the armies provided an investment opportunity, as can be seen from the examples of the Antwerp merchant Hans de Witte and the London–Amsterdam based merchant house of Calandrini–Burlamachi.[20] Similarly it was more often than not the hope of financial gain which motivated the individual soldiers who volunteered for these forces. Sydenham Poyntz, who in 1645 became Colonel-General and commander of Parliament's Northern Army in the English Civil War, absconded from his apprenticeship in the 1620s in order to seek his fortune as a soldier in the Netherlands, eventually rising through the ranks to become sergeant-major in the Imperial army in Germany during the Thirty Years War. As an English bachelor and former apprentice Poyntz was not an atypical soldier serving in the Netherlands during this period, but he was far from being a typical recruit for the early modern armies of northern Europe.[21]

Some recruits were impressed vagabonds and criminals who opted for military service to avoid punishment and imprisonment. England and

Spain in particular appear to have boosted the size of their armies by using felons and convicted criminals. In England between 1585 and 1602 an average of between 5,000 and 6,000 men were raised annually by such measures, and undoubtedly caused many contemporary English writers to despise professional soldiers as being the basest of the common people, no more than rogues and vagabonds.[22] Most soldiers, however, were like Sydenham Poyntz: single, young men who were tempted, not so much by the pay which was known to be low and irregularly paid, but by the bounty or signing-on fee. They were mainly unemployed or so-called masterless men and they originated primarily from either the mountainous or marginal regions of Europe where living conditions were harsh and hopes of material improvement low or they came from the war zone itself. Some of the latter may well have found it safer to be inside an army rather than among the civilians exposed to it, as claimed by some historians.[23] But like the marginal areas of Europe, regions devastated by prolonged warfare offered little hope of improvement or employment for the civilian population. For them, as much as their colleagues from the mountainous regions, becoming a soldier may not have been so much an option as a necessity forced upon them by unemployment and hunger. In other words the growing armies of the sixteenth and early seventeenth centuries consisted predominantly of volunteers from the poorer regions of Europe or those deprived and cast adrift by the consequences of warfare. Soldiers' provenance was geographically diverse and virtually all armies consisted of a mixed bag of nationalities. When Gustavus Adolphus landed in Germany his army consisted predominantly of Swedes and Finns, but only two years later the need to expand and substitute troops meant that by then Swedes and Finns only constituted 12 per cent.[24] Considering that recruitment generally took place in towns and cities we should not be surprised to find that most registered soldiers appear to have come from an urban environment. Volunteers from the countryside would, of course, have signed up in the nearest town which accordingly was listed as their place of provenance, thereby giving the often misleading impression that the urban environment provided the most lucrative area for recruitment.[25]

However, no armies in early modern Europe consisted exclusively of combatants. Most soldiers were accompanied by prostitutes, mistresses, wives and children, servants, camp-hawkers and sutlers. Camp followers in the Spanish army of Flanders appear to have constituted more than half its number,[26] out of whom female followers formed a minimum of 28 per cent. As can be seen from the broadsheets produced by Dürer's pupil,

Hans Sebald Beham in the 1530s, this was typical of armies of the sixteenth and early seventeenth centuries. Portraying a *Wounded Man in the Army's Train* (Plate 3.4) Beham offers insight into the chaotic conditions of an early sixteenth-century army on the march. In between the infantry mingle women on horseback and on foot carrying cooking utensils and food on their backs and heads, not to mention the presence of live chickens and a cock crowing. At the back a couple of sutlers on horseback can be seen while at the front of the broadsheet a wounded soldier on a small, decrepit looking horse is offered a drink by his heavily loaded mistress. A similar message is conveyed by Beham in the complementary broadsheet *Women and Knaves* (Plate 3.5) where the number of marching pike- and broadsword-men is matched by the number of women marching behind them clutching household utensils, flasks and fowls, not to mention the odd lapdog.[27]

No doubt the growing armies with their large numbers of camp-followers caused great anguish among the civilian population even if they were not under attack. They could only passively watch such motley crowds march through their localities or, worse, camp within them. By then armies often numbered in excess of 10,000 men which made them larger than most early modern towns – a frightening number to contemporaries for whom such armies must have represented devouring locusts sent as a punishment by God. Such interpretations would have been supported by the reading of the Book of Revelation (9:3–11) where the locusts are represented by a human army.

Early modern armies could only be properly supplied by boats and barges along either coastlines or navigable rivers, or exceptionally when troops moved along an already known route like the 'Spanish Road' suitable victuals could be prepared and stocked beforehand. The provisioning requirements were, however, staggering: an army of 30,000 men would need 20 tons of bread, 20,000 gallons of beer, and 30,000 pounds of meat every day. These figures do not include the requirements of the around 20,000 horses needed by the cavalry, the officers, the baggage wagons, and the growing number of artillery guns. These animals needed 90 tons of fodder or 400 acres of grazing daily.[28] In theory these early modern armies were supposed to be supplied centrally or supply themselves locally through payment. The reality, as was commonly known, was totally different. Badly supplied and paid troops resorted to regulated plundering and billeting which often developed into unlicensed pillaging and looting. No wonder the adage that 'every soldier needs three peasants: one to give

Plate 3.4 Hans Sebald Beham, *Wounded Man in the Army's Train* (c. 1530)

Plate 3.5 Hans Sebald Beham, *Women and Knaves* (c. 1530)

up his lodgings, one to provide his wife, and one to take his place in Hell', became popular in the German countryside during the Thirty Years War.[29]

The sufferings of peasants in times of war had by the Thirty Years War become a major topic for graphic artists such as Jacques Callot and Hans Ulrich Franck who dedicated whole series of prints to this motif. Their portrayals bear similarities with Johann Sadeler's earlier print from the last quarter of the sixteenth century, but Sadeler is far more interested in the ability of war to turn the world upside down than in acts of violence *per se*, as can also be seen from the title of his print combining two passages from Isaiah: 'O my people, your leaders mislead you' (Isaiah 3:12), your 'watchmen are all blind', 'dumb dogs cannot bark' (Isaiah 56:10) (Plate 3.6). At the back of the print a town is ablaze, while its inhabitants are fleeing. Some of the soldiers from the army marching past are busily plundering the farm in the foreground. Lambs are being killed and slaughtered while one soldier attempts to shoot the fleeing shepherd. The peasant's wagon stands packed with his belongings ready to be taken away by the marauding troops, some of whom find time to thresh corn in the barn, while another is busy feeding the chickens, all of which is being silently watched by the dog and the cock who would normally have warned and protected both the peasant and his farm. Thus war and soldiers are not seen to be at the root of this torment and desolation, but instead they are depicted as actors punishing a sinful world, something which is emphasised by the quote from Isaiah and the Protestant psalm sung by the army chaplain, which points to the fact that redemption can only be obtained through faith and grace.[30]

The association between soldiers, death and the Devil was already common by the early sixteenth century. Dürer, as we have seen, had used it to great effect in 1513, and his follower the Nuremberg artist Erhard Schoen introduced it with similar effect in his broadsheet from 1532 *Army train* (Plate 3.7).[31] Here in the train among supply-carts, prisoners of war, and pikemen death is represented by two skeleton lansquenets carrying scythes instead of pikes, while the Devil with the wings of the fallen angel as described in the Book of Revelation (12:7–9) sits on a tired nag, holding an hour-glass in his hand and wearing a crown of thorns or spikes with a serpent in it. The crown neatly juxtapositions the Devil with Christ while apparently identifying him with Antichrist. The inclusion of the serpent is a reference to Genesis 3 where the serpent seduces Eve and is seen as the cause of Man's first sin, and as such representing an embodiment of the Devil. This is an iconography which would have been easy to comprehend for contemporaries with their fairly detailed knowledge of the Bible, while

O mein Volck / die dich weisen / verfüren dich / deine Wechter seind alle blind / stumme Hund / mögen nit bellen / Esai.3. & 56.

Plate 3.6 Johann Sadeler, Plundering Soldiers (late sixteen-century)

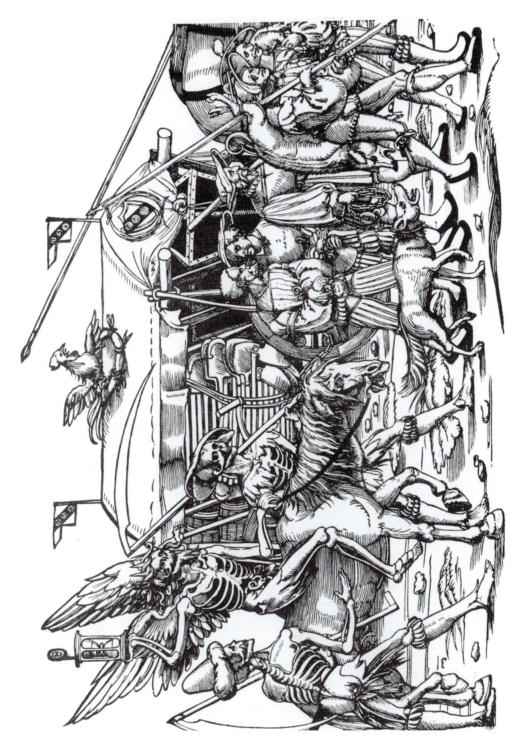

Plate 3.7 Erhard Schoen, Army train (1532)

the underlying apocalyptic message would have been enhanced by a reading of 1 John 2:10: 'Little children, it is the last time: and as ye have heard that antichrist shall come, even now are there many antichrists; whereby we know that it is the last time.' That Erhard Schoen should let Antichrist/the Devil appear in an army train would have made sense to contemporaries and confirmed their fear and anxiety of the impending Day of Judgement indicated by the growing incidence and destructive effects of war.

In order to guarantee supplies and make sure that the troops did not resort to widespread looting and wanton acts of destruction which would quickly lay waste the countryside and prevent any army from remaining in any given locality for any length of time, a system of regulated plundering gradually became the norm during the late sixteenth and early seventeenth centuries. It became known as the *kontributionssystem* and reached its most developed form in Germany during the Thirty Years War. In effect it was a form of taxation levied on all local communities in an army's vicinity in either cash or goods. The punishment for late payments or shortfalls was severe. The threat of having their property destroyed or torched was real in most war zones during this period. The figure of the *brandmeister* with his oversized, burning torch was an easily recognisable figure for contemporaries and often represented in popular prints. It could take the more dramatic form showing the *brandmeister* with burning buildings behind him from which women and children were fleeing, as portrayed by Leonhard Fonsperger in his *Kriegsbuch* from the Thirty Years War, or just a figure on horseback with his torch, supplemented by a brief text indicating the brutal nature of his enterprise, as shown in the woodcut by Erhard Schoen from the 1530s (Plate 3.8).[32]

The city fathers of Nördlingen in Germany did their utmost in order to protect the city's inhabitants against the Catholic and Protestant armies which passed the city during the Thirty Years War, or, as in 1634, laid siege to it. They met nearly all the cash demands by the Imperial and Swedish officials who led these forces, as well as demands for money from the troops themselves. For the city council such forms of controlled extortion appear to have been preferable to the risk of direct uncontrolled plunder, even if the burden of war proved detrimental to municipal finances after 1625. Despite such willing cooperation by the city authorities Protestant Nördlingen could not avoid a devastating siege, when Imperial and Bavarian forces besieged the city in the summer of 1634. Repeatedly bombarded and attacked, the city, by then overcrowded with refugees from the countryside, suffered food shortages and a prolonged attack of epidemic

Pranntmayster.

¶ Im Püntischen zug ward ich erke
Do ich vil raubschlösser verprent
Die wyder den pundt hetten gehandt
Das niemant sicher vor jn wandt
War durch manicher hantwercks me
Sein narung kaum gewynnen ke
Ich wolt das ich solt noch anzinden
Die raubschloß all die ich möchtf
(do)

NM

Nicolas Meldeman briefmaler zu Nürnberg bey der Tan am brückin

Plate 3.8 Erhard Schoen,
Brandmeister (c. 1530)

disease. When eventually the Swedish forces were defeated outside its gates
the city was forced to surrender. Unprecedented taxes were imposed on its
citizens while hundreds of Imperial soldiers were quartered in their homes
at the same time as plague continued to rage within its walls. One of those
who survived the experience claimed that in those days it was considered a
blessing to die from the plague rather than to survive and suffer such terrible punishment.[33]

In order to prevent wanton destruction and pillaging, princes and commanders alike sought to tighten military discipline. Consequently this

period witnessed the issue of an increasing number of more detailed military codes, not primarily for the sake of the long-suffering civilian population, but rather to preserve the armies and to prevent them from uncontrolled suicidal actions which would devastate the theatre of war and prevent further military action. The 'Lawes and Ordinances of Warre' issued in 1642 by the Earl of Essex, then general of the Parliamentary forces in England, are typical of such codes. They threatened soldiers who extorted victuals and money from the civilian population with the death penalty, while those who destroyed farms, orchards, trees, cattle and crops were threatened with severe punishments; likewise unlicensed and premature pillaging also merited the death penalty.[34] Lack of food and provision more often than not presented greater dangers to an army than did enemy action. Together with the lack of pay it led to a constant and dangerous wastage of armies through desertion, or worse by collective action of its soldiers in the form of mutinies.

For the civilian populations in the war-zones mutinies were often more dangerous than when being besieged or attacked by enemy forces. Unpaid and hungry soldiers who mutinied were often totally out of control and caused greater devastation to towns and countryside than did troops plundering in a systematic and orderly fashion with the consent of their officers. The sixteenth and seventeenth centuries are riddled with mutinies, starting with the famous and much publicised sack of Rome in 1527 by Emperor Charles V's unpaid German mercenaries, many of whom were evangelically inclined, which sent an apocalyptic trembling through a Catholic Church already weakened by the growing evangelical movement in north-western Europe. Later the Spanish army of Flanders mutinied no less than 45 times in the period between 1572 and 1607, and at least 21 times during the next 40 years – some of the mutinies lasting over a year.[35] The sack of Antwerp in November 1576 shocked not only Protestants in the Netherlands and across Europe, but also Catholics, and served to bring together the rebel provinces in the north with the hitherto loyal ones in the south in an alliance – the Pacification of Ghent – against Philip II.[36] Even the generally well-disciplined Swedish army of the Thirty Years War suffered a number of major mutinies. In the spring of 1633, despite the signing of the Heilbronn League, the Swedish army in south Germany mutinied and before Chancellor Oxenstierna had managed to satisfy the troops' arrears most of the campaigning season had been lost. Two years later Oxenstierna was held hostage in a military camp near Magdeburg by mutinous German troops serving in the Swedish army who wanted to make sure that they would be paid for their services. For the civilian populations, however, mutinies in their immediate areas or neighbourhoods held the prospect of even greater sufferings than those caused by the relatively orderly extortions and plunderings by regular armies.

The demobilisation of such increasingly large armies presented similar problems for civilian society. The threat to society, whether perceived or real, from the ex-soldier, either alone or in groups, sometimes in criminal gangs, became a growing problem from the sixteenth to the seventeenth century. Both contemporaries and their governments tended to identify the growing number of so-called sturdy and threatening beggars who threatened law and order with ex-soldiers. Of the many Elizabethan Acts dealing with the punishment of vagabonds and sturdy beggars in England, two issued in 1593 and 1598 dealt specifically with disorderly, idle and maimed soldiers returning from the wars. Their timing might well reflect the problems recently caused by the many demobilised English soldiers returning from France in 1590. According to a local official in Rye they were a miserable lot, 'some wounded, some their toes and feet rotting off, some lame, the skin and flesh of their feet torn away with continual marching, and all without money and clothes'.[37] In fact the Elizabethan JP William Lambarde considered poor soldiers a new category of poor which constituted a significant part of the general increase in poverty. As he put it: 'There were always poor leprous, poor lazarous, aged poor, sick poor, poor widows, poor orphans, and such like, but poor soldiers were either rarely or never heard of till now of late.'[38]

In the United Provinces similar problems were associated with discharged soldiers during the first years of the Twelve Years Truce with Spain (1609–21) and again in the years immediately after the end of the Thirty Years War and the conclusion of the Peace of Münster in 1648. Considering the many English, Irish and Scottish soldiers who served in the Dutch armies in the late sixteenth and early seventeenth centuries it is hardly surprising that we find a high number of these nationals among those who were arrested for vagrancy and theft across Holland and Zeeland during this period. They were, after all, as opposed to their Dutch and German colleagues, far from home when they were demobilised at the start of the truce with Spain. Finding themselves out of work and penniless they resorted to begging and petty crime and were repeatedly arrested by the local courts and banished.[39] We may never know to what extent early modern armies served as magnets for convicted criminals, but we can be certain that they served to criminalise a fair proportion of the people who served in them.[40]

The scourge of war and marauding soldiers caused the often long-suffering rural populations in particular to take action. More often than not they would do so on an *ad hoc* basis attacking and killing stray troops. The surgeon Ambroise Paré who accompanied his employer the Vicomte de Rohan with the French expeditionary force which assisted the German Protestant princes in their conflict with their Habsburg Emperor, Charles V, in 1552, vividly described the terrible injuries suffered by a hungry soldier who had tried to extract 'victuals by force or love' from local peasants. He returned with no less than seven serious wounds to the body and a sword stuck deep in his skull. His commanding officer wanted to end his sufferings immediately, since the army was to march on the following day and because he feared that the local peasantry would show the injured soldier no mercy, but brutally massacre him if he was left behind. It is evident from Paré's description that the French forces were finding it difficult just to find enough victuals to prevent mass-starvation, because of the hostility and precaution of the local peasants who had removed all their cattle and supplies from their rural abodes to the relative safety of nearby cities and castles.[41] Similarly the Catholic Imperial forces under the command of Count Pappenheim who arrived too late to prevent Spanish forces from surrendering the city of Maastricht in August 1632, were forced into a hurried retreat because 'the boores round about rose vp in Armes against him, not willing to suffer the insolences of his Souldiers, who neere Visell had murdered some of their peasants, in revenge whereof the bores cutt the throats of some of his stragglers, he bethought himselfe, and returned back againe to his own quarters'.[42] In many places, however, peasants rose in what is best described as armed neutrality to prevent their localities from becoming battle-zones, attempting to prevent armies from crossing or moving into their territories. This was certainly the case with the risings of desperate English peasants, known as clubmen, who in 1645, after three years of civil war, took up arms to protect their local communities against the Royalist as well as Parliamentarian armies, in places such as Shropshire, Worcestershire, Herefordshire, Wiltshire and Hampshire, just to mention a handful of the counties where they became active.[43]

WEAPONS

For contemporaries the many changes and improvements in military technology which enhanced the potential for destruction in our period had obvious apocalyptic implications. Luther himself had acknowledged as much in an Advent sermon in 1522 when he had emphasised that among the main apocalyptic determinants of the age was the fact that 'the skill of waging war hath so much increased that more cruel and desperate arms and weapons of war, and other warlike instruments can hardly be invented then are now'.[44]

Apart from the much larger armies which were in action for longer periods and more frequently from the late fifteenth century until the end of the Thirty Years War in 1648, technological innovations served dramatically to change the nature and scale of warfare in this period. The day of the heavily armoured cavalryman, a feudal knight or nobleman, whose suit of armour would have cost the equivalent of a small farm, and who reached the peak of his military efficiency around 1450, was over by the sixteenth century. By then he had proved no match for infantry pikemen, fighting together, in tightly knit units or squares. This had already been proved by the Swiss who with their heavy eighteen-foot pikes had crushed the Burgundian heavy cavalry in 1476 and 1477. Consequently, the pike in a lighter, slightly shorter and more wieldy format of thirteen feet came to dominate the European battlefields by the first decades of the sixteenth century. Detailed pictorial instructions for how to handle such weapons were widely published as can be seen from Jacob de Gheyn's seminal and highly influential work, *Wapenhandlinghe van Roers* (1607) (Plate 3.9).[45]

Of far greater significance for the changing nature of war, however, was the growing number of firearms employed in the theatres of war during this period. Already by the 1520s it had become generally accepted that handguns could wreak havoc on the massed bodies of pikemen who had by then controlled the battlefield for the last forty years. As a result by 1570 the Spanish army had one handgun for every three pikemen, while thirty years later it had as many pikes as handguns, while by 1590 the Dutch army, by then the most modern in Europe, had two handguns for every pike. The growing number of handguns and cannons used also changed the nature of warfare dramatically, making combat less direct and causing greater and more atrocious injuries to combatants and civilians alike.

In the sixteenth century the most common type of firearm was the arquebus. More than four feet long and weighing around twelve pounds the arquebus was fired by pulling a trigger which lowered a piece of smouldering cord into the gunpowder in the priming pan. The matchlock, as this mechanism was called, was an unreliable firing mechanism and the rate of misfire may have been as high as 50 per cent. Still, the matchlocked arquebus represented a relatively cheap and effective tool of

Plate 3.9 Jacob de
Gheyn, *Pikeman* (1607)

destruction with reasonable accuracy when fired inside sixty yards, as
compared to other available weapons at the time. Often, however, the
unreliable matchlock proved as dangerous to the soldier firing it, as to the
enemies he intended to harm. The gunpowder in the priming pan might
explode, causing 'a flash in the pan', and when doing so might perma-
nently blind the soldier and inflict horrendous burns on his face in particular. It may well have been such injuries Ambroise Paré encountered while
serving as a surgeon in the French army during the Turin campaign of
1537. Entering a stable in order to find shelter for his horse, immediately
after the enemy had withdrawn, Paré encountered three soldiers who

> were leaning against the wall, their faces wholly disfigured, and neither saw nor
> heard, nor spoke; and their clothes did yet flame with the gunpowder which had
> burnt them. Beholding them with pitty, there happened to come an old soldier,
> who asked me if there were any possible meanes to cure them, I told him no: he
> presently approached to them, and gently cut their throats without choler.
> Seeing this great cruelty, I told him he was a wicked man, he answered me that
> he prayed to God that whensoever he should be in such a case, that he might find
> someone that would doe as much to him, to the end he might not miserably
> languish.[46]

Plate 3.10 Jacob de
Gheyn, *Musketeer* (1607)

From the middle of the sixteenth century the longer and heavier musket which needed a metal fork for support gradually replaced the arquebus. It was a far more powerful weapon than the arquebus. It fired a two-ounce ball which would kill a man in shot-proof armour a hundred paces away or bring down a horse at the same distance, while loaded with scattershot it was horribly effective at close range. It was, however, considerably more difficult to handle than the arquebus and musketeers were consequently better trained and paid (Plate 3.10).[47] This again may explain why muskets were relatively slow in replacing arquebuses. Thus by 1600 there were still more arquebusiers than musketeers in the Spanish army of Flanders.

Obviously such major technological changes affected battlefield tactics. Some were introduced gradually such as longer battlelines and less compact formations, while other and crucial changes were introduced in the United Provinces in the 1590s by Maurits of Nassau and Willem Lodewijk of Nassau. A technique which permitted a group of arquebusiers or musketeers to subject the enemy to continuous fire, known as volley fire, was introduced. The so-called counter-march was devised, initially placing the arquebusiers in rows ten deep; later with better weapons and ammunition this was cut to six rows. This method allowed the Dutch forces to fire their weapons and then walk to the back to reload, thus maintaining continuous fire. Having been at war with Spain for more than twenty years the Dutch were keen to maximise the effect of their resources and troops, by spreading them as thinly as possibly on the ground while compensating for such deployment with better training. Drills became standardised and formed part of the daily routine for the troops of the United Provinces by the end of the sixteenth century. It was exactly such drills and regular training which saw the Dutch forces under the command of Maurits of Nassau see off the superior Spanish infantry on the beaches near Nieuwpoort in June 1600.[48] Dutch drill and tactics became reknowned throughout Europe, not least via the pictorial drill manual *Wapenhandlinghe van Roers* produced by Jacob de Gheyn in 1607, which was widely disseminated and copied either by people such as Henry Hexham, who had served in the armies in the Netherlands, in his *Principles of the Art Militarie* (1642) or Dutch emigrants such as John Cruso in, among others, his *Instructions Militarie* (1632).

Forty years later during the Thirty Years War the Swedish monarch Gustavus Adolphus added his own improvement to the Dutch counter-march, by reversing its order. By getting each rank to advance before firing it became possible to use this manoeuvre in an attacking form even if initially its success was somewhat limited. Furthermore, the Swedish soldiers proved faster at reloading thus making it possible for Gustavus Adolphus to cut the number of rows of musketeers needed in order to maintain continous fire. Likewise Gustavus Adolphus proved innovative in his extended use of field-artillery. Using smaller and lighter cannons in greater numbers, he achieved greater mobility for his artillery during battle, and was thus able to concentrate fire where needed to a degree not seen before. Where the Dutch army had deployed only eight cannons at the battle of Nieuwpoort in June 1600, thirty years later Gustavus Adolphus was deploying no less than eighty cannons.[49] It was, however, not as field-guns that artillery pieces had come into their own in the late fifteenth century but as siege-guns. The fact that initially they were very cumbersome to move, often being extremely heavy, weighing several tons, and being as long as three metres, had much to do with this. Lack of mobility, however, did not matter in the siege context. The French king, Charles VIII's, invasion of Italy in 1494–5 proved important for the added significance which contemporaries began to attach to artillery in sieges. His army of 18,000 troops supported by forty siege guns drawn by horses quickly overpowered the Italian strongholds and fortifications he laid siege to. High walls and castles proved of little use against cannons, something which had been realised by some military engineers such as Leon Battista Alberti since the mid-fifteenth century.

The popular fear which these large guns generated is probably best illustrated by the names, not only given to certain types of artillery, such as basilisks and falcons, but also to individual cannons such as 'Monster', 'Lion' and 'Messenger'.[50] Erhard Schoen's broadsheet from around 1535 (Plate 3.11) showing two large field-guns being prepared and loaded by their gunners depicts the awe in which such large cannons were held. Their size and ornamental design demonstrate their importance while their names 'Fierce Buck' (*Scharpff Hiersz*) and 'Brutal Butcher' (*Scharpffe Metzs*) imply their potential danger. Two verses detail their potential for causing havoc and destruction: where 'Brutal Butcher' is put in action 'he will dance across moats, through ring walls, inner walls and bastions, through churches, houses, cellars, kitchens. He will move through halls, living-rooms, bedrooms' and what he does not destroy directly will fall indirectly through his 'kiss'. In other words, he is not only a serious threat to other soldiers and armies, but he will wreak havoc on civilians too, who will find no shelter from him in their churches or their homes.[51]

It was in response to the success of such siege-guns that a number of Italian states began to build fortifications capable of withstanding artillery bombardments during the last decades of the fifteenth century. Out went stone walls and moats and in came a major change in military architecture which was to last in one form or another until the twentieth century, the angled bastion, or the *trace italienne* as it became known in northern Europe due to its geographical origin. This was an expensive defensive option demanding large and extensive engineering works in order to construct a network of thick, low bastions sloping backwards, built of earth, rubble and stone, in order to present a glancing surface to cannon balls. When this Italian phenomenon finally spread north of the Alps during the 1530s, the Dutch added their own design and covered their bastions in turf in order to absorb artillery shot better. By the end of the Thirty Years War only a handful of major towns in the Dutch Republic had not been supplied with bastions. The introduction of bastions also contributed to the overall

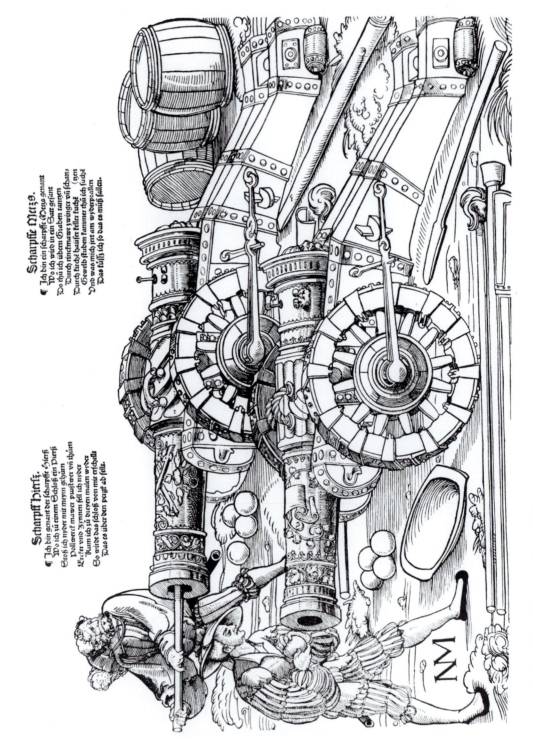

Scharpffe Metze.

¶ Ich bin ein scharpffe Metze genant
Wo ich würd in ein Satz gesant
Do thů ich über Graben rauffen
Durch trinck mawer zwinger vñ schan
Durch fürcht pawſe teller fücht qen
Grewlb ſtauben ſammer thů ich sücht
Vnd was mich jrrt am wyderprallen
Das fůll ich ſo bas es můß fallen.

Scharpff Hirtz.

¶ Ich bin genant der scharpff Hirtz
Wo ich zů einem Schloß ein Pirtz
Stoß ich nyder mit meynn gschütz
Dolluert mawer pawſterer vñ thůrn
Lecker vnd Zynnen fell ich nyder
Kum ich zů bayern malen weder
So wirdt das ſchloß von mir erſchellt
Das es über den pргft ab fellt.

Plate 3.11 Erhard Schoen, *Loading two fieldguns* (c. 1535)

growth of armies. More soldiers and guns were needed to defend the new bastions which were far more extensive than any previous defensive works, while besieging armies needed many more troops in order to undertake sieges which became longer and less conclusive. Consequently it became imperative for an advancing army to lay siege to such newly fortified cities simply because they were too dangerous to by-pass. Thus the new *trace ital-lienne* served not only to prolong sieges, but also to minimise the number of normal, open battles which took place in areas where the new bastions had been introduced. This explains why we find so few battles compared to sieges in the Eighty Years War between Spain and the Netherlands and during the Thirty Years War in some areas of Germany.[52]

The Imperial city of Regensburg, as portrayed in Mattheus Merian's print of 1648, demonstrates how a complex network of sloping bastions were considered necessary defences by most major cities by then. Regensburg had, of course, just been exposed to a fair dose of war, having first been captured by Protestant forces in 1633, then re-taken by Imperialist forces the following year, and finally shelled by the Swedes during the meeting of the Imperial Diet in 1641. This experience caused the city to accelerate work on its defences. As in the case of most early modern cities, which were not newly founded, the new bastions surrounding Regensburg were added in front of the city's already existing medieval walls and towers (Plate 3.12).[53]

Sieges, of course, also served to create an often dangerous mixture of military and civilian objectives and attitudes within the besieged town or city, leading to open conflict between the two groups about the aims and directions of the campaigns, as can be seen from Christian III's siege of Copenhagen during the civil war (1533–6), which secured his accession to the throne. Having suffered terrible deprivation and hunger over a considerable period, which they had tried to alleviate initially by the less than charitable action of driving their poor out of the city, only to see them driven back by the besiegers, a major movement for peace arose among the citizens of Copenhagen. Eventually a considerable number of the citizens gathered in one of the city's main squares trying to convince their civic leaders that surrender was now the only option. However, no agreement could be reached and a scuffle broke out between the minority pro-war faction and the majority desperate for peace which caused the foreign mercenaries defending the city to open fire on the unarmed civilians, killing many while pursuing others into their houses, where they hacked the inhabitants to death and plundered the premises.[54]

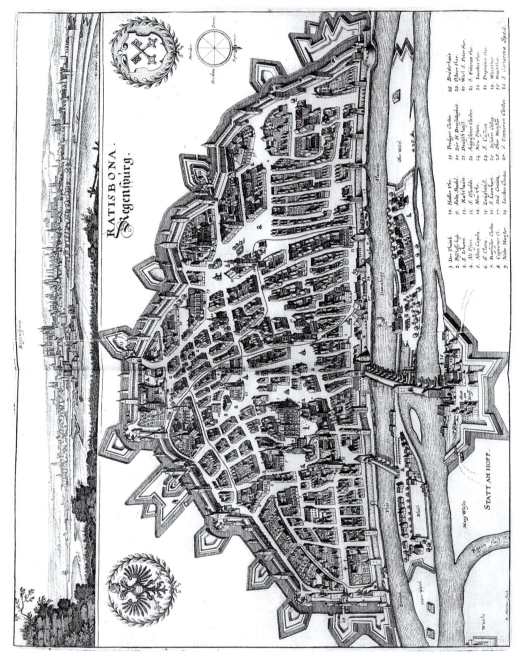

Plate 3.12 Mattheus Merian, *Regensburg*, from his *Topographia Bavariae* (1648)

By the sixteenth century the days of glorified hand-to-hand battle were rapidly disappearing and medieval chivalry associated with the fully armoured knight was vanishing. What chivalry survived draped itself in allegorical pageantry rather than real warlike action. Thus the jousting in elaborate armour which Elizabeth I of England witnessed her loyal knights indulge in was little more than Renaissance pageantry and bore no relation to its original purpose, namely training for the battlefield.[55]

When the Danish Latin poet and theologian, Erasmus Lætus, described the festivities celebrating Christian IV's birth and baptism in 1577, he provided a detailed explanation why no tournament and jousting took place. He stated that nowadays, when chivalry has lost its significance and 'most things are decided through dissimulation and cunning, and when guns are appreciated above all other weapons, physical strength and military prowess have by nature lost all their former lustre, since the bravest, strongest and most forceful men are torn away from this wretched world in their early youth if not childhood. Only few opportunities are provided to show bravery when weapons have become no more than a shortcut to crime.' Lætus then added that these days when the bravest was more likely to be killed by the greatest coward than the other way round, a victory which was not achieved through horrible murders and bestiality was considered worth nothing. In particular, Lætus was disgusted by the military practice whereby guns were loaded with fat which was lit together with the gunpowder, and which when penetrating the body with the bullet resulted in the injured and dead burning horribly. This sight was so ghastly that more often than not it caused even their enemies to feel pity for them.[56] Lætus undoubtedly romanticised the chivalry of an earlier age in order to emphasise the horrible nature of early modern warfare.

But, as can be seen from an illustration in the Anglo-Dutch military writer John Cruso's work, *The Art of Warre* (1631) (Plate 3.13) burning missiles were not new inventions connected with gunpowder, but had long been fired by catapults and crossbows, even if the two burning barrels, chained to the flaming cannon-ball, look a far more serious proposition than any of the other 'instruments to cast fireworks' shown by Cruso.[57] For contemporaries, however, there could be little doubt that the period's much increased technical ability to cause large-scale mutilation and destruction, combined with new and terrifying weaponry and tactics, was a cause for serious concern and anxiety. In the context of the apocalyptic mood of the age such changes to the way war was conducted must have been seen as further confirmation that the Last Days were indeed imminent.

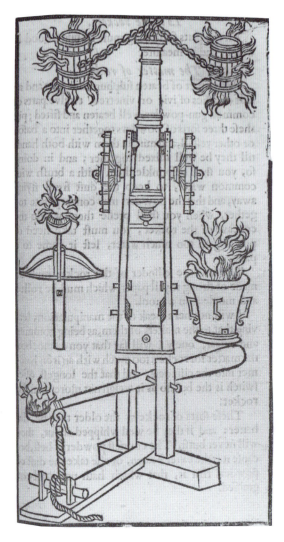

Plate 3.13 John Cruso,
*Divers instruments to cast
fireworks*, from his *The Art
of Warre* (1631)

WOUNDS

These new and enhanced weapons of destruction obviously added to the
general anxiety and apprehension of the age, not least because of the injuries they caused. We may not be able to talk of wounds of an apocalyptic
nature, but the character and range of injuries sustained in war during this
period can only have added further to the impression that these were
indeed the last and horrible battles forecast in the Bible to take place before
the return of Christ. How else were laymen, physicians and surgeons to
deal with wounds and injuries on a scale and of a nature they had never
encountered before?

Certainly, the horrors of early modern warfare did not leave the relatively few physicians, who gained direct experience of it, unaffected, as can be seen from the reactions of the Venetian physician Alessandro Benedetti. In his description of the battle of Fornovo in July 1495 between the invading French army of Charles VIII and the pro-Habsburg Italian army, Benedetti noted how the dead and dying on the battlefield were plundered by local peasants as well as friend and foe:

> Very many wounded were found naked among the corpses, some begging aid, some half-dead. They were weakened by hunger and loss of blood and wearied by the heat of the sun and thirst; with tongues thrust out they begged for water. In this affair no form of cruelty seemed to be lacking. There were about 115 of these; some Frenchmen were mingled among them, begrimed with mud and blood and looking like slaves, and these without distinction were brought into the Venetian camp and attended by the surgeons at public expense. Some still breathing after hands and feet had been amputated, intestines collapsed, brains laid bare, so unyielding of life is nature.[58]

With the increased use of gunpowder the injuries to combatants grew worse and posed new problems for the growing number of army surgeons who sought to treat them during this period. They included injuries such as gunshot wounds, burns and compound fractures. The French surgeon Ambroise Paré (1510–90), who served in more than forty French military campaigns and who wrote a number of best-selling medical/surgical treatises, became the leading exponent of new medical approaches in surgery which led to significant improvements in a number of fields. The most important of his books, *Method of Treating Gunshot Wounds*, first published in 1545, publicised his new technique for treating gunshot wounds and performing battlefield amputations. Describing in detail the damage and harm caused by guns, Paré emphasised the significance of the names given to such instruments of destruction such as 'Culverines, Serpentines, Basilisques, Sackers', reminding his readers that these were instruments of mass-destruction which everyone ought to detest. He went on to point his finger at mines and burning or explosive missiles in particular which blew up so many soldiers while causing others 'to burne in their harnesse, no waters being sufficiently powerfull to restraine and quench the raging and wasting violence of such fire cruelly spreading over the body and bowells'.[59]

More by accident than design Paré caused a major advance in the treatment of gunshot wounds. Until then surgeons had believed that such wounds were poisoned by the gunpowder carried into the body by the bullet, as can be seen from the influential *Book of Surgery* (1497) by the Alsatian army surgeon, Hieronymus Brunschwig. However, Brunschwig's suggested treatment of drawing a silken cord through the wound to remove the poisonous powder, did not gather support. Instead, surgeons followed the advice of the Spaniard, Joannes de Vigo, and cauterised the wound with boiling oil, if necessary sealing any severed arteries by the application of a red hot iron – as explained in Vigo's *Practica copiosa in arte chirurgica* (1514) which went through no less than forty editions. The myth of the poisonous gunshot wound, probably had a lot to do with the fact that the most efficient firearm of the day – the musket – fired lead balls, which due to their softness, weight, deformity and slow speed generated horrific wounds. Even without the further complication of fractured bones such wounds were difficult to deal with. They needed to be enlarged in order to remove the bullet, which increased the risk of infection significantly. Matters were not improved by the fact that physicians as well as surgeons embraced the doctrine of suppuration which had come about as a result of a mistranslation of Hippocrates and Galen. Consequently they tended to stuff the wound with all sorts of material in order to produce this effect considered necessary for healing.[60]

It was during his first campaign in 1536 that Ambroise Paré stumbled over a new treatment of gunshot wounds which convinced him that such wounds were not poisonous and that cauterising them with boiling oil caused more harm than good. After the assault by French forces on the castle of Villane, Paré and his fellow-surgeons had to treat a large number of soldiers with gunshot wounds. Being inexperienced and young, Paré treated his patients, like the other more senior surgeons, according to the instructions of Vigo, despite the realisation that it caused great pain to the victims, until he ran out of oil. Consequently, he decided to apply a dressing to the wounds of the remaining injured, which consisted of egg-yolk, oil of roses and turpentine. The next morning he found that those treated with this linament had fared much better than those who had had their wounds cauterised. They had not only slept well, but had no fever, and their wounds were not inflamed, in contrast to those who had been cauterised. From then on Paré advocated the use of soothing linaments and bandages instead of boiling oil, while emphasising the need to remove dead tissue and foreign matter in order to prevent infection. Similar methods were advocated by other leading military surgeons from the middle of the sixteenth century, such as the Englishman Thomas Gale, and Felix Wurtz of Zurich.

Likewise, Paré was also able to introduce a new and improved treatment of burns. Considering the much higher incidence of such injuries as a consequence of the increased use of gunpowder, this proved an important discovery. Early modern cannons were, after all, quite liable to explode, killing and burning the gunners badly, while insufficient cleaning of barrels caused a high incidence of flashburns among the crews. Equally, musketeers under stress often poured too much powder into the flashpans of their weapons, causing minor explosions which left them with severely burned faces.

In this particular case Paré appears to have indulged in a human experiment. A kitchen boy had accidentally fallen into a caldron of boiling oil during the Turin campaign of 1537, and on his way to treat him Paré stopped at the nearest apothecary to pick up 'refrigerating medicines commonly used in this case'. An old country woman overhearing his request told him to try to use a dressing consisting of crushed onions and salt instead, which, according to her, would reduce the blistering and scarring. Paré took the opportunity to experiment on 'this greasy scullion' as he put it, covering part of his burns with the onion paste and the other with the traditional remedies. The next day he discovered that the area covered with the paste was free of blisters while the other was full of them. The success of this ointment can be seen from the fact that it is supposed to have remained in use among Russian army surgeons as late as the Second World War.[61]

Ambroise Paré also took the lead in introducing better amputation techniques. Together with other military surgeons such as William Clowes, who served the Earl of Leicester's expeditionary corps in the Netherlands in the 1580s, he reintroduced the practice of ligature prior to amputation, which had been lost since Celsus in the second century. This reduced the risk of the patient bleeding to death, and William Clowes claimed to be able to remove legs, yet causing his patients to lose less than four ounces of blood in the process. Due to its labour intensiveness, however, this proved a practice which only gained ground slowly. Other improvements included covering the stump of the amputated limb with flaps of skin and muscle, as advocated in Hans von Gersdorff's, *Feldbuch der Wundarznei* (1517), which helped prevent infection, while the risks of gangrene were reduced by amputating well above the wound.[62] According to Paré there were also important aspects such as the patient's future mobility to consider when amputating. Even if only the foot had to be amputated Paré argued that the leg should be cut off 'five fingers breath under the knee. For so the patient

may more fitly use the rest of his Legge with less trouble, that is, he may the
better goe on a wooden Legge; for otherwise, if according to the common
rules of Art, you cut it off close to that which is perished the patient will be
forced with trouble to use three Legges instead of two'.[63]

Not all serious leg injuries, however, necessarily caused surgeons to
amputate immediately. During the siege of Breda in 1637 Colonel George
Goring managed to keep his left leg despite a gunshot which hit him 'in the
iuncture, where the foote is fastened to the legg, brake assunder all the
vpper Sinnews, toore away a great deale of his flesh, bruised the huckle
bone, and broke the end of the great shinn-bone, where it ioynes vnto it'.
Clearly a nasty wound and at first the surgeons had wanted to amputate,
but observing Goring's courage, 'good health and temper', they decided to
wait, considering the immediate risk of gangrene minimal, and after only
two dressings of the wound they abandoned all thought of amputation.[64]
Thus George Goring survived with his left leg intact to take his part on the
Royalist side in the English Civil War.

Amputations of arms had to be dealt with in a different manner, and here
it was essential to remove as little of the 'sound parts' as possible. Paré,
however, did not restrict his interests and innovations to the surgical
aspects of amputations, but took a considerable interest in the construction of artificial limbs. This can be seen from a number of illustrated editions of his works, where he would supply detailed instructions for the
construction of wooden legs 'for poor men' (Plate 3.14), and far more
complex artificial limbs made in iron, often of an intricate mechanical
nature (Plates 3.15 and 3.16). Likewise, Paré also offered detailed and
graphic instruction for how to deal with fractures and how best to set dislo-
cated bones (Plates 3.17 and 3.18). Amazingly, he even found time to
engage in something akin to plastic surgery, for example developing
special brackets for sewing together deep facial cuts (Plate 3.19).

Even if surgeons such as Paré and Clowes were exceptional in the sixteenth century and their improved techniques and treatments only filtered
through slowly to the rank and file of military surgeons, soldiers must have
nevertheless stood a good chance of surviving amputations as can be seen
from the many pictures of the period which depict limbless ex-soldiers,
who survived to beg on the streets. Thus the problem of maimed soldiers
returning from the wars to a life of vagrancy and begging was considerable
in late Elizabethan England, and Parliament passed no less than three Acts
concerning such people between 1593 and 1601. Pensions collected by the
churchwardens were to be supplied by the local parishes where such

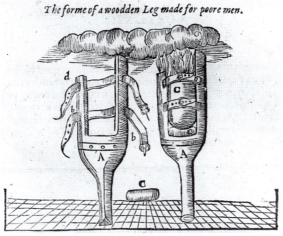

The forme of a woodden Leg made for poore men.

Plate 3.14 Ambrose
Paré, *The forme of a wooden
leg made for poore men*,
from his *The Works of that
famous Chirurgion* (1634)

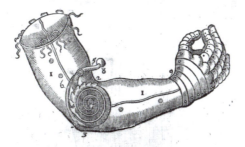

The forme of an arme made of iron very artificially.

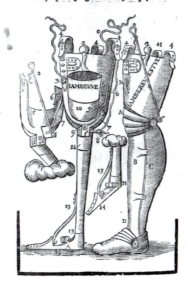

The description of legs made artificially of iron.

Plate 3.15 Ambrose
Paré, *Artificial arm and leg
made of iron*, from his *The
Works of that famous
Chirurgion* (1634)

The forme of an hand made artificially of iron.

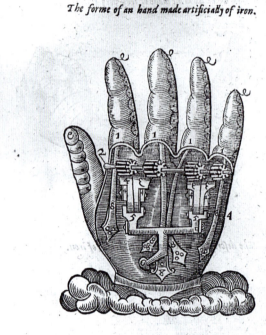

This figure following sheweth the back-side of an hand artificially made, and so that it may be tyed to the arme or sleeve.

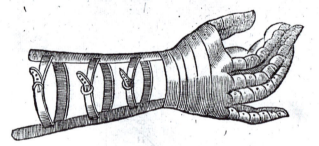

Plate 3.16 Ambrose Paré, *Artificial hand made of iron*, from his *The Works of that famous Chirurgion* (1634)

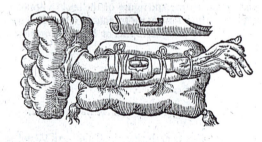

Plate 3.17 Ambrose Paré, *The figure of a fractured Arme, with a wound bound up, and seated, as is fit*, from his *The Works of that famous Chirurgion* (1934)

Plate 3.18 Ambrose
Paré, *An expression of the
first manner of putting a
shoulder into Joynt*, from
his *The Works of that
famous Chirurgion* (1634)

Plate 3.19 Ambrose
Paré, *How to sew a facial
wound*, from his *The Works
of that famous Chirurgion*
(1634)

soldiers, who had 'adventured their lives and lost limbs or disabled their bodies', had been recruited.[65]

Obviously, the injured soldier's survival depended to a considerable extent on the quality and availability of medical care. Apart from princes and great noblemen who were attended by their personal physicians and surgeons, only a limited number of barber-surgeons were available to the rank and file in the sixteenth and early seventeenth centuries. However, the number and quality of barber-surgeons continued to improve throughout our period. The Danish king Christian IV encouraged surgeons to settle throughout his kingdom, providing a net of such people stretching from Copenhagen across all major provincial towns of his realm, often ignoring the reservations of local guilds. This was done as much to guarantee that his army and navy might be well supplied with such qualified medical personnel, as to provide the provincial population with reasonable access to medical care. Thus, in 1611 the king instructed a number of provincial towns to provide him with a specified number of surgeons by Easter, and similarly in 1645, when a naval force was being equipped, the king informed his local administrators that a number of cities and towns were to be prepared and ready to send surgeons to the capital 'with well-supplied chests' at short notice.[66] The title-page of William Clowes's tract, *A Prooved Practice for All Young Chirurgians* (1588), shows what an army surgeon's chest looked like and what instruments it included (Plate 3.20).

Similarly, the primitive working conditions army surgeons had to contend with when in the field are portrayed in a print emphasising Clowes's own observation that surgeons above all needed a good eye, a strong arm and a stout heart.[67] The print shows a surgeon probing for the bullet in the shoulder of a soldier injured by a gunshot wound, who is being restrained by a colleague or the surgeon's assistant (Plate 3.21).

Likewise, it is noteworthy that when Christian IV appointed an army-physician in 1644, not only was the physician Jørgen Willomsøn ordered to stay with the army and carry a considerable supply of drugs with him, but it was specified that officers were to pay him for his services, whereas his annual salary of 500 thalers was intended to cover his services to the rank and file.[68]

Military service, however, did not always, for obvious reasons, appeal to the best surgeons who if chosen often tried to supply a substitute who was usually considerably less skilful. Clowes undoubtedly came close to the truth when he complained about the many deaths caused by incompetent

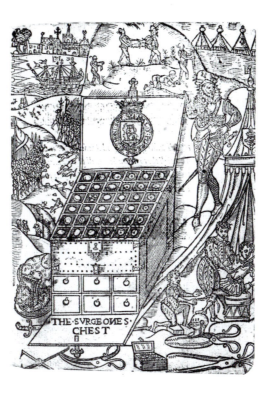

Plate 3.20 W. Clowes, *The surgeon's chest*, title-page from his *A prooved practice for all young chirurgians* (1588)

Plate 3.21 W. Clowes, *Surgery in the field*, from his *A prooved practice for all young chirurgians* (1588)

surgeons. Low pay as well as the possible danger clearly served to discourage potential candidates. This was realised by the English Privy Council in the 1580s, when it responded to suggestions from officers in the English expeditionary corps in the Netherlands by improving salaries considerably for surgeons – doubling them from one to two shillings a day – thus enabling them to employ several assistants, simultaneously doubling their actual number. On an average surgeons were better paid than many officers to judge from the figures quoted by the military writer John Cruso. According to Cruso quartermaster-generals in the armies of the United Provinces were paid 6 shillings 8 pence per day while the chief surgeon received 4 shillings, and surgeons were paid 2 shillings 6 pence a day, the same amount as quartermasters.[69]

The growing significance of military surgery in the sixteenth century is also in evidence from the growing number of vernacular works on the subject which were published: nearly fifty works written by barber-surgeons wholly or partly concerned with military surgery reached the bookmarket. Similarly, the sixteenth century witnessed the beginning of the publication of pocket book compendia of anatomy, in the vernacular and with medical illustrations, clearly aimed at army and navy surgeons. Ambroise Paré's *Anatomie Universelle* was published in this format in 1561, while a more typical example can be found in the military surgeon, Joseph Smidt's *Mirror of Anatomy* (1601).[70] The growing incidence of war and the increasing number of barber-surgeons serving in them clearly created a market which printers and book-sellers rushed to fill.

Early modern soldiers, however, were far more likely to die from diseases such as dysentery, typhus, smallpox, malaria or plague than from wounds sustained in battle. Other dangers to their health and battle fitness were 'foot rot', known in the twentieth century as 'trench foot', which besieging troops encountered on a considerable scale, and stress induced by violent explosions, which in the twentieth century has become known as 'shell shock'. During the siege of the castle of Hedin in 1553, the constant blasting of the French forces within the castle by the Habsburg artillery had dire indirect consequences for the defending troops according to Paré who served as surgeon to the commander of the French forces, the Duke of Bouillion:

> Now through this diabolicall tempest of the Eccho from these thundring Instruments, and by the great and vehement agitation of the collision of the ayre resounding and reverberating in the wounds of the hurt people, divers dyed, and others because they could not rest by reason of the groanes and cryes that they

made, night and day; and also for want of good nourishment and other good usage necessary to wounded people.[71]

In order to avoid outbreaks of epidemic disease among their forces military commanders appear to have paid increasing attention to matters of hygiene in their military codes. Thus the disciplinary code of the Earl of Leicester for his troops in the Netherlands stipulated that soldiers were only to use appointed places – latrines – to relieve themselves, while animals were only to be slaughtered at appointed places outside camps and garrisons. All carrion and entrails were to be buried, while all personnel were warned not to 'defile the waters adioyning, but in the lower part of the streame some good distance from the Camp, upon payne of imprisonment'. At the same time it also became recognised that to camp near bogs and moors exposed the troops to unnecessary risk of disease 'by the stenches and infectious vapours thereof'.[72] Lack of basic hygienic measures among the troops in Christian IV's headquarter at Tangermünde on the river Elbe in 1625 – the dreadful stench coming from the camp was emphasised by a contemporary chonicler – evidently served to reduce their strength through epidemic disease well before the King encountered the Imperial forces under Count Tilly.[73]

The period also witnessed a number of new initiatives in medical care for soldiers, even if far from all of them were acted upon. Thus the Elizabethan government ignored the call of Thomas Digges to create a permanent pool of carriages and drivers for ambulance service in times of war.[74] Likewise, military hospitals were slow in being established. The first appears to have been established in 1567 in the city of Mechelen by the Duke of Alva upon his arrival in the Netherlands. Initially the hospital only survived for a year, most likely due to lack of funds. It is, however, noteworthy that the lack of proper medical care for the troops, including a hospital, featured prominently among the complaints of the Spanish mutineers between 1574 and 1576. In 1585 the military hospital in Mechelen re-opened with a staff of around 50 and 330 beds. It appears to have treated not only combat injuries, but also diseases such as malaria and the pox, and psychological disorders like battle trauma. The Spanish government appears to have paid most of the expenses connected with the hospital, but the veteran Spanish and Italian troops, for whose benefit it had been established, contributed one real of their monthly salary.[75] Gradually, more military hospitals came into existence during the early seventeenth century. Thus in 1638 the Swedish government created a military hospital in the former monastery of Vadstena. However, this institution seems to have been closer to the institutional, nursing home for crippled and maimed soldiers established by the Spanish government at the Garrison of Our Lady of Hal.[76] During major sieges or campaigns something akin to field hospitals were often established. They were generally recognised and protected by the warring parties, as can be seen from events surrounding the siege of Maastricht in 1632. When the articles of surrender between the Spanish forces, who had defended the town, and the Prince of Orange were concluded, an article was included which stated that all injured and sick soldiers and officers could remain in the town, privately with their hosts or in their respective hospitals until fully recovered.[77]

Occasionally, medical expertise appears to have been able to play a more unusual and pro-active role in the military events of the day, as when a soldier's wife coming from the besieged Spanish garrison in Maastricht was arrested for the second time by soldiers from the Prince of Orange's army under suspicion of carrying letters to other enemy forces. Despite a thorough search of her body and clothes no letters could be found, but theatened with hanging she confessed to having swallowed two copper-boxes with letters. Whereupon the chief-physician of the States General's army 'gave her some pills in, the which wrought so well with her, that the next morning they were found, washed opened (and the letters found)'.[78]

The growing incidence of warfare combined with the increased use of more destructive weapons such as cannons and muskets in particular, aided by tactical and technical developments, caused greater and more horrific injuries to soldiers, as well as civilians, in the sixteenth and early seventeenth centuries than ever before. This might to some extent have been allieviated by the discovery of better treatments and techniques by the growing number of barber-surgeons who were employed in early modern armies and navies. Often forced by circumstances, as we have seen in the case of Paré, many surgeons were willing to consider innovative and unorthodox approaches and remedies in order to save their patients. Many, like William Clowes, were positively inclined towards Paracelsianism, not surprisingly when it is borne in mind that Paracelsus had himself started his medical career as an army surgeon and among his most famous works was his book on surgery, *Grosse Wundarznei*, published first in 1536. Paracelsus's advice to the surgeon to protect the wound by keeping it clean and open and not sealing it off obviously inspired Clowes and others, even if they may not have taken on board the full millenarian implications of the natural philosophy of Paracelsus.[79] But, as the surgeons themselves admitted, early modern warfare with its extensive use of guns and gunpowder caused suffering and injuries on an unprecedented and horrific scale, which was more often than not beyond any relief. As such it also affected the views and attitudes of the leading thinkers and theologians of the day.

WAR AND RELIGION: THE RESPONSE OF CHRISTIAN HUMANISTS AND PROTESTANTS

Not surprisingly the growing incidence of war and its increased effects on contemporary society affected humanists as well as evangelical reformers. Christian humanists such as John Colet, Erasmus of Rotterdam, Sir Thomas More and Juan Luis Vives repeatedly voiced their criticism of the period's increased warfare. The general acceptance of warfare as having a role in political life, being a continuation of politics by other means, and the accompanying doctrine of a just war which reached back to the *Corpus Juris Canonici* and the *Summa Theologica* of Thomas Aquinas, was forcefully rejected by them. Instead, they pointed out that war was fratricide and undermined the establishment of a true Christian commonwealth towards which all Christian governments should work. John Colet, who had travelled in Italy in the 1490s and quite likely personally witnessed some of the many conflicts which ravaged northern Italy in this decade, first voiced his rejection of violence and war in his lectures on the Epistle of St Paul to the Romans in 1496: 'For it is not by war that war is conquered, but by peace and forbearance, and reliance in God. And in truth by this virtue we see that the apostles overcame the world.'[80] Seventeen years later Colet reiterated his views, this time in a sermon preached before Henry VIII which was clearly meant as a warning to the king not to continue the war against France which had commenced in 1511. Erasmus of Rotterdam, Colet's protégé who was then living in England and who may well have been present, reports that,

> Colet preached a noble sermon before the King and his Court on the victory of Christ, exhorting all Christians to war and conquer under the banner of Him their proper King. For they, he said, who through hatred and ambition were fighting, the bad with the bad, and slaughtering one another by turns, were warring under the banner, not of Christ, but of the Devil. At the same time he pointed out to them, how hard a thing it was to die a Christian death, how few entered on a war unsullied by hatred or love of gain; how incompatible a thing it was, that a man should have that brotherly love without which no one would see God, and yet bury his sword in his brother's heart.[81]

According to Erasmus a degenerative process had been at work after the initial disruption of Man's prelapsarian state of peace until finally warfare had become chronic in society. Not only had it, according to Erasmus, reached an unprecedented peak by the time he was writing his tract against war in 1515, but it threatened to become even more pervasive unless 'wise men' could halt this downward trend of human history. For Erasmus there was nothing glorious or chivalrous in early sixteenth-century warfare with its large armies. Describing an imaginary battle, he emphasised

> the unlovely murmur of so huge a multitude; the eyes sternly menacing; the bloody blasts and terrible sounds of trumphets and clarions; the thundering of the guns, no less fearful than thunder indeed, but more hurtful; the frenzied cry and clamour, the furious and mad running together, the outrageous slaughter, the cruel chances of them that flee and of those that are stricken down and slain, the heaps of slaughters, the fields overflowed with blood, the rivers dyed red with man's blood.[82]

However, not only was warfare as such odious to Erasmus and the Christian humanists, but professional soldiers in particular were despicable. According to Erasmus these mercenaries were 'the dregs of all men living', who hardly deserved to be labelled humans, or as he put it 'if we must needs call such . . . monsters men'.[83] Such views were shared by the Carmelite monk and Christian humanist Paulus Helie who drew on the experiences gathered during the peasant revolt in Scania in Denmark in 1525. Here a regiment of foreign lansquenets, having briefly skirmished with a group of peasants in the countryside, stormed a local town despite it having already surrendered and opened its gates. The mercenaries then brutally murdered all the citizens and plundered the town, not even sparing 'the holy places'. As Helie put it, 'thus raged the executioners of Hell, who themselves deserved all the punishments of Hell. In these times they are the only people to benefit from the madness of the princes'.[84]

For the Christian humanists all this energy was better spent on bringing about a universal peace among all Christian princes which could lay the foundation for a *Pax Ecclesiae* which would herald a golden age of reform and the creation of a truly Christian society. These millenarian expectations reflect an optimism and apocalyptic expectancy that was not to be promoted again until a century later on the eve of the Thirty Years War, but then by Protestant theologians.

By the early 1520s, due to the growing threat to Western Christendom by the victorious Ottoman armies, the Christian humanists began to abandon their pacifism even if they continued to argue forcefully for a comprehensive peace among Christians. No longer, however, was this to be done in order to bring about a golden age, but solely for the sake of preserving

Christianity. In August 1521 the Turks had captured Belgrade and were laying siege to the supposedly impregnable island-fortress of Rhodes and Erasmus was wondering what would be the result of this 'great tumult of war'. He found princes in both Church and State insincere in their plans for a crusade against the Turks, which, he claimed, only provided them with yet another pretext for robbing and taxing their subjects who were already seriously oppressed. Significantly, however, he added that he was not opposed to war against the Turks if they attacked, but he emphasised that any war fought in Christ's name should be conducted with Christian methods and in a Christian spirit.[85]

The fall of Rhodes to the Turks in December 1522 was a major blow and caused great anxiety within contemporary Western Christianity. Consequently in April 1523 the Pope proposed a truce between Henry VIII of England, Francis I of France and Emperor Charles V in order to make a common front against the Turks. But to no avail! A few years later the impending catastrophe to Western Christendom, brought about by the fratricidal strife among Christian princes, and predicted by the humanists, seemed imminent after the battle of Pavia in February 1525 which saw the French king Francis I become a prisoner of Emperor Charles V.[86] Combined with the rapid progress of Ottoman forces through the Balkans and Hungary which led to the fall of Budapest in the wake of the battle of Mohács in August 1526, where Suleiman the Magnificent defeated the forces of the Hungarian King Louis II, this incident caused deep despair in humanist circles.

Juan Luis Vives, temporarily back in Bruges, published his work *De Europae dissidiis, & republica* (1526) to which he added a tract dealing with the European conflicts and the Turkish war (*De Europae dissidiis et bello Turcico dialogus*). Here he voiced the commonly held fear that the expected invasion of Italy by the Turks would signal the end of all Christendom. A situation he, like his humanist friends, considered had been brought about primarily by the greed and insanity of secular rulers as well as the popes.

That year Luther entered the debate about whether or not war was permissible among Christians when he published *Ob Kriegsleute auch in seligem Stande sein können* (1526) (*Whether soldiers, too, can be saved*). The pamphlet resulted from the reformer's discussions with the knight Assa von Kram, councillor to Duke Ernst of Braunschweig-Lüneburg, who had commanded Saxon forces in the recent Peasant War and participated in the decisive battle at Frankenhausen (15 May 1525) when the peasants had been totally routed. However, its time of publication coincided not only with a renewed Ottoman threat to Western Europe after the fall of Budapest in August, but also with a circular letter from Emperor Charles V, written in the wake of his victory over Francis I at Pavia, calling on the Catholic princes of the empire to exterminate the Lutheran heresy. Based on his teaching on the two kingdoms – the spiritual and the secular – Luther emphasised that:

> For the very fact that the sword has been instituted by God to punish the evil, protect the good, and preserve peace (Rom. 13:1–4; 1 Pet. 2:13–14) is powerful and sufficient proof that war and killing along with all the things that accompany wartime and martial law have been instituted by God. What else is war but the punishment of wrong and evil? Why does anyone go to war, except because he desires peace and obedience?

Similarly Luther claimed that the office of soldier was God-given, pointing out that it was of the greatest importance to make sure that those who served society in this capacity were upright and Christian citizens who did not abuse civilians and plunder indiscriminately, but were satisfied with their wages. As opposed to his Christian humanist critics Luther had no qualms about accepting mercenaries.[87] They and their office did not differ materially from other occupations:

> A craftsman may sell his skill to anyone who will have it, and thus serve the one whom he sells it to, so long as this is not against his ruler and his community. In the same way a soldier has his skill in fighting from God and can use it in the service of whoever desires to have it, exactly as though his skill were an art or trade, and he can take pay for it as he would for his work. For the soldier's vocation also springs from the law of love. If anyone needs me and calls for me, I am at his service, and for this I take my wage or whatever is given me.[88]

Luther, however, realised that it was difficult to find the upright and God-fearing men needed for the military profession. Unfortunately a 'great many soldiers belonged to the devil' a fact which, he admitted, more often than not manifested itself in their ungodly language and swearing. Likewise, Luther recognised that many vagrants and sturdy beggars were mercenaries who were temporarily unemployed. Such former soldiers might ultimately become 'scoundrels and robbers', but it was Luther's hope that they might be encouraged to take up a civilian vocation and earn their living until such a time as their rulers needed their services once more.[89]

Towards the end of *Whether soldiers, too, can be saved* Luther stated that he wished to say something about the war against the Turks, not only because the Ottoman threat had moved so much closer by 1526, but also because his Catholic opponents had accused him of being opposed to war against the

Turks.[90] This was a reference to Luther's *Explanations of the Ninety-five Theses* which he had published in 1518 and where he had argued that taking up arms against the Turks amounted to resisting God who had sent this rod to punish Christians for their sins.[91] Christian humanists such as Erasmus shared this view with Luther, at least until their disagreements by the mid-1520s. Erasmus had posed the question how Christians by waging holy war on the Turks could hope to convert them by murder and pillage, adding that he preferred 'a true Turk to a false Christian'.[92] What Luther and Erasmus clearly agreed upon was that war against the Ottomans should and could not be a holy war – a crusade, religiously motivated and led by the Church. If anything it was the Christian humanists who at this stage advocated pacifism, not Luther.

By the late 1520s such overlapping views did not prevent Thomas More from attacking Luther for what he perceived to be Luther's misconstrued pacifism in the face of Turkish aggression, while ironically according to More, Luther was advocating the use of force against other Christians:

> It is a gentle holiness to abstain for devotion from resisting the Turk, and in the meanwhile to rise up in routs and fight against Christian men, and destroy as that sect hath done, many a good religious house, spoiled, maimed, and slain many a good virtuous man, robbed, polluted, and pulled down many a goodly church of Christ.[93]

In spite of the growing Turkish threat, both perceived and real, it was not, as had been expected, Ottoman forces who eventually sacked Rome in 1527. This 'apocalyptic' event which rattled Catholics across Europe, including the Christian humanists, was conducted by Emperor Charles V's unpaid German mercenaries, generally perceived to consist of evangelical or Lutheran heretics. For Thomas More and his friends this incident neatly served to unify their particular antagonism to Luther and his evangelical followers with their general hatred of war and mercenaries. In his *Dialogue concerning Heresies* More provided a graphic description of the horrors perpetrated in Rome by these mercenaries who because they were heretics had behaved doubly monstrously. Thus they had forced elderly, honourable Roman citizens naked into the streets with their hands tied behind their backs, pulling them by cords attached to their genitals. Some of the mercenaries had then positioned themselves with their pikes pointing towards these defenceless civilians while their colleagues had pulled them towards the pikes. Faced with the laughter and jokes of these cruel mercenaries the poor Romans were left with the unpalatable choice of impaling themselves on the pikes or having their genitals torn off.[94]

In his timely pamphlet from April 1529, *On War against the Turk*, published only five months before the Turks laid siege to Vienna and thus once more heightened the anxiety within Western Christianity, Luther finally answered his critics within the Catholic Church.[95] He pointed out that the popes had never seriously intended to wage war against the Turks. Instead the whole scheme for crusades had been a smokescreen for extorting and robbing the laity in Germany of their money, only for the sums collected to be spent by the Curia in Rome. The attacks on Luther had resulted not from his rejection of a holy war against the Ottomans, but because he had exposed the real intent of the pope. Luther then went on to point out that repentance was the only way forward, because God had justly given 'us into the hands of the devil and the Turk'.[96] The reformer clearly considered the Turkish threat part of the great apocalyptic scheme which was imminent, emphasising that:

> I and my followers keep and teach peace; the pope along with his followers, wages war, commits murder, and robs not only his enemies, but he also burns, condemns, and persecutes the innocent, the pious, the orthodox, as a true Antichrist. And he does this while sitting, in the temple of God (2 Thess. 2:4), as head of the Church; the Turk does not do that. But just as the pope is Antichrist, so the Turk is the very devil incarnate. The prayer of Christendom against both is that they shall go down to hell, even though it may take the Last Day to send them there; and I hope that day will not be far off.[97]

In his two broadsheets from 1530 and 1532 respectively, Dürer's pupil Erhard Schoen illustrates the apocalyptic horrors commonly associated with the recent Ottoman siege of Vienna. In the first (Plate 3.22) a verse by Hans Guldenmundt from Nuremberg requests God to witness the atrocities committed by the Turkish soldiers, shown by Schoen impaling innocent babies, hacking others to death while wading through the bodies of the killed mothers, and to show mercy on His people. In the second (Plate 3.23) entitled: *A lament to God about the many and horrible frenzied deeds committed by the bloodthirsty Turks and request for merciful help*, a victorious Turkish army is shown ravaging the surrounding Viennese countryside, killing innocent children while dragging their prisoners in neck-irons behind their horses.

Luther went on to urge the princes and political leaders of the empire to make up their differences and unite under the leadership of Emperor Charles V. According to him it was important not to underestimate the Turks, and only a considerable and well-armed force could hope for victory. Individual kings and princes stood no chance as recent events in Hungary had proven. Luther concluded his pamphlet by stating the hope

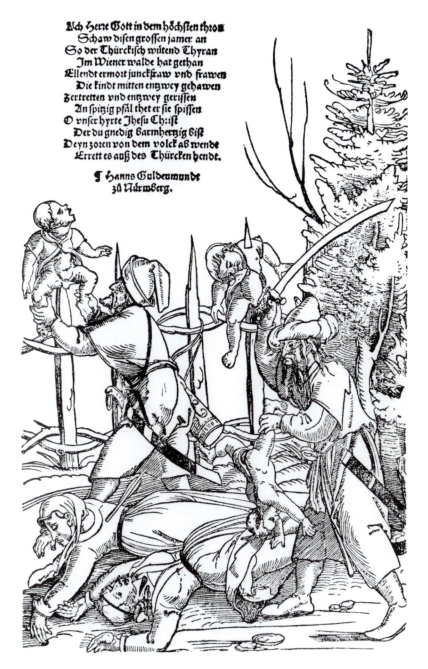

Ach Herre Gott in dem höchsten thron
Schaw disen grossen jamer an
So der Thürckisch wütend Thyran
Jm Wiener walde hat gethan
Ellendt ermort junckfraw vnd frawen
Die kindt mitten entzwey gehawen
Zertretten vnd entzwey rerissen
An spitzig pfäl thet er sie spissen
O vnser hyrte Jhesu Christ
Der du gnedig barmhertzig bist
Deyn zoren von dem volck ab wende
Errett es auß des Thürcken hendt.

¶ Hanns Guldenmundt
zů Nürmberg.

Plate 3.22 Erhard
Schoen, *Turkish Atrocities*
(1530)

Plate 3.23 Erhard Schoen, A lament to God . . . (1532)

that his advice would be taken; if it failed to work 'then may our dear Lord Jesus help, and come down from heaven with the Last Judgement and strike down both Turk and pope, together with all tyrants and the godless, and deliver us from all sins and from all evil'.[98]

Calvin agreed with Luther that it fell to Christian magistrates to wage war in order to defend their citizens against evil and intruders. Quoting Augustine, Calvin stated that rulers:

> whether they have to take up arms against an enemy, that is, an armed robber, they must not readily catch at the opportunity, nay, they must not take it when offered, unless compelled by the strongest necessity. For if we are to do far more than that heathen demanded, who wished war to appear as desired peace, assuredly all other means must be tried before having recourse to arms.[99]

War, in other words, was a necessary evil which Christians had to resort to in the last instance. Preaching on the Book of Samuel in the years 1562–3 shortly after the Wars of Religion had begun in his native France, Calvin might well have been inspired by recent French events, but he still emphasised that war was a major scourge for most of Europe, when he told his congregation:

> We have already seen battles for such a long time. There is no end to them. And even apart from battles, we have seen how many people have been killed by wars. This has not been the case merely in one place and in a single army, but has gone on among princes who claim to be Christians and Catholics – and yet they are killing an infinite number of people. And then the war has swept through one country like a storm. One sees poor people dead among the bushes, and others who are left have to endure hunger and thirst, and heat and cold, and many deprivations – to such a degree that if you cut their throat, you would do them a favour. For they are suffering and will die ten times, so to speak, before death strikes a final blow.[100]

It is noteworthy that Calvin's distaste for war is built as much on its indirect as its direct effects, emphasising the pain it inflicted on poor and innocent civilians whose sufferings had increased not only from the growing incidence of war in the sixteenth century, but also from the much wider physical impact warfare had on the countryside and local economies because of the continuous and longer campaigns by much larger armies.

Considering this social and intellectual climate it is hardly surprising to find that Heinrich Bullinger, Zwingli's successor in Zurich, dedicated one of his sermons to the issue of war. Bullinger's sermon 'Of War', probably written during the 1540s, went through numerous publications and translations. The sermon differs distinctly from both Luther and Calvin in its tone and use of belligerent language. Like the other reformers Bullinger points out that God has given 'the sword into the magistrate's hand, to be a defence for harmless people against unruly cut-throats' adding that it fell to them to kill 'rebellious people, seditious citizens, and barbarous soldiers' who according to Bullinger differed little from 'wild beasts'.[101]

The fact that Bullinger personally had experienced the horrors of war in 1531, when he and his family had been forced to flee Bremgarten for Zurich after the Zurich troops had been defeated at Kappel in October, is evident from the sermon's focus on the negative aspects of military conflict. He admonished magistrates to consider the 'endless troop of mischievous evils' which accompanied even a war 'for just and necessary causes'. He emphasised:

> By war both scarcity of every thing and dearth do arise; for highways are stopped, corn upon the ground is trodden down and marred, whole villages burnt, provision goeth to wrack, handicrafts are unoccupied, merchandise do cease, and all do perish, both rich and poor.

And then continued:

> for wicked knaves are promoted to dignity, and bear the sway, which abuse mankind like savage beasts. Hands are wrung on every side; widows and children cry out and lament; the wealth that hath been carefully gathered to help in want to come, is spoiled and stolen away; cities are rased, virgins and unmarriageable maidens are shamefully deflowered, all honesty is utterly violated, old men are handled unreverently, laws are not exercised, religion and learning are nothing set by, godless knaves and cut-throats have the dominion; and therefore in the scriptures war is called the scourge of God.[102]

Heinrich Bullinger, however, differed from his co-Reformers in other and more significant aspects: he was an advocate of religious war. Here he was at odds with the other leading Reformers such as Luther and Calvin who both would have rejected such a policy as a dangerous mixture of the spiritual and the secular domains, something they both accused the papacy of. It is in fact difficult to spot the qualitative difference between Bullinger's holy war and the papal crusades against heretics. Such worries do not appear to have affected Bullinger, who in this respect appears to have been deeply affected by the climate of confessionalisation which set in after the failure of the Colloquy of Regensburg (1541) to reach a compromise between Catholics and Protestants and the subsequent meeting of the Council of Trent (1545).

When it came to holy war the *antistes* of Zurich was prepared to advocate offensive war. Such wars should be undertaken in defence of 'true religion

against idolaters and enemies of the true and catholic faith'. He also took
the opportunity to underline that those who (Luther and Calvin?) claimed
that no war could be undertaken in defence of religion were mistaken.
Such wars could be undertaken, defensively to assist co-religionists and
offensively 'to defend the Church in danger to be drawn by any barbarous
prince from true religion unto false idolatry'.[103]

Not surprisingly such holy wars could not, according to Bullinger, be
undertaken by the common mercenaries of the age who were often
'wicked, covetous and blaspheming warriors', but had to be undertaken by
godly soldiers who were 'faithful and courageous'. In fact Bullinger
pointed out that the use of irreligious mercenaries explained why the Turks
were overrunning Christian Europe and Christians made subject to 'devilish Mahometism'. The remedy was to field an army of godly soldiers, commanded by a pious general on a par with Old Testament warrior-kings such
as Joshua and David. He was to be assisted by godly ministers, for 'the Lord
had appointed priests and ministers of true religion to attend and serve in
wars'.[104]

Undoubtedly Bullinger's emphasis on predestination and covenant-
theology, developed in a period of increasing confessionalisation, naturally led to advocacy of holy war. If the Reformed were God's chosen people
– having replaced the Jews as the true covenanters – then Old Testament
examples were highly relevant, as was the idea that God is 'a man of war'
who leads his people into battle in order to preserve true religion – which
could easily be transported from biblical time into present and historical
time.

These aspects of Bullinger's work became extremely influential among
Reformed Englishmen towards the end of the sixteenth century.
Bullinger's *Decades* (including *Of War*) were quickly translated into English
and went through numerous editions. In 1586 Archbishop John Whitgift of
Canterbury ordered that every learned minister in England should possess
a Bible or a Latin or English copy of Bullinger's *Decades*.[105] England's confrontation with Spain during the reign of Elizabeth which, apart from the
Spanish Armada in 1588, held out the prospect of a final apocalyptic clash
between the leading Catholic continental power and Protestant England,
affected the overall religious and popular outlook of the Elizabethan
period and beyond. It was an experience which led Francis Bacon to accept
the idea of pre-emptive, offensive war for the sake of religion. According to
Bacon Spain wanted to subject England in order 'That they would plant the
Popes Law by Armes as the Ottomans doe the Law of Mahomet'.[106]

The Elizabethan divine, Stephen Gossen, fully agreed with Bullinger, pointing out that wars in defence of the true religion were truly godly causes in which God intervened directly, aiding his troops to fight more courageously, while protecting them in battle in order to give victory to His chosen people (i.e. the Reformed).[107] Not surprisingly it fell to early seventeenth-century English, Puritan clergymen such as William Gouge to amplify and develop Bullinger's Old Testament model for holy war. In his work, *Gods Three Arrowes: Plague, Famine, Sword, in Three Treatises*, published in 1631, Gouge showed himself as one of the leading crusade-minded Calvinists of the age. When discussing what wars were lawful, Gouge first emphasised:

> There have been wars extraordinarily made by express charge from God. As the wars in Moses his time against Sihon and Og, and the Midianites (Num. 21:21, 33 and 31:1) and the warres in Ioshuahs time. No question must be made of them, because they had the best warrant that could be made, *Gods command*. If any will make those wars a patterne to root out kingdomes and nations as Moses and Ioshua did, let them shew the like warrant.

Obviously such a command justified offensive warfare for Gouge as did the maintenance of 'truth and purity of religion'. This had caused the 'Israelites in Canaan' to take up weapons against their 'brethren on the other side of the river Jordan'. Quoting Daniel and the Book of Revelation Gouge pointed out that this was the reason why the princes of the earth were encouraged to go to war against Antichrist. Published at a time when Protestant fortunes had just began to improve after the intervention in the Thirty Years War by the Swedish King Gustavus Adolphus in 1630, Gouge's work is a cry to war – holy war or God's war – against an Antichrist who by then needed no further identification, namely Counter-Reformation Catholicism and Catholics under the leadership of the pope.[108] The threat was everywhere for Gouge:

> Both the Palatinates, Bohemia, Moravia, Silesia, Hungary, and almost all Germany: Rochel, Montauban, Montpellier, Nimes, and other townes, cities, and countries in France: Bredaw in the Low Countries, and many other places in Christendome haue felt deepe wound of warre, whereby idolatry hath thrust out Piety, Superstition is set in the roome of Religion, Vsurpers have entered on the rites of the true Lords and Inheritours, the bloud of many millions hath beene shed, more have beene exiled, and all things turn'd upside downe.[109]

In such wars, Gouge claimed, God would lead the godly as their 'chiefe Captaine and generall' while those who followed his call to battle demonstrated their true faith. In fact such 'holy warriors' could look forwards to something approaching guaranteed salvation should they lose their lives in this cause: 'O how gloriously do such with victory returne from war! how blessedly do such as Martyrs die in battell.' For a clergyman like Gouge to write that 'For a souldier to die in the field in a good cause, it is as for a preacher to die in a pulpit', it evidently meant that in terms of achievement and hope of salvation nothing better could be hoped for.[110]

Already since the mid-1620s Gouge had been encouraging godly Englishmen to arm themselves and undertake military exercises. He wondered 'at the blindnes, carelesnes, improvidence, and security of this our age, in neglecting and disrespecting a matter of so great consequence', and recommended that every city and corporation, if not town and village, in England should be provided with trained bands and 'Artillery Gardens' where they could exercise. Furthermore, in order to encourage as many as possible to participate, he proposed that those who 'offered themselves to these Military exercises' should receive a 'publique allowance', putting these activities on a par with other government activities such as 'the mending of High-waies' and the building of bridges.[111]

In his advocacy of holy war he was joined by many of his clerical colleagues such as Thomas Barnes and Alexander Leighton. Such wars according to Leighton were 'grounded upon the absolute command of God, for the revenging him upon his enemies, or the delivery of his friends. . . . The like warrant is given to war against the Whore and her confederates'.[112] Both Leighton and Barnes considered it a religious duty for England and Englishmen to side with continental Protestantism and enter the Thirty Years War, thereby contributing to the war against a dangerous resurgent Counter-Reformation Catholicism, playing their proper part on the side of Christ and true religion in the apocalyptic drama unfolding before them.[113]

The response among Christian humanists to the increase in warfare and its horrific social consequences was, as we have seen, a cry for unity and eirenicism, at least among Christians. Such a move would, according to them, facilitate a truly Christian, unified and necessary defensive front in the face of the Ottoman threat. This was still a realistic option by the early sixteenth century before the Reformation had broken up Western Christendom. However, when it was re-launched a century later this Christian humanist eirenicism was adopted and reshaped to further Protestant unity only by a number of Lutheran and Reformed theologians, such as the English Calvinist minister John Dury and the leader of the Bohemian Brethren Amos Comenius. However, initially it found little if any sympathy with either Luther or Calvin who both considered war a necessary and acceptable evil, even if they agreed wholeheartedly with the humanists in rejecting the concept of holy war. Instead, Luther pointed to the need for political unity under the leadership of Emperor Charles V to successfully fight the Turks. Unlike the Christian humanists, however, Luther considered the office of soldier to be God-given and on a par with other occupations. However, Luther's apocalyptic views of the pope as Antichrist and the Turk as the Devil incarnate, who would both return to Hell at the end of time, which he considered to be rapidly approaching, would appear to have opened the door for a religiously justified war against these two monsters of the Apocalypse, even if the best weapon against them, according to Luther, remained true repentance.

Heinrich Bullinger had no such qualms and advocated defensive, as well as offensive warfare in defence of true religion, i.e. holy war. A similar rationale lay behind the eschatological advocacy of the Huguenot leader Philippe de Plessis-Mornay for a pre-emptive strike against the Catholic forces of Antichrist in the first decade of the seventeenth century.[114] Obviously such godly wars could not be undertaken by common mercenaries, but had to be sustained by true believers, as pointed out by Bullinger. Furthermore, those who fell in such godly causes were to be counted among God's elect people and could, as true martyrs, expect to be saved, as argued by William Gouge.

It would appear that a growing and intransigent body of Protestant theologians were arguing the case for pre-emptive, as well as holy, war from the middle of the sixteenth century until and including the first decades of the seventeenth century. Furthermore, their rationale was more often than not rooted in eschatological and apocalyptic expectations. They were, however, not alone in advocating such views. Catholics, such as the Catholic convert and polemicist Kaspar Schoppe in his *Trumpet Call to a Holy War* published in 1619, were advocating similar aggressive steps to be taken by the Catholic powers. Schoppe would have had a supporter in the prominent Jesuit adviser to Emperor Ferdinand II, William Lamormaini, who considered the Emperor to be God's tool in His quest to restore Catholicism in Germany. Referring to his Protestant adversaries in 1630, Lamormaini wrote: 'With God's aid we will devour them. Let us stand firm, and he will fight for us.'[115]

Similar views generated and guided Catholic antagonism towards their Huguenot compatriots during the Wars of Religion in France. Many of the Catholic perpetrators of the St Bartholomew's Day Massacre of 1572 were convinced that they were carrying out God's orders when killing the Huguenots. Militant sermons by priests such as Simon Vigor served to raise the religious and eschatological temperature in Paris on the eve of the massacre while self-proclaimed prophets such as the nun or lay sister who announced to the Parisians that their city would be destroyed if they did not kill all the Huguenots added fuel to the general apocalyptic anguish amongst the predominantly Catholic population of the city.[116] Eschatological expectations fuelled by astrological predictions and popular almanacs provided the ideological rationale behind the Catholic League's revival in France in 1584, whose members considered themselves to be God's soldiers fighting a holy war.[117]

THE EXPERIENCE OF WAR

The Eighty Years War

We now have to explore to what extent this apocalyptic and eschatological dimension – the Red Horse – was present and ideologically significant in the two major and longest lasting conflicts of the age, the Eighty Years War and the Thirty Years War. From a Reformed perspective there was little doubt that all the major wars of this period were, if not eschatological, then definitely religious, in nature. Mathew Newcomen, the minister of Dedham in Essex in England, put it forcefully in a fast sermon preached in 1642:

> Many goodly bloudy fights hath Antichrist glutted his cruell mind with. The funerall piles of England in Queen Maries dayes. The Massacre of France. The Warres of Germany (including the Netherlands). The butcheries of Ireland. Goodly fights in the eyes of Antichrist.[118]

The Dutch Revolt was initially caused by a mixture of religious, political and economic grievances against the rule of Philip II of Spain and his representative in the Netherlands, his half-sister Margaret, Duchess of Parma, Governess General in the Netherlands from 1559 to 1567. It began as a movement of opposition among the local nobility to Margaret's chief adviser Cardinal Granvelle, a loyal servant of Philip II, and his main religio-political aims, namely the reorganisation of the local bishoprics in order to improve their economic and administrative strength, supplemented by the introduction of the Inquisition in order to halt the advance of Protestantism in the early 1560s. Margaret's attempt to enforce Philip II's heresy laws in a proclamation of 20 December 1565 raised the religious temperature and caused open rebellion to break out under the leadership of William of Orange.

By mid-summer 1566, however, the mainly noble confederates had lost the initiative in the rebellion to Reformed preachers and their supporters many of whom had returned from exile in Germany, France, England and Geneva. It led to a Calvinisation of the revolt, causing an outburst of iconoclasms starting in the southern and gradually spreading to the northern provinces, perpetrated by militant Calvinists, creating what in Dutch Reformed tradition became known as the 'wonderyear'. The initial success of the Reformed rebels caused Philip II to take strong measures. He ordered his leading general, the Duke of Alva, to take his troops from Italy to the Netherlands to bring the situation under control. What had begun as a series of local disturbances and small-scale revolts was quickly developing into a major war, which with interruptions was to continue for around eighty years. Alva who had served Emperor Charles V in the Schmalkaldic War in Germany sought to break the back of Protestantism and the rebellion simultaneously. The accelerating economic hardship caused by the war, directly as well as indirectly, and the accompanying religious persecution instituted by Alva's Council of Blood, as it became known, forced around 100,000 people of the Reformed faith to flee the Netherlands for Germany and England in particular.

In Dutch Reformed mythology the Duke of Alva quickly came to represent the pope's or Antichrist's henchman. From as early as 1569 he was repeatedly portrayed in a series of popular broadsheets and paintings as the representative of the Devil and Antichrist, who not only had enslaved the seventeen provinces of the Netherlands, but who, inspired by Cardinal Granvelle, had brutally tortured and murdered the evangelicals. Repeatedly Alva was shown as sitting on a throne waiting for the Devil to crown him, presumably as king of Spain and the Netherlands, while Cardinal Granvelle, who bellowed advice in his ear, was offered the papal tiara. In the background Protestants were being tortured, hanged and broken on the wheel, while in some cases towns were put to the fire. Evidently, Alva was seen as an apocalyptic figure who, as some versions stated, served as 'the rod of God' punishing the people for their sins (Plates 3.24 and 3.25). The myth of Alva as an instrument of the papal Antichrist proved incredibly durable in the revolt and lasted well into the seventeenth century.

Encouraged by his success in dealing with the revolt in the southern Netherlands Alva headed north with the intent of quickly forcing these

Plate 3.24 Anon., The throne of the Duke of Alva (1569)

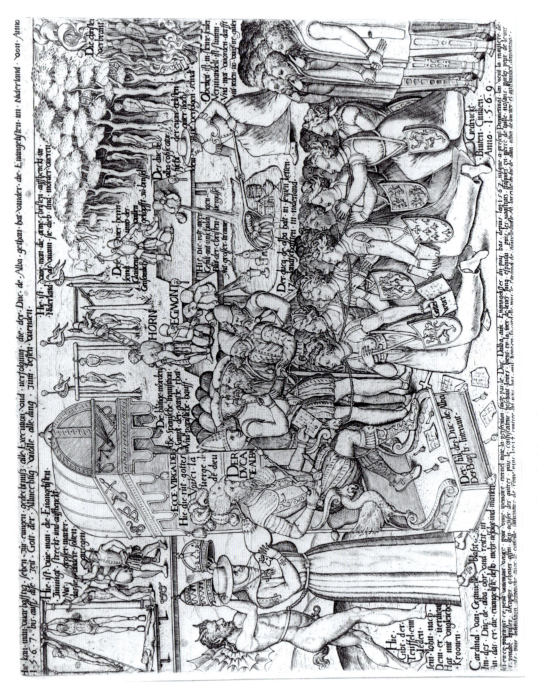

Plate 3.25 Anon., *The throne of the Duke of Alva* (1569)

Plate 3.26 Anon., *The slaughter of Zutphen* (1620)

provinces to submit. On 14 November 1572 he took Zutphen in Gelderland, sacking the town and killing several hundreds of its population of around 7,500. 'The Slaughter of Zutphen', together with the butchery of nearly the whole population of Naarden the following month, had a dramatic effect on popular imagination in the Netherlands. These events achieved symbolic significance as prime examples of Spanish cruelty and persecution of godly Reformed civilians. They were repeatedly used to portray the atrocities committed by the anti-Christian Spaniards against innocent and pious Protestants, as can be seen from this popular print issued towards the end of the Twelve Years Truce in 1620, showing mass hangings and naked men and women with their hands tied being pushed into the river Isel to their icy death in its frozen water (Plate 3.26).[119]

Shortly after having committed the atrocities in Naarden, Alva laid siege to Haarlem. This proved one of the longest and most bitterly fought sieges in the Eighty Years War. Where Alva's brutal suppression of the rebels had served to discourage further opposition in the south and north-east it hardened the opposition in Holland and Zeeland where the local population had been significantly reinforced by returning and deeply committed Calvinist emigrants. The Dutch community in London provided money and ministers for the churches under the cross in these provinces.[120] In

May 1573 the minister Bartholdus Wilhelmi informed his former London colleagues from Dort that while Haarlem was still besieged there were many soldiers about who had pillaged and burnt half the town of Nuyss nearby. Middelburg had been plundered by the Spanish general Philip de Lannoy, who apparently intended to ship his booty past Flushing to Antwerp. The Orangists, however, were watching him and had taken an oath to take his ships when they set out.[121]

Haarlem with its quite formidable fortifications and strongly committed garrison and militia proved a far more formidable opposition than anything Alva's forces had hitherto encountered. The Spanish besiegers were constantly harassed by the defenders, and stuck in their trenches during the bitterly cold winter months they suffered heavy losses while the Madrid government incurred enormous expenses. When Haarlem finally fell in July 1573 it had done much to restore self-belief within the rebel forces while simultaneously denting Spanish reputation and morale.[122] Alva may have lost as many as 10,000 troops in the siege, as much from the effects of the severe weather and disease as from the military activities of Haarlem's defenders. Shortly after Haarlem's surrender the Spanish regiments mutinied for their arrears, having been refused permission to sack the city.[123]

The intensive military activity leading up to the fall of Haarlem in July is evident from the minister Godfried van Wingen's letter written from the town of Woerden in Holland in that month. Having arrived in the town twelve days earlier with his wife he had only recently realised that the surrounding villages were occupied by the Duke of Alva's soldiers, who had pillaged the neighbourhood and constructed fortifications. He informed his friends that the attempt to relieve Haarlem had failed and that Woerden was about to be besieged while the Prince of Orange was pouring troops and ammunition into the town in order to secure it.[124] His former consistory colleague Pieter de Carpentier wrote back to London in November 1573 from Schiedam in Holland and despite stating that 'the Lord is vexing us more than ever by enemies' and asking them to pray for him and the town, he appeared relatively optimistic. Even if Alva's soldiers were quartered less than half an hour's distance from Schiedam, they could do little except in frosty weather, since the town was surrounded by water. Having recently received no less than 500 pounds of gunpowder from Rotterdam and being well provided with soldiers and artillery the town was evidently well defended. The only worry seemed to have been the many people from the surrounding countryside who had sought shelter in Schiedam and clearly put a strain on provisions. However, Carpentier thought that the deprivation suffered by the Spanish forces in the field would eventually force the enemy to withdraw because of hunger.[125]

Hand in hand with intensified warfare followed a higher incidence of disease, especially plague, and dearth as can be seen from a request for assistance from the 'community under the cross' in s'Hertogenbosch in Brabant sent to the Dutch community in London in February 1574, where they pointed out that 'the plague is raging among us, and the want of our poor is very great in these times of dearth', adding that 'the rich separate from us and abandon the Word of Christ'.[126] This lack of Christian solidarity among the Reformed under the cumulative pressure of war, famine and disease proved far from unusual as can be seen from a letter written by the leaders of the Reformed community in Brussels in spring 1580. Describing how many of their members had died of plague and other diseases during the last twenty months they added that the church had also lost many people who simply wanted to escape the burdens and effects of warfare.[127]

The Duke of Alva was relieved of his command in the Netherlands in November 1573, but the death of his successor as Governor-General, Don Luis Requesens, in March 1576, at a time when Philip II's finances were stretched to breaking point trying to pay for the war against the rebels while simultaneously fighting the Turks in the Mediterranean, led to a collapse of Spanish finances in the Low Countries. Still it took some months before the Spanish army began to fall apart. Thus unsupplied and unpaid Spanish troops continued the siege of Zierikzee in Zeeland until the town surrendered in July 1576. The effects of this siege were described in a letter written by the Reformed leadership in Zierikzee the following October: 'We live here in a destitute town, situated in an inundated region, in which we have neither sowed nor mowed anywhere; which town moreover the incomprehensible but just judgement of God had deprived of all wealth in various ways.' They emphasised the great costs they had been forced to bear during the recent siege which had lasted nearly a whole year, paying first for the twelve companies which defended the town and then after its surrender finding the money for the large ransom of 100,000 guilders. On top of that they had to feed their starved conquerors, who then mutinied and left a devastated town whose leaders feared that great multitudes of its poor would perish through hunger if they received no external help.[128]

The mutiny spread quickly and at the beginning of November the main body of mutineers attacked Europe's leading commercial capital Antwerp. Despite the hurriedly executed defensive works, a ditch and a rampart, dug between the city and the nearby citadel built by Alva in 1567, the troops and militia in Antwerp proved unable to resist the attack and for several days the city was subjected to widespread pillage and slaughter. The material destruction was bad, though the number of civilians killed only ran into hundreds rather than thousands as reported at the time, but this was of little significance for the religious and political consequences, which these real or perceived atrocities promoted. Among the Reformed families who experienced the 'Spanish Fury' the experience came to achieve prominence within family history and mythology. The London physician Baldwin Hamey, Junior, whose family had fled Bruges in 1567, described the terrors of the pillage in detail in his family history written towards the middle of the seventeenth century. He evidently had been told the story by his mother, Sarah Oeils, who again must have been told the story by her parents since she was only eleven months old when Antwerp was sacked and

> her father's house was torched and burnt down, and as the flames raged round their most precious possessions it was doubtful whether they or the soldiers were the most savage. All hope of refuge was cut off, for the conquerors stood shouting in every street, armed with torches and drawn swords. In the space of three days they wrought upon their enemies, women and treasures all that the extreme of anger, covetousness and lust suggested to them.[129]

News of the 'Spanish Fury' quickly spread across the Netherlands and most of north-western Protestant Europe, where it added to the growing body of anti-Catholic and anti-Spanish propaganda, the so-called 'Black Legend'. It was effectively broadcast in broadsheets, prints, pamphlets and plays which were repeatedly reprinted and reshaped during the Eighty Years War.[130] One of the most poignant prints even portrayed that well-known scourge of godly Protestants, the Duke of Alva, Antichrist's assistant, as being responsible for the destruction of the city and its inhabitants (for propaganda purposes it seems to have mattered little in 1616 that the Duke of Alva had in fact left the Netherlands by the end of the year 1573). The viewer is confronted by a giant death-like Alva, a figure of truly apocalyptic proportions, tramping on two dead or dying citizens within the confines of the citadel of Antwerp which the Duke had been instrumental in building in 1567 (Plate 3.27).

The Spanish war effort intensified in the 1580s. Writing in November 1584 from the predominantly Catholic city of Brussels which, however, was under Reformed and Orangist control, the Calvinist minister, Daniel de Dieu, provides an interesting insight into the pressures, fears and anxiety which gripped significant strands of the local population. De Dieu

45.

Ecce ALBA exsultat; vanáq, ab imagine sperat   En pede monstra premit, domitor modò sculptus in ære,
Æternas populi laudes quas fama negaret ,   Gloria ficta fuit, tenuesꝗ evasit in auras .

Plate 3.27 G. Baudart, Statue of the Duke of Alva in the citadel of Antwerp, in his *Les Guerres de Nassau* (1616)

informs us that the citizens were now deeply impoverished having to maintain no less than twenty companies of soldiers, twelve English and eight French, the latter presumably being part of the Duke of Anjou's troops. Fortunately these companies were not complete and in his opinion the fewer soldiers present in Brussels the better since he considered them far from reliable, referring to their recent treachery in Lier and Cambrai. He added that 'among the French soldiers there are, moreover, many beggars, and the Papists report that the French are all in their favour, as being unwilling to fight against the Malcontents'. These Malcontents consisted of mutinous troop contingents often under the leadership of Catholic nobles who had turned against the States General without yet having reconciled themselves with Philip II of Spain. De Dieu concluded his letter by informing the recipients that Alexander Farnese, Duke of Parma, was quartered with an army of 12,000 soldiers around nearby Nienhoven, emphasising that even if he threatened Brussels they feared 'treason from within more than open force'.[131]

Two years later when Alexander Farnese blockaded the city De Dieu informed his friends in London that he had been unable to write to them for some months 'owing to the present critical times' when misery was reigning in Brussels. Despite the negative effects of the Spanish blockade some food was still reaching the city and even if the Reformed community was falling into poverty, because there was no longer any demand for their lacemaking and knitted socks, they were in good courage, which was so much more remarkable since De Dieu reported a number of cases of fevers and catarrhs among them. However, the Catholic majority in the city did their utmost to discourage resistance, pointing out that there were already 10,000 Spanish and Italian troops on their way to Flanders and the whole province would soon be in the hands of Philip II. This assurance they derived from an Almanac for that year by Jan Franc of Antwerp, who found the present year indicated in the words of Psalm 21:

> In thy strength the king rejoices, O Lord. It is surprising that such stupid, false and seditious books are allowed to be printed here. I have no doubt as to the wish of the enemy, but the Lord who formerly protected Israel against Pharao, and us, so long against the Spaniards, still lives in Heaven.[132]

By January 1584 the Spanish blockade had had a more severe impact on Ghent than Brussels. In Ghent the leading citizens had considered the best way of tackling the blockade by Parma was by seeking to deprive the Spanish soldiers of victuals in the vicinity of the city. Hence they had

torched all houses, corn, mills and castles in their immediate neighbourhood and laid the countryside waste. They had expected that these measures would compel the enemy to depart, but to their great disappointment
they had just heard that 'the Deputies of the United Provinces' had allowed
Parma's forces unhindered to take in supplies of victuals during the next
four months which would carry Spanish troops through the difficult winter
months permitting them to continue their blockade with ample provisions
while the population in Ghent could expect to starve. Bitterly they pointed
out that: 'We need not tell you how serious this report is to all lovers of the
Christian religion, as it seems as if a sword were put into the enemy's hand
wherewith to slay us.' The Reformed leaders in Ghent feared that many of
their people would perish as a consequence of deep poverty, cold weather,
hunger and general misery.[133] Undoubtedly the drastic measures the
blockaded and besieged more often than not were forced to take combined
with their physical isolation, which served to nurture rumours, could easily
undermine local confidence and create anxiety and hysteria.

Even if no shots were fired against the walls of Ghent the situation within
the city deteriorated quickly and by mid-summer there was widespread
starvation. The fact that thousands of people from the surrounding countryside had sought shelter within the walls did nothing to ease the situation. The Reformed minister in Ghent, Jacob Regius, a former alumnus of
the London Dutch community, which by then wanted to recall their former
student to serve in London, replied: 'It would distress me to tear myself
away from this community, and besides at this moment we are so closely
besieged that nobody can leave the town without the gravest danger. In this
hour of trial the eyes of the community are naturally directed towards their
shepherds, and who of us could forsake them?' Faced with an imminent
attack by Spanish troops the unity and sense of purpose among this religiously divided community was weakening and Regius emphasised: 'We
witness here great dejection and unspeakable sadness and anxiety. We have
been surrounded by the enemy for several months, are badly and treacherously ruled from within, abandoned by our allies, menaced by evil-minded
persons and slandered by our neighbours.' The situation was evidently
grim and the leaders of Ghent may well have started negotiations for surrender with the Duke of Parma at this stage. Ghent finally surrendered a
couple of months later, on 17 September.[134]

Half a year later it was the turn of the great metropol of Antwerp. A
request for assistance was forwarded by the Reformed community to its
sister-church in London.

> You know what heavy and intolerable burden this town has to bear through this long war, not only because lately the whole of Flanders and Brabant (except Antwerp, Bergen and Mechelen) has fallen into the hands of the enemy, and all the poor of these regions have migrated to us, but through the siege which has lasted since 9 July last, which has caused the merchants to depart, and all trade and manufacture to cease. The taxes for defraying the costs of the war are incredible, and fall mostly upon the middle classes (and others who are not so wealthy), as the principal and wealthiest people have left us. The river being closed to us all the necessities of life are becoming dearer every day, so that we are compelled to beg for assistance, whereas formerly we were able to help others.[135]

Apart from Ostend which was by then the only town in Flanders still in rebel hands, the portrayal of the situation by the Antwerp leaders was correct. Brussels had surrendered to the Duke of Parma only the week prior to their plea for help. As opposed to the brutal treatment meted out by Alva, Parma showed considerable restraint and leniency in his dealings with the rebels. Nevertheless this seems to have done little to improve Spanish reputation either in the Netherlands or abroad. Daniel de Dieu, writing from Flushing in Zeeland, informing his friends in London of Brussels's surrender, told them how all the Reformed ministers and schoolmasters were escorted out of the city with their families to Bergen-op-Zoom. According to De Dieu, however, this unexpected leniency on the part of the Spaniards had only been shown in order to lure other towns to surrender. It seems that there was little the forces of Philip II could do to erase the effects of the 'Black Legend' – even positive actions were seen to have ulterior and dark motives, seen with Reformed eyes at least.[136]

The situation in the totally isolated town of Ostend was obviously difficult. The Reformed community in the town had already received assistance from London for their poor members the previous year. 'They were grateful since trade had already come to a total standstill while the richer citizens were leaving the town', as they seem to have been doing all over the southern Netherlands. The garrison in Ostend, as opposed to so many other towns in Flanders and Brabant, proved loyal and took 'an oath of adhering to Holland and Zeeland and those who preserved the faith' – i.e. the Reformed religion. A year later the civil and military leaders in Ostend sent Captain Zuderman and a minister to London to raise financial support and troops for their struggle from the Dutch immigrant communities in England. They quickly recruited 200 men mainly from Norwich and Colchester who by early September 1585 had arrived safely in Ostend, whereas the ship with provisions of corn and English beer dispatched from London was seized by privateers from Dunkirk who operated under Spanish protection.[137] A year later the civic leaders of Ostend once more had recourse for help from London:

> We have not forgotten your former benevolence, but the groaning and lamentations of our poor do not cease, and we are unable to relieve them. Hence we trust you will listen to the complaints of your brethren, who are so sorely tried by diseases and famine. You know, no doubt, that the garrison is paid tardily, and that those who have come lately from England have never before been subjected to such suffering. We pay taxes to the uttermost, but are unable to meet all the requirements. In the approaching winter we shall probably be constrained to abandon our poor altogether.[138]

Who were these men who, having already emigrated to England, now volunteered for service back in their home-country? Far from all of them appear to have been committed Calvinists who returned to fight for what they considered a godly cause. Thus, the soldier Joos Lupaert who served in Lillo in Brabant in 1591 had enlisted in London seven years earlier because of slack trade in the city. He had left his wife and child behind, initially for a year, but later when he had asked her to join him she had refused to go to the Netherlands because 'she feared hard times' there. That at least was Joos Lupaert's version of events. His brother-in-law, however, considered him 'a blasphemer and a worthless fellow', while his wife complained that he had abandoned her, a claim substantiated by Joos's relatives in London. Since she had received no tidings from him she had presumed him dead. Subsequently she had re-married an Englishman four years earlier, with whom she now had two children. Consequently she had no intention to return to her first husband, Joos Lupaert.[139]

The Eighty Years War, however, did not solely affect areas which were part of the seventeen provinces of the Low Countries. By 1590 Wesel, situated in Cleves, being part of the Holy German Empire and a centre for German Calvinism, claimed to have suffered not only from the soldiery of Spain, but also from troops fighting for the United Provinces. It had lost most of its trade and many of its citizens were ruined. As was the case in most of the cities and towns which had been either blockaded or besieged in Flanders and Brabant it was the poor in Wesel who suffered most while the majority of the well-to-do had left the town. The citizens of Wesel, despite having no part in the conflict, claimed that they were harassed by nearby Spanish garrisons because they received wounded English soldiers who had been fighting for the United Provinces.[140]

By 1598 the town of Bergen-op-Zoom was still holding out as the last major outpost for the United Provinces in Brabant, but its citizens were paying a high price for their loyalty and were urgently in need of assistance.

> As for nearly sixteen years our town has been a frontier-town, the enemy has caused us great trouble. Our best land has been inundated for our own protection and that of Zeeland, and our higher land may be cultivated only as far as our artillery can protect it. Last summer the plague and diarrhoea raged here, and our soldiers mutinied. And though our Magistracy has prevented further harm, yet we are greatly burdened by our large garrison, whose wives and children we have to maintain besides the widows and orphans. Our town-council and the Deacons have now erected an orphanage, but as our citizens cannot defray all the expenses we request your help.[141]

Bergen-op-Zoom, in other words, had experienced all the horrors which early modern urban dwellers could expect to be confronted with during a prolonged military conflict or siege: food shortages, epidemics, mutiny, financial strain and greatly increased poverty levels. The damage caused by the troops employed for the town's protection with their considerable train of family and camp-followers, often seemed greater or equivalent to that caused by the enemy.

Ostend shared the experience of Bergen-op-Zoom. For long it had been the only town in Flanders which had remained loyal to the United Provinces, only to see itself coming under renewed and intensive Spanish pressure in July 1601 when a large Spanish force commenced what became an epic siege which came to symbolise the struggle in the Low Countries. The siege acquired European fame and many young European noblemen included a trip to Ostend in their Grand Tour to acquaint themselves with the new military techniques and tactics on display there.[142] Not surprisingly its siege was later to feature prominently in the rapidly growing military literature of the early seventeenth century.[143]

Maurits of Nassau tried to relieve the beleaguered town of Ostend on several occasions. In March 1603 all the captains of the Zeeland garrisons were ordered to bring their companies up to full strength recruiting 'reliable and religious persons'. A campaign was clearly imminent. However, according to the leaders of the Reformed community in Middelburg, such godly people were sparse on the ground in Zeeland where they could only expect to recruit beggars and vagabonds. Instead they hoped to be able to enlist such people from the Dutch immigrant communities in England who had previously been able to provide them with soldiers, especially since they had heard that the Dutch and Walloon workmen in England found it increasingly difficult to find employment.[144]

The following June the town of Flushing which served as a staging post for supplying Ostend with fresh troops and provisions, while also providing the initial treatment of the sick and wounded soldiers arriving from Ostend and Sluys before they were transported further back from the frontline, found itself under severe strain. Not only did they have to provide care for the many wounded coming from Ostend, but plague had recently carried off 4,000 of the town's inhabitants; consequently they had totally run out of linen for bandages. The deacons and directors of the local hospital pointed out that they also provided care for many wounded and sick coming from Sluys, 'who sometimes are sent to other towns, but require to be treated at least once before they can be transported, which we are unable to do on account of the want of beds, linen and blankets'. Their request to their Dutch Reformed brethren in London was met and a couple of months later they expressed their gratitude for the linen for bandages they had received, while requesting the Londoners to buy white 'Northern Karsey' with the money collected for them. This was evidently going to provide clothes for the many orphans and poor citizens in Flushing. A further gift of £25 and linen for bandages was gratefully received in Flushing in December 1604, a few months after Ostend's surrender to the Spanish commander Ambrosio Spinola: 'Which though destined for the soldiers coming from Ostend (which it has pleased the Lord to prevent) serves us now for the sick soldiers coming hither from Sluys, Yzendijke and elsewhere.'[145]

Even towns such as Tiel in Gelderland which did not see much military action were seriously affected by the protracted conflict. Often, from the civilian perspective, it was difficult to see that your own soldiers were preferable to those of the enemy. It was the secondary effects of war which put local resources under considerable pressure in Tiel where 'the army of the States' had been quartered for a number of years. It had caused considerable devastation and damage to the surrounding countryside, while the magistracy had to provide for a growing number of sick and poor. Furthermore, Tiel was garrisoned by English and Scottish soldiers, for whose widows and orphans the town's deacons found it increasingly difficult to find the necessary support.[146]

For the Puritan MP for West Looe in Essex, Geoffrey Gates, there was no doubt that the conflict in the Netherlands was a sign of the Last Days as described in the Book of Revelation and symptomatic of the great apocalyptic struggle the world was then engulfed in.[147] In December 1578 he finished his pamphlet, *The Defence of Militarie Profession*, [148] which vigorously defended war as a godly occupation when undertaken in defence of true religion. The book also served as a warning to Elizabethan England. 'The experience of other mens harmes, warneth the wise to be ware. The experience of forren evils, warneth England to watch it selfe out of securitie, and to be watchfull, and wisely to take it selfe.'[149]

Geoffrey Gates was evidently well informed about recent Protestant history, particularly about the most recent incidents in the Dutch Revolt. He emphasised that

> By armes also, hath the Lorde God of hostes entred foot in Belgia, and there taught the ignorant handes to fighte, and the slowe couraged to be bolde and hardie. Whereby the pride of the enemyes is daunted, and their glorye abated, (and that before oure eyes) in such apparent and wonderfull maner, as wee may wel say that the Lorde of hostes is abrode with his armyes, to pourchase to himselfe honor and prayse, for the yeere of his redemed is come: neither will he geue ouer the fielde any more, til he hath utterly destroyed his ennemyes and confounded the wicked for euermore and giue perpetuall rest to Israel, according as it is written.[150]

Gates then proceeds to offer an interpretation of recent Protestant history as an apocalyptic event where God (in true Old Testament style) wracks his enemies and defends the new Israel by the sword.

> And now let us father beholde with discretion what worke the Lord is entered into by Armes, in these last dayes of the worlde: And how martiall prowesse and industrie hath mightely served to advaunce the name and glorye of God, and so giue passage to his Gospell, where it lay prostrate and troden under the feete of Antichrist and his consorts. For when the time was come in the yere of our Saviour Christ 1517 that the Lord set foote on earth to restore his Sanctuary he beganne his businesse by a poore ministrie (i.e. Luther) under the couert & protection of the most worthie prince Duke Frederick of Saxonie, and so encreased under the defence of the most noble Princes, John Duke of Saxonie, & Philipe Lantgraue of Hesse, & of the famous and warlike cities, Augsburg, Strassburg, Ulmes, Magdeburg etc. And when the champions of the kingdome of darknesse (under the conducts of the most renowned Emperor Charles V) seemed to renge [reign] the hoste of Israel under a terrible victory: then did the Lorde of hostes bestirre himselfe, and frustrating the councels, and dispersing the forces of his enemies, he vanquished the troupes of the Philistines by the Armed hand of his chosen captain Maurice, Duke of Saxony: who by the vertue of Martial prowesse ayded by the Lord God of hostes, brake the teeth of the ungodly, and restored the worde of God to a free passage throughout all Germanie.[151]

In his chronological survey of God's wars Gates provides a detailed account of the ongoing conflict in the Netherlands and wonders how it is that God has taken command of Orangist forces in their 'quarrell of truth and righteousnesse' and encouraged them 'not to feare the multitude of their enemies'. He emphasises how God has 'stood by the Hollanders in their honest cause and hath justified their quarrell', while predicting that God will support them till the End.[152] Geoffrey Gates was far from unique among godly Reformed Englishmen in holding these opinions. They were widely shared by his Puritan contemporaries and early seventeenth-century successors as can be seen from the writings of among others Edmund Calamy and Stephen Marshall.[153]

Directly, as well as indirectly, the experiences of the Dutch Revolt had a major impact on the way knowledge of the art of war and its consequences was disseminated.[154] From the late sixteenth century a growing number of works reached the market, often going through numerous print-runs. Most famous was Jacob de Gheyn's widely translated and pirated drill book, *Wapenhandelinghe* (1607), which consisted of only four pages of text supplemented with no less than 119 pages of woodcuts illustrating the often complex drill movements.[155] Often writers of such military manuals would draw upon their personal experiences of military action, which obviously added to the book's credibility while making them more market-able. This was the case with Thomas Fisher's *The Warlike Directions* (1633) and Captain Henry Hexham's *The Principles of the Art Militarie* (1637) which drew on their authors' long service with some of the English regiments fighting for the United Provinces in the Netherlands.[156]

Captain Henry Hexham, a firm Calvinist and a member of the English Reformed churches in The Hague and Delft, started his literary career as a translator of a couple of theological treatises by the Leiden professor of theology Johannes Polyander before writing on military matters, then, upon his retirement from the army in Holland in 1648, he became the first Anglo-Dutch dictionary maker.[157] Hexham dedicated his translation of Polyander's *The refutation of an Epistle* (1610) to his commander, Sir Horace Vere, while his friend, John Burgess, minister to the English Reformed church in The Hague provided a letter to the reader: 'and in my opinion so much the more agreeable vnto you, by how much you declare yourself a zealous louer of that Truth which this author maintaineth, and haue with losse of blood and hazard of life, defended with your sword, what this man by his pen'.[158] The temporary cessation of hostilities in the Netherlands caused by the Twelve Years Truce (1609–21) had evidently left Sir Horace Vere's quartermaster with plenty of spare time and provided him with an opportunity to translate Polyander's pamphlets, the second of which he dedicated to Lady Vere.

Worthie Reader, for varietie sake, to employ my idle time to some vse, and to
offer my mite vnto the Church of God, that the graue and learned men of our
nation may see, that the ministers of other reformed churches, marche pouldron to pouldron with them vnto the Lords combate: I haue vndertaken this
translation, free from ostentation: onely my ambition is (in tracing after the
stepps of my Author) to haue one flurt [a fencing foil – a fleuret] at Antichrist,
and one push at the fall of the great whore of Babylon, and so much the rather,
because mine eyes haue seene some of her fornications, which some others
haue but heard.[159]

Evidently, Hexham considered the struggle against Spain as part of the
great apocalyptic battle against Antichrist and saw himself as one of
Christ's soldiers marching into battle for the Lord.

Later, after Hexham had served as quartermaster to Horace Vere's regiment during the siege of Maastricht in 1632, he published an account of
what had proved a high-profile victory for the Dutch in taking the great
fortress of Maastricht.[160] Hexham counter-balanced his story by giving a
brief account of the Duke of Parma's siege of Maastricht over fifty years
ealier in 1579. He underlined how the Spaniards had taken the town by
storm after having besieged it for eight months. During the assault they
killed not only many of the town's defenders but also many women and
children. The Spanish soldiers deliberately drowned hundreds of civilians
by throwing them off the bridge leading over the river Maas, an episode
which bore similarities to the earlier events in Zutphen. Those who fled
'into the steeples and turrets of churches and cloisters' to save their lives,
crying out to the soldiers to spare their lives were not shown mercy, but
instead fired on by the musketeers, evidence of which, according to
Hexham, could still be detected by the many musket-balls stuck in the
walls fifty years later.[161]

It seems, however, that God fought for the Dutch in all weathers. The
siege of 1632 was much shorter, but took place during an unusually wet
summer, which initially caused the besiegers some difficulties, but later
assisted them considerably in preventing a Spanish and Imperial relief
army under the command of Count Pappenheim from attacking their
siegeworks at the beginning of July.

About this tyme it was a very wet season, & great store of Raine fell so that the
River swelled, and the Enemye could not forde it over, till our works, double
entrenchments, Ditches, Skances, Ravelings, and halfe-Moones on the other
side of the River, were defensible, which made vs believe, that as God fought for
vs before the Busse (s'Hertogenbosch) with drye weather, so now hee did the
like by wett weather, & made the heavens to favour vs.[162]

Having taken the trouble of emphasising the Spanish cruelty fifty years earlier it is somewhat surprising that Hexham says that Maastricht nearly suffered the same fate only three days before it surrendered on 23 August. During the assault on the town on 20 August the Dutch forces nearly broke through the defences and would, had they been successful, have pillaged the town despite the pleas for mercy from its citizens.

The fall of Maastricht combined with the fact that the local peasantry had taken up arms against his troops 'cutting the throats of his stragglers', as a consequence of their plunderings, caused Count Pappenheim temporarily to withdraw from the province of Limburg. A week later Pappenheim, however, returned with an army of around 7,000 men to take revenge. It proved a brief incidence of sustained pillage, 'where his men committed cruell Insolences, breaking up Churches, Cloisters & Gentlemens houses, spared not the Romish Catholiques themselves, especially his men payd those of the Reformed Religion' before they returned to the theatre of war in Germany. According to Hexham not much had changed over the last seventy years – Spanish and Imperial troops were still perpetrators of evil and anti-Christian deeds whose brutality did not even spare their own co-religionists.

The victory was celebrated by two services in St Matthew's church in Maastricht which was packed by soldiers and inhabitants. When the preacher to the States General, Conrad Merkinius, left the pulpit after the afternoon's sermon he was embraced by an old woman, 'whom God had preserved from death' when the town had been taken by Parma in 1579. Being a Calvinist she had been so overjoyed upon hearing the pure Word of God preached again that she caught the preacher in her arms – like 'Symion did to our Saviour' causing much rejoicing among the bystanders. The fall of Maastricht was in other words a momentous victory for the forces of godliness and the United Provinces.[163]

The Thirty Years War

If God's hand was immediately visible to contemporaries, especially Protestants, in the prolonged confrontation between Catholic Spain and its rebellious, former subjects in the United Provinces, fighting under a Reformed banner, then all the signs of the imminence of the Last Days and the great apocalyptic battle between Christ and Antichrist, prophesyed in the Book of Revelation, were even more evident to contemporaries in the Thirty Years War, especially during its first fifteen years.[164] The London minister Edmund Calamy expressed it forcefully in a fast sermon preached in 1641:

Some Nations are chastised with the sword. Others with famine, Others with man-destroying Plague. But poore Germany hath been sorely whipped with all these three iron whips at the same time, and that for about twenty yeares space. Oh, let us make use of this Bucket, and draw out water, and poure it out before the Lord this day; let us send up our cries to Heaven for Germany. It is a signe that we are not true members of the body of Christ, because we have no more fellowship of the miseries of the same body. A dead member hath no sense of its own misery, or of the bodies distemper. If wee be living members, we will simpathize with the calamities of God's people.[165]

If the figure of Antichrist's adjutant, the Duke of Alva, loomed over the Reformed perspective on the Eighty Years War, it was by contrast the figure of the Messianic prince who would arrive to institute a Protestant millennium in connection with the return of Christ, which came to dominate Protestant eschatological expectations in the Thirty Years War. These expectations were, as we shall see, successively applied to Frederick V of the Palatinate, Christian IV of Denmark and, finally and most forcefully, to Gustavus Adolphus of Sweden.

From the end of the Twelve Years Truce beween Spain and the United Provinces in 1621 the Eighty Years War and the Thirty Years War became entangled and difficult to separate. Thus in July 1622 Count Spinola and his Spanish forces laid siege to Bergen-op-Zoom immediately after having concluded their successful campaign in the German Palatinate and in Jülich-Cleves. Spinola's army was more than 20,000 strong and seems to have had an even greater train of camp-followers accompanying it, if the report of the Calvinist ministers in Bergen-op-Zoom can be trusted. As they put it 'such a long tail on such a small body never was seen', emphasising their surprise at seeing 'such a small army with so many carts, baggage horses, nags, suttlers, lackeys, women, children and a rabble which numbered far more than the army itself'.[166] Even if the number of camp-followers of the Spanish army in Flanders was notoriously high, occasionally matching the number of troops, this was undoubtedly an exaggeration on the part of the Calvinist ministers; we can, however, safely assume that the number of people directly or indirectly involved in the siege of the town would have been well over 30,000.[167]

The siege proved a costly failure for Spinola whose army dwindled from its original 20,600 men to a little over 13,000 in less than three months, when in early October Spinola was forced to abandon the siege, mainly due to mass desertions. It serves to illustrate that sieges not only imposed terrible hardship on besieged civilians and defending soldiers, but could become unbearable for the besiegers too. No less than 2,500 of the Spanish deserters were so desperate that they fled into the city they were besieging, begging for asylum. They claimed to have received no pay and no food from their superiors. Conditions must have been miserable in the trenches outside Bergen-op-Zoom to generate desertion on this scale during what proved a short summer siege. The response of a deserter, staggering up to the walls of Bergen-op-Zoom in order to surrender, is illustrative. When challenged by the watch, asking from where he came, he responded: 'Hell'.[168]

However, the siege of Bergen-op-Zoom was far from a typical siege in the early modern period. Most significantly it does not appear to have affected the civilian population of the area to the extent warfare and sieges of this period normally did.

Among the first civilians to suffer the devastating effects of the Thirty Years War were the leaders of the Reformed communities in the Lower and Upper Palatinates, whose ruler, the young Elector Palatine, Frederick V, had been instrumental in bringing about the war in the first place, by accepting the Bohemian crown. After the defeat of Frederick's army outside Prague on 29 October 1620, the Lower and Upper Palatinates were quickly occupied by Imperial, Bavarian and Spanish forces respectively, sending most of the leaders of the Reformed churches and schools into exile. Realising, as they did, that they were without any Imperial, legal protection, since the Reformed faith had not been included in the Religious Peace of Augsburg in 1555, the pastors, schoolmasters and their families fled, often having been actively persecuted by the occupation forces. This important confessional aspect of the war was further enhanced when the Emperor published the Edict of Restitution on 6 March 1629, which was directed against the Reformed in particular, while generally promoting Catholic Counter-Reformation policies.[169]

Relying on charity these refugees settled primarily in and around Hanau and Nuremberg. By the autumn of 1629 the refugees congregated in Hanau had exhausted all sources of assistance, informing their friends in London that, 'the sight of our afflicted brethren and their families bereft of medical aid and daily bread, is pitiable. They are so exhausted by illness that they cannot help each other.'[170] Flight, anxiety and exile in an alien city threatened by war was obviously taking its toll. In and around Nuremberg conditions appear to have been better at this stage. Here the leaders of the refugees pointed out that:

> Some seem to look upon our sojourn in these places as idleness, and think that we ought to search for some employment or manual labour. But our leisure, in

which we have to struggle with hunger, false brethren and a thousand difficulties and dangers is very irksome to us.

The war, however, was gradually coming closer to Nuremberg, as the refugees were only too aware, when they added: 'meanwhile the Imperial army blocks up all our roads to such an extent that none of us can leave this neighbourhood without running the greatest danger'.[171]

The following year Sweden and Gustavus Adolphus intervened on the Protestant side, evidently not discouraged by the disastrous intervention in the conflict five years earlier by its rival for Baltic hegemony, Denmark–Norway, under the leadership of its king, Christian IV. Like Gustavus Adolphus, Christian's reason for entering the war had been partly religiously motivated. Evidently Christian IV saw himself, or wanted to be seen, as the saviour of Protestantism. While staying at the castle of Rothenburg in December 1625 Christian had had a vision during his morning prayer. While praying for the embattled evangelical churches in Germany Christ had appeared blood-stained, tortured and derided before the king. For Christian and his subjects, since the king took care to have his vision publicised, this was a clear sign that God wanted him to come to the defence of the suffering evangelical communities in Germany.[172]

This was not a novel experience for the king. Christian IV had already received a much publicised portent from God some ten years earlier when a large supernatural fish had been caught off the coast of his duchy of Holstein (Plate 3.28). There was nothing exceptional in this – a herring with a warning inscription had after all been presented to Christian's father Frederik II in 1578. Furthermore, Man's fate, at least in a figurative sense, was repeatedly linked to that of fish in the Bible (see for instance Ecclesiastes 9:12 and Habakkuk 1:14) and prophetic wonder-fish and whales played a significant part in the popular mythology of the fishing nations surrounding the Baltic and North Sea.[173]

This martial-looking fish caught in 1615 with sword and halbards sticking out of its body, combined with its somewhat obscure inscription: (*WEWEWEDENME*: Woe – Woe – Woe – Denmark?), indicated some approaching military disaster to Christian IV and his kingdoms unless the king and his people mended their ways and showed sincere repentance. Taking its departure from Luke 19:40 this was clearly a last warning from God via an inarticulate being or object after His warnings sent through His church and ministers had been disregarded.[174]

It is significant that Christian IV continued to have similar visions until he was defeated by the Imperial commander Count Tilly at Lutter-am-

Plate 3.28 Anon.,
Wonder-fish (1615)

Barenberg in August 1626 – a defeat which finally deflated this Protestant
dream. Considering this evangelical emphasis it is surprising that
Christian IV never made a conscious effort to promote his evangelical
crusade in Germany among his subjects. Unlike Gustavus Adolphus of
Sweden, Christian never indulged in any significant anti-Catholic propaganda. He only made use of public days of general prayer to promote the

Protestant cause. Not until 1623 when he issued a statute against 'cursing and swearing' did he admonish the general public that such blasphemous behaviour inevitably invoked 'the certain signs of God's wrath', such as dearth, war, rebellion and plague, as could be seen in neighbouring countries.

His defeat in 1626 and the subsequent occupation of Jutland by the Imperial Catholic army of Wallenstein served to actualise these and even worse apocalyptic visions for the population. A feeling of having offended God prevailed, and it was recognised that His anger and punishment might only be averted through penance and prayer. It was as a consequence of this defeat and his own growing piety and faith in Christ's redeeming grace that Christian IV from around 1629 began to have himself portrayed in both texts and pictures as a parallel to Christ betrayed by Judas (his allies?) and convicted and humiliated by Pilate and the Pharisees (the Emperor?).[175] Christian and his government were not alone in praying for divine intervention on their side in this moment of crisis. In February 1628, while occupied by Wallenstein's troops the inhabitants of the south Jutland town of Sønderborg saw a peculiar sight in the sky. From the north a great army was seen marching south, fully armed with muskets and cannon. Over the town it clashed with another army coming from the south. A major battle then raged in the sky lasting several hours and witnessed by several hundred people who were trembling with fear. The army from the north eventually stood victorious, clearly signalling that a distressed Protestant people was still to be saved from its predicaments.[176]

God's punishment, however, was not meted out on the Danes by Imperial troops alone. The Danish forces who fled ahead of them in considerable disorder up through Jutland, plundered many of the market-towns on their way, starting with the town of Kolding, which despite the presence of Christian IV, desperately trying to halt the military collapse, was severely pillaged. It is, in fact, difficult to determine whether Imperial or Royal troops did more damage to the towns and countryside in Jutland before the Treaty of Lübeck (1629) brought an end to Danish involvement in the war.

Dismay and dread dominated life in Jutland over the next couple of years nurtured not only by rumours of real and perceived troop movements, but also by news of armed gangs of displaced people and vagabonds touring the countryside, preying on civilians and soldiers alike. The destruction of major market-towns such as Vejle where most of the major buildings were destroyed or burnt and the remaining population deeply impoverished, while most of the town's considerable hop gardens and surrounding forests were laid waste, demonstrates the damage wrought by the mercenaries.[177] When the region of Salling was finally occupied by Imperial troops in October 1628 their arrival was preceded by a supernatural event, which indicated that this was all part of a divine scheme of punishment. The day before the troops' arrival the area was hit by an unusually violent snowstorm, where hail the size of musket-balls and even the size of proper balls killed many of the younger cattle in the fields.[178]

Compared with what followed in Germany the sufferings of the Lutheran population in Jutland proved relatively mild in comparison. A wealth of broadsheets and pamphlets testify to the suffering of the peasant population in Germany during the Thirty Years War. Typical of these mass-produced broadsheets is one from around 1620 entitled: *The Lord's Prayer of common peasants against the merciless soldiers*, juxtapositioning the Common Man and the Lord's Prayer against the men of violence (Plate 3.29). The etching shows a village being plundered by musketeers. In the foreground a musketeer is grabbing the purse of a frightened peasant while his heavily loaded mistress watches, supporting herself on his musket-rest. This violence against the defenceless is reflected in a tableau at their feet where the chickens are fleeing a dog who is killing one of them. To the left scared, elderly peasants are watching and praying, while to the right another musketeer is raping a peasant woman. The text informs us that such acts are against the law of God and that the soldiers may go to blazes.[179]

More than any other event, however, it was the total devastation of one of the Holy Roman Empire's most prominent Imperial cities – Protestant Magdeburg in 1631 – which struck Protestant contemporaries in particular as an event on the biblical scale of disasters, only matched by the destruction of Jerusalem itself. Despite a considerable propaganda effort to convince his own subjects, as well as the Protestant princes and Imperial cities of the Holy German Empire, of his Protestant credentials and motives, Gustavus Adolphus was slow in winning allies in Germany. The Imperial city of Magdeburg, which had survived a protracted siege by Wallenstein the previous year, became Sweden's first ally when signing a treaty with Gustavus Adolphus in August 1630. However, the Swedish king proved unable to come to the assistance of his strategically and confessionally important ally, despite his many public pledges to do so. Magdeburg was captured by Imperialist forces under Tilly the following May.[180] The city was immediately sacked by Tilly's forces which had suffered heavy losses during the siege and a significant part of the population was massacred,

while even more succumbed to the fire which broke out soon after the city's fall. The destruction of Magdeburg was widely portrayed in both text and prints, as for instance in this broadsheet showing the last stage of the siege and the storm of the city (Plate 3.30).[181]

The dramatic events were recorded by an Imperial soldier in a diary of his experiences of the war. He was part of the forces which successfully took the city by storm early in the morning of 20 May. Having avoided injury in getting into Magdeburg he was shot twice just inside the 'neistadter' gate. He was then carried back into the camp where he was bandaged. It is noteworthy that what appears to have been a relatively effective first aid system had been set up among the Imperial troops. Our writer had first been shot in the stomach, but fortunately for him the bullet had passed straight through him and had come to rest in his shirt. Then, however, he had been hit in both shoulders. Back in the camp he was attended by a barber-surgeon, who had cut the bullet(s) in his shoulders out with a chisel, after having bound his hands behind his back. In a period which knew nothing of anaesthesia this was the only option. No wonder that the soldier was eventually taken back to his hut more dead than alive. Despite his severe injuries he still expressed his sadness that 'this beautiful city' had suffered such a terrible fate. Unable to take part in the plunder of the city himself, his wife entered it intent on obtaining a carriage for his transport, bedclothes for him to rest on, and linen for bandages. While she was gone he was lying next to his sick baby daughter Elisabeth, who had only been born the previous year while Tilly's army had camped in the vicinity of Wiesbaden. But before his wife had returned he had been deeply troubled by agitated rumours in the camp, claiming that most of the buildings in the burning city had collapsed and killed many of the plundering soldiers and female camp-followers. Fearing, as he claimed more for the sake of his sick child than for his own wounded self, that his wife may have perished, he was greatly relieved when she returned half an hour later in the company of an old woman who had helped her carry the loot. It consisted of bedclothes, a large pitcher full of wine, two silver belts and clothes which the soldier later sold for 12 thaler in Halberstadt. By the evening when his horses arrived the soldiers in his company had each given him either a thaler or half a thaler. Evidently a tradition existed whereby soldiers in a regiment felt a collective responsibility for those of their colleagues who were injured, providing assistance for their maintenance and medical treatment.

Four days after the fall of Magdeburg all the injured Imperialist soldiers were transported to Halberstadt. Casualties appear to have been high since

Plate 3.29 Anon., *The Lord's Prayer of common peasants against the merciless soldiers* (1620)

Plate 3.30 Anon., *The fall of Magdeburg* (1631)

our soldier informs us that there were around 300 injured from his regiment alone, who surprisingly all recovered. Seven weeks later the soldier was himself fully restored, but his sick baby daughter was not so fortunate. Elisabeth died in Halberstadt. Putting a cross next to the sentence reporting her death the soldier expressed the wish 'that God would grant her a happy resurrection'.[182]

If the experience had been a brutal one for many of Magdeburg's attackers it proved an even more devastating occasion for the city's mainly Protestant population of 20,000, many of whom perished in the sack. For the minority, who managed to escape, the experience made a life-long impact. Johann Daniel Friese, son of the town-clerk and only twelve years old at the time, later described the traumatic events in detail in his autobiography, informing us how the family managed to avoid both the Imperial troops and the fire engulfing the city, spending the whole day fleeing to safety.[183] The merchant Simon Prinz, who actively took part in Magdeburg's defence as a gunner, found his own house plundered when he returned from the walls. Trying to save his family, among them his mother who had been badly injured, Prinz was held up by Imperial soldiers who demanded money and valuables in order to spare his life and let him go, only to see his apprentice, who prayed the soldiers to give him quarter, hacked down with an axe in front of him. Narrowly avoiding getting killed on several occasions Prinz and his family were eventually given quarter by a lieutenant-colonel who escorted them out of the burning city. However, he was forced to leave his injured mother behind, not knowing what eventually happened to her, adding: 'The Almighty God give her a happy Resurrection'.[184]

The minister Christopher Thodaenus was responding to a request to attend a Protestant colonel who lay seriously injured in a nearby hostel when the Imperial soldiers were storming through the streets of Magdeburg. Here he was quickly joined by his wife and maid who did not dare to remain alone in their own house. Groups of marauding soldiers quickly broke into the hostel demanding money and valuables. A musketeer who very appropriately looked like the Devil nearly killed Thodaenus when he was unable to satisfy his demands. Only his wife's determined intervention made sure that the bullet aimed at him went over his head and hit the wall. However, the minister was less fortunate with his next encounter with an enemy soldier, who hit him on the head with his sword causing him to bleed profusely. This soldier led the three of them out into one of the main lanes of the city which was packed with thousands of moving and screaming people, not to mention many dead bodies. In the confusion they eventually managed to secure quarter from a colonel who personally led them out of the burning city on the promise of ransom.[185] Similarly, the engineer Otto Gericke, who later served in the Swedish army, nearly perished in the sack of Magdeburg while losing most of his possessions.[186]

There was nothing unusual about the level of brutality applied at Magdeburg – it was normal practice to sack a town that resisted – but the scale of the slaughter was uncommon. For the first time in the war a major city of 20,000 people had been plundered and destroyed. A city which was furthermore a capital of Protestantism. No wonder the event assumed great and apocalyptic symbolism among Protestants and Catholic alike. Twenty newspapers, more than 200 pamphlets and over 40 illustrated broadsheets, describing the brutality and comprehensiveness of the sack, were published across Europe. By early June detailed information had reached Cologne via the United Provinces which was related in the newspaper, *Niederlendischen vnd auss andern Orthen Post- | zeitungen des 1631. Jahrs.* The paper claimed that since the destruction of Jerusalem the world had hardly witnessed a more dreadful spectacle than the recent events in Magdeburg. The conquering of the city had seen many thousands of women and children throttled, burnt and brutally killed in the basements. More than 1,500 peasants from the surrounding countryside had sought shelter in the city as had many nobles, who together with the population of more than 20,000 people had lost their lives in the sack.[187]

The new French weekly newspaper, the *Gazette*, also reported the sack of Magdeburg by early June:

> Magdeburg, this eye of the Empire has been torn out and its burghers have with their brave decision made the story of Sagunt and Numantia creditable. The day after its capture a muster revealed that only a thousand souls still remained in this once populous city. A fine example of the fickleness of human affairs: the work of several centuries is transformed into ashes in less than a day. Considering the constant blissfulness of a city which had hitherto never been captured the few burghers who survived the sack are hardly given leave to complain. Similarly their present misery is so great that even their destroyers, if they are not to be considered inhuman, cannot deny spilling true or simulated tears for them.[188]

God clearly had a hand in the sack and destruction of Magdeburg. A Catholic and Imperial pamphlet published in 1632 also referred to the destruction of Jerusalem, when claiming that the world had not witnessed a more terrible act and punishment by God until the destruction of

Magdeburg. The brutal plundering of the Imperial soldiers had, according to this pamphlet, been of short duration. It was only when the plunder had come to an end, that 'God's anger and chastisement had begun in earnest, and fires broke out and mines exploded, so that within a few hours this beautiful city with all its great riches was reduced to ashes.'[189]

Many of the Protestant pamphlets which dealt with the disaster provided a detailed description of the horrors which had taken, or were supposed to have taken, place. *Copey eines Schreibens Auss Magdeburg* (Copy of a Letter from Magdeburg) or as it was entitled in its second edition, *Warhafftiger vnd ausführlicher Bericht* (True and detailed Report) both published in 1631, is in many respects typical. Describing the city's capture it informs us that far from all the defenders who asked for quarter were granted it by Tilly's soldiers. Count Pappenheim's troops appear to have been particularly brutal and among them especially his Walloon regiments who conducted themselves in the most unChristian manner, much worse than Turks! Rather than showing mercy the Walloons had not only put the surrendering troops to the sword, but had begun to chop down innocent women, children, pregnant women not to mention clergy wherever they came upon them, whether it be in their houses or in the local churches. Such unChristian behaviour shocked the already hardened troops in Tilly's army who were deeply upset. The author expressed the pious hope that never again would the Lord visit the Protestant side with such a dissolute and devilish people as Tilly's soldiers. However, in the view of the pamphleteer, the people of Magdeburg were not totally blameless for what had happened. The educated elite, and in particular the city's governors, had behaved in an arrogant manner, disregarding sermons warning them and encouraging penance. Similarly some of the clergy in the city had been more concerned with self-promotion and their own worldly glory rather than serving God and their congregations. Thus it became unavoidable 'that Christ was crucified and that much innocent blood was spilt by such ungodly lansquenets'.[190]

Other pamphlets went even further in terms of the dire details they offered their readers. Thus *Kurtzer, Jedoch warhefftiger eigentlicher, Bericht. Wie es mit eroberung vnd Zerstörung der vhralten weitberühmten, Stadt Magdeburg hergangen* (1631) (Short, but true and proper report. How the capture and destruction of the ancient and famous city of Magdeburg took place), describes how two Imperial soldiers found a small child lying in the street crying, and how they each grabbed one leg and ripped the child apart. Having provided this gruesome vignette the author informs the reader that the Imperial soldiers dealt with their female prisoners in such an evil and depraved manner that it was impossible for him to describe it. According to the author it is a wonder that God did not dip the perpetrators in pitch and sulphur and let this barbarous act go unpunished, but, as he added, they might still get their just deserts.[191]

Whether true or not, such dramatic reports of inhuman cruelties served to fuel a growing anxiety and added to the apocalyptic speculations of the period. It certainly resulted in a number of sermons, many of which were later published in a number of Protestant, German cities, which not only lamented the destruction of Magdeburg, but offered consolation and urged people to do penance and mend their ways before it was too late.[192] Similarly popular prophetic pamphlets such as *Die Jämmerlich, betrübte Prophetin Frau Sybilla Magdeburg* (1631) (The wretched, distressed prophet lady Sybilla Magdeburg) added to the general sense of doom and impending apocalyptic disaster. They claimed that the fate that had befallen Magdeburg was only the first sign of the impending destruction not only of the Holy Roman Empire, but the whole Catholic Church. Like the comet of 1618 the sack of Magdeburg in 1631 was a sign of terrible things to come.[193] There were, according to the pamphlet, good historical reasons for Magdeburg's recent and terrible punishment. In Roman times its citizens had worshipped a picture of Venus, which should have led them into sodomy. This 'unchaste, devilish picture' had remained in Magdeburg for 800 years and should have caused its citizens 'to commit even greater sins through venereal sodomy and unchastity'.[194] Magdeburg's destruction was part of God's great eschatological plan which would eventually lead to the fall of the pope and the Roman Church.

The anxiety and general fear of an impending apocalyptic war had been prominent in Augsburg, another of the great Imperial cities, since at least 1615. Here, as elsewhere, the comet of 1618, which appeared in the sky with a long tail of fire behind it in December added to the eschatological expectations and speculations (Plate 3.31).[195] The Augsburg brewer Jerg Siedeler noted the event in detail in his diary and quoted the interpretation provided by Elias Ehinger, teacher at the high school and the city's librarian, in his *Astrological Judgement* published that year. Here Ehinger pointed out that the comet signified 'a great change of government within some years accompanied by terrible wars and rebellions by the common man and great persecutions. The whole world would be affected by misery and wretchedness, through war, bloodshed, robbery, murder and conflagration, great dearth, hunger and plague.'[196]

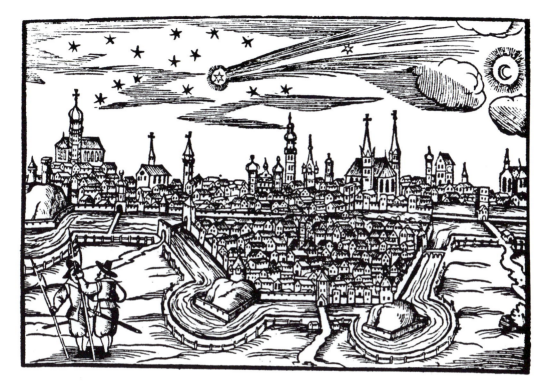

Plate 3.31 J. Senfft, *Comet seen over Augsburg in 1618* (1619)

Considering that Augsburg had been confessionally divided between Lutherans and Catholics since the Peace of Augsburg in 1555 it is surprising that the peaceful co-existence between the two groups managed to survive the growing, apocalyptic hysteria which surrounded the start of the Thirty Years War. It was not until the Edict of Restitution, issued by the Emperor in March 1629, that this long-standing religious equilibrium broke down. The Edict immediately served to bring the religious element back to the forefront of the war. Despite the fact that the Imperial Free Cities were excluded from the Edict which banned all Protestants other than Lutherans and granted ecclesiastical rulers the same right to enforce religious uniformity on their subjects as secular princes,[197] it had severe consequences for Augsburg, not least due to the pressure both Emperor Ferdinand II and the local bishop were able to exert on the city council. All Protestant councillors were replaced on a city council which for generations had been finely balanced between Catholics and evangelicals. Protestant services were prohibited in early August 1629 while soldiers loyal to the now Catholic city council dispersed the crowds which gathered outside the Protestant churches. Goaded by Ferdinand II the council then proceeded to close all Protestant churches and force the Protestant ministers to leave Augsburg. The population was instructed to attend Catholic mass while being served notice to avoid all dispute about religion and rebellion. Furthermore, it was announced that paupers who were or remained Protestants were excluded from poor relief – indoor as well as outdoor, while orphans maintained by the city were escorted to church by soldiers in order to make sure they attended Mass.[198] The Protestants in Augsburg chose only passively to resist the unrelenting persecution they suffered through such Counter-Reformation measures, while desperately looking for some supernatural sign explaining the reasons for their sufferings and, more importantly, when they could expect them to end. Meanwhile the outside world came to see Augsburg as a prime example of what the Emperor and the Catholic Counter-Reformation intended to do to Protestants and Protestantism through the Edict of Restitution.

Generations of Protestants had nurtured a chiliastic dream, since at least the mid-sixteenth century, of a Messianic prince or king who would come from the north – described as the lion from the north or from the country of the midnight sun – and not only save the true believers, i.e. Protestants, from the threat of Antichrist and the 'Babylonic whore', i.e. the pope and the Catholic Church, but institute the beginning of the 'Protestant' millennium. This was a dream which had a solid biblical base. Due to the fact that the house of David, and Judah in particular, are described as the 'lion' and 'lioness' in the Old Testament, the Davidic messiah by extension was likened to a lion in the Book of Revelation (Revelation 5:5). Likewise, Jeremiah had predicted that Babylon would be laid waste by a great people coming from the north (Jeremiah 50:3) and that Israel would be punished for her sins by a lion coming from the north (Jeremiah 4:6–8).[199] At the outbreak of the Thirty Years War some of these expectations had focused on Frederick v of the Palatinate who, when he accepted the Bohemian crown in September 1619, had become the champion of German Protestantism. However, it was the successful intervention in 1630 of Gustavus Adolphus on the then despairing Protestant side in the Thirty Years War which served to give renewed impetus to this apocalyptic vision of the lion of the north, who on behalf of God would lead the righteous, i.e. good Protestants, to victory and punish the ungodly, i.e. Catholics.[200] The image acquired particular significance after Gustavus Adolphus's victory at Breitenfeld on 17 September 1631. It was forcefully promoted in England by the author of the *Swedish Intelligencer* who claimed:

> The first Part I undertook, to cheere up the long-exercised expectations of such well-affected English, as desired in their dayes, to see some ease and consola-

tion to the miserably afflicted Churches of Germany. In that poore Booke, our Nation first read That God had begun to send a Deliverer vnto his people. This (me thoughts) in a time of my leasure, was a work not altogether beneath me: and that to bring glad tidings, was next unto the Preaching of the Gospel.[201]

It also inspired direct action from repressed Protestants in the empire. Thus a peasant rebellion broke out in Upper Austria in September and October of 1632.[202] Where Gustavus Adolphus acquired messianic characteristics among Protestants in Germany, Catholics came to see him as the scourge of God bringing the punishments announced by the comet of 1618.[203] In this context Catholic apocalyptic expectations were growing too, and the general fear and hatred of Gustavus Adolphus, the great Protestant icon, caused Catholics to identify him with Antichrist. This view appears to have been promoted by the Jesuits in particular, who according to the author of the *Swedish Intelligencer* 'comforted their credulous Novices with his being Antichrist, and that he should raigne 3 yeeres and a halfe, and no longer'.[204]

Such sentiments evidently affected the population of Augsburg in particular in the autumn and winter of 1631 when the war was moving closer to the city. The citizens were forced to pay contributions towards the Imperial army of Count Tilly and by March 1632 many were forced to have troops quartered in their houses. Anxiety and tension were growing in this religiously divided city where Protestants only three years earlier had been disenfranchised and prevented from public worship. The battle of the River Lech on 5 April, which saw Gustavus Adolphus defeat Maximilian of Bavaria and Count Tilly, opened up the way to Augsburg whose defences were both outdated and inadequate. While the evangelical leaders within the city were trying to organise an opposition to the Catholic council the city surrendered after Gustavus Adolphus had struck a deal with the city's garrison which allowed it to leave the city with all its weapons upon opening the gates for the Swedes. The Swedish soldiers were particularly warmly welcomed by the Protestant women of the city, according to the Catholic priest from the nearby village of Oberhausen who had sought safety within the walls of Augsburg. This is certainly also the impression given by the broadsheet issued in 1634 to celebrate the city's 'liberation' by the Swedes (Plate 3.32), which depicts a scene of civic joy showing the citizens of Augsburg acclaiming Gustavus Adolphus.[205] According to the Catholic priest they welcomed the Swedish king and his soldiers as 'God's angel and their redeemers', offering them an abundance of food and drink. Initially, this vision of Gustavus Adolphus as the saving Protestant lion

Plate 3.32 Anon., *Augsburg liberated by the Swedes in 1632* (1634)

from the north leading a godly army appears to have rung true and the Swedish troops impressed the citizens of Augsburg with their piety, regular prayers and psalm singing.[206] Despite their recent brutal conquest of the Imperial city of Donauwörth,[207] and disregarding the fact that the Imperial garrison there had decamped the city prior to the arrival of the Swedish army, Gustavus Adolphus's army was at this stage perceived to be a different, civilised and truly godly army, at least among German Protestants.

This godly army was seen to react in a tempered and 'humane' manner, as opposed to the Imperial armies which treated the civilian population with great brutality, as can be seen from a letter written from Nuremberg in December 1631. Referring to the recent and unexpected victories of Gustavus Adolphus it described how Tilly had raised a new army after his defeat at Breitenfeld near Leipzig and was marching towards Nuremberg. Surprised by the speed with which the Imperialist army had approached the city many of the refugees from the Upper Palatinate who had sought refuge in the surrounding countryside had been unable to reach the safety of the walls of Nuremberg. Some had been fortunate enough to be able to hide in the woods, but many 'were overtaken by the enemy and mal-treated'.[208]

Gustavus Adolphus's victories caused great optimism among the many Reformed refugeees in Germany who interpreted this new development in biblical terms, seeing themselves as holders of the new covenant and as God's chosen people who were in the process of being delivered from their 'babylonian captivity':

> Not unlike the joy which the captives of Babylon felt at their unexpected delivery is that which the Exiles of the Palatinate feel now at the prospect of freedom while the power of the enemy is so far diminished, that some have already returned to their former abode. But in the same way that the Jews felt embar-rassed by the desolation of their country, the long and perilous return home, and the want of all necessities, so are we perplexed by the sad aspect of our fatherland, which, for ten years has been devastated, and is even now a prey to military licentiousness.[209]

By 1 May 1632 this view of the Swedish army as a godly, particularly well-disciplined and pious force was rapidly evaporating among many Protestant communities which had had direct experience of the recent warfare. The exiled Reformed community in Hanau reported that their 'evils' were increasing despite the splendid victories of Gustavus Adolphus. For while the king of Sweden had marched into Bavaria, their own country, the Palatinate, was being devastated by Bavarian and Spanish troops. Furthermore, the Swedish troops left behind by Gustavus Adolphus to garrison the towns and cities of the Palatinate had proved disturbingly similar to other mercenary forces, often plundering the civilian population they were supposed to defend. By May this was still put down to the fact that Gustavus was no longer present to instil the necessary godly discipline. A few months later, however, such excuses were no longer ventured when the refugees in Hanau bluntly stated that, 'not only are we oppressed by the tyranny of the Imperialists, but the licentiousness of the Swedish soldiery is so great that we hardly know who is our friend'.[210]

The image of Gustav Adolphus as the long awaited saviour of Protestantism who as God's instrument had entered the chiliastic struggle of the Thirty Years War in order to bring about a Protestant millennium, was actively promoted in a massive wave of both texts and pictures, in the form of cheap and mass-produced pamphlets and illustrated broadsheets, following the king's conquest of Augsburg. Two broadsheets were issued together in 1632.[211] One under the title The oppressed city of Augsburg (Die betrangte Stadt Augsburg) graphically depicted the effect of the Imperial Edict of Restitution on the city (Plate 3.33). The city is shown as besieged by the two apocalyptic beasts mentioned in the Book of Revelation: 'And I saw a beast rising out of the sea, with ten horns and seven heads, with ten diadems upon its horns and a blasphemous name upon its heads' (Revelation 13:1). This beast which was 'to make war on the saints and to conquer them' has arrived at the gates of Augsburg and is here shown as wearing papal tiaras, identifying the pope with Antichrist, spewing out priests over the city while demonstrating its power by encircling Augsburg with its tail. Facing it on the other side of the city is 'another beast which rose out of the earth; it had two horns like a lamb and it spoke like a dragon.' (Revelation 13:11). Considering that the Book of Revelation states that this beast 'exercises all the authority of the first beast in its presence, and makes the earth and its inhabitants worship the first beast', it is most fittingly given a beretta to wear, disgorging the storm-troopers of the Counter-Reformation, the Jesuits, over Augsburg. These enemies of Christ are thus busily promoting the Counter-Reformation, while the text informs the reader about the banishment of the city's evangelical clergy in August 1629, a move which preceded its forcible re-Catholicisation.

The second broadsheet entitled The city of Augsburg delivered by the grace of God (Die durch Gottes Gnad erledigte Stadt Augsburg) shows the two apocalyptic beasts slain by Gustavus Adolphus, 'God's faithful tool from the north'

Plate 3.33 Anon., The oppressed city of Augsburg (1632)

(Plate 3.34). This is a direct reference to the long awaited chiliastic saviour of all true Christians, the lion of the north. The tail of the mortally injured seven-headed papal beast now stretches towards the Catholic strongholds of Freising and Munich, which were captured by Gustavus Adolphus during May 1632. The text of the broadsheet refers directly to the Book of Revelation (13:5–6), adding that 'this most wonderful termination of the late unjust oppression at Augsburg (as well as at many other places) clearly gives the true meaning of the glorious Revelation of John regarding the nature of the aforementioned two beasts'.

Despite elevating Augsburg to an icon in Protestant apocalyptic expectations and using its printing presses for a major propaganda effort Augsburg's experience of being 'liberated' by the lion of the north proved deeply traumatic. What Gustavus Adolphus termed its 'papist' magistracy was immediately ousted and replaced with committed Protestants. More problematic, however, was the Swedish king's insistence that the city construct new and expensive fortifications, consisting of a system of modern bastions, while simultaneously finding a monthly contribution of 30,000 florins to pay for the 4–5 Swedish regiments garrisoned in the city. By August 1632 most of the citizens were bankrupt. Unpaid, the soldiers of Gustavus Adolphus's army proved that their Protestant piety and arduous psalm singing was no more than a thin veneer. Confirming the view already voiced from Hanau they proved no better than their Imperialist counterparts. They descended on the impoverished city and plundered it so thoroughly that they made off with everything which was not immovable or bolted down. Augsburg's desperate situation is reflected in the fact that the city's population dropped from a total of around 80,000 in 1632 to less than 18,000 three years later. Three-quarters of Augsburg's population either fled, died from starvation and disease, mainly plague, or fell victim to the city's 'liberators', deliberately or accidentally killed, by Swedish soldiers.[212] Undoubtedly the German broadsheet from these years, picturing some of the soldiers serving in the Swedish army as deeply grotesque and dangerous characters, is rooted in the apocalyptic significance, in this case negative, which contemporaries attached to it (Plate 3.35). The superhuman and deeply threatening persona of the Lapp, Livonian and Scottish soldiers shown here belong naturally to the imagery of the Book of Revelation. The reindeer on which the Livonian is sitting, 'unknown to all Germans' as the text points out, looks more like an apocalyptic monster than a real animal and is supposed to possess supernatural strength. The Lapp, Livonian and Scottish soldiers are superhuman beings, 'strong as

Plate 3.34 Anon., *The city of Augsburg delivered by the grace of God* (1632)

Plate 3.35 Anon., *Picture of the supernatural people to be found in the Swedish army* (c. 1630)

steel, immune to shot and thrust, and able to withstand frost and hunger'. No wonder that the accompanying text ends with a prayer to God to protect Germany.[213]

Another Imperial city and a Protestant ally of Sweden, Nuremberg, began to suffer increasingly from the war during the autumn of 1632. Until then the city, which was well fortified, had remained untouched by the war. Gustavus Adolphus arrived with his army in June and constructed a vast fortified camp, linking up with the city's defences where his army could rest secure. The presence of Gustavus Adolphus caused Wallenstein and Maximilian of Bavaria to unite their armies and blockade the city until it was relieved by other Swedish forces in August.[214] By September, however, Nuremberg was once more besieged by Wallenstein's troops who by now had the city fully surrounded, making it near impossible for the inhabitants and the refugees within its walls to find the food they needed. Two months later the number dying from starvation and plague was rapidly rising.[215] Three months later matters had deteriorated further. The plague was still raging while the city was hemmed in on all sides. The leaders of the Reformed refugee community in the city reported that 'freebooting is going on all around us, and the country people are leaving us, so that there is a great scarcity of necessities and dearness of everything'. Furthermore, those who recovered from the epidemic were attacked by a strange and insatiable hunger to such an extent that some even died from gluttony.[216]

The villages surrounding Nuremberg suffered in particular during these extended sieges and many sought shelter from the marauding Imperial troops within the walls of Nuremberg. On his flight to Nuremberg in July 1632 the minister of Vach, Johann Georg Renner, fell into the hands of a group of 'Krabaten' – Croatian soldiers – who were infamous for their brutality and disregard for human life. Renner gave them most of the valuables and money he carried with him and thought himself lucky to get away with his life, knowing that a number of his colleagues had not been so fortunate. Having safely reached Nuremberg he watched how the Imperial troops put the surrounding villages to the torch. The countryside around Nuremberg appears to have been nearly depopulated from July to October and hardly any villagers dared return or venture out with the result that the dead lay unburied for days. When Renner eventually returned to Vach he personally experienced the plunder conducted by Imperial cavalry in early November. They forced Renner out of bed despite the fact that he claimed to be mortally ill (however, he survived for another ten years). He was then badly beaten by the soldiers until he was drenched in blood and watched helplessly while the soldiers drove off all the cattle belonging to the locals. Subsequently he found himself imprisoned for six weeks until he had paid a ransom of 400 thalers. Renner blamed one of his female parishioners for his misfortune, suspecting that she had informed on him to the Imperial troops, claiming that he was a wealthy man who could muster a hefty ransom.[217]

The minister in Eltersdorf and Bruck, Andreas Spiegel, remained among his flock and personally witnessed the destruction caused by the Imperial troops, pointing out that they robbed and plundered all the villages around Nuremberg, injuring and killing many civilians. Subsequently, due to fear and anxiety no one dared work the fields or return to their villages with the result that the Word of God was only seldom heard in the rural areas. For Spiegel there was no doubt that God's punishing hand lay behind all this suffering. Thus, when during the winter of 1633/34, a large owl had settled in the church tower in Bruck where its horrible hooting throughout the nights kept the locals awake, Spiegel was convinced that this signified God's warning about the immediate destruction of both village and region. Referring to Isaiah 13:21–2, with its distinct apocalyptic flavour, he prayed that God would show mercy to the people of Bruck and avert the approaching disaster. The fact that the community was hit by plague the following August would indicate that his prayers went unanswered.[218]

By March 1633 the leaders of the Reformed refugees in Nuremberg apologised to their benefactors in London for not having written sooner, but, as they explained, all roads were blocked by the enemy and letter-carriers were lucky to escape from the city unless protected and assisted by a powerful military escort. They themselves were in deep despair, threatened from all sides by the enemy, while hearing nothing but rumours of devastation, 'freebooting and incendiarism'. The sloth of the Swedish garrison only served to encourage the enemy while increasingly they were as scared of their defenders as their besiegers who, they had no doubt, were intent on robbing them.[219]

Despite the many Swedish victories and the leadership provided by the Swedish Chancellor Axel Oxenstierna in the wake of Gustavus Adolphus's death at the battle of Lützen in November 1632, the refugees in Nuremberg remained dejected about their prospects. Like so many of their fellow Protestants they considered the death of the 'lion of the north' a near irreversible setback for the godly cause. Protestants, however, were not alone in interpreting Gustavus Adolphus's death in a distinct religious light. Emperor Ferdinand viewed the death of the Swedish king as a response to his prayers, especially since he, relying on God to support the Catholic cause, recently had rejected a scheme to assassinate Gustavus Adolphus.[220] For Protestants the outlook, however, remained bleak and not even the formation of the Heilbronn League in April 1633 could make the Reformed refugees in Nuremberg take a more optimistic view.[221] Some of them aired their despair in a letter:

> The Evangelical States have renewed their compact with the Swedes for continuing the war, and restoring Religion and the State to their former freedom. But the latter (the Swedes) on account of the difference in Religion, seem rather slow and difficult in helping the Palatinate, and they do as much harm to the Lower Palatinate as the enemy.[222]

Even before the major Swedish mutinies, which occurred between April and August 1633, and which were caused, as with so many other instances, by the troops' arrears in pay, the myth of the godly and well-disciplined Swedish army had obviously been deflated. In May the refugees stated that they lived in a city beleaguered by robbers who were willing to spare neither property nor lives, and that their own soldiers were not much better. The war, which had ground to a halt after Gustavus Adolphus's death and developed into minor skirmishes, appears to have continued in that mould. Agriculture had now come to a total standstill and the Swedish garrison scarcely did more than to make the occasional excursion, while the Bavarian besiegers immediately retreated into their fortresses, avoiding the risk of battle.[223]

Despite these disappointments the rout of the Swedish army at the battle of Nördlingen in September 1634, which left more than 12,000 Protestant soldiers dead on the battlefield, had a devastating effect on Protestant aspirations. In a letter of January 1635 the Reformed refugees in Nuremberg referred to the 'unfortunate battle' at Nördlingen, which had until then made it impossible for them to forward any letters with safety, adding that it would anyway have been impossible for them to describe their misery in a letter.[224]

In Hanau, which was soon to be the only city holding out for the Protestant cause in the Rhineland, the effects of the defeat at Nördlingen were disastrous, as can be seen from a letter written from the city in November 1634:

> In the time of the Apostles Agabus predicted a great famine. We have no prophets, but we fear that a great dearth is coming over us, for the Imperial war of 14 years has exhausted and impoverished our whole country and that of our neighbours, while lately a multitude of troops caused great damage and interfered

with agriculture. And as some of our towns were captured, we also feared an attack or siege, so that we took in a large garrison, which will reduce our citizens to poverty and prevent them from aiding our poor. All handicrafts are stopped to the great inconvenience of our workmen, especially as the plague caused great misery among us. Hanau has hitherto been an asylum for many of our exiled brethren and sisters, but now our means are exhausted, and we live in fear of famine and poverty.[225]

When a year later the minister to the Dutch community in Hanau wrote to London the city had already been under siege by Imperialist forces for months and he himself was amazed that Hanau still existed. Considering that its citizens were mainly craftsmen, they ought long ago to have been utterly ruined by 'the three plagues', the enemy within, by which the minister meant the garrison, the enemy without, the Catholic forces, and epidemic disease. The devastation of the countryside around the city by the Imperialist army meant that the surrounding villages had been totally depopulated, while all cattle and corn had been consumed by the besiegers. 'The sword of the Lord' had killed around 12,000–13,000 people over the summer and among these casualties of the epidemic were most of the principal inhabitants of the city. The only consolation was the recent defeat of the Imperial General Gallas, which temporarily had caused the siege to be lifted. This divine intervention had made it possible for the inhabitants 'to gather in so much of the remaining fruits' that they would have enough supplies to see them through winter.[226]

Meanwhile the Lower Palatinate was suffering from the occupation of Spanish troops. By the autumn of 1636 Franckenthal was so impoverished that only 60 citizens ate 'their own bread'. Not only was the countryside around the city totally devastated by war and plundering, but in some places the bodies of people who died a year ago of hunger still remained unburied.[227]

War-weariness caused by the extensive destruction and plundering by the different armies was rapidly spreading in Germany during the late 1630s. A number of popular prints and pamphlets were published, which lamented the horrible effects of the prolonged war. The anonymous print entitled *Picture of the merciless, abominable, cruel and monstrous Beast, which without mercy and lamentably has harried, exhausted and ruined the greater part of Germany within a few years* is representative of this response, with its often strongly apocalyptic flavour (Plate 3.36).[228] Looming large in the centre of the print is the Beast of war, part man, with its arm holding the instruments of war, burning torches, a pistol and a halberd, while resting its armoured

Abbildung des unbarmhertzigen / abscheulichen / grausam / und grewlichen Thiers /

Welches in wenig Jahren / den grösten Theil Teutsch-landes erbärm- und jämmerlichen verheeret / auffgezehret und verderbet. Beneben einem Bericht / woher dasselbe seinen Ursprung / wer solches erzogen / ernehret / ꝛc. Endlich durch was Mittel seiner wieder loß zu werden. Männiglich an Tag gegeben.

Plate 3.36 Anon., The abominable monster of war (late 1630s)

leg on the throat of a fallen soldier, but predominantly animal, with its wolf-head consuming all sorts of worldly riches, jewellery, gold- and silver-ware which it stuffs into its mouth with its lion's paw, its other leg that of a horse, while dragging a long rat-tail behind it. This apocalyptic beast, reminiscent of the second beast in Daniel's dream (Daniel 7:5) or the beast of Antichrist which according to the Book of Revelation shall rise from the bottomless pit and make war, conquer and kill (Revelation 11:7), has caused widespread destruction, leaving burning villages and towns in its wake (backgound, left). A cavalryman is seen pursuing and killing fleeing civilians, while death in the form of a skeleton is embracing a naked and exhausted woman and her children; in the foreground snakes, lizards, slugs, snails and toads are jumping from the beast's rat-tail, symbolising the starvation and epidemic diseases caused by war (left). It is noteworthy that at a time when the religious and apocalyptic antagonism of the Thirty Years War was fading, war continued to be seen and portrayed in an apocalyptic light, even when the confessional dimension had gone.

The prospects of peace and the death of the Beast are held forth in the right side of the picture. At the back the sun rises behind undisturbed towns and villages while the slain beast's stomach is slit open and all the silver, gold and precious stones are rolling out for the civilians once more to gain their wealth.

By the summer of 1641 the Dutch Reformed inhabitants of Franckenthal did not consider their prospects much better. They had heard a lot of talk about peace, but to them 'the civil war was only increasing in intensity'. They expressed the vain hope that the princes of the empire would take 'precautions against the enemy which is threatening us from the east, and which is, if not drawn on, at any rate increased by the discords of the Christian Princes. But many who grow rich by the loss of others, seek to prolong the war, while publicly they cry for peace.' A considerable war-weariness was evidently taking hold among Calvinists, many of whom had now begun to favour Christian unity and eirenicism over victory for the godly, especially when faced with the renewed Ottoman threat from the east. Referring to the calling of the Long Parliament they commended Charles I of England for acting 'more prudently by extinguishing the sparks of the dangerous flame'. Not surprisingly they emphasised that if their own princes had done the same, Germany would not now be in such a sorry state.[229]

Their expectations of a peaceful outcome of the growing confrontation between Puritans and anti-Calvinists in England proved, as we know, unduly optimistic. Within a year of their pronouncement the Red Horse of war was riding across England too, and belatedly the country came to share directly in the pervasive early modern experience of anxiety, suffering and destruction while the country was engulfed in a growing chiliastic mood. In 1650, looking back on the recent Civil War in England, the soldiers and non-commissioned officers of the English army in Scotland declared that it had been the Book of Revelation which had sustained the godly during Archbishop William Laud's persecutions and continued to nurture and motivate them through the years of conflict. Accordingly they had been

> stirred up by the Lord, to assist the Parliament against the King, being abun-
> dantly satisfied in our judgements and consciences that we were called forth by
> the Lord to be instrumental to bring about that which was our continual prayer
> to God, viz., the destruction of Antichrist and the deliverance of his Church and
> people. . . . – we were then powerfully convinced that the Lord's purpose was to
> deal with the late King as a man of blood. And being persuaded in our con-
> sciences that he and his monarchy was one of the ten horns of the Beast (spoken
> of, Rev. 17:12–15), and being witness to so much of the innocent blood of the
> Saints that he had shed in supporting the Beast, and considering the loud cries
> of the souls of the Saints under the altar, we were extraordinarily carried forth to
> desire justice upon the King, that man of blood.

Considering this apocalyptic rationale for their actions it can hardly sur-prise that the English soldiers went on to warn the Scots that they were not normal professional soldiers, 'soldiers of fortune or merely the servants of men', but godly warriors, led by Christ himself in his capacity as king of the Saints, who had now come amongst the Scots 'as a refiner's fire and as a fuller's soap'.[230] This was a direct reference to the prophetic and eschato-logical statement in Malachi 3:2 about how at the Second Coming Christ will cleanse the world: 'who may abide the day of (the Lord's) coming? and who shall stand where he appeareth? for he is like a refiner's fire and like fuller's soap'.

4 The Black Horse: Food, F(e)ast and Famine

And when he had opened the third seal, I heard the third beast say
Come and see. And I beheld, and lo a black horse;
and he that sat on him had a pair of balances in his hand.
And I heard a voice in the midst of the four beasts say,
A measure of wheat for a penny, and three measures of barley for a penny;
and see thou hurt not the oil and the wine.

(Revelation 6:5–6)

The pair of balances is the icon of the market-place, where food is traded. It is a good image for our consideration of food, fast/feast and famine in this apocalyptic period, for as we shall see the state of the food supply in Europe, speaking generally, was neither too little (dearth) nor too much (glut). Surprisingly, it was approximately in balance. There was enough food for all most of the time. A penny was a notional day's pay, and representing the value of wheat as three times that of barley is reasonable. But, as we shall also see, the right to a share of the food was deeply unequal. What the penny bought varied immensely, and whether the grain one ate was wheat or was barley depended on one's position in the social hierarchy as much as on where one lived. For, 'during famines not all suffer equally: some die of starvation, others suffer less, and still others are fairly well nourished and even derive profit from the tragedy of the victims.'[1]

The period 1498 to 1648 was one of growing wealth and provision – and hence of expectation – all over Europe. It was also a period of massive population increase all over Europe. Yet famines occurred frequently. In a context of rising general wealth and a growing population, famines have a stronger impact than in times of continual shortage. The poor get even poorer, and they starve, they even starve to death. In an age of faith, such as this was, there can be a great willingness to look to the divine message that famines seem to represent. In such times, social and economic relationships, structures and experiences get unconsciously translated into, and experienced as, events of great religious significance. The divine plan for the world seems to be working itself out, and the distress for societies and

individuals that famines bring with them, was interpreted as divine punishment and taken as a sign of the rapid approach of the Last Times. Taking
famines as crisis-points in normal economic relations within the society,
as we do here, will offer a handle to explore something of the economic
structures of the period, and their relation to ideological ones.[2]

We shall take famine as meaning 'an acute, that is, short-term and severe
deterioration of the nutritional status of the community, from a background which may or may not have been one of chronic food shortages'.[3]
In distinguishing famine from dearth, we shall follow the characterisation
of the people of the sixteenth century: that in times of dearth food stuffs are
in short supply and thus become extremely expensive, but in times of
famine, food stuffs cannot be bought at all, however rich one is.

There were many occurrences of famine in our period, mostly local in
impact, sometimes national, and occasionally across the whole of Europe.
A study of famines in Russia over a thousand years indicates that there has
been one significant famine or hunger year somewhere in Russia on
average once every five years: they were 'a regular but unexpected
calamity'.[4] The Russian experience of famines continued for centuries
longer than it did in the West, and can thus be treated as reasonably typical
of what would have happened in a Western state in our apocalyptic period.
In England there were significant shortages in the years 1527–8, 1550–2,
1555–6, 1557–9, 1596–8 (the 'Great Hunger' which killed up to 10 per cent
of the population), and 1623–4. In Paris, to take a major town on the continent, we find records of dearths or famines in 1520–1, 1523, 1528–34, 1548,
1556, 1560, 1565, 1572–3, 1574, 1587, 1590, 1595–8, 1621, 1625, 1629 and
1631–2.[5] The modern historian of agriculture, Slicher von Bath, has
written that 'On an average, there was a risk of a bad harvest every four
years, with disastrous consequences in areas with poor transport facilities
where people relied to a great extent on the local market.'[6] So we can take
famine – not just dearth – as something that most people would experience
at least once in their lives, if not more, wherever they lived in sixteenth-
century Western Europe. It was an ever-present fear.

The whole question of what people ate in the past, and the occasions
when they could not eat at all, as in famine, is still at an early stage of historical study. Even in a literate society, dearths or famines – all but the most
extreme ones – by their nature leave little direct trace. Unlike epidemic diseases, whose incidence was different to that of famines, dearths or famines
did not prompt a great deal of ephemeral writing or of pictures. Only a few
people offered their advice in print on how to cope with a present dearth or

avoid an impending one, though some such literature does exist, as we shall see. But certain administrative records can be used to detect the likelihood of instances of dearth or famine having occurred, such as the grain prices set by town authorities, or government orders to restrict the export of grain, or the like. Where high grain prices can be correlated with evidence of unusual numbers of deaths, then dearth or famine can be inferred. Parish records were kept fairly assiduously in England, France, Italy and Switzerland from the early sixteenth century, and can be used for this purpose. As historical demography is still a relatively new branch of history, it has only recently been possible to ask (as Peter Laslett did in 1965) 'Did the peasants really starve?'[7] The answer seem to be: yes, in famines they did. And they starved believing God had sent this agony as a punishment for sin.

FAMINES: NATURAL OR MAN-MADE?

Until quite recently it was taken for granted by historians that famines were simply natural checks on the population. That is to say, when the size of the population outstrips the capacity of the land to support it, then famine follows inevitably. Episodes of bad weather, it was thought, merely triggered famines, thus turning a situation in which the population had literally been living on the bread-line, into a full crisis, in which people died of hunger. When mass death from starvation had reduced the population again to a size that the land could support, then (it was thought) famine disappeared. Famines, therefore, were seen by historians as being acts of Nature, bringing the population back into balance with the food supply. This view of famines comes ultimately from the Reverend Thomas Malthus, writing at the end of the eighteenth century. In his book *An Essay on the Principle of Population* (1798) Malthus argued that famine, disease and war are 'positive checks' on the expansion of population, which it would be foolish to fight. As the population increases geometrically, he argued, so it outruns the possible food supply, which can only increase arithmetically: famine is a positive and natural check which re-establishes the balance. Human suffering, while regrettable, is thus inevitable and natural – and, indeed, for Malthus the clergyman, part of God's scheme of things. Malthus was initially writing not a technical treatise on population, but a political tract. His targets were on the one hand those English supporters of the French Revolution who believed society could be bettered in the long term. The 'principle of population' was Malthus's answer to show that it could not. The revolutionaries were therefore misguided. Malthus's other target was the then-current Poor Law legislation, which he claimed supported the poor during dearths and famines and allowed them to breed, thus subverting the natural 'positive check' that famines and epidemic diseases were intended to provide. For Malthus the Poor Laws were, in this sense, unnatural, and against God's order of things. Interestingly enough, as we shall see, the Poor Laws that Malthus was campaigning against had been introduced in our apocalyptical period by people with a very strong belief in God, precisely in order to relieve the distress of dearth and famine. While no historian of demography would today take the moral line of Malthus, nevertheless until very recently demographic history has been conducted in an exclusively Malthusian context, taking famines to have been a 'positive check' on the growth of population, but arguing about how precisely this check operates, whether it operates efficiently, and if so with how long a time-lag in the operation of the 'positive check' between the famine and its effect on population numbers.

However, in recent years some historians have interpreted famines as due to the *structure*, that is, the social and economic structure, of the society in which they occur. David Arnold has claimed that 'Famine has come to be seen more as a symptom than a cause, a sign of a society's inner weaknesses and not just a consequence of temporary climatic aberrations.'[8]

One observer of present-day food production in peasant societies has given a radical reconsideration to the origin and structure of famines. Although this approach is still essentially Malthusian (and has been criticised by Arnold for being so), it too looks at the structure of particular societies as the key to their experience of dearths and famines, and it presents a more positive prospect of change than Malthus. This approach has been developed by Ronald Seavoy.[9] Peasant societies of past and present, Seavoy argues, are by their very nature *subsistence* societies: they produce enough to subsist on, with a small surplus of food in good years, but with no means of coping with a series of bad harvests. As subsistence cultures they survive in good times, but since peasants are, as peasants, indolent and non-entrepreneurial (it is not in their interest to work harder than necessary to provide a subsistence food supply), they take little thought either for the morrow or for improving their long-term food supply. Inevitably, Seavoy claims, the high fertility typical of peasant societies means that the number of mouths to feed repeatedly overtakes the available food supply. Dearths and famines are thus unavoidable.

The only way in which a peasant society, past or present, can get out of this loop, Seavoy claims, is by becoming a *commercial* society, producing food primarily for sale to the market, rather than just for the subsistence of the peasant producers themselves.

> In its broadest sense, commercializing agriculture meant extracting an enlarged food or commodity surplus from the peasantry. The extractions from the peasantry were not usually in the form of food or commodities levies, but in the form of money taxes . . . Second to money taxes . . . was fencing (enclosure) of arable land . . . Land withdrawn from communal control was put into commercial tenure, and the products it produced were for market sale.
>
> These money obligations could only be paid by growing crops for market sale. Fencing, combined with commercial land tenure, ends subsistence land use . . . In order for these changes to be successful, they must be strongly enforced by central governments.[10]

Such a transformation involves not only a radical change in the economic relations of producer and consumer, but also in motivation and attitude. For Seavoy, the only way of assisting Third World economies today to get out of the cycle of famines typical of subsistence societies, is for the leaders in those countries to take political action to introduce a commercial market and modern agricultural technology.

Seavoy also demonstrates that just such a transition from a subsistence to a commercial agricultural society has occurred in all Western societies, rendering them to all intents and purposes immune from peace-time famine, as is our own society today. In particular he demonstrates that England was the first early-modern state which became a commercial society with respect to its agriculture. It reached this stage, he claims, between the end of the fifteenth century and the early decades of the seventeenth century, that is, precisely over the course of the period we are studying here. As a consequence England could increase per capita food production to meet current needs with an adequate surplus, and thus not suffer episodes of famine. In later years (as in the eighteenth and nineteenth centuries) its birth rate could also significantly increase, yet it did not suffer from the famine cycle ever again. The move from subsistence to commercialised agriculture meant that many more mouths could be fed from the same land, that a large non-rural population could be maintained from the labour of the rural agricultural worker, and that the whole process could be significantly more efficient because it produced regular food surpluses which prevented peace-time famine, whatever the weather.

Controversial though it may be, Seavoy's thesis makes a great deal of historical sense, and we shall adopt it here to understand the ravages brought by the Horseman on the Black Horse. For on the basis of Seavoy's thesis we can see that Europe's fields as a whole in our period were still being cultivated on a subsistence basis, and hence suffered the repeated dearths and famines typical of a *subsistence* peasant society. Put in another way, the famines were a side-effect of the fundamental social and economic structure of the society, in the context of a continued population increase. Dearths and famines were inevitable – inevitable side-effects of the population increase of the time, given the subsistence form of agriculture. While gradual changes were made in this subsistence agriculture by those tilling the land in order to increase food production to some degree, they were not enough to prevent the regular disasters of dearth and famine when the climatic conditions, or other triggering impulse, upset the delicate balance between food and mouths. Moreover, we can see from Seavoy's account that the one society which, on his account, in this period moved over furthest to a *commercialised* agriculture, England,[11] was able, as a result, to move once and for all out of the famine cycle. The famine of 1623–4, he writes, was 'the last peace-time famine in England'.[12] But this made England unique:

> By about 1650, most of English agriculture was commercialized, even though the subsistence pattern of land use continued. The key index of commercialized agriculture is fertility behaviour. The population of England stabilized about 1650 and remained stable for the next 100 years. This occurred approximately 200 years before France achieved demographic stability (about 1850), and like England in 1650, the stabilization of the French birthrate was due to the commercialization of agriculture.[13]

It can be appreciated on Seavoy's explanation of the relation of subsistence farming and population pressure, that it could hardly be the actions of individuals alone that transformed economies subject to famines into economies not subject to famine. The transforming process was on a much larger scale, and it arose in part from the process of 'monetisation': the introduction of an economy with money as the primary means of exchange, to replace a feudal economy with services and labour as the primary means of exchange.

By the beginning of our period a change from a primarily feudal economy to a primarily money economy had been in process across Western Europe for some time, affecting some areas more strongly than others. This change in the economic basis of society brought with it a change in the nature of social relationships. Instead of the primary economic and social relationship being between feudal superiors and inferiors, with all the duties, obligations, labour burdens and payment in kind that went with this relationship, increasingly these feudal burdens were being transformed into rent burdens. In some ways this made the peasant more free. While landless peasants had only their labour to rent out, those peasants who did own a little land could rent out their labour too. For the poor and landless, this money economy allowed some of them to slip out of their feudal ties altogether, and to build up trading. But the negative side of the money economy was that incomes were now subject to inflation – and there was to be enormous inflation in the course of the period – and it meant that people could become indebted. In particular, as we shall see, the advent of the money economy meant that the food purchase became the critical exchange.

Moreover, the increase in population which continued during this period had a significant effect on small landholdings. Where heritable land was partible, it came to be subdivided into ever smaller parcels, the smallest of which could not support a family from its produce. Where land was not partible, the sons who did not inherit became landless squatters and labourers. Both processes meant that more people were more vulnerable to harvest failure. According to the historian Jan de Vries:

> A growing population that divides its land into smaller holdings must introduce more labor-intensive techniques; these place a downward pressure on labor productivity. During the transition the likelihood of more frequent famine crises is increased and the peasants on the smaller holdings may find, as *morcellement* [i.e. the subdividing of land] continues, that they cannot support themselves on their holdings: they enter the labour market periodically as day laborers to supplement their inadequate income from the land.[14]

As Andrew Appleby has written of this process in England during the course of the sixteenth century:

> Population growth had created a large impoverished group at the very bottom of rural society, a group that may have always been at subsistence level and was certainly pushed towards starvation at the end of the century. Put simply, there were too many people in rural England at the end of the sixteenth century to be fed, given the inequitable distribution of land and the existing agricultural technology.[15]

All these changes mean that the status of the staple food became ever more critical, and lives became more vulnerable if the staple crop was endangered: these changes themselves meant that dearth and famine were more likely, and that coping with them for the poorest in society would be more, not less, difficult. Thus the danger of starving was greater. For if one is a landless labourer in a monetary economy, you have less chance of getting food in famine conditions than do labourers still tied to the land, since it is in the interest of the owner of the land to keep his workers alive, even if they are serfs, whereas if someone earning a money wage loses his employment he is unable to purchase food at all.[16] The twentieth-century Russian experience of moving from a (feudal) subsistence agricultural system to a market-based agricultural system, is a recent example which shows how the likelihood of famines and shortages gets greater rather than smaller during this transition process.[17]

There are and were three possible triggers for visitations of the Black Horse of famine: climate, war and disease, either of humans or of plants.

Climatic conditions which acted locally and only over a short period, such as excessive rain or drought, had medium-term effects. For instance, two consecutive years of excessively wet summers ruining the crops would have had effects lasting up to seven years before the harvest cycle was fully recovered. Recently, by putting various meteorological and agricultural measurements together, historians of climate have begun to demonstrate that there has been general long-term climatic change as well, and that 'climatic change can alter the course of civilizations'.[18] It appears that climate change in the long term is rapid rather than gradual, and that 'a cooling and variable climate brings serious problems for food production'. The evidence indicates that there had been a long warm period, peaking around 1200, and thereafter a general cooling until the mid-fifteenth century. From that low point there was 'a rather short warming trend that peaked around the end of the sixteenth century'. A subsequent cooling in the seventeenth century has been called a 'little ice age', running to about 1850, marked, among other things, by the advance of low-reaching Alpine glaciers.[19] In other words, our apocalyptic period is one where the climate changes for the better – that is, for the warmer – from the 1470s to approximately the 1580s or 1590s, when a long cooling period begins. Such warm periods 'are associated with above-average population levels', since it is likely that 'grain yields increase, along with measures of fertility and life expectancy at birth (though only slightly), leading to an upswing in the population growth rate'.[20] Then, with the advent of cooler climatic conditions, we could expect serious problems for food production, since 'the obvious impact of a long period of cooling is to lower the elevation where crops can be effectively grown, in effect decreasing the land available for cultivation and leading in turn to either a decline in total output or more intense cultivation and lower yields.'[21] So we might expect an increase in the frequency or intensity of famines from the end of the sixteenth century, bringing a general decline in nutrition.[22] This is generally what we find, with the two greatest and most widespread famines of our period occurring in the 1590s and the 1620s. Of course, while not every local climatic disaster in which short, intense periods of rain or drought brought on famine conditions can be put down to the general climatic trend, yet the *general direction* of climatic change had significant effects on the *general incidence* of dearth and famine conditions. So it may well be the case that the long-term warming trend in the climate made the increasing population levels of the period 1490–1590 possible, and the cooling period which followed produced the unfavourable conditions which threw most of Western European society into repeated crises and famines from the 1590s onwards.

With respect to war, we have seen some of the effects of this man-made disaster already in Chapter 3. Armies live off the land, or despoil the crops and reserves of the local population; they lay waste and pillage. This certainly has medium-term effects on the food supply, and it could take several years to recover the full harvest cycle. It has been estimated that in the course of the Thirty Years War (1618–48) the German lands lost a large proportion of their population, perhaps as much as 40 per cent, through wars and their consequences such as famine and epidemic disease.[23] As we shall see below, armies could also lay siege to a town and induce a completely artificial famine killing far more people than were killed in resisting the siege.

Finally, with respect to disease as a cause of, or trigger for, famine, it is certainly the case that a severe local outbreak of epidemic disease affecting humans would affect the workforce, and at crucial times of the year would affect the planting or the harvesting, and hence the final crop. But the effect of famine in itself providing the conditions in which epidemic disease might thrive, was likely to have been far greater than that of disease in triggering famine.[24] Plant diseases could not only kill a crop or render it inedible, but a particular fungal disease typical of rye regularly induced the deadly agonies of 'holy fire' or 'St Anthony's fire', as it was called, or 'ergotism' as it is known today. Common in France, it spread to Germany in 1581. Its agonies are fearful: 'convulsive ergotism twists and arches the body as massive seizures in the muscles bring tearing and unbearable pain', and sufferers try and kill themselves to escape the pain. With wheat, the rust fungus is the worst of the fungal diseases, flourishing in wet summers and, at its worst, turning the rain red. It reduces the harvest and damages its quality for bread-making and for the next year's seed.[25]

Although, as we have seen, repeated dearths and famines were the inevitable side-effect of a growing population in a subsistence economy, the people of the period naturally saw dearth and famines as direct acts of God. For the episodes of terrible weather which triggered dearth and famine could not be anticipated, and there seemed to be no natural reason for their occurrence or their continuance. It was obvious therefore that God was working through the stars and the weather to affect the crops and animals, in order to send messages to mankind about mankind's sins and failure to acknowledge and worship the true God.

Before we turn to the conditions under which famines occurred, it is first desirable to look briefly at the food and feasting of the period, since it will become apparent not only that the food resources were distributed in a most unequal way, but also that there was one particular feature of the general diet of everyone which made the lower orders of society yet more vulnerable to famine and starvation than they might otherwise have been.

FOOD

What was available to eat in the Europe of 1498 to 1648, and how was it consumed? Our knowledge of the diet of the rich and well-to-do is better than our knowledge of the diet of the poor: 'The dietary situation of the majority of the population who lived in the rural world is largely a matter of speculation and inference', according to modern historians of diet and consumption in the German lands of the period,[26] and the same is true for everywhere else in Europe too.[27] Obviously, the first (but far from the only) determinant of what was available to eat was what grew locally. For although this was an age of bulk transport of foodstuffs by water, as in the case of grain, and by land, as in the case of cattle on the hoof, perishable foods could not be moved very far because transport along poor roads was slow and greatly increased the cost. The important types of farmed food were grains, vegetables, fruit, dairy produce and oils, meat, fish and spices. The greatest variety of foods was typically available to the richer inhabitants of the largest cities, both from the long-distance trade in luxury goods, and also because around the largest towns forms of market gardening were being developed.

A variety of vegetables was available in season, such as cabbage, leeks, sorrel, lettuce and endive, and onions. While beans in particular provide a high-energy diet, like other vegetables they were not held in high esteem by most people, and many people thought that they were food 'more meet for hogs and savage beasts to feed upon than mankind'.[28] However, vegetables came to be eaten in greater quantity in the course of the sixteenth century, including melons, pumpkins, cucumbers, parsnips, carrots, cabbage and turnips. The potato, which was later to become the great standby vegetable amongst the poor, was imported into Europe in the 1580s, but was not widely grown until the seventeenth and eighteenth centuries, so it had no presence on the table in this period. Amongst available fruits were apples, pears, plums, cherries, peaches and, in warmer climes, oranges and lemons.

If one lived in an area with abundant rainfall, flattish terrain and good soil – which in general means Europe north of the Mediterranean countries – then cow's milk, butter and cheese could be available. In more mountainous areas milk and cheese could be got from sheep and goats, while eggs were also often available. In southern Europe vegetable oil played the part of dairy produce.

Freshly slaughtered meat was available mostly in spring and autumn: in spring when the surplus new-born animals were killed, in autumn when those animals unlikely to make it through the winter were slaughtered. Beef, lamb and mutton, goat and especially pig – that food recycling machine – could be eaten fresh. So could poultry such as ducks, geese and other birds kept for food, such as pigeons and pheasants. At the great autumn slaughtering, much of the meat was preserved, by pickling in brine, by direct salting, by smoking, or by both salting and smoking. Beef, lamb, goat and especially pig, were preserved in these ways, as were game birds and game animals.

Fresh fish was available within a few miles of the coast, and to towns up navigable rivers where it could be brought quickly by boat. A manor could have its own pond or fishery, as many monasteries and noble houses did, and rivers were also a ready source of fresh-water fish. Preserved fish could be transported in barrels any distance, either dried, salted, smoked, or both smoked and salted. The two fish species which were prepared like this on a great scale were cod, which could be fished from the Mediterranean to the Baltic (*baccalà*, the Italian salt cod, is still widely eaten around the Mediterranean), and herring above all. Herring came from the North Sea, the Baltic and the north Atlantic. Cod was preserved in two forms: white, which was salted; and red, which was both smoked and salted.[29]

Some spices and condiments were local products of Europe. Mustard and garlic could be grown anywhere. But sophisticated spices such as pepper (from India), saffron (cultivated around Barcelona, in Germany and in eastern England) and cinnamon (from Ceylon), could only be afforded by the rich.

With these foodstuffs, one could say that there was a sufficient, if restricted, range and quantity available in times of peace.

But the foodstuff which was most important to all but the very wealthiest people, whose diet was usually the most varied, was grain for making bread. Bread was, quite simply, the staple food, to an extent it no longer is anywhere in Western Europe today.[30] The income and spending of a relatively well-to-do town craftsman, an assistant mason, living in one of the richest areas of Europe, Antwerp, around 1600 has been analysed.[31] More than three-quarters of the income of this typical skilled urban worker was spent on food in one form or another. Half of his entire income – not half of what he spent on food, but half of *everything* he spent – went on grain to make bread or on bread itself.[32] As it provided the staple food, grain was crucial to everyone, in a way that no other foodstuff was. It gave people the strength to work. So if there was a shortage of grain, for any reason, the effect on the diet of everyone was immediate and very noticeable, and it also directly affected everyone's capacity to work. A severe shortage of grain in effect constituted a famine. Failed harvests were one – but only one – of the reasons for such shortages, as we shall see. The unique position of grain in the diet of everyone meant that it was the foodstuff whose absence could provoke riots and social instability. And the sight which provoked food riots was that of wagons carrying grain out of the starving area, as we shall see later.

Of the grains, wheat[33] was the most highly valued for bread.[34] Wheat is also the grain which was used for the various forms of pasta in southern Europe. Whether it is more nutritious than other grains is an open question. It was preferred for its taste, texture and colour. Long the staple bread corn of the Mediterranean lands, wheat was the bread grain of choice of the landed and richer classes in the north of Europe. It was not until the eighteenth century, even in England, which was at that time the most innovative country in agricultural terms, that wheat became the primary bread grain of most of the urban population. While the varieties of wheat mean that it will grow in widely varying climatic conditions, it always needs good quality soil. Moreover, wheat was an inefficient crop since it was known to 'drain the soil', and so the ground had to lie fallow one year in three or four. Less fertile fields require marling or liming, both of which are expensive, if they are to produce wheat. Wheat does less well on poorer soils than other grains. Even on land which today would be seen as suitable for wheat, other bread grains were often grown, primarily rye and barley, not just because they had a better or more reliable yield, but because they were the customary bread grain of the peasantry. Rye was probably the most widely used bread grain. Often wheat was mixed with rye to produce a basic bread flour known as 'maslin' (mixed corn) in English, *miscelin* in French, *Mengcorn* in German. Either one could sow rye and wheat together, which was thought to ensure a crop, since the rye would succeed even if the wheat failed through the shortcomings of the soil or the weather or both. Or one could mix the 'pure' grains of wheat and rye after harvesting, to make a bread of mixed corn, also known as maslin bread. Wheat and rye were 'winter corn': they were sown in autumn and reaped the following summer. They were thus at the mercy of the weather for many months.

Barley and oats, by contrast, were 'summer corn', being planted in spring and harvested a few months later. But these, both of which grow on poorer soils than wheat and rye, were the bread grains of necessity, not of choice. Barley was the main 'drink corn', used for meeting the enormous demand for beer and ale, while oats was mostly used as provender for horses, except in those regions, such as Scotland, where it was of necessity the main bread grain.

Spelt, a grain related to wheat, was often grown in southern Europe and as far north as southern Germany, and was often mixed with rye either in the planting or in the making of bread.

Maize ('Indian corn') was introduced in the 1490s from the Americas by the Spanish, and was increasingly grown in Spain and France during the sixteenth century where it was used for bread, although it was not highly thought of.[35] It was grown in north Italy from at least the 1560s, when it was also consumed as a ground meal called polenta.

For a few, living in the Valencia region of Spain, rice was the staple grain; and rice had also been introduced around Pisa in the mid-fifteenth century, becoming important in north Italy and in southern France in the course of the sixteenth century. This new cereal has been described as 'the corn of the marshes'.[36]

Within a household, people of different status would eat according to their differing position in the hierarchy. A Yorkshire farmer in 1641, for instance, used best wheat for the family's pies, maslin for the family's bread and the piecrusts of the servants, with brown bread made from rye, peas and barley for the workers on the farm.[37]

Much was considered to hang on the type of grain from which one's bread was made, and over the period in wealthier areas wheat came to be preferred by the urban population. Only under the stress and duress of dearth would people make their bread from what they considered to be an inferior grain. 'Barley is in time of scarcity the bread-corn of the poor', said an English proclamation of 1622, forbidding the use of barley to make ale.[38] Similarly William Harrison said, in his *Description of England* of 1587:

> The bread throughout the land is made of such grain as the soil yieldeth; nevertheless, the gentility commonly provide themselves sufficiently of wheat for their own tables, whilst their household and poor neighbours in some shires are enforced to content themselves with rye or barley, yea, and in time of dearth, many with bread made either of beans, peas or oats, or of all together and some acorns among, sith they are least able to provide themselves of better.[39]

Thus, at very worst, one was reduced to making bread from inferior 'grains' or seeds: peas, beans, millet, and even acorns.

The centrality of grain to the diet is shown by the fact that daily menus of the period, insofar as they can be reconstructed, indicate that grain of one kind or another was eaten in some form at every meal of the day. In addition to being eaten as bread, grain was eaten as a filler for soups and other dishes, as it still is in peasant economies of Europe today. It was, primarily in the form of barley, the basic ingredient of ale or beer, which was the preferred drink of most households.[40]

To fill the demand for grain from a continually growing population, the available land was expanded. In some areas this was accomplished by the digging of polders for drainage (especially by the Dutch), and improved irrigation.[41] Marshes were drained, moors and wasteland ploughed, grazing land was put under the plough again. In other areas, marginal lands which had been abandoned after the Black Death of 1348 were brought back into cultivation. In the short term, while their fertility was good, such lands helped produce an increase in grain, but when their fertility was exhausted, which happened soon enough, they gave little return for the work invested in cultivating them. In the longer term, those people most dependent on the cultivation of marginal land were those most vulnerable to poor harvests, and hence to dearth and famine.

Staple foods have both positive and negative features. While the staple food of a particular culture will have been chosen through force of circumstances and not through an act of deliberation, it will always be a food which grows locally, which constitutes a bulky food to eat (so that you feel full, not hungry), which gives one energy and strength to carry out one's work, and which is at least fairly pleasant to eat. It will almost always be a carbohydrate. Once adopted as a staple, that particular crop will be given privileged attention, and the important moments in the annual cycle of producing it (usually its planting and harvesting) will be ones which involve the whole local community, and they will probably also accrue particular celebrations and ceremonies around them, whether that staple be a grain, which is most common, or a bean, a tuber, a fish or a bird. So the staple food makes particular demands on the society, and in most years it repays that society by nourishing it. Reciprocally, time and attention given to nurturing the staple crop is time and attention not given to alternative crops. We have already seen how vegetables in general were held in low esteem, and cultivated in a desultory way in this period. It has been estimated that up to three-quarters of all land planted with crops was devoted to corn.[42] When the staple crop failed, therefore, there was little in the way of alternative sources of food which could take the place of the staple food in the general diet: Appleby has commented that 'it seems highly unlikely that the poor had any cheap alternative foodstuffs in time of grain shortage'.[43] This is another typical feature of most subsistence agricultural economies.

The local staple food is not necessarily the one which would grow best in a given area, and tradition has a lot to do with the persistence of particular staples in the diet. For instance, in our period in Northern Europe, rye was often grown on land which would have been suitable for wheat, simply because rye was traditionally the staple grain of the peasantry there. Sir William Ashley, the historian of bread, points out:

> a country like Germany, which at the beginning of the medieval period is a rye-growing and rye-eating land, continues to be in the main a rye-growing and rye-eating land [up to the nineteenth century], because it continues to be a country of peasant proprietors, and mostly of relatively small peasant proprietors. On the other hand, in England rye yields much earlier to wheat . . . largely because in England capitalist farming first developed.[44]

So the Germans, or at least the north Germans,[45] were eating first rye then maslin over our period as the staple grain for their bread, while the English were eating maslin then pure wheat as theirs.

A further limiting factor about a staple food is that its special role means that if a society is to develop economically, and land is to be given over to other kinds of crops, for market or industry, then the staple has to be provided from elsewhere. Staple foods are not abandoned just because other foods are available: indeed, one condition of economic and agricultural development in a society seems to be that the supply of the staple food must be maintained, at least in the short term. This importing of staple food happened most markedly in our period in the Netherlands, where the development of different industries in the sixteenth century meant that much arable land was used to provide raw materials for products such as flax, hops and linseed, and thus was lost to grain production for food.[46] So when the burgeoning population outstripped the immediate food supply in Holland in the mid-sixteenth century, its needs could be met by Dutch merchants importing bread grains from the Baltic every autumn. The role of the Baltic as the reserve bread-basket of Western and Southern Europe increased throughout this period. By the 1580s the Dutch merchants alone were sending over a thousand ships a year to Danzig, as well as ships to the other Baltic ports of Elbing and Königsberg. Most of these carried grain on their return journey, either wheat or rye or barley, and the Dutch shipped the grain not only to Amsterdam for themselves and for reshipment to other northern countries, but also developed a trade with the Mediterranean lands, bringing bread grains to the Italians and Spaniards. The irony of the situation is that while this grain was exported through the Baltic ports from the Polish Republic of Nobles and from both Royal and Ducal Prussia in order to feed a western population undergoing the modernising changes of monetarization and the commercialisation of agriculture, yet the owners of the manorial estates on which it was grown in such quantities had to reintroduce feudalism and even enserfment in order to meet the demand for the labour-intensive grain cultivation for export.[47]

It is the existence of a grain staple food tradition across Europe which meant that dearths and famines were so strong in their impact, and that they affected the poorest most hard. For throughout this period 'grain prices fluctuate more strongly than the prices of other products and wages. Over a shorter period wages do not vary as much as grain prices, and wage-earners are at a disadvantage when grain prices go up.'[48] Gregory King in the seventeenth century calculated that a shortfall of 10 per cent in the grain harvest leads to the price going up by 30 per cent. When the shortfall is 20 per cent, the price rise is 80 per cent and, catastrophically, when half the harvest is lost, then the price of grain goes up by 450 per cent!

Unfortunately for the poorest, prices of grain did indeed go up in a remarkable way in the course of the sixteenth century, in what has been termed the 'Price Revolution' – or inflation. Some contemporaries believed that the inflation was due to the excess of gold and silver brought to Europe from the Spanish territories in America. More recently, historians have argued over whether the leading element in this inflation was the level of rents. A German broadsheet from 1621 entitled *The Sad complaint of the poor against the domination of inflation* (Plate 4.1), blamed the rich for causing immense suffering to the poor through their speculations. The author of the text puts the worldly misery in a religious context, where the poor are promised God's assistance, while the rich are guaranteed to suffer in hell. In the middle of the picture we see a poor man attacked by a wealthy man, who in turn is being bitten by the monster of avarice, Belial, who is sitting on sacks and boxes of gold. In the left-hand corner, the mouth of hell gapes open and the rich can be seen in the fires of hell; in the right-hand corner, the poor woman with a baby is sitting on a box, possibly evicted from the house.[49]

This inflation affected the price of bread grains dramatically: 'in most of western and central Europe wages lagged far behind rents and the price of food'.[50] In other words, real wages declined: you could buy less with the money you got from your wages. And as bread grains were the most important item in the budget of the poor and middling sort, the real cost of bread went up. When people could not afford even the cheapest of grains, they suffered personal experience of dearth and might even be forced to become beggars. Then, in this situation, came the worst famine period of the whole century: the 'Great Famine' of the 1590s, which we shall deal with below.

The general dependence on a staple grain also meant that the countryside was a far worse place to live during dearth or famine, than were towns, even though the countryside was where the food was produced. For grain always moved – more correctly, was moved – from areas of low purchasing power to areas of high purchasing power, irrespective of the relative degree of hunger and need. The governors of the greatest trading ports such as Venice, London or Amsterdam could import grain by ship for their populations during emergencies. But all towns could in practice monopolise the supply of the grain of their hinterland through their superior purchasing power, and through their willingness to deploy armed guards and legal coercion when necessary. Civic authorities were also able to organise grain supply within towns and, to a certain extent, also its market price, even for the urban poor, much better than could be done in the countryside. In times of epidemics, the town was the place of death. But in the times of famine, the towns gave the better chance of life.

F(E)AST

Food and its consumption have highly symbolic roles as well as nutritive ones in human societies. What you eat, when you eat it (especially in

Plate 4.1 *The sad complaint of the poor against the domination of inflation*, 1621 (Trawrige Klage der Armen wegen der übermachten Geltsteigerung)

celebrations) is very important. As, of course, is the act of deliberately not eating: fasting has particular roles in communal life, and especially with respect to the professional religious such as monks and clerics. Refusing to eat, for whatever reason, was a positive act, then as now. Personal fasting – voluntary periods of self-denial of food and drink – had long been part of the ascetic tradition within Christianity. Fasting and abstinence were practised not just in the monasteries and nunneries whose inhabitants had dedicated themselves to asceticism in the cause of greater spirituality, but also in the wider secular world. At certain times, in order to control the senses or to discipline the body through denial of the senses, 'both men and women fasted or adulterated what food they ate in order to destroy any pleasure they might experience in it'.[51] Food and its taste were associated with luxury, and hence indulgence in them was often associated with sin, and over-eating was regarded as a 'sin of the mouth' by Catholic clerics.[52]

Feasts are a recurrent feature of civil society, celebrating significant moments in the year, in the life of the individual, in the life of groups, in the life of the society as a whole. Feasts were made when someone joined a brotherhood, when a guild annually celebrated its foundation, when people got married, when major contracts were made, when students graduated. Feasts marked ties of power, dependence and obligation. Wilhelm Abel tells of great feasts in Cologne in the 1570s and 1590s, where enormous quantities of food were produced and consumed. Three new doctors of theology and their guests, for instance, consumed at a sitting an ox, three stags, three hundred hens and game birds, two hundred pounds weight of fish, as well as pastry, bread and vegetables.[53]

Feast and fast also had important roles in marking and celebrating the Catholic Christian calendar. While food of course has significance of some kind in most religions, in Christianity the connection is particularly strong. The celebration of a meal – the thanksgiving memorial service of the eucharist or mass – was at the very heart of Catholic religious life: eating sanctified bread and drinking sanctified wine in accordance with Christ's instruction, 'Do this in memory of me', with the bread being turned into his flesh, the wine into his blood. The story of Christ's life was itself bound up with, and in part expressed through, food culture. He called himself the bread of life for believers (John 6:35). He is recorded as attending the marriage at Canaan where he performed the miracle of turning water into wine; he fed the five thousand with five barley loaves and two fishes. And, as part of his personal spiritual journey, the Gospels record

Christ going on a fast of forty days in the wilderness. The Church's liturgical year, the series of feasts and seasons revolving round the life of Christ, was central to the life of everyone in Europe. The feasts were moments of celebration, the fasts were acts of penitence and physical mortification for exercise in temperance and the health of souls, especially in preparation for the great annual event of the Christian calendar, Easter. While, with the coming of the Reformation, the stipulations for fasting were abolished in Protestant areas, the practice of fast days often continued, with meat being avoided on Friday and Saturday usually, and Lent fasting continuing.[54]

Feasts were held on saints' days in the Catholic tradition. But the greatest communal feast was associated with Christ's own forty-day fast in the wilderness, and the Christian community practised a remembrance of this in its own fasting during Lent. The preparation for this fasting was a period of Carnival (literally, farewell to meat), crowned by a great feast, still marked in the calendar by the day known in some countries as Mardi Gras ('Fat Tuesday') and in others as Shrove Tuesday ('to shrive' was to hear confession and give absolution, in preparation for the fasting). All the products of animals that walk on the land had to be consumed: the meat, the eggs, the milk, the butter. Today making pancakes remains a popular way of using up these products. John Taylor, the self-styled 'water-poet' of early seventeenth-century London, in 1617 characterised Shrove Tuesday as a greedy person:

> Always before Lent there comes waddling a fat gross bursten-gutted groom, called Shrove-Tuesday, one whose manners shows that he is better fed than taught: and indeed he is the only monster for feeding amongst all the days of the year, for he devours more flesh in fourteen hours, than this whole kingdom [of England] doth (or at the least should do) in six weeks after. Such boiling and broiling, such roasting and toasting, such stewing and brewing, such baking, frying, mincing, cutting, carving, devouring, and gorbellied gormandizing, that a man would think people did take in two months provision at once into their paunches, or that they did ballast their bellies with meat for a voyage to Constantinople, or to the West Indies.[55]

After the feast came the forty days fasting, in which Christians were not permitted to eat during most of the day, having only a small meal at noon. At this meal abstinence was practised: that is to say, the contents of this one meal were restricted, following the dietary restrictions of the book of Leviticus. Generally speaking there was a prohibition against meat, meat products (dairy produce and eggs), oil and wine. However, during the Lenten fast, Sundays were exempt from fasting.

The painter Pieter Breugel the Elder (c.1528–69), an Erasmian Catholic, depicted in striking fashion what he called *The fight between Carnival and Lent* in Brussels and the Southern Netherlands in a painting of 1559 (Plate 4.2). Carnival is personified in the left foreground as a fat man on a barrel, pushed by two men in festive garb, and his weapon is a spit with a roasted animal on it. Lent is personified as a skinny crone on a little cart pulled by two women, and her weapon is a baker's shovel (used to put bread in the oven) but on it are just two little fishes. The painting as a whole has carnival activity on the left, and lenten activity on the right. Gluttony and self-indulgence face sobriety and good deeds. Meat, beer and pancakes confront fish, water and pretzels. John Taylor, in his jocular characterisation of Lent, claimed that usually, no sooner had people had a taste of the Shrove Tuesday pancake, 'that sweet candied bait', than they ran riot. 'Straight their wits forsake them, and they run stark mad, assembling in routs and throngs numberless of ungoverned numbers, with uncivil civil commotions.' Young men armed themselves and 'put playhouses to the sack, and bawdy-houses to the spoil'.[56] Such riotous behaviour is represented here too in Breugel's painting, and is contrasted with the sobriety of behaviour in the fasting period. The centrality of fish to the Lenten scene is striking, since this perhaps most typified the diet of Lent. Salted herring from the North Sea was the primary substitute for meat. Only one other creature could be eaten during Lent, if it could be obtained: the barnacle goose, since it was believed to develop from a fish.

The situation with Protestants was different. From the 1520s there were no obligatory fasts in the liturgical year. It was clear to the magistrates of Basle in 1534, for instance, that Lenten fasting and the prohibition of certain foods were as lacking in biblical warrant – and hence 'uncommanded' by God – as were the veneration of saints or clerical celibacy.[57] Ideally, the attitude to fasting that Protestants were to adopt was that outlined by the Danish Lutheran reformer Peder Palladius, who defined 'true fasting' in his visitation book of 1543, which set out all the practicalities about running a Protestant church. True fasting, according to Palladius, is not limited to a particular time of year, neither before nor after Easter, nor is it more important on Fridays, or Sundays, or Saturdays or Mondays, 'but all days should be the same to a good Christian'. Nor, he claims, does fasting mean eating fish but not pork, nor eating bread without butter on it, or eating expensive herbs and not fish nor pork: 'that is a liar's fast, a monk's fast, a devil's fast, and none of that is mentioned at all in the Scriptures'.

Plate 4.2 Pieter Bruegel the Elder, *The fight between Carnival and Lent* (1559)

> But a true fast is to eat and drink nothing. As long as you do that, then you are fasting . . . Fasting is hunger, hunger, hunger. When our Lord Jesus had fasted he was hungry. When our monks, copying Him, used to fast before Easter, then they were more fat and more chubby at Easter than they had been in Lent. . . . At other times, when you are not fasting, eat and drink for your natural preservation beef, pork, fish, or anything else God has given you, on Friday as on Sunday, and thank God for His generous gifts. We are not bound to this or that day, as in the time when we were under the pope and the monk.[58]

Thus, as Palladius's advice shows, individual fasting by choice was still legitimate for Protestants. Communal fasting, by contrast, had no biblical authority. However, customs die slowly, and it is certainly the case that Protestants and Reformed still engaged in fasts, even in the Lenten fast (as can be seen from John Taylor's account above), and in times of great national calamity even Puritans called for and engaged in fasts to seek God's forgiveness for national sin and for mercy in dearth and famine.

FAMINE AS DIVINE PUNISHMENT

Just as both feast and fast had immediate religious connotations in this apocalyptic period, so too did famine. For, 'according to the Christian concept that stamped western civilization for hundreds of years, the fruits of the soil are a gift, and food is a loan, from God. Conversely, failure of the harvest was viewed as God's punishment. In his struggle for food, therefore, man should not only work but pray.'[59] God punished Adam for eating the fruit of the forbidden tree in the garden of Eden, by cursing the ground: 'cursed is the ground for thy sake; in sorrow shalt thou eat of it all the days of thy life; thorns also and thistles shall it bring forth to thee; and thou shalt eat the herb of the field; in the sweat of thy face shalt thou eat bread, till thou return unto the ground'. The Bible contains many stories of God sending what God Himself called 'the evil arrows of famine' (Ezekiel 5:16) as a punishment for the sin and disobedience of the chosen people and of particular individuals. Solomon, at the dedication of the temple, covenanted with God on behalf of the people that 'when heaven is shut up, and there is no rain, because they have sinned against thee . . . If there be in the land famine, if there be pestilence, blasting, mildew, locust, or if there be caterpillar', then God in heaven would hear with special compassion the prayers and supplications made in the temple (I Kings 8:35–9). That famines and dearths were sent as divine punishments, was known as the doctrine of judgements.[60] That such judgements on sinful mankind might be withdrawn by God as an act of mercy, if the people were truly contrite and humbled themselves and prayed to God, was established by Solomon's pact with God. Thus devout Christians did not suffer passively during dearths and famines, but believed they should be active in expressing repentance and turning to God for forgiveness. We have a rather interesting perspective from a Catholic canon of Bologna, who in 1602 declared that God sent three kinds of punishment for sins: famine, war and pestilence. But famine was the least terrible because it generally spared the priesthood, so one could generally confess one's sins before dying![61]

Preachers regarded it as their role to call the attention of men of state to the true causes of famine, and hence to its true cure. For instance, the Puritan preacher of Kingston-upon-Thames in England, John Udall, in 1596 published a series of sermons on the book of Joel, 'wherein the counsel that the Holy Ghost gave the Israelites to redress the famine which they felt . . . is applied in particular unto our present time'.[62] He pointed out to the Earl of Warwick, a member of the Privy Council, that without a proper view of the true cause, government attempts to deal with famines could only make matters worse, because their plans 'are framed in the shop of human policy only'. What needs to be recognised, he said, is that 'all enormities and disorder do proceed from sin, and every breach in a state, from the displeasure of the Lord for the contempt or neglect of his holy commandments'. Udall uses Joel as his text:

> I think the doctrine that then fitted them [in the time of Joel], to be very necessary for us, upon the like occasion, for as the hand of God was upon them in the want of bread, so (though not in the like measure) is it upon us: as they had little sense, or feeling thereof, to acknowledge it, the punishment of God upon them for their sins, but ascribed it to other causes, so do we, imputing it, some to the hardness of wise men's hearts, some to the thievery of transporting [i.e. removing grain from stricken areas], and some to the unseasonable times, but few look into themselves, and their sins, that procure the Lord to turn the hearts of men, and the benefit of heaven and earth from us: as the Lord having sent famine, which prevailed not with them, to their conversion, did threaten to send a more violent and forcible rod, the invasion of strangers upon the land: so doth he by many warnings and tokens threaten the same upon us, and (lastly) as the Lord prescribed unto them, if ever they looked to have his judgements present, removed, or those that hanged over their heads, turned away, they must meet the Lord, and prevent his wrath, by fasting and prayer, which might be as means to bring them to the true humiliation of their souls, so we, that by the same sins, are punished, and threatened in the same manner, by the hand and rod of the same jealous god, if ever we look to be reduced [i.e. brought back] soundly again into his favour, must take the same course, that he (which did know the best way) prescribed unto them.[63]

So the preacher must be listened to, Udall says, as he points out the sins of commission and omission of the people, including the abusing of the fat of the land by 'superfluity in banqueting', vanity in dress, and wasting thousands of quarters of wheat, which God ordained for the food of man, by turning it into 'that most devilish device of Starch' for cuffs and collars, 'a sin so abominable that it doth cry so loudly in the Lord's ears for vengeance, as his justice must needs proceed against us for it, without speedy repentance'. Famine is directly brought on by sin and luxury, and can only be averted by repentance.

Another Reformed preacher, Lodovike (Ludwig) Lavatere (1528–86), a minister of Zurich, had spoken similarly of the cause and cure of famine in 1571.[64] God is the first cause of all disasters, and works through a whole variety of second causes to bring about dearth and famine. Sorcerers and witches do not have the power to do this, only God:

> For God being the Lord of nature, ruleth as himself pleaseth, without, yea, and against the rules of nature . . . Of all other, the greatest enemies to corn in many Countries are Locusts . . . in *Anno* 1542 they oppressed both *Polonia* and *Silesia*, in so great heaps, that the inhabitants, though in vain, went about to scare them away with the ringing of bells, sound of trumpets, and ringing of basons. As great hurt also hath been done to the fruits of the earth, both by hail, sometime falling from heaven as big as Hens Eggs, killing under them both man and beast . . . as also by storms, tempests, whirlwinds, and inundations, either rotting the seed, or pinching the blade, or shaking the ears of corn . . . Oft times again it happeneth that the cause of *Dearth* may come by continual Rain, the seed perishing by too much wet:[65] wherein God having opened his bottles, as he himself speaketh, Job. 38.37 hath made the clouds which should drop *fatness*, Psalm 65.12 to pour down the moisture of *rottenness*. Joel. 1.17, so that sowing Wheat, we have reaped thorns, Jere. 12.13 . . . Wars also make a great scarcity, both for the present, and afterward, all the Corn either being wasted with fire, or trampled down with Horses, or carried away by the Enemy . . . Too many there are who think *Famine* and *Dearth* to come by chance, they say there hath always been an intercourse of things, War followeth peace, and *Dearth* plenty: and this interchange shall hold on to the worlds end. But we out of the scriptures have learned, that nothing comes by chance, but even the least things are guided by God's providence.[66]

Lavatere thought (like Udall) that people mistook the second cause for the first, and vice versa, believing that it was the actions of men profiting from dearth and famine which were to blame – or even the Reformed religion itself – while they failed to think of the true cause, their own sins:

> The common multitude with one consent lay all the fault upon the oppression of Landlords enhancing their rents, the malice of Farmers grudging without

cause, unmercifulness of Usurers grinding without pity, the intolerable licenses of *Monopoles* and *Solesales*, engrossing without measure, the covetousness of hoarders keeping up their grain without mercy; (all which no doubt, are principal outward means whereby God doth bring it to effect), but of corruption in manners, of vices and vileness of life, of the *Immunity* and *Impunity* of sinning, without shame, without restraint, not one word . . . In this and the like calamities, the whole fault for the most part is laid upon Religion, certain Miscreants and Varlets, crying out of the Pulpit, in the open Market, at their public Feasts, that the new Religion (for so they entitle the preaching of the Gospel) is the only cause of this *Dearth*. Since there hath been a separation, and that the Saints departed, have not their *Due honor*, and the *Old manner of worshipping God* (for so they call their *Romish superstition*) is abandoned, the world hath been still in a *Deluge of Calamity* from which, *forsooth*, we should be freed, if we had kept the [religious] profession of our forefathers . . . The holy scripture doth in plain terms set down, that the *Dearth of Victuals* is the scourge of God, for the manifold and enormous sins, principally *Atheism* and *Idolatry*.[67]

In addition to atheism and idolatry, Lavatere claimed that God was using famine to punish the sins of private gain, perjury and oppression, covetousness, cruelty, pride, drunkenness and over-eating, and (an unusual one) neglect of the payments of tithes.

Because famines were sent as divine punishment it was indeed possible to pray and fast an imminent famine away. William Gouge claimed this had happened in 1626 in England and Wales. We should take note, he says to his readers,

how it standeth us in hand, when there is cause to fear a famine, or when a famine is begun, to search out the causes thereof, to confess before God our sins, to turn from them, humbly, heartily, earnestly, extraordinarily, with weeping, fasting, and prayers to supplicate mercy of the Divine Majesty. We have late evidence of the efficacy of such means used. For in the year 1626 it rained all the spring, and all the summer day after day for the most part, until the second of August, on which day by public Proclamation a Fast was solemnly kept throughout the whole Realm of England, and Principality of Wales, as it had by the same Proclamation been solemnised in the Cities of London and Westminster and places adjacent, on the fifth day of July before. On the said second of August the sky cleared, and rain was restrained, till all the harvest was ended: which proved a most plentiful Harvest. Thus the famine threatened and much feared was withheld. So as God's ordinances duly and rightly used are now as effectual as ever they were.[68]

God's greatest punishment with famine was to induce cannibalism, and especially to thereby induce starving mothers to eat their own babies. To contemporary observers this grossest of depravities was fascinating. To be reduced to eating one's own baby was a terrible warning for others: unless we repent and thus avert God's just punishment for our sins – famine – then God will punish us yet further by inducing us to commit this unspeakable sin, as we have been warned in the Bible. For in Leviticus 26 it is recorded that God promised Moses that if the children of Israel walked in His statutes and kept His commandments, all would be well with their harvests and their bread:

> Then I will give you rain in due season, and the land shall yield her increase, and the trees of the field shall yield their fruit. Then your threshing shall reach unto the vintage, and the vintage shall reach unto the sowing time: and ye shall eat your bread to the full, and dwell in your land safely. (Leviticus 26:4–5)

But, God said, if the children of Israel would not for all this hearken unto him, but walked contrary to Him:

> then I will walk contrary unto you also in fury; and I, even I, will chastise you seven times for your sins. And ye shall eat the flesh of your sons, and the flesh of your daughters ye shall eat. (Leviticus 26:27–9; see also Deuteronomy, 28:53–7)

The direct connection between sin, famine and the punishment of eating one's own offspring, could hardly be clearer for a Christian.

Moralists could find instances of this depravity in most famines of the period. For instance, Martin Parker, warning the English in 1638 to avoid the punishment of war and subsequent famine that God was currently visiting on the Germans, relates in execrable verse a recent German case of the devouring of a new-born babe by its mother:

> At *Hornebash* a woman had a child
> Of which she had lain in not long before,
> Hunger, that wild things tames, makes tame things wild,
> Oppressed this woman and her babe so sore,
>   That she food lacking, milk it needs must want,
>   And both for nutriment did feebly pant.
>
> The woman seeing in what deep distress
> Her tender Infant was through want of food,
> And famine did her body so oppress,
> That what to do she in amazement stood.
>   Motherly pity for the babe did plead,
>   Necessity cries out it must be dead.
>
> Necessity prevails, she takes a knife,
> (My heart doth tremble while I write of it)
> Wherewith she wrest the Innocent of life,
> And of the flesh made many a savoury bit.
>   O famine there's no plague compares with thee,
>   Thou art (by odds) the worst of all the three.[69]

The moral is to abandon our sins:

> Let's all consider 'tis th' Almighty's hand,
> That striketh others, and doth spare our land,
> And that his love, (not our desserts) are cause,
> Why from our Nation he the stroke withdraws.
>
> Let's hate our lovèd sins, our vain excess
> Of (Luciferian) pride, sloth, drunkenness,
> Extortion, avarice, and luxury,
> Let's feed and clothe Christ in necessity,
> I mean in's little ones, what's done to them,
> His own words ratify, as done to him,
> This is his will, to do't let's all endeavour,
>   And he (no doubt) will give us peace for ever.[70]

Such depravities, such transgressions of normal social behaviour, such repudiation of one's most fundamental social conditioning, are typical of the psychological effects of famine. An expert on present-day famines comments that 'As famine progresses, normal social behaviour is increasingly affected. Initially there will be mutual help between family or families but at a later stage everybody tends to care only for themselves . . . children and the elderly are usually the first victims.'[71]

FAMINE IN THE SIEGE OF SANCERRE, 1573

Of the many famines of the period, we shall limit our account of how famines struck, what effects they had, and how they were interpreted, to three: the first two were famines entirely man-made through the effects of war, when towns were put under siege. Such famines linked the Red and the Black Horses in double punishment. The other one was the most widespread famine in its incidence and effects: that of the 1590s – widely referred to as the 'Great Famine'.

For the first of our famines resulting from war, we have an eye-witness account of the effects of the famine on the individuals and the community under siege. From this we can gather something of the distress and the extremes of behaviour which people were driven to by hunger. Famine hunger is very painful, physically and emotionally. Pitirim Sorokin, sociologist and witness of the Russian famine of 1919–20, sees it almost as a law of famine, that 'hunger tends to suppress all activities that either hinder or fail to promote its satisfaction'.[72] He claims that hunger conditions generate extremes of behaviour: both acts of the greatest selfishness, as well as acts of self-sacrifice. Similarly, he claims, one finds in famines violent rejection of religion and ethical codes side by side with 'the emergence of an apocalyptic mentality, in mysticism, in religious revivals, in the diffusion of a spirit of penitence and asceticism, and in a disposition to burn or give away one's worldly possessions'.[73] Physically, famine victims are often affected by depression and apathy as they lose their body fat and then their muscle. The skin turns grey and the hair begins to fall out. If the starvation is slow rather than sudden, the stomach bloats out, and just before death from starvation bloody diarrhoea ('bloody flux') appears. When a third of the original body weight has been lost, then death from starvation occurs.[74]

Sancerre, a Reformed town in the Loire valley of France, was put under siege in 1573 by the Catholic royal forces in the course of the French Wars of Religion. In the course of the eight-month siege some 84 people died from the military effects of the siege, but more than 500 people died of famine. Our source for the ravages of this famine is the account given by Jean de Léry, a Huguenot minister who was himself in the town during the siege.[75] The town of Sancerre is built on a hill, making it relatively easy to lay siege to. Léry had had some experience of short famines in Brazil, and thus felt he could claim that this famine in Sancerre was unlike any other in modern times for its severity, and that it was comparable to the famine of Samaria recounted in 2 Kings 6:25 etc. As a minister of religion he also naturally compared it with the famine in Jerusalem in 67 AD, recounted by Josephus in *The Jewish War*, in which 'a mother and honourable woman, hardening herself against the laws of nature, killed and ate the fruit of her own womb'.

The siege began in January, and the terrible famine began to take effect in March. First meat ran short. So a horse which had been hit by a cannon shot on 19 March, was skinned, cut up, carried away and eaten by the guild of wine-dressers and boatmen, who claimed never to have eaten better beef. Then a donkey was slaughtered, boiled and roasted and made into pâté. Within a month all the many donkeys and mules in the town had been eaten, and then most of the horses were killed and eaten too. The town council set the price for horse meat in the butchers' shops: the best meat should sell at 3 sols a pound, the worst 2. But these prices were not observed by some 'who did not recognise the hand of God in these most calamitous times', and by the end of July a pound of horse meat sold at from 18 to 22 sols. 'As the famine increased little by little at Sancerre, the cats also had their turn, and were all eaten in a short time, such that the supply of them dried up after a fortnight.' Because of the dearth, some people set to catching rats, and the hunger which drove them on inspired them to invent all sorts of rat traps, and the poor children were well satisfied when they could have some mice to eat, which they cooked on the coals. 'There was no tail, paw or skin of rat which was not seized upon to serve as nourishment for a great multitude of suffering poor folk . . . The dogs were not spared, and they were killed without emotion, like sheep normally are.' In June the council resolved that the bread ration should be half a pound a day; after eight days this was reduced to a quarter of a pound, constantly decreasing until all supplies of grain and flour of the garrison had been exhausted by the end of the month. At the beginning of July, some people were urged on by 'the belly, which has no ears, and necessity, the mother of invention', to try eating leather, using all sorts of cooking methods. It tasted a bit like tripe. When the leather was all consumed, people turned to trying parchment 'not only white blank parchment, but also letters, title-deeds, books printed and hand written, having no difficulty in eating even those a hundred or a hundred and twenty years old'. They were soaked, chopped, boiled for a day and a half, and then they were fricasseed like tripe, or cooked with herbs and spices. After paper, people turned to eating the hooves of horses and cattle and the horns of cattle. They ate the harness of the horses, especially the white leather. They ate their own belts. Those who had gardens supplying herbs for flavouring, had to guard them at night with arms, to protect them against marauders. By the beginning of July there was so little grain that three-quarters of the population had to give up eating bread. Some tried to make bread out of straw, or of the shells of nuts, roasted and ground. The final 20 horses were slaughtered in July, and the flesh fetched virtually its weight in gold, selling for 20 or 22 sous a pound. Every part of the horses found a hungry buyer. Even the blood sold for 28 francs: blood puddings were made from it, with a few herbs, and these were sold for 80 sols each. The cupidity of those with some foodstuff to sell was unbelievable: they would not heed the word of God, Léry said, which warned that they would lose it all – as they did when the enemy soldiers confiscated all their money at the fall of the town.

As the famine continued, conditions got progressively worse:

Alas! As the prophet Jeremiah said in the book of *Lamentations* about the inhabitants of Jerusalem, those who had been accustomed to eat delicate food perished in the streets, and ate the dung of men and of beasts during the siege. Was not the same seen and practised in Sancerre? For I can affirm that dung and human excrement were piled up and collected to eat. And I saw some who, having filled their pots with horse shit, ate it with such avidity that they claimed to find it as good as if it had been made with bran-bread.

But the worst depravity was yet to come: mothers eating their own babies, as warned about in the Bible.

> But, O God eternal! Here was the height of all the misery and judgement of God. For as he says in his Law that he will reduce those who do not obey his commandments to such a condition that during a siege he will make the mothers eat their own children: those walled-up in Sancerre (even if they may have been walled-up not because of their sins, but rather on account of their dispute over religion and for their witness of the faith), not having profited from the knowledge that God had given them, nor having profited from other rods and punishments – and be it as it may that it is through the good will of God – saw this great crime, barbarous and inhuman, committed within their walls. For on the twentieth of July, it was discovered and established that a wine-dresser called Simon Potard, his wife Eugène, and an old woman who lived with them called Philippes de la Feüille, had eaten the head, the brains, the liver and the entrails of their daughter aged about three years, who had died from hunger and a lingering disease.

Léry himself saw the evidence: the bone, the head of the poor girl cured and gnawed, the ears chewed, the tongue cooked, all the limbs put in a pot ready to boil with vinegar, spices and salt. He was so shocked that 'all my entrails were disturbed': in other words, he vomited. The father was burned alive as punishment, the mother strangled and burned, and the old lady, who had died in the meantime, was dug up and burned. What else could the magistrates do? Léry asked: otherwise, as the famine got worse, everyone would be killing each other in order to eat them!

At the height of the famine, Léry saw 25–30 people a day dying of hunger. But the young children seemed to be most vulnerable. He believed that their natural heat, which normally encouraged them to eat, was extinguished by their cold stomachs, and caused their deaths. They died slowly and in pain: 'they survived and breathed until their bones pierced their skin, making piteous cries before they gave up the spirit. How we die of hunger! Where is the heart (it would have to be harder than a rock or loadstone) or the ears, which hearing such sounds would not have been affected?' The pain of hunger affected the limbs. Léry himself suffered from being unable to sleep since one could not stretch one's limbs for the cramping pain, and the spleen gave extreme pain to those whose flesh had melted away as a result of hunger.

Léry witnessed one of the phenomena that Sorokin has remarked on in famine: that while some are reduced to cursing God, others become stronger in their faith. 'Constantly in the middle of this great distress and famine', Léry recorded, 'you can see some marvellously constant people, exclaiming "Dear Lord, deliver us from these scourges and rods of famine and of war with which you punish and chastise us on account of our sins. Have pity on your poor people, and in the midst of your anger remember your mercy. If it please you that we die thus, give us the grace to trust in you until our last breath." And then there were others who would not be subdued, and who did not leave off following their bad ways.'

In June, in the midst of the despair of famine the Consistory arranged for public prayers to be said six days a week at five o'clock in the church of St John, and urged everyone to be present 'to implore God's aid and his mercy in this urgent necessity'. More practically, the council made arrangements that the poor lying in the streets should receive alms at eleven o'clock, each in their own quarter of town, from those who wanted to exercise charity. By the beginning of June, however, all that could be distributed to the poor was soup, leather, skins and wine. Not only was bread in extremely short supply, 'but one no longer mentioned it'. Eventually, after more than 500 deaths, the siege was lifted and the famine relieved. This was one of many sieges of the French wars of religion, in which the defenders of a town were subjected to the torture of famine as a military strategy.

FAMINE IN THE GREAT SIEGE OF PARIS, 1590

Perhaps the worst siege of those wars was the 'Great Siege of Paris' of 1590, our second example of famine induced by siege. The new king, the Huguenot Henri IV (Henri of Navarre), put the capital under siege from May until August. The Holy League (the Sainte Union), sworn to return France to true Catholicism, had established Paris as its base. The League had been opposed to Henri III, the Catholic king, for his lack of true Catholic commitment, and Henri had had the League leaders murdered and was in turn assassinated in 1588. The League was now implacably opposed to his Huguenot successor, Henri IV, whom they regarded as nothing less than a heretic. Thus, by contrast with the siege of Sancerre, here a Protestant French monarch besieged a Catholic – indeed ultra-Catholic – city. We can again rely on the account of an eye-witness who lived in Paris throughout the siege, Pierre de l'Estoile, who held the positions of Audiencier de la Chancellerie de Paris, Conseiller du Roi, Notaire and Secrétaire du Roi, and who kept a journal from 1574 until his death in 1611. His accuracy and reliability are well-known, and of the events of the famine of 1590 he writes: 'What I record about this I either saw with my own eyes or I have it on the word of men of good faith, including a poor man who, for a piece of bread, brought me news of everything unusual or interesting.'[76]

The first act of the royal army on 7 May, was to take the suburbs and burn down all the mills around Paris. At the beginning of the siege the authorities inside Paris estimated that there were about 220,000 people in the town, and that the available wheat, if rationed, would last for about a month, after which barley could be used. The Spanish were supporting the League, and they helped in various ways such as giving money to the poor so that they could buy bread. After a month, on 15 June:

> Don Bernardino Mendoza, Spanish Ambassador . . . in an assembly called to find a way to deal with the famine which was growing from day to day in Paris . . . made a strange proposal, the like of which had never been heard, namely, to put through the mill the bones of the dead in the [cemetery of the] Innocents, to reduce them to powder, which could be mixed with water and made into bread to be used for nourishment for those who had no grain and no way to get any, an opinion which was received in such a manner that not a man in the assembly was found to oppose this suggestion.

By 20 June no wheat could be found for the poor anywhere in town, and they were reduced to eating oat cakes, which were themselves very expensive, 'which increased their cries and complaints'. On 24 June the Archbishop of Lyons and the Spanish Ambassador threw money to the people in front of the palace, but the people called for them to throw them some bread instead: they were dying of hunger, they said, and this money was useless to them because they could not find any food to buy with it. It was resolved to make a visitation of all the religious houses in the town, and in every one of them was found more provisions than would be required for the inmates for half a year. The Jesuits were particularly well-stocked with wheat, biscuit, salted meat, vegetables and other food 'in greater quantity than in the four greatest houses in Paris'. Each religious house was ordered to distribute food daily to the poor of the quarter. The poor-houses, meanwhile, were obliged to bring out all their cats and dogs, which were killed and cooked in great pots and the resulting stew distributed to the poor 'with a piece of flesh of dog or cat, and a piece of bread'. Poor and rich were now dying in the streets, as much from the badness of the nourishment as from the dearth of provisions.

In July the nearby League town of St Denis, which had also been under siege, fell to the king, and its inhabitants were able to eat again: 'stews of the meat of horses, asses, and mules began to be sold in stalls on the street corners; people fought to get them'. Meanwhile in Paris itself, 'horse meat is so expensive that the poor can't buy it; they chase dogs and eat them, and eat grass that grows in the streets, which is a hideous and pitiable sight'. According to l'Estoile, 'the only thing that is cheap in Paris is the sermons, where the preachers fill the poor people up with wind, that is with lies and stupidities, giving them to understand that it will endear them to God if they die of hunger. They even say that it is better to kill one's own children if you didn't have anything to feed them with, than to receive a heretic King.' Rumours began of child-eating. Apparently a very rich woman, unable to find food at any price, and having seen her two little children die of hunger, had hidden their bodies and had them salted by her servant, and the two of them ate their flesh in place of bread. Visions were seen. The Duke of Savoy's men saw serpents in the streets. A Jesuit and a bishop were asked what the significance was of the appearance of these poisonous creatures in town. A courtier blurted out, 'On my faith, my lord, it is a judgement of God. I have a great fear that these beasts are coming to eat us in our homes.' But the Bishop of Ast said that these creatures were an effect of magic, they were an illusion by which the Devil was trying to discourage the Catholics, and given that was the case, then he preferred to be devoured by serpents than to let the cursed heretics into the town. L'Estoile estimated that 30,000 people had died of famine by the end of July. Crowds of poor people ran out from the besieged city to eat the herbs and grass around it, putting themselves at risk of being killed by the besiegers, because they were unable to find any herbs or skins of even the vilest animals in the town itself, 'having already eaten the donkeys, dogs, rats, the bones of the dead'.

August began with a procession to ask God to favour the aims of the Duke of Mayenne (the leader of the League), and to send immediate help for the people's misery and calamity. A week later there was a tumult at the Palace, of people whom hunger had driven there, as hunger drives the wolves from the woods, who were armed and who demanded 'La paix ou le pain', 'Give us peace or bread'. But the next day, when they assembled again, 'instead of bread they got blows; instead of peace they got the gallows'. In the middle of the month, on 16 of August, it was announced 'that anyone could leave the city, because hunger was so acute. The bread made of the bones of our fathers [from the cemetery of the Innocents] began to be used. But it didn't last long because those who ate it died; some said that was what it was made for.' As the people's murmuring became daily more insistent that peace needed to be made with the king, the leaders of the League became more strident in their claims that it was better to kill one's children, to gobble them up, than to recognise a heretic king.

During the last days of the siege, according to l'Estoile, 'you could see the poor, dying, eating dogs on the street; others ate animal garbage that had been thrown in the river, or rats, or meal made of bones'.

> Finally, necessity growing, two or three days before the siege was lifted, some soldiers, people completely barbarous and inhuman, dying of awful madness of hunger, began to chase after children as if they were dogs, and ate three of them, two at the hôtel Saint-Denis and one at the hôtel de Plaiseau; and this cruel and barbarous act was committed within the walls of Paris, so much had the anger of God been inflamed over our heads.

L'Estoile could not believe this at first, but after he found it to be true, 'confessed and witnessed by the mouths of the soldiers themselves'.

The siege was lifted on 30 August. Immediately the price of food reduced to a quarter of its value in the last days of the siege. Henri IV was not able to take Paris on this occasion. For this he had to wait until July 1593 after he had discovered a more efficient way of taking the city than by laying siege to it with the death of so many of its inhabitants. In 1593 for the second time he converted to Catholicism – and it was then, when the Parisians joyfully greeted him as king as he went to mass in the cathedral of Notre Dame, that he is said to have made his famous remark: 'Paris is worth a mass!'

THE 'GREAT FAMINE' OF THE 1590S

We saw earlier how the 'price revolution' or inflation of the late sixteenth century meant that real wages fell, and that as a result the real cost of bread – how much bread your wages could buy – therefore went up. In a money economy, as Europe increasingly was by the late sixteenth century, access to bread (and hence survival) depends on access to money. And in the course of the sixteenth century the money value of corn went up compared to every other possible commodity. Thus the rise in the relative cost of bread, whatever grain one made it from, whether wheat, rye or barley, meant that purchasing one's daily bread called on a greater and greater proportion of one's wages, leaving little for any other expenses. As demand for products other than food is depressed, so workers in industries such as textiles become redundant and join the queue for bread. Moreover, as the population continued to increase through the second half of the sixteenth century, there were ever more mouths to feed. Thus by the 1590s the situation was unstable, and everything depended on the size and regularity of the harvest if dearth and famine were to be kept at bay.

Unfortunately the 1590s saw some of the worst harvests of our entire period and, tragically, these disastrous harvests ran in succession over three, four or even five years, thus allowing no opportunity of recovery. The early 1590s were worst in the south of Europe. In Sicily, Naples and mid-Italy there were poor harvests in 1590–2. In Spain the worst years were 1593–4. The south of France suffered in 1590–3 and in 1596–8; in 1597 in the Lyonnais food was so dear that some villages sold their bells to feed the poor.[77] In England the run of poor harvests began in 1593 and lasted until 1597. In Scotland the years 1595–8 were famine years. In the Low Countries the harvest failed in 1594–6. In northern France the worst years were 1596–8. Further north, in Sweden and Norway, the poorest harvests were also in 1596–8: in Sweden a contemporary wrote in 1596 that 'People were found dead in the houses, under barns, in the ovens of bath houses and wherever they had been able to squeeze in, so that, God knows, there was enough to do getting them to the graveyard, though the dogs ate many of the corpses. Children starved to death at their mothers' breast, for they had nothing to give them suck.'[78] The crop failures mainly arose from unremitting rain during the springs and summers, which rotted the crop in the fields and caused floods, but in some places such as mid-Italy the causes were wet winters and dry summers. With these repeated failed harvests famine conditions were widespread. A few years of good harvests then followed in 1598 (in some areas), 1599 and 1600, in which recovery was accomplished, but 1601 was another very poor harvest and famine reigned again in places such as Ireland.[79]

While the 'Great Famine' struck all across Europe, its incidence in some places was more severe than others, and usually it was worse in the country than in the town. The famine disaster years of 1594 to 1597 in north-west England have been investigated by Andrew Appleby in a celebrated study. Appleby's area of study, the counties of Cumberland and Westmorland, was almost exclusively rural; the towns were of little consequence, the villages small. The region is mountainous, and most of the farmers had – if anything – only a small area of arable to grow their corn and vegetables. But in order to buy their grain or bread the farmers relied in normal times mostly on income from selling the cattle and sheep they reared on the hills. A report of 1570 said that 'the country consists most in waste ground [i.e. common pasture] and is very cold and barren . . . yet it is very populous and breedeth tall men and hard of nature . . . [whose] greatest gain consists in breeding of cattle'.[80] As in many areas of Europe at this time, the population of the area had doubled over the period from 1563 to the 1590s. It is obvious that the economic position of the poor husbandman was going to be precarious in times of crisis in such an area of marginal cultivation and with many more mouths to feed. Appleby's study shows that in these years famine caused death on a significant scale in Westmorland and Cumberland, enough to bring on a demographic crisis. From the end of 1596 (that is, from after the first failed harvest), right through 1597 and into early 1598, the number of burials shot up, reaching in the spring of 1597 three and even four times the norm in some parishes.

When the series of poor harvests began to bite throughout England, the Oxford preacher George Abbot in his *Exposition on the Prophet Jonah* (1600) wrote:

> I see that all is not well. He is blind who now beholdeth not that God is angry with us . . . Behold what a famine he hath brought to our land, and making it to persevere, yet hitherto doth increase it. One year [1594] there hath been hunger; the second year [1595] there was a dearth; and a third which is this year [1596], there is great cleanness of teeth.[81]

Even the hard-headed members of the Privy Council, who recognised the role of speculators – 'more like to wolves or cormorants than to natural men' – in forcing the price of corn up, in a 1597 pronouncement also recognised the hand of God in the nation's misery:

> Almighty God hath mercifully and favourably withdrawn His heavy hand, wherewith we were deservedly punished by an universal scarcity through the unseasonable weather, and hath now yielded us with His blessed hand a change thereof in this latter end of summer, to great comfort of all sorts of people.[82]

One of the Englishmen who offered public advice on how to cope with the famine was Sir Hugh Platt whose book of *Sundry new and artifical remedies against famine* opened with a motto from St Augustine: 'There is no way to flee from God when He is irate, except to God placated' (Non est quo fugias a Deo irato nisi ad Deum placatum). Naturally, 'the first and principal, and most Christian counsel' that Sir Hugh could offer 'in these threatening days of sword and famine', was

> by hearty prayers from a zealous heart to call upon the name of the great and almighty JEHOVAH, and of the gracious and merciful God of Israel, that it may please him to forget and forgive our manifold sins and transgressions, which have turned his favorable countenance so long from us, and brought down from heaven so many clouds of wrath upon the fruits of the earth, as that the great hope of our harvest is smitten and daunted already, and that it would please him

of his fatherly goodness by such means as shall seem best in his own eyes, for the relief of these our present wants, to turn this our penury into plenty, and so to bless us with his bountiful hand, that we may all sing a full song of thanksgiving unto him.[83]

For Sir Hugh the famine was made worse by greedy landlords and merchants, and his hope was that 'by these our joint labours we should frustrate the greatest part of these covetous complots, and by new and artificial discoveries of strange bread, drink and food, in matter and preparation so full of variety, to work some alteration and change in this great and dangerous dearth'. The main 'new and artificial remedies' he proposed were ways of taking away the unsavoury taste of those most disliked substitutes for bread corn such as beans, peas, beechmast, chestnuts, acorns, vetches and the like. 'If this may in some good measure be performed', he wrote, 'then I doubt not but that the bulk and body of our meal and flour will be much increased and multiplied, at the least for the poor man's table.' He also suggested ways of taking away hunger pains by sucking allum, tobacco or liquorice.

RESPONSES TO FAMINE

'When God travails his people by famine, the government of communes is very difficult', wrote an inhabitant of Puy-en-Velay in 1529.[84] This was certainly true throughout this period. For people threatened by, or suffering from, famine were faced with desperate situations and they took desperate measures. When the poor of the town or the country ran out of first food and then money, they faced the threat of starving to death. Either they could starve quietly – and the way in which continued under-nourishment saps one's energy made this the route frequently taken – or they could try and do something about their situation. Eating the seed-corn was the first resort of starving peasants. This meant of course that there would be nothing left to plant for the following year. In this way a severe shortage in one year could have hunger effects which lasted several years. Once the seed-corn was eaten, peasants could try and migrate to the nearest town. While towns were able to commandeer grain reserves through their high purchasing power, the arrival there of poor peasants simply worsened the situation of the town's own poor and made lawless behaviour more likely. It might be possible to petition the local or national government. It might also be possible to take direct action, action which all governments regarded as illegal and dangerous. What elicited such direct action most frequently was the sight of grain being moved out from a region where hunger and dearth were being experienced. Thus demonstrations and riots against the transport of grain occurred most frequently in areas where grain was grown. Peasants, armed or not, would 'stay' – that is stop or hinder – wagons or boats moving grain. Occasionally they would seize the grain, but the penalties for doing this were very severe, and grain riots would often end with the ringleaders being imprisoned and hung. Naturally enough, the poor of country and town assumed that merchants and governments were hoarding grain against an increase in prices. Often they were right. A French contemporary wrote:

> In a year of bad harvests the peasant farmer in the country is not the most outspoken in his complaints . . . The real sufferer is the day labourer; he finds himself caught, as the saying goes, between the devil and the deep blue sea, and doesn't know which way to turn. The price of bread has gone up, but he cannot hope for a corresponding increase in wages. He despairs, and despair breeds riot.[85]

When a government faced rioting or the fear of lawlessness they would often issue regulations against hoarding, and seek to fix market prices for grain in order to try and ensure the people got fed.

In many towns the buying and selling of corn in times of want were centralised by government, so that its price and supply could be controlled. In London, for instance, the government placed the responsibility for financing the importation of grain into London to meet times of dearth, upon the city companies:

> They were ordered to lend to the civic authorities sums of money . . . to be repaid when the corn was sold. Then soon after 1514 a great establishment, with granaries, mills, and even bakeries, was established on London Bridge, and this Bridge House became the centre of the corn administration. Later, the companies were themselves compelled to purchase the grain in prescribed quantities, and store it in the Bridge House.[86]

The constant supply of bread corn was so important in the keeping of the peace that even outside times of stress governments continually tried to regulate its price and to forbid certain unfair practices. In the 'Assize of bread', a short digest of the laws on bread supply which was repeatedly issued in England from at least 1500, the legal weight of a loaf was computed against the price of corn. If the price of corn went up, then the penny loaf would weigh less, and vice versa, and the 'Assize' specified the legal quantity (Plate 4.3). Bakers selling short weight would be punished, being put into the stocks for their third offence. Punishments were also detailed for forestallers and regrators. The forestaller attempted to buy corn before it reached the market, 'to the intent to make the victual or corn dearer in the market, in hurt and prejudice of the king's people'. The regrator bought up as much of the corn on sale in the market at the regular price as possible, in order to corner the market, and then he 'selleth it again dearer in the market in hurt of the king's people'.

Perhaps surprisingly, out of the problems of a rapidly expanding population, of an unreformed agricultural system barely able to keep pace with demand, and of the resulting frequent food shortages, there came the basic structures of early modern European social welfare, expressed as schemes of poor relief, usually established through the legal structure of Poor Laws. Where simple direct repression of beggars and vagrants had been the pattern of governmental response at the end of the fifteenth century, from the 1520s onwards rulers and municipal authorities fundamentally reformed their social policy. 'The period 1520 to 1535 was the turning-point. Until then the necessities of life were relatively abundant and famines relatively rare, but the dearth year 1521–2 showed the writing on the wall. Demographic growth without "problems" proved incompatible with the structure of agrarian production.'[87]

The immediate spur for communal action was often a famine. In Venice, for instance, it was the widespread famine of 1527–9 which led to the enactment of a new Poor Law. Famine in the region had led to peasants and villagers moving into the towns of the Veneto: 'a great part of the country has come hither', the Vicenza annalist Luigi da Porto wrote, 'so that, with death and the departure of the people, many villages in the direction of the Alps have become completely uninhabited'.[88] As poor harvest succeeded poor harvest, the Venetian Senate passed a law in April 1529 designed 'to watch over the welfare of the poor and the health of the sick, to give bread to the hungry, and not to fail to aid and favour those who are capable of earning their own living in the sweat of their brows'. To achieve these goals, all 'foreign' beggars were to be expelled to their places of origin. The Venetian poor unable to work were to be put into hospitals or other places of refuge, while the distribution of charity to widows and orphans was to be the responsibility of priests and lay deputies in each parish. Every year each parish had to elect a small committee to appeal for and collect a voluntary tax, which was to be used to support the poor and thus prevent 'the divine Majesty [i.e. God] to be offended in their parishes, as far as that is possible'.[89]

Co-ordinated social policies were initiated in some 60 different towns between 1522 and 1545, following much the same pattern in each. The

¶ Ye ſhall vnderſtande to rede the Aſſyſe of breade alwayes to the farthynge waſtell, ꝛ from one colume to another / throug he

¶ The quarter of wheete.	A farthynge Waſtell.	A farthynge Symnell.	A farthynge Whyte lofe.
¶ The quarter of wheete at. xii. d.	vi. li. xvi. s. wey enge. lxi. ounce and a half and ii. d. troye.	vi. li. xiiii. s wei enge. lx. oūces and quart ꝗ di. and ob. troye.	vi. li. xviii. s. weyeng. lxii. oū ces. iii. quarter and. i. d. troye.
¶ The quarter of wheete at. xviii. d.	iiii. li. x. s. viii. d weyeng viii. oū ce quart ꝗ di. ꝗ a. ob. troye.	iiii. li viii. s. ꝗ, viii. d. weyenge liii. ounce ter. i. d. ob. troy	iiii. li. xii. s. viii d. weyenge. lb. ounce ꝗ di. and i. d. troye.
¶ The quarter of wheete at. ii. s.	iii. li. viii. s. wei enge. xl. oūce. iii quarter and a. i. d. troye.	iii. li. vi. s wey eng. xxxix. oūce and di. and. ii d troye.	iii. li. x. s. wey enge. xlii. ounce troye.
¶ The quarter of wheete at. ij. s. vi. d.	liiii. s. v. d. wey enge. xxxii. oūce di. and di. quar ter ꝗ, ob. troye.	lii. s. v. d. wey eng. xxxi. ounce quart di. ꝗ. i. d. ob. troye.	lvi. s. v. d. weien ge. xxxiii. ounce iii. quarter and ii. d. troye.
¶ The quart of wheete at. iij. ſhyllynges.	xlviii. s. weyēg xxviii. ounce. iii quarter / and a i. d. toye.	xlvi. s. weyeng xxvii. oūces di. and. ii. d. troye.	l. ſhyllynges / weyeng. xxx. oū ces troye.

Plate 4.3 The assize of bread. From *Here begynneth the Boke named the Assyse of breade, What it ought to Weye after the pryce of a quarter of Wheete. And also the Asssyse of Ale, with all maner of wood and Cole, Lath, Bowrde, and tymbre, and the weyght of Butter and Chese* (London, 1540). Reprinted in Mr Ashbee's *Occasional Fac-simile Reprints of Rare and Curious Tracts of the 16th and 17th centuries* (London, 2 vols., 1868–72), vol. I

begyn at the quarter of wheete/ and so to the nexte colume to
the out both sydes of the leafe/ as the boke openeth.

A halfepeny whyte lofe.	A halfepeny wheten lofe.	A peny wheten lofe.	A halfepeny houscholde lofe,
xiii.pounde. xvi s. weyēg.c.xlb. ounce dī . and/ ii.d.troye.	xxii.ħi. xiiii. s. weyeng two.c. xlviii.ounce/ a quarter dī.and a.ob.troye.	xli,ħi viii.s.wei enge.iiii.c. lxxx and.xvi.ounce: iii.quarter.i.d. troye.	xxvii,ħi,xii,s, weyenge, iii ,c, xxxi,ounce dī,a i,d,ob,troye,
ix. ħi.v.s. iiii.d. weyenge.c.li.oū ce dī. quarter ꝛ i.d.ob.troye,	xiii.ħi.xviii.s. weyeng.c. lxvi. ounce.iii quarꝼ and.i.troye.	xxviii.ħi.xvi.s. weyenge.iii.c. xxxiii,ounce dī, and.ii.d.troye.	xviii.ħi.weieng ii.c,xvi,ounces troye,
vii.ħi. weyenge. lxiiii.ounces troye.	x ħi.x.s. weyen ge.xxvi ounces troye.	xi.ħi.weyeng,ii c.iii.ounce troy	xiiii,li,weyeng c,lxviii. ounces troye,
v ħi.xii.s.x.d. weyēg.lxvii. oū ce dī ꝛ dī. quar= ter.i.d.ob.troy.	viii.ħi.xix. s.iii d, weyeng.c.vii ounce dī.ꝛ.i.d. troye.	xvii.ħi.xviii. s. xi,li,v, s,viii,d bi,d, weyeng.ii weyeyg,c,xxxv c.xv.ounce and ounce quarꝼ dī, ii.d,troye. and,ob,troye,
v.ħi.weyeng.xl. ounces troye.	vii.ħi x.s.weyē ge.lxxxx.ounce troye.	xv ħi,weyeng, iii, scoꝛe ounce troye,	x x,li,weyeng a,c xx,ounce troye, troye,

common timing of all these new schemes in different parts of Europe has been interpreted as part of 'the triumph of commercial capitalism', with charity, social control and labour regulation all linked in the interests of the early capitalists.[90] While this may have been the case, it is noteworthy that these are also the early years of the Reformation and of the Catholic response commonly termed the Counter-Reformation. In all areas where such reconstructions of social welfare provision took place the ideology of renewed Christian commitment underlay the measures to maintain the poor: though brought into existence by demographic and economic causes, dearths and famines were responded to in Christian and communal terms.[91] In Catholic regions, first the 'modern devotion' (*devotio moderna*) movement of the late fifteenth century, and then the new religious orders of the Counter-Reformation, preached what has been termed an 'aggressive evangelism'[92] and equally practised a greater communal concern for the poor and needy. In Lutheran communities, the civic authorities now saw it as their role to take on themselves the care of the poor which had hitherto been the voluntary responsibility of charitable givers. Amongst Reformed Swiss towns, the changes in Zurich were the pattern for the other cities. In Geneva, for instance, begging was outlawed, the magistrates united the city's hospitals into one *Hôpital Général* (1536) in which the poor were to be housed and fed, and also the sick poor cared for. Deacons were appointed as stewards of communal alms, to manage properties whose income went to the support of the poor, and to raise funds from the inhabitants on a regular basis.[93] In England too, Poor Law legislation was first passed in 1531 after the famines of the 1520s, and by 1536 it constituted a scheme to control begging and to set the poor to work, while arranging for them to be supported on parish collections.[94] The various statutes for care and control of the poor in England were ultimately consolidated in the Parliamentary legislation of 1598 and 1601 enacted in the wake of the Great Famine of the 1590s. In this the obligation to support the poor was laid on the wealthier members of each parish, with support of paupers in their own homes, rather than in centralised institutions as on the Continent. In general, one can summarise, the poor were now forbidden to beg; they were either housed in large municipal institutions or they were given cash or food to survive at subsistence level; and they were to be persuaded by one means or another to adopt an ethic of work not begging. To finance these schemes the richer members of society were taxed in a voluntary or obligatory system. The worst effects of dearth were thus mitigated in their effect on the poor, as well as the effects of economic slumps and epidemics.

ESCAPING PEACE-TIME FAMINE

There were two areas of Western Europe which, by the end of our apocalyptic period, had just become free of the cycle of population growth occasioning periodic peace-time dearth or famine. They were the two areas in the forefront of trade and industry and of the commercialisation of agriculture. Naturally, they were the two areas which had most freed themselves of feudal ties and land-tenure in the countryside. They were England, especially the south-east, and the Netherlands, especially the western and northern provinces. It was, as Seavoy's analysis demonstrates, because they were able to abandon subsistence agriculture, that these two regions were able to slip out from the cycle of peace-time famine. They are also the two areas where the population first stabilised, which Seavoy takes as a marker of the arrival and success of commercialised agriculture.[95] By contrast, other areas either continued to experience the tragedy of the subsistence-farming/famine cycle or became increasingly subject to the threats of dearth and famine, as their subsistence agriculture was unable to feed their continually growing populations. In the south of Europe the situation got progressively worse. From the early sixteenth century to the 1590s, first Portugal, then Spain, then Italy, found that their harvests were becoming unequal to the task of feeding their populations. In Italy, corn had to be imported from the south, from Apulia (Puglia) and Sicily, and then from Turkey. Eventually, in the great crisis of the 1590s, the Tuscans and the Venetians, like the Portuguese and Spanish, were obliged to buy Baltic corn to stave off famine, corn which arrived in Dutch ships. For the next 30 years only the annual flotillas of grain ships from the Baltic kept the population of the northern Mediterranean from starvation.[96]

England and the Netherlands took different routes to reaching this food and population stability. In England among the great social upheavals which marked and assisted the transition were the *enclosure* of common fields and common grazing by individuals, with the loss of such land to the community as a whole; and the *engrossing* of one holding with another, with the house on one of the consolidated holdings subsequently demolished or left to decay. Contemporaries, including the government, saw this as a tragedy, taking enclosure and engrossing as signs not of the population growth and agrarian improvement which actually prompted them, but as signs of decay and impoverishment, and they treated them as the causes of the depopulation of the countryside and of the shortage of bread corn.[97] Enclosure and engrossing were interpreted as simply the products of sheer greed on the part of large farmers. William Harrison, for instance, writing in 1571, deplored the apparent decay of parishes which he associated with engrossing (or encroaching). It was, for him,

> so notable and grievous an inconvenience growing by encroaching and joining of house to house and laying land to land, whereby the inhabitants of many places of our country are devoured and eaten up and their houses either altogether pulled down or suffered to decay little by little, although sometime a poor man peradventure doth dwell in one of them, who, not being able to repair it, suffereth it to fall down and thereto thinketh himself very friendly dealt withal if he may have an acre of ground assigned unto him whereon to keep a cow or wherein to set cabbages, radishes, parsnips, carrots, melons, pompions [pumpkins], or suchlike stuff, by which he and his poor household liveth as by their principal food, sith they can do no better. And as for wheaten bread, they eat it when they can reach unto the price of it, contenting themselves in the meantime with bread made of oats or barley: a poor estate, God wot! Howbeit, what care our great encroachers?[98]

As for enclosure, even in market towns, Harrison lamented,

> the ground of the parish is gotten up into a few men's hands, yea, sometimes into the tenure of one, two, or three, whereby the rest are compelled either to be hired servants unto the other or else to beg their bread in misery from door to door . . . Certes a great number complain of the increase of poverty, laying the cause upon God as though He were in fault for sending such increase of people or want of wars that should consume them, affirming that the land was never so full, etc., but few men do see the very root from whence it doth proceed. Yet the Romans found it out when they flourished and therefore prescribed limits to every man's tenure and occupying.[99]

What such observers were witnessing, however, was what has been called 'the undoubted poverty that was a concomitant of economic growth'.[100] A major part of that economic growth came from the 'agricultural revolution' which England (like the Netherlands) was experiencing, especially in the decades after 1560. The introduction of fallow crops (such as clover), marsh drainage, manuring, stock-breeding, the floating of water meadows, and, most of all, the system of 'up-and-down husbandry' (i.e. putting land alternately into tillage and pasturage), all led to a great improvement in the yields of both arable and pasture, together with a great expansion in industrial crops such as wool, flax and woad.[101] While England in the later sixteenth century still had to import corn in times of dearth, especially from the Baltic, yet the success of this agricultural revolution in the longer term meant that England again returned to being a net exporter of corn in the later seventeenth century.[102] And 'not the least of the fruits of agricultural innovation was the general and great prosperity reflected in rising prices, profits, wages and rents after the mid-1560s'.[103] The successes of the innovations were preached by certain English gentlemen, self-styled 'improvers' of agriculture in the 1620s to 1640s, seeking to get the government and their fellow farmers to embrace and further this agricultural revolution.[104]

The route taken in the Netherlands to population stability, and hence to escape from the threat of peacetime famine, was different. Here population growth did not lead to the crises familiar elsewhere in Europe. Instead, 'population growth . . . reacted with the particular endowments of the region to provoke a restructuring of the rural economy'.[105] One essential difference from almost anywhere else, was that most of the peasantry of the Low Countries was essentially free of feudal ties from as early as 1500.[106] Starting early in the sixteenth century, the rural economy of the northern Netherlands came to be transformed by specialisation, amounting in effect to an 'agricultural revolution'.[107] Industrial crops such as flax, hemp, hops and rape-seed began to replace bread grains in many areas. The bread grains to feed the population were now imported cheaply from the Baltic, in Dutch ships. Farming itself was made more efficient and productive. As the population continued to increase, so the excess population of the countryside could migrate to the towns, where it could be employed in new or expanding industries such as textiles, sugar refining, brick-making and, of course, ship-building. The population of the largest towns, Amsterdam, Leiden and Haarlem, increased fourfold over the period 1570 to 1647 by such migration from the countryside, especially from the south, from Protestant Germany and from the eastern provinces.[108] The transformations of the agricultural economy thus fuelled the urban industry and the shipping, fishing and commercial trade of the Netherlands which expanded so greatly in this period and came to dominate European trade as a whole, making the population of the Dutch Republic the richest in Christendom.

Even in the severe crises brought on by the weather in the 1590s and 1621–4, the Netherlands were able to cope. Food prices were certainly high, but, as the historian van Deursen has written,

> actual famine did not occur, for the Amsterdam grain trade [with the Baltic] guaranteed that there would always be something to eat in Holland. In 1581 the synod of Middelburg cited 'the general difficulties' that would require the proclamation of a day of worship or fasting: war, plague, dearth and religious persecution. The synod said nothing about famine . . . In Holland and in the Republic as a whole, people did not die of hunger . . . [though] dearth could become quite fearsome.[109]

Thus in the commercialised agricultural system of England and the Netherlands, by 1648 the regular tragic loss of life that followed from visitations of the Black Horseman could at long last be avoided – at least if he did not come in company with the Red Horseman of war. But there is no simple equation to be made between a modernised economic system and a modernised ideological system. For, as Charles Webster has shown, it was in England, the most modernised economic entity in early seventeenth-century Europe, that the apocalyptic vision remained most powerful, and continued to shape the ambitions of improving Puritans through from the 1620s to the 1660s.[110]

5 The Pale Horse: Disease, Disaster and Death

And when he had opened the fourth seal, I heard the voice of the fourth beast say, Come and see. And I looked, and behold a pale horse: and the name of him that sat on him was Death, and Hell followed with him. (Revelation 6:7–8)

SEXUAL DISEASE

'As Almighty God saw the sins of Italy multiply, especially in her ecclesiastical and secular princes', God 'was unable to bear it any longer and decided to cleanse his Church with a great scourge.' Thus wrote the Dominican friar Girolamo Savonarola in 1495 in a book justifying to the pope and others his apocalyptic preaching and prophecying in Florence. Among his other servants God had chosen Savonarola for this task and God saw to it, Savonarola recalled, 'that I came to Florence in 1489 at the command of my superiors. That year, on Sunday, August first, I began to interpret the book of the Apocalypse in public in our Church of San Marco. Through the whole of the same year I preached to the people of Florence and continually stressed three things: first, the renovation of the Church would come in these times; second, God would send a great scourge over all Italy before that renovation; and third, these two things would happen soon.'[1] Savonarola began to hear divine messages which he introduced into his preaching, such as: 'Thus says the Lord God – the sword of the Lord will come upon the earth swiftly and soon'. And there were others:

> Rejoice and exalt, O you just; but prepare your souls for temptation by reading, meditation and prayer, and you will be freed from the second death. And you evil servants, filthy as you are, stay filthy still; let your belly be filled with unmixed wine, your loins rotted with lust [*renes vestri dissolvantur luxuria*], your hands defiled with the blood of the poor.[2]

In a vision of 1492 Savonarolo saw the Lord's punishing sword lowered towards the earth: 'It rained swords and hailstones with dreadful-sounding thunder, as well as arrows and bolts of fire. On earth war, pestilence, famine, and countless tribulations arose.'[3]

Savonarola's apocalyptic preaching in San Marco in Florence caused a great stir, and events rapidly seemed to confirm the validity of his prophecying. The punishment of God seemed to have arrived in the figure of Charles VIII of France and his army, coming over the Alps in August 1494, though Savonarola was soon to see Charles as inaugurating the New Jerusalem for Italy. The Medicis fled from Florence and a republic was installed in their place, under Savonarola's personal moral and political leadership, heading a party called 'The Weepers' (the *Piagnoni*), and with Savonarola building the famous 'bonfire of the vanities' to burn the luxuries of the penitent Florentines. But then, unfortunately for Savonarola, eleven months of rain caused harvest failure, so Florence was haunted in 1496 by famine, and in 1497 by plague. The weakened populace rioted, and the pressures of foreign politics led to the Medicis regaining power in 1498, and to Savonarola himself being hanged and burnt for heresy and false teaching.

But a further one of Savonarola's prophecies did come true, regarding a new pestilence, though in a way that he could not have expected (since he was in this case using pestilence as a metaphor for the rule of evil prelates).[4] It was his prophecy that the loins of the Lord's 'evil servants' would begin to rot as a result of that great medieval vice, *luxuria* – which is licentiousness and indulgence, and hence came also to mean lust. For a fearful new disease had arrived in Italy. This is how the Fourth Horseman made his entrance in the 1490s, bringing disease, disaster and death. These themes will provide us with a window on to the social dimensions of this apocalyptic age, by seeing the different perceptions of epidemic disease, the varying responses of different social orders to disease, the varying availability of care, and the different vulnerability of the social orders. An 'epidemic disease' is one which, literally, 'falls on the mob', which appears *abruptly*, which kills or severely disables *many* people, *suddenly* and over a short period, and usually in a particularly dramatic and *unpleasant* way.[5] Our account of the visitations of the Pale Horse must of necessity be selective with respect to different epidemics, to geographical outbreaks and to coverage in the time period.

The new disease was one affecting the loins – it was sexual, and soon recognised to be so by some people – and it was a disease which came to epitomise indulgence and lust. It caused in its time as much concern and anxiety as AIDS is doing today. And it produced an immediate and continuing series of publications from academic physicians, and also from sufferers, recounting their tribulations and their desperate search for a cure. For this new disease did not spare the literate class of men: it attacked humanists, scholars, courtiers of kings, princes, bishops and popes, as much as it affected common soldiers; and it affected courtesans and royal mistresses as much as common prostitutes. It was as at home in the hovel as in the court, and Francis I of France, Henri III of France, and the Emperor Charles V are all thought to have suffered from it.[6]

The first large outbreak of it occurred in 1494, in the army of King Charles VIII of France which had recently been occupying Naples. Given this first appearance, it is no surprise that the French called it the Neapolitan disease, while those to whom it was spread equally naturally called it the French disease. Others were to call it the Polish disease, the German disease or the Spanish disease. The variety of early names that this disease was given indicates how its arrival was perceived: that it originated from outside, and that it was spread especially by soldiers. One of the earliest broadsheet portrayals of pox shows a soldier suffering from the disease (Plate 5.1). It is a Nurnberg broadsheet recalling a prophecy made in 1484 by a doctor, Theodoricus Ulsenius, M.D. of Paris, about a 'scabies epidemic which would rage through the whole world'. The artist is said to be Albrecht Dürer, the artist of the Four Horsemen of the Apocalypse. Through soldiers and other travellers the pox spread at terrifying speed: according to a modern historian of the disease, Claude Quétel, it spread across the whole of Europe within five years, reaching Nuremberg and Strassburg by 1495, Geneva and Paris by 1496, England and Scotland by 1497, Hungary and Russia by 1499.[7] As early as 1506, Albrecht Dürer could write from Venice to a fellow artist back home: 'Give my willing service to our prior. Tell him to pray God for me that I may be protected, and especially from the French sickness, for there is nothing I fear more now and nearly everyone has it. Many men are quite eaten up and die of it.'[8]

At first the disease had no technical name. It was referred to most often in Latin as *morbus Gallicus*, the French disease. More commonly it came to be called 'the great pox', in contrast to the small pocks that came from smallpox, and the Spanish often called it 'bubas', like the bubo of plague. It was, not surprisingly, a French physician, Jacques de Béthencourt, who suggested in 1527 that the disease should be called the 'venereal disease' (*morbus venereus*) rather than the French disease, arguing that it should be named after what was by then seen as its main (though not exclusive) cause, sexual intercourse with a diseased person. Another French physician, Jean Fernel, in 1546 put forward the Latin name *lues venerea*, venereal plague, which was often adopted by medical men.

Plate 5.1 Albrecht Dürer,
Soldier with the pox,
Nurnberg broadsheet,
1496

When the disease first broke out it was fearsome and extraordinarily painful, causing its sufferers to scream with pain all day and, even more so, all night. We shall follow here the account of Ulrich von Hutten, a humanist in the service of the Archbishop of Mainz, who had contracted the disease while a soldier in Italy in 1509 or 1510 aged about 21 or 22, and who suffered grievously from the disease for many years. According to Hutten, the physicians would at first have nothing to do with the disease because it was so horrible. For when it first began:

> it was of such filthiness, that a man would scarcely think this sickness, that now [i.e. in 1510] reigneth, to be of that kind. There were boils, sharp, and standing out, having the similitude and quantity [i.e. size] of acorns, from which came so foul humours and so great stench, that whosoever once smelled it, thought himself to be infect. The colour of these pustules was dark green, and the sight thereof was more grievous unto the patient than the pain itself: and yet their pains were as though they had lain in the fire.[9]

There was considerable variation in the manifestation of symptoms, but the pustules usually started, in males, on the penis.[10] The astrologers predicted that the disease would only last seven years and then disappear, but instead after seven years the disease turned into a somewhat milder form, without the acorn-like pustules or so much stench. But the pain continued to be excruciating. 'If any thing may cause a man to long for death, truly it is the torment of this sickness', Hutten wrote. 'For this pestilence besides all his vexations and torments (which pass far all other) only with his foulness and loathliness is able to make one weary of his life.'[11] Hutten felt driven to the sin of suicide under the pain, and only hesitated when he remembered his Christian duty of manfully suffering great torments and pains for Christ's sake.

The pain was in the joints, but it also came from the running sores all over the body, and from the holes that appeared in the flesh as it putrefied, so that one could see the bone and watch it being eaten away. Plate 5.2 shows a bedside scene in which a man and a woman are being treated for the pox. The green pustules are very evident. A physician inspects the urine of the woman, while a surgeon anoints the pustules of the male patient. According to von Hutten, there were agonising sores in the bladder, the liver and the stomach. Ulrich von Hutten's case of the disease began in his left foot. As it rose up his leg the skin over the shin began to rot in many holes, very painfully, and over these holes 'was a knob so hard that a man would have thought it a bone', exceeding painful. He could hardly stand up because of the pain; the calf and knee were very cold, the thigh consumed

Plate 5.2 Treatment of pox-sufferers, 1498. Anon., from B. Steber, *A Mala Franzos Morbo Gallorum, Praeservatio ac Cura* (Venice, 1498)

Plate 5.3 Infant Jesus sending arrows of disease, 1496. Title-page from J. Grunpeck, *De Pestilentali Scorra, sive Mala de Franzos* (Augsburg, 1496)

and worn away; one buttock virtually withered away. The pain in his left shoulder was so great that he could not raise his arm, and both shoulders were withered. There was a constant voiding sore below his ribs on the right side, and a constant stream from the top of his head, running down his back. If you touched the place where this filthy stream began, it felt as though the skull was fractured. His face was very painful too. In all this litany of pains Hutten, unlike most other writers, did not mention any lesions or pain in his genitals.

Like all diseases of the early modern period, the French pox had a hierarchy of causes. The *primary cause* in most people's view was God punishing sin. The pox was God's punishment: *flagitium Dei*. The infant Christ, on his mother's knee, was portrayed as sending the arrows of disease on to sinners (Plate 5.3). The Emperor Maximilian declared, in an edict published at Worms in 1497, that in sending the French pox God was punishing blasphemy, the taking of God's name in vain. For while famine, earthquakes and plagues have traditionally been God's punishments, Maximilian declared, yet now 'there attacks ferociously that new and most grievous disease of men which they call the French Disease, arisen in our days, unheard of in the memory of mankind'.[12] Hutten started his treatise with the words, 'It hath pleased almighty God', *Visum Deo est*, 'that in our time sicknesses should arise which were unknown to our forefathers'.[13] This view was shared by medical men. In apocalyptic terms the court physician in Ferrara, Corradino Gilino, wrote in 1499, 'We also see that the Supreme Creator, now full of wrath with us for our terrible sins, punishes us with this cruellest of ills which has now spread not only through Italy but across almost the whole of Christendom. Everywhere is the sound of trumpets; everywhere the noise of arms is heard. How many devices of bombardment and machines of war are being made! What unheard-of iron weapons are now constructed to replace stone balls! . . . Let us say, with the Prophet in the sixth psalm, "Lord, do not censure me in your anger nor in your wrath afflict us". This I believe is the cause of this savage plague.'[14] Some theologians claimed the sin in question was *luxuria*, being duly punished by God: 'seeing that the guilty organ [i.e., the penis] is the organ which suffers, the theologians admire that just and equitable maxim, for a like sin a like penance'.[15]

Below this supernatural cause, the second level of cause, through which God expressed His anger, was taken to be the creation of a poison by *natural* events.[16] Typically in an epidemic the poison was perceived as arising from a corruption (or rotting) of the air, which in turn corrupted other things, including humans. 'All do agree', wrote Ulrich von Hutten, 'which is very evident, that through some unwholesome blasts of the air, which were at that time, the lakes, fountains, floods, and also the seas were corrupted, and thereof the earth to receive poison, the pastures to be infected, venomous vapours to come down from the air, which living creatures in drawing their breath received. For this disease was found in other beasts like as in men. The astrologers fetch the cause of this infirmity from the stars, saying that it proceedeth of the conjunctions of Saturn and Mars, which was not long before, and of two eclipses of the sun.'[17] Some astrologers noted that the disease arose under the sign of Scorpio, the sign of the zodiac which dominated the genital area of the human body.[18] Nicolò Leoniceno, professor of medicine at the University of Ferrara, where the disease was the subject of disputes in the medical faculty as to whether it was new or had been known to the Ancients, wrote in 1497 that 'about the time of the breaking out of this new Distemper, there happened a great overflow of waters through all *Italy*, not sparing even *Rome* itself. The *Tiber* so swelled as to become navigable: Such vast showers of rain falling round about the countries that year, that the earth thus polluted with the stagnant water, it was no wonder (a very sultry season especially coming after, and joining in with so much moisture, which in the opinion of Philosophers as well as Physicians, are the parents of putrefaction) such Sickness should arise?'[19] Similarly, according to Leonard Schmaus, writing in 1517, in the summer of 1494 the air had been intemperate, being hot and humid, and there was a quite exceptional flooding of all the waters of the whole of Europe: the air had reached 'that hot and humid condition which gives rise to all putridities'.[20] Thus the climatic conditions which caused the dearth which put an end to Savonarola's apocalyptic reforming mission, were the same ones which gave rise to the apocalyptic disease of the pox.

According to the physicians, the poison thus generated – that is, the venomous vapours – acted on the human body by making one or other of the four 'humours' of the human body (black bile, yellow bile, phlegm and blood) superabundant and acrid, and this sharpness spread to the outer parts of the body, where it burnt and dried the skin and filled it full of scabs; or, if the heaviness of the humour had been increased, then it spread to the joints, where it caused the great pain and swellings. This was the third level of cause, the 'immediate' cause. The general view, and one which was to remain associated with this disease until modern times, was that it was a disease of 'unpure blood', blood which was putrefying.[21] Given this view of how an outbreak of French pox could begin, it was no surprise to contemporaries, at least in the early years of the disease before it was so directly linked with sexual intercourse, to find that monks and other ecclesiastics, right up to the level of bishops, cardinals and even popes (Alexander VI and Julius II), suffered from the disease.

But there was another widely and simultaneously held view of the origin of pox, one again consistent with contemporary medical theory and giving an alternative 'natural' account of its cause. In this understanding, the pox was seen, like many other diseases, as having been produced out of two pre-existing diseases: a man with a 'leprous' (i.e. leprosy-like) disease has intercourse with a woman with 'sores' in her womb. The result is to generate, in the woman's womb, a new disease, the pox. Together the man and the woman made the pox in an orgy of lust, *luxuria*; and this creative event of generating the pox could be repeated by other afflicted couples at other times and places, whenever there was a luxurious diseased sexual encounter. But once it had been generated (either by this mode through diseased sex, or through the corruption of the air), the disease of pox thereafter lurked in the woman, awaiting the approach of an innocent man to attack. 'This thing as touching women', Hutten wrote, 'resteth in their secret places, having in those places little pretty sores full of venomous poison, being very dangerous for those that unknowingly meddle with them. The which sickness gotten by such infected women, is so much the more vehement and grievous, how much they be inwardly polluted and corrupted.'[22] Similarly, Joannes de Vigo, a surgeon writing in the 1510s, wrote that 'This disease is contagious, chiefly if it chance through copulation of a man with an unclean woman.'[23] Such infected women were the most desirous of intercourse, and this theory neatly explained why sex with a prostitute – 'filthy lust' – could so easily lead to the pox for a man.[24]

Thus although the disease could be made naturally in this way by a man and woman together, it was publicly suffered only by men (the relative silence throughout the sixteenth century about women suffering the disease is remarkable). By the 1520s, moreover, the phenomena of babies being born already suffering from the pox, and of the transmission of the pox from wet-nurses through breast-feeding, had been noticed. Woman's role was thus to be the harbourer of the disease and tempter of men. This is of course a replaying of the Fall, where a woman led a man into temptation. However, a parallel tradition also saw woman as the potential cure of the great pox, at least if the woman was a virgin or of chaste life and habit, and tales were told of men being cured either suddenly or gently over time by sexual relations with pure women. An early account of how a pure woman kept her poxy husband from death for many years by intercourse with him (and not catching the disease) is told by the famous humanist Jean Luis Vives, and the veracity of his tale is ensured by the fact that the couple in question were his parents-in-law.[25] This is a striking example of a disease being 'gendered' in its very origin, with quite different roles and values in transmitting the disease and in suffering from it, being ascribed to the two sexes.

As the first cause of this new disease was God's angry punishment of sin, the first act of cure and prevention necessary was to repent and place oneself under divine protection. Since the thirteenth century Mary, mother of Christ, had had a role as a tutelary figure, that of Mary, Mother of Mercy, the 'Misericordia'. The Virgin is portrayed crowned, arms outspread, holding out her cloak under which suppliants kneel, seeking her protection. This image had been familiar against plague since the fourteenth century, when it had been frequently painted on the inside walls of churches. Now it appeared repeatedly in woodcuts in the printed literature about the pox (Plate 5.4). But public repentance and confession of sins did not necessarily bring immediate results. The pious Duke of Ferrara, Ercole I d'Este, scrupulously put into effect in 1496 all the moral and civic reforms that Savonarola called for, to avert the wrath of God from his court, including measures against blasphemy, sodomy, games of chance and prostitution; but all three of his sons had nevertheless caught the pox by 1497 at the carnival in Mantua.[26]

For the treatment of the French pox most physicians could not find anything that looked like guidance in the classical medical writers, Hippocrates and Galen. Hence it is understandable that a pious medical man with a strong sense of the divine origin of the disease could, like court laymen, be put in mind of the agonising attack of 'sore boils from the sole of his foot unto his crown' that God had allowed Satan to impose on His perfect servant, Job, to try him. The Ferrara ducal physician Lodovico Carri advised the Duke's eldest son and heir in 1498 to act like Job had done when God first sent a trial, and to shave his head in order to promote his cure.[27]

With respect to natural cures, however, as the disease evidently affected the skin, the first resort of medical men was usually to the use of mercury, which the Arab physicians had used for skin complaints. Thus the skin was rubbed with mercury-based ointments. But as the new disease was seen as a poison which needed to be expelled, mercury was also taken in another form: the patient inhaled the vapour from a bowl of warm mercury, usually under the direction of a surgeon. The effect was striking. Not only did the

Carmen Dicolon Tetraſtrophon ex ſapphico endeca ſillabo et adonio dimetro F Conradi R C ad clementiſſimā dominā noſtram Mariam ut nos a gallico morbo intactos preſeruet incolumes

Plate 5.4 Mary Misericordia. Anon., from Conrad Reitter, *Mortilogus* (Augsburg, 1508)

patient find his guts were stimulated to expel the poison, but in particular his saliva increased dramatically. After a month of such treatment, however, the patient began to tremble uncontrollably, his teeth began to loosen and fall out, and paralysis sometimes ensued. Hutten recalled that under the mercury treatment 'the disease voided both by the nose and the mouth' and the patients found that 'all their throats, their tongues, the roofs of their mouths, were full of sores, their jaws did swell, their teeth were loosed, and continually there voided [i.e. voided out] the most stinking scum and matter that could be, and whatsoever it ran upon and by it was polluted and infected'.[28] This cure was as bad as the disease, so the victims desperately turned wherever they could, and even accepted treatment from illiterates such as cesspool emptiers who proposed cures based on poisons such as arsenic.

And then in 1517 a miraculous cure was discovered, or so it seemed. It was a piece of wood from Espagnola (Haiti) in the West Indies. It was miraculous because it worked in a way beyond the physicians' understanding of natural operations; and also because it was provided directly out of God's mercy, as sufferers such as von Hutten believed in their joy at discovering its powers for themselves. 'If we ought to give thanks upward unto God, both for good and evil', Hutten asked, 'how much are we bound for the gift of Guaiacum, yea, how much doth the gladness and joy of his benignity towards us pass the sorrow and pain of that infirmity?'[29] In Espagnola, according to the information that people like von Hutten had, all the Indians suffered from the French pox at some time in their lives, just like Europeans all suffer a childhood attack of measles or smallpox, which they usually survive. The remedy they use in Espagnola, which carries them through this disease, is this wood called guaiacum. It is a very dense wood, denser and harder than any previously known; when it is burnt it has a sweet odour and it exudes a resin which dries very hard. The treatment requires the preparation of a decoction: shavings of the wood are soaked in water for a day and a night and then gently cooked until the water reduces to half (Plate 5.5). The scum is kept for anointing the sores. The water, which looks rather muddy, is drunk twice a day at mealtimes. This course of guaiacum drinking is the heart of the cure – 'this wood by itself is sufficient to pluck up this disease by the roots'[30] – but the patient needs to follow a course of treatment, which involves being kept in an overheated room (a 'stew') for up to thirty days, on a much reduced diet, drinking the guaiacum decoction regularly. The effect of the guaiacum is to induce copious sweating in the patient, sweating out the poison little by little: 'the nature of this medicine is to purify and cleanse the sores underneath and under the flesh . . . the nature of this medicine is not to break or pluck away the blood, but by little and little to amend and purify it (in which blood being corrupt, resteth all the force and strength of this disease) and to expel and divide from the body the hurtful humours that are nourishments of this disease, from some [people] in their urine and sweatings, and from other some in their sieges [i.e. stools] . . . by means of which it fetcheth out and voideth marvellous foul filthiness . . . And therefore the physicians say, that the virtue of this medicine is to heat, to dry, and to amend the faults of the blood and of the liver.'[31] It worked for von Hutten, at least at his first use of it, which he celebrated by publishing his book announcing the wonders of the new drug, after which he turned his restored energy towards assisting the Lutheran Reformation.

Plate 5.5 Method of
preparing the blessed
wood (guaiacum), by
Francisco Delicado
(1525)

In the next two decades of great demand for this wood, fortunes were waiting to be made, and the Augsburg banking business of the Fuggers – sellers of papal indulgences to Germany – became even richer on their monopoly of the trade in lignum vitae, the wood of life, also known as the holy wood, the lignum sanctum, and as the wood from the Indies, lignum indicum. Guaiacum was administered by physicians, and came to be used mainly by richer patients; the poor, attended by surgeons and unskilled people, were restricted to using mercury and other poisons.[32] The claims of guaiacum as the specific cure for the French pox were to be challenged later again by mercury. China root and sarsaparilla, used as a sudorific and blood purifier respectively, were introduced in the 1530s, the one from China and the other from the West Indies, and were sometimes used as specifics in the pox where guaiacum was unavailable or unsuccessful. The Emperor Charles V was supposedly cured by China root when guaiacum had brought him no relief.[33]

Was the French pox a new disease, as its early sufferers thought? Certainly no one had seen anything like it before, and attempts even by professors of medicine at universities to trace it in classical medical works were not very successful. The strangest origins were proposed for it. One charlatan even claimed that the disease was a result of cannibalism at the siege of Naples.[34] It was more than 20 years after the first outbreak of the French pox before anyone suggested that the disease had been brought to Europe from abroad, from the New World. This view of its origin rapidly came to be accepted, and by the 1540s it was widely thought that it had been brought to Europe by some of Columbus's returning sailors landing at Barcelona in 1493, who had then joined Charles VIII's army as mercenaries, thus taking the disease to Naples. It was assumed that it was then spread via the prostitutes who always followed the army, thus in a short time reaching all classes of society. The question of the origin of the disease has been raised again in the early twentieth century, and it continues to be a question of controversy among modern syphilologists and historians of medicine whether the disease was imported or whether it was an old European disease which just assumed an exceptionally virulent form in the 1490s. Despite the passion with which the argument is still conducted, the evidence is inconclusive for either view. The view that the disease was one native to the West Indies, and which was brought to a Europe which had never experienced it before, came to be promoted hand in hand with the guaiacum cure, itself brought from the West Indies. The miracle wood cure was discovered and promoted in Europe only from 1516, and may have derived from a mission sent to the Indies by Matthew Lang, Cardinal of Gurk (Kärnten in Austria) and Bishop Coadjutor of Salzburg, and himself a sufferer from the disease. At least three publications (in addition to von Hutten's personal account of 1519) were produced quickly thereafter, all in and around Augsburg. Augsburg, in addition to being the city of the Fugger banking family, who gained the monopoly on the sale of guaiacum, was also a great publishing centre. First was published in 1517 an anonymous work whose title could be rendered in English as 'A Recipe for Using a Wood for the French Disease and other running open Sores, translated from Spanish into German'.[35] A couple of weeks later, again in Augsburg, the physician Leonard Schmaus issued a little work on the French disease 'and its newly-discovered cure with Indian wood'.[36] Again in 1517, the imperial physician Nicolaus Pol wrote in Latin (probably in Innsbruck) a tract 'On the Method of Healing with that Indian Wood called Guaiac the Bodies of Germans who have Contracted the French Disease'.[37] The person who put forward the claim that the pox originated in the West Indies was Gonzalo Fernandez de Oviedo y Valdés, who wrote about it in his work on the natural history of the Indies, published in 1526 and 1535. 'Such is the divine mercy', Oviedo wrote, 'that wherever it permits us to be afflicted for our sins, it places a remedy equal to our afflictions.'[38] It was recognised in classical medical theory, that for diseases local to a particular region God often placed the cure next to the disease. But the effect of the making of the myth of the origin of guaiacum in Espagnola (Haiti), where the entire population supposedly traditionally suffered from the disease, encouraged a stereotypical view of the American Indian as lascivious and immoral, which assisted the Christian conscience when attacking the Indians. The disease was also blamed by some on the Jews: it was claimed that leprosy, to which the Jews were traditionally liable, as the Bible sup-posedly revealed, had turned into a new disease in the course of the Diaspora created by Ferdinand and Isabella's expulsion of the Jews from Spain in 1492.[39]

The period around 1520, when guaiacum became the miracle cure, was when the French pox first came to be characterised as a divine punishment primarily for personal (as opposed to communal) sin, and as usually being acquired from illicit sexual intercourse. The cycle from sin to cure is illus-trated in Plate 5.6, where the patient in bed is reminded by a picture of the sin which started his illness: on the right the attendants cut and prepare the wood. The period around 1520 was also the period when pox was recog-nised as a disease where the sins of the parents were visited on the children,

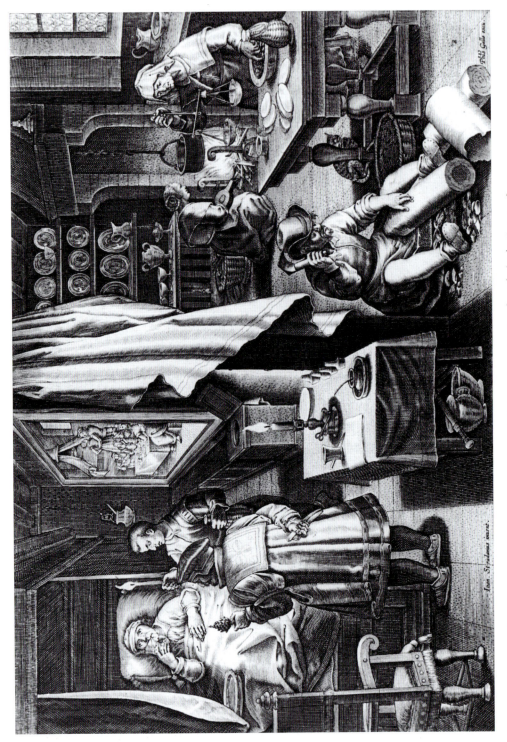

Plate 5.6 Sufferer from the pox, 1570s. Copperplate published in 1570 by Jean Galle, after a design by Hans van Straet

for children of infected parents could be born with the disease, or acquire it through the milk of infected wet-nurses. Generations were thus cursed by the ravages of the pox, the first disease which was known to be hereditary.

It is possibly only when the disease was recognised as hereditary that a precise historical and geographical origin was sought for it. In the two views of the origin of the disease which we have discussed, arising from poisoned air, or from a combination of two other diseases in a diseased sexual encounter, the pox could arise anew whenever conditions were appropriate. A precise and localised origin for pox, whether located in the Americas or in ancient Europe, was only required when it was seen to be a persistent disease which was acquired only by transmission from a person who already had the pox.

The mortality of pox was nowhere as great as its social impact: after the first terrifying epidemic outbreak of the disease, pox became familiar as a constant presence in society, and the bodily lesions and stinking breath typical of it became commonplace. It is possible also that the disease changed its nature after its first outbreak in 'virgin soil' (as the epidemiologists call a population hitherto not exposed to a particular infectious disease), and as the population gained some resistance to it, so the disease itself may have lost its initial high mortality.[40] But while it did not kill significantly, it certainly would have contributed to weakening the population as a whole. Doctors and surgeons, and quacks of all kinds continued to proclaim new treatments for it, and it continued to be the disease which claimed most public attention. It continued also to be thought of as related to sin and licentiousness, and it has been claimed that in some of the plays of Shakespeare the image of the pox represents individual, social and political corruption and decay.[41]

As the link between having sexual intercourse with an infected person and getting the pox became more firmly recognised, so the individual increasingly came to be seen as having a responsibility to avoid getting and spreading the pox. As with early cases of AIDS in the late twentieth century, there were stories that some sufferers were motivated by revenge in seeking to infect as many people as possible. In 1529 Erasmus wrote that 'we observe that this disease is accompanied by a mortal hatred, so that whoever is in its clutches takes pleasure in infecting as many others as possible, even though doing so is no help to him'.[42] Precautions could, however, be taken, and by the mid-sixteenth century the more pox-aware physicians were advising men to wash their genitals after sex, and to keep the penis wrapped in a little linen cap soaked in various medicaments.[43]

In 1530 a practitioner at Verona, who had been educated in medicine at the celebrated medical university of Padua, gave this disease a poetical, classical-style name, that he coined himself, which has become the name by which we know it today: syphilis. The account of the disease that Girolamo Fracastoro (Hieronymus Fracastorius) gave, he chose to write in the form of a Latin poem, 'Syphilis, or the French disease' (*Syphilis, sive Morbus Gallicus*).[44] He began to write it while living in the country in about 1510, driven there by the plague and it filled his leisure hours for several years. The poem opened by asking 'what seeds conveyed this strange disease, unknown of any through long centuries?' 'The seat of the evil must exist in the air itself . . . The air, indeed, is the Father of all things and the Author of their being. Often, too, it brings grievous maladies to mortals; born in many ways, it starts corruption in the tender body, easily receiving the taint and passing it on' (1.123–9). Conjunctions of planets corrupt the air, leading to new diseases.

Initially Fracastoro's poem had dealt only with the nature of the pox (book 1), and the regimen and therapeutics to be adopted (book 2). Mercury he dealt with at length since 'A wondrous virtue in that Mineral lies' (2.271) in the cure of the pox, and he gave the discovery of mercury a suitably mythical origin. Cardinal Bembo, to whom the poem was to be dedicated, suggested in 1525 that Fracastoro add something on the new cure by guaiacum, so Fracastoro added a third 'book' to the poem:

> But now the verdant Blessings that belong
> To new discover'd Worlds [i.e. America] demand our Song.
> The sacred Tree must now our Muse employ,
> That only could this raging Plague destroy. (3.4–6)

The poet describes how

> This Plant the Natives conscious of its use
> Adore, and with religious Care produce;
> On ev'ry Hill, in ev'ry Vale 'tis found,
> And held the greatest Blessing of the ground
> Against this Pest that always Rages there,
> From Skies infected and polluted Air. (3.47–52)

The natives prepare the bark and treat themselves with it: and as they sweat,

> All Parts (o prodigy!) grow sound within,
> Nor any Filth remains upon the Skin;
> Fresh youth in ev'ry Limb, fresh vigour's found,
> And now the Moon has run her monthly Round. (3.85–6)

What gods taught the natives these practices? Here Fracastorius introduces his mythical story, couched in terms of classical characters, about a shepherd called Syphilis. A fleet of ships (clearly a mythologised version of the expedition of Columbus) reaches a western land where the voyagers witness the natives conducting a religious ceremony to cleanse a large crowd of diseased people of their own race:

> And now within the sacred Vale were set
> Each Sex, and all degrees of Age were seen,
> But plac'd without distinction on the Green;
> Yet from the Infant to the grizled Head,
> A cloud of Grief o'er ev'ry Face was spread,
> All languish'd with the same obscene Disease,
> And years, not Strength distinguished the Degrees;
> Dire flames upon their Vitals fed within,
> While Sores and crusted Filth prophan'd their Skin. (3.236–9)

Animals are sacrificed and a shepherd character stands by the altar where he is ritually drenched with bull's blood. The natives tell the voyagers that their ancestors had ceased to worship the gods and had been punished by an earthquake and

> In that dire Season this Disease was bred,
> That thus o'er all our tortur'd Limbs is spread:
> Most universal from its Birth it grew,
> And none have since escap'd or very few. (3. 282–4)

Syphilis, a shepherd who had complained to the sun, the chief of the gods, that the sun's pitiless heat showed no regard for humans or animals, in his anger had begun the cult of the mortal king, raising altars to him. Thus, for his impiety, Syphilis was the first to be punished with this disease:

> And first th' offending Syphilis was griev'd,
> Who rais'd forbidden Altars on the Hill,
> And Victims bloud with impious Hands did spill;
> He first wore Buboes dreadfull to the sight,
> First felt strange Pains and sleepless passed the Night. (3.327–30)

As the disease spread amongst the populace, they sought the advice of the oracle, the Nymph Ammerice, who urged the people to annual sacrifice and to look for the cure of the disease in the green woods. Marvellously, this sacred tree straightway began to put forth green leaves:

> 'Tis sacred Truth –
> These Groves that spread so wide and look so green
> Within this Isle, till then, were never seen,

> But now before their Eyes the Plants were found
> To spring, and in an instant Shade the ground. (3.359–60)

The ritual sacrifice of Syphilis was substituted by sacrificing a bull and drenching a shepherd with its blood.

But alas, as the natives were telling the voyagers this tale, some of the voyagers' ships had returned to Europe, where the disease was suddenly found to be raging:

> Till now the Ships sent back to Europes shore,
> Return and bring prodigious Tidings o'er.
> That this Disease did now through Europe rage,
> Nor any Med'cine found that cou'd assuage. (3.382–6)

Some of the sailors, who had contracted the disease even as they returned from Europe to this mythical America, were treated in the native way and recovered. It was obvious that this wood had to be taken to Europe:

> ... not forgetful of their Country's good,
> They freight their largest Ships with this rich Wood,
> To try if in our Climate it would be
> Of equal use, for the same Malady. (3.396–9)

This wonderful tree must be celebrated:

> Hail heav'n-born Plant whose Rival ne'er was seen
> Whose Virtues like thy Leaves are ever green;
> Hope of Mankind and Comfort of their Eyes,
> Of new discover'd Worlds the richest Prize.
> Yet if my Streins have any force, thy Name
> Shall flourish here, and Europe sing thy Fame. (3.405–7; 410–13)

Fracastoro's poem was greatly admired in its time as a masterly piece of Latin verse, a Renaissance poem beautifully modelled on the *Georgics* and *Aeneid* of Virgil.[45] However, the suitability of the name 'syphilis' for the disease did not so impress Fracastoro's contemporaries, and it was not generally adopted as the technical name for the disease until the nineteenth century.[46] The use of the vehicle of Latin verse to write polished hexameters about a grisly disease appealed to Renaissance literary taste in a way it no longer does. After all, Apollo was the god of poetry as well as of healing. Indeed, Fracastoro's was not even the first but the fourth account of the disease to be published in poetic form.[47] Although deliberately distanced from immediate sixteenth-century concerns by its classical format, Fracastoro's account nevertheless portrays the disease as imposed as punishment by the gods for irreligion, and shows the use of guaiacum as a ritual purification in a religious setting, part of an expiation for the sins of the people, and in these ways it echoes the experience of his contemporaries who saw the disease as punishment for sin, and the cure as given by a forgiving God. Fracastoro's account does not, however, suggest that he thought the disease was brought to Europe from America by Columbus's sailors: for Fracastoro the European outbreak was purely coincidental with the Europeans' discovery of the American cure.[48]

For pox, at the beginning, when it first broke out, all forms of social mixing were deemed to be very dangerous. At Paris the first regulations ordering the infected to be confined to their own homes or, if poor, to a special rented house in the suburb of St Germain, were made by the Parlement in March 1496: 'Whereas there are many sick persons in this city of *Paris* infected with a Disease called the *Great Pox*, which for these two years past has spread very much in this Kingdom, as well at *Paris* as in other places, so that there is cause to fear lest its violence should increase now in the Spring season, it is thought proper to make some provision against it.' Strangers had to leave Paris on pain of death if they returned before they were fully cured. Guards of the infected poor in the rented house were ordered that 'they suffer none of the infected to walk abroad, converse or hold any communication in the City; and that if any such be met with in their walks, that they immediately cast them out of the city, or throw them into prison to be corporally punished'. An edict of the Provost of Paris issued in January 1498 reinforced these regulations: strangers affected with the pox, both men and women, were to return to their homes 'under pain of being thrown into the river, in case they are ever hereafter found therein'.[49] In other places pox victims were treated much more kindly and in all significant towns certain hospitals, or certain rooms in the common hospitals, were set apart for those suffering from the pox.

General hospitals had been in existence since the twelfth century, which took in the poor, the aged and the sick. They were built round individual charity, for Christ had said in Matthew 25 that the only way to heaven for the rich was to support those in need: 'I was a stranger and you took me in: naked, and ye clothed me: I was sick, and ye visited me'. The poor, sick and needy represented Christ Himself, for Christ had said, in the same place: 'Inasmuch as ye have done it unto the least of these my brethren, ye have done it unto me'. In carrying out these works of mercy, donors had built hospitals large and small, usually giving land whose rent income provided long-term support. Treatment and food were free for those in need. Care was usually provided by a religious order (either professed or lay) whose members dedicated themselves to nursing the sick and looking after their spiritual welfare. These institutions were at the same time both religious in nature and were also meeting social needs. Many large towns in France had their Hôtel Dieu, with that in Paris being the largest of all, offering beds to hundreds of sick, poor and needy. But except for leprosy houses (lazarettos), demand for which was decreasing in this period as leprosy became less common, none of these institutions catered exclusively for the sick, or just for one class of disease. The arrival of the pox thus led to the creation of new kinds of hospital, dedicated just to the sufferers from this one disease, where treatment could be offered (unlike in lazarettos which had been institutions simply to segregate the leprous or plague victims).

In German lands a new hospital of this kind was usually called a *Blatternhaus* ('Pox-house'), or more commonly a *Holzhaus* ('Wood-house'), named after the guaiacum wood which was used for treatment in them. Some 20 of these have been traced in German-speaking areas, founded between 1497 and 1540, either as new foundations, or as converted leper houses, or as specialised wards of general hospitals.[50] There were pox hospitals by 1540 in Erfurt, Prague, Hamburg, Strassburg, Frankfurt, Augsburg, Zurich, Bern, Dresden and other towns. But because the pox was such a disgusting disease in contemporary eyes, and those suffering from it (especially the poor) were shunned, donors did not voluntarily come forward to found these new hospitals. Instead, it was usually the municipal authority in Northern Europe who had to establish and maintain them, to meet this sudden, urgent and new social need. These hospitals had separate wards for men and women, and usually offered both the mercury and the guaiacum treatments, under the care of a barber-surgeon. The Fugger family themselves, merchants and monopolists of guaiacum, founded a famous little hospital complex of some 50 dwellings, at Augsburg in 1519, which came to be called the *Fuggerei*, and which included a *Holzhaus* for treatment of the pox, which could accommodate 18 patients.[51] Most of the German pox hospitals were small, with about a dozen beds. The largest of them was the Augsburg one, which by 1629 had 122 beds. With regard to the curative regime, the report of the governor of the Strasbourg *Blatternhaus* claimed in 1544 that

> We have in the past year [15]44 accommodated in the hospital [*bloterhus*] 118 persons, not including servants, pensioners and workers, among them 54 men and 64 females. Among [the patients of] both sexes are 11 who stayed during the whole year, the majority half a year or more, some three months, a few twenty

weeks and more. Even fewer are those who did not stay longer than 6, 8 or 10 weeks.

It has been estimated that about one in four of the patients in these hospitals left feet first. So they could certainly be seen by sufferers as offering positive regimes of treatment.

In the south of Europe the foundation of new hospitals for pox sufferers was more closely linked to the (Catholic) Church than in the north. In Italy the new hospitals for those suffering from the pox usually had the ominous title of *Incurabili*, the Incurables.[52] In Bologna, Ferrara, Genoa, Rome, Naples, Florence, Brescia, Venice and Padua, hospitals were founded in the period from the 1490s to the 1520s, open to those rejected by the traditional hospitals. They were frequently dedicated to the curious historical figure of St Job, the Old Testament sorely tested servant of God, but given an honorary sainthood in the Christian tradition. A confraternity dedicated to St Job had been established in Ferrara as early as 1499, which planned to establish a hospital to treat those affected with the French disease.[53] The founding of the pox hospitals in Italy was often associated with the Company of Divine Love, a lay religious movement begun in the 1490s in Genoa, whose members dedicated themselves to exercising Christian love on their fellow men, to prayer, and to flagellating themselves in private as penance for their own sins. The Company of Divine Love had nobility and high ecclesiastics in its membership, who thus became involved personally and financially in supporting the pox hospitals. The *Incurabili* hospitals came to receive special attention also from other reforming associations who were in the sixteenth century dedicated to a renewed Catholic Christian mission, including the Jesuits, the Friars Capuchin (Cappuccini), and the Ministri degli Infirmi. In time such orders also tried to reform prostitutes, who were deemed to be a main means of transmission of the disease. The Italian pox hospitals varied in size, with one of the largest being that of Naples, which had 600 patients by 1535. The hospital at Rome, the San Giacomo, received over 1,400 males and over 330 females in 1569, with even higher admission figures later in the century.

In some towns, such as in the Milan Spedale Maggiore, and in Vicenza, Verona, Orvieto and elsewhere, a ward of an existing hospital was set aside for sufferers from the pox. In Rome the pope himself, Leo X, in 1515 issued a bull authorising the change of use of an old hospital for pox patients. The bull spoke of the poor suffering from the disease who flocked to Rome 'in such great numbers that they cannot gain entrance without difficulty to the hospitals of the city because of the multitude of such people and they give offence to the sight and sense of smell. Thus the said poor people, who are afflicted with an incurable disease, are obliged for the whole day to look for food through the city, sometimes dragging themselves along on little trolleys and vehicles, giving offence to themselves and blocking the way of those whom they encounter.'[54]

SIEGE DISEASE

While pox took the greatest share of public fear and attention, it was far from being the only new epidemic disease visited on Europe in this period. The new modes of warfare brought with them their own diseases, thus linking the threat from two of the Horsemen of the Apocalypse.[55] As an army settled in to besiege a town, its soldiers often began to suffer 'camp fever', a fever sometimes called 'typhus', a Greek term associated with the stupor that came with this fever, for stupor with extraordinary headache was one of its main characteristics, together with red pustules (*petechiae*) resembling flea bites or lentils all over the trunk of the body and the limbs. Not just the besieger, but also the besieged suffered from this new disease, which the besieged would sometimes call 'famine fever' as their food supplies ran out. Its association with armies is indicated by its alternative sixteenth-century names: Hungarian disease, Swedish disease, and many others. It killed many more soldiers than the fighting ever did, and vastly more than the pox. It was a fever which killed by the thousand.

The classic description of the disease of typhus comes from the Verona physician Girolamo Fracastoro, in 1546, who wrote that

> this disease invades so very gently that the sick are hardly willing to call in a doctor . . . soon, however, the symptoms of malignant fever began to show themselves. For though, according to the nature of fevers of this sort, a moderate heat was felt, nevertheless a sort of internal disturbance became obvious, then prostration of the whole body, and a lassitude such as follows overexertion; the patient could only lie flat on his back, the head became heavy, the senses dulled, and in the majority of cases after the fourth or seventh day, the mind would wander . . . About the fourth or seventh day red, or often purplish-red spots broke out on the arms, back and chest, looking like flea-bites, though they were often larger and in the shape of lentils, whence arose the name of the fever ['lenticulas'].[56]

Those affected lost all capacity to help themselves and lay prostrate until death or, more rarely, recovery occurred.

Another outbreak of this or another similar disease, also called 'Hungarian disease' (Pannonica), attacked the Christian armies defending

Europe against the Turks in the 1560s and again repeatedly in the 1590s. This 'dry death' (*sicca mors*) killed more soldiers than the attacks of the enemy did. It was a disease endemic to the region ('proper to the Hungarian soil'), and no one in the army was familiar with the local conditions. Hence the soldiers were confronted with air in a condition they were not accustomed to, together with unusual food and drink, and these together brought on the disease. It was worst in June, July and August. As reported by Tobias Corberus, an army surgeon in the 1590s, it was a deadly langour, with severe stomach upset:

> In itself it is a langour rather than a disease, since at the beginning it does not immediately disturb the usual actions of life, but introducing little by little an incapacity to the functions, it shows its danger only after the person is already prostrate and confined to his bed all day. Then, coming from elsewhere, as it were, as if it had overrun the defences, it turns out the victor, leading him to death.[57]

It had apparently appeared first in 1489–90 during the wars in Granada between Ferdinand and Isabella and the Moors.[58] The Italian physician Fracastoro, writing in 1546, believed it had first appeared in Italy in 1505 and 1528, but that in Cyprus and other places it had been known a long time. Camp fever appears to have struck the French forces besieging the army of Charles V in Naples in 1528, forcing them to withdraw.[59] The wars with the Turks in the 1490s, and then again in the 1520s to the 1550s in particular saw severe outbreaks of the 'Hungarian disease' among the troops. According to Hans Zinsser, the historian of typhus:

> One of the earliest really decisive typhus epidemics was that which dispersed the army of Maximilian II of Germany, who was preparing with 80,000 men to face the Sultan Soliman in Hungary. In the camp at Komorn, in 1566, a disease broke out which was undoubtedly typhus. It was so violent and deadly that the campaign against the Turks was given up . . . The Thirty Years War was in all its phases dominated by deadly epidemics . . . [In one particularly crucial episode] in 1632 Gustavus Adolphus and Wallenstein faced each other before Nuremberg, which was the goal of both armies. Typhus and scurvy killed 18,000 soldiers, whereupon both the opposing forces marched away in the hope of escaping the further ravages of the pestilence.[60]

An outbreak of this disease or something similar in Oberammergau in Bavaria in 1631 led to an unusual outcome. Swedish troops had been devastating the country for a long time, and after months of an outbreak of 'wild headache', the council of the Catholic village made a vow to God as an act of penance and as a petition for deliverance that if God relieved them, they would produce a Passion Play every tenth year. The vow was made on behalf of themselves and their descendants. God evidently heard and honoured the vow, since afterwards no one died of the disease. The play is still performed today.

Camp fever was perceived as new. As one author later observed of the recentness of its appearance: 'of old great Armies were led up and down in *Europe, Asia,* and *Africk,* without any notable Contagion, and their Musters were commonly not much diminished; but now, no sooner is a Siege begun, but immediately the Besieged die within, and the Besiegers also without, by some strange popular Pest; and when the Siege is over, hardly a Company, or Troop, marches forth, but there follow Wagons laden with sick men'. This same author suggested that this new contagion resulted from a mixing of fever with the lurking ferments of the pox. This is similar to one supposed origin of pox itself, as a mixture of two pre-existing diseases. 'Immediately the Fever associates it self with the Venomous reliques (or *lurking Ferments*) of that *French Lues,* from which it borroweth Poisons, which produce that Fever called the Malignant and Camp-Fever; after which, the Contagion propagates it self, even upon such persons as are free from the said French Lues; and having the Fever as it were for its Father, and the *Lues* for its Mother, the new-born Monster being a Mongrel begotten of two distinct Diseases, starts up a Third Thing different from both its Parents.'[61]

THE ENGLISH SWEAT

Amongst the other numerous and frequent epidemics which struck Europe throughout this period, there was one which originated in England and seemed to limit its attacks mostly to English people, the 'English sweating sickness' or the 'English sweat'. Breaking out first in September 1485, just before the battle of Bosworth, among the troops of the future Henry VII in Wales, it spread to London and then over the whole kingdom, killing the rich and powerful as readily as the poor and weak, and with an unusual pattern of striking particularly at well-nourished men in the prime of life. It reappeared in epidemic form in 1506 in London, in 1517 when it spread from London to the rest of the country, in 1528–9 again beginning in London and spreading to the whole country, and on this occasion it appeared also in Germany, Denmark, Norway and Sweden, the Netherlands and Vienna. The Burgomaster of Leiden in 1530 reported that 'Now that it is hard to come by food in the town, there is great poverty and terrible hunger. The wretched people are suffering all the time and every day someone says, "O dear God, do not pass over us with our 'hot sickness' but give us quick release, for we would rather die than go on living".'[62]

Then it appeared for the last time in 1551, in England, when it began at Shrewsbury and proceeded into Wales and then to Winchester, Coventry, Oxford and other towns in the south to London, and from there to the towns of the east and north of England. It reached Calais (an English territory) and Antwerp, but only the English people living there seem to have been affected. After these five outbreaks it has never reappeared.[63] John Caius, a Padua-trained physician then practising in London and in the royal court, who witnessed the 1551 outbreak, wrote a book about it in 1552, *A Boke or Counseill against the Disease commonly called the Sweat or Sweatyng Sicknesse.*[64] 'The sweat' was particularly fearsome because it attacked and killed within one day. Caius wrote of it that for its 'sudden sharpness and unwonted cruellness [it] passed the pestilence' (p. 9), since unlike plague it was so sudden. This disease 'immediately killed some in opening their windows, some in playing with children in their street doors, some in one hour, many in two it destroyed, and at the longest them that merrily dined, it gave a sorrowful supper. As it found them so it took them, some in sleep, some in wake, some in mirth, some in care, some in fasting and some full, some busy and some idle, and in one house sometime three sometime five, sometime seven and sometime eight, sometime more, sometime all, of the which, if half in every town escaped, it was thought great favour' (p. 10). The disease was a fever, with pain in the back and limbs, the liver and the stomach, with pain and madness in the head, and 'passion of the heart'. Flushing and windiness were followed by extreme drowsiness. Sweating was profuse, thick and with a vile smell, which even the decorous Caius called an 'ungentle savour or smell' (p. 17). Its mortality was very high: virtually everyone who suffered the disease died from it, and within a day. Holinshed's *Chronicle* records of Henry VII's soldiers that 'suddenly a deadly burning sweat so assailed their bodies and distempered their blood with a most ardent heat, that scarce one amongst an hundred that sickened did escape with life; for all in manner as soon as the sweat took them, or within a short time after, yielded the ghost'.[65]

Caius believed the disease to have a double cause. First arose an infection in the air, coming from evil mists and exhalations drawn out of the ground by the heat of the sun. In 1551, Caius recalled, a mist in the region where the disease began 'was seen [to] fly from town to town, with such a stink in mornings and evenings, that men could scarcely abide it' (p. 14). The second cause was the impure spirits in people's bodies, which had been corrupted by repletion, that is by overeating of the wrong foods. 'Repletion I call here', Caius wrote, 'abundance of humours evil and malicious, from long time little by little gathered by evil diet, remaining in the body, coming either by too much meat [= food], or by evil meat in quality, as infected fruits, meats of evil juice or nutriment, or both jointly. To such spirits, when the air infective cometh consonant, then be they distempered, corrupted, sore handled and oppressed, then nature is forced, and the disease [is] engendered' (p. 15). This double causation explained why the disease was unique to the local conditions and way of life of the English, and why it struck the well-nourished middle-aged man as much as the poor man. Excess of bad food or (in the case of the poor) of ale, laid up evil humours in the body, 'good sweating stuff' (p. 17) as Caius called it. Caius railed against 'the intemperance or excessive diet of England' (p. 21), urging the adoption of a moderate diet and temperance. Caius concluded his little book by saying, 'If other causes there be supernatural, them I leave to the divines to search, and the diseases thereof to cure', as a matter outside his competence as a physician (p. 36).

PLAGUE

Among the innumerable epidemics of the period, a major problem continued to be the most feared of all diseases, the disease to which other epidemics were often compared in order to convey their horribleness: plague. It was regularly represented as an arrow sent from God (Plate 5.7). The years 1348–9 had witnessed the pandemic of plague now known as the 'Black Death', which killed probably a third of the population of Europe. While never again occurring on that scale, plague nevertheless continued to break out in epidemic form repeatedly, and it is, unfortunately, safe to assume that in every year between 1494 and 1649 plague was killing its thousands and its tens of thousands suddenly and horribly somewhere in Europe. The modern historian of plague, Jean-Noël Biraben, has written that from 1348 to 1670 'the plague raged in Europe every year, sometimes across vast regions, sometimes only in a few localities, but without omitting a single annual link in this long and mournful chain'.[66] It was not to be until 1665 in England and 1720 in Marseilles, that plague would make its last epidemic appearance in Europe.[67]

In the period from 1494 to 1648 with which we are concerned here, plague broke out on 17 occasions on a scale which reached across virtually the whole of Europe; this averages about once every nine years. The very

Plate 5.7   The plague.
Painting on wood (1510)

worst of these Europe-wide outbreaks were in the years 1522, 1564, 1580, 1586, 1599, 1604, 1625, 1630 and 1636.[68] In a world where life expectancy was about 35 years, this meant that a Europe-wide outbreak occurred in the lifetime of most people.

But in addition to these very large trans-regional outbreaks, every locality experienced its own pattern of frequent outbreaks. In the Dutch cities, for instance, during the period 1493–1649 plagues broke out with great frequency[69] (Table 5.1). In Amsterdam there were 24 outbreaks, in Leiden 27, in Rotterdam 20, in Dordrecht 18. Sometimes God let the plague visit three or four years in a row, as in Amsterdam in the years 1557, 1558 and 1559, again in 1601, 1602 and 1603, again in 1616, 1617 and 1618, and yet again in 1623, 1624, 1625 and 1626. Sometimes, by contrast, God spared a city for over two decades at a time, as Amsterdam was spared between 1493 and 1522, and again between 1575 and 1599. Plate 5.8, shows God sparing the city of Lyons. The mortality in a town like Amsterdam was high: in the years of the worst outbreaks of the epidemic, such as 1624 and 1636, it has been

Table 5.1 Outbreaks of plague in Dutch towns, 1450–1668

Place	Years
Amsterdam	1469, 1471, 1483, 1493, 1522, 1534, 1550, 1554, 1557, 1558, 1559, 1573, 1574, 1599, 1601, 1602, 1603, 1616, 1617, 1618, 1623, 1624, 1625, 1626, 1629, 1635, 1636, 1652, 1653, 1654, 1655, 1656, 1657, 1663, 1664, 1665, 1666 (37 years).
Leiden	1483, 1508, 1509, 1515, 1517, 1518, 1519, 1524, 1525, 1526, 1538, 1556, 1557, 1567, 1568, 1572, 1573, 1574, 1599, 1602, 1603, 1604, 1605, 1617, 1624, 1634, 1635, 1636, 1652, 1653, 1654, 1655, 1664, 1666 (34 years).
Rotterdam	1467, 1468, 1469, 1557, 1573, 1574, 1593, 1594, 1595, 1596, 1598, 1601, 1602, 1603, 1604, 1618, 1624, 1625, 1626, 1634, 1635, 1636, 1637, 1655, 1656, 1657, 1660, 1664, 1665, 1666 (30 years).
Dordrecht	1450, 1452, 1458, 1469, 1482, 1484, 1509, 1530, 1564, 1574, 1575, 1579, 1584, 1587, 1599, 1600, 1602, 1603, 1604, 1618, 1623, 1635, 1636, 1637, 1655, 1656, 1657, 1664, 1665 (29 years)
Gouda	1480, 1494, 1509, 1513, 1518, 1521, 1527, 1574, 1588, 1593, 1600, 1602, 1603, 1616, 1617, 1624, 1625, 1629, 1635, 1636, 1637, 1655, 1657, 1663, 1664, 1665, 1666, 1668 (28 years).
Gorinchem	1481, 1489, 1502, 1519, 1523, 1526, 1555, 1568, 1583, 1599, 1600, 1602, 1603, 1606, 1635, 1636, 1637, 1652, 1653, 1655, 1664, 1665, 1666, 1667 (24 years).
Hoom	1493, 1509, 1515, 1528, 1558, 1562, 1567, 1575, 1577, 1580, 1586, 1590, 1599, 1600, 1601, 1602, 1603, 1624, 1635, 1652, 1656, 1663, 1664, 1665 (24 years).
Schiedam	1518, 1519, 1526, 1537, 1558, 1571, 1594, 1599, 1602, 1603, 1625, 1633, 1634, 1635, 1636, 1652, 1653, 1654, 1664, 1666 (20 years).
Haarlem	1493, 1509, 1516, 1519, 1525, 1526, 1531, 1557, 1572, 1573, 1574, 1581, 1635, 1636, 1637, 1655, 1664 (17 years).
Delft	1537, 1557, 1558, 1567, 1573, 1574, 1594, 1601, 1624, 1625, 1627, 1635, 1636, 1655, 1662, 1664 (16 years).
Alkmaar	1599, 1602, 1604, 1624, 1635, 1636, 1650, 1656, 1657 (9 years).
The Hague	1513, 1574, 1635, 1654, 1655, 1656, 1661, 1663, 1664 (9 years).
Heusden	1603, 1604, 1624, 1625, 1634, 1635, 1636, 1637, 1664 (9 years).
Brielle	1538, 1557, 1573, 1604, 1664 (5 years).
Noorderkwaiter	1624, 1625, 1655, 1656 (4 years).
Oudewater	1572, 1573, 1574, 1575 (4 years).
Geertruidenberg	1603, 1604, 1605 (3 years).
Vlaardingen	1602, 1665, 1666 (3 years).
Delfshaven	1557, 1558 (2 years).
Egmond	1516, 1605 (2 years).
Het Gooi	1596, 1598 (2 years).
Den Helder/Huisduinen	1604, 1605 (2 years).
Koedijk	1602, 1604 (2 years).
Langedijk	1602, 1604 (2 years).
Naarden	1655, 1656 (2 years).
St. Pancras	1602, 1604 (2 years).

Source: From Leo Noordegraaf and Gerrit Valk, *De Gave Gods: De Pest in Holland vanaf de late Middeleeuwen*, 1988.

Plate 5.8 The city of
Lyons preserved from
the plague

calculated that over one in ten of the city's population died from the
disease: the population was literally decimated. Even in a year like 1635,
one of the least severe outbreaks, when only about one in 16 of the population died, the social and emotional impact of plague would have been enormous.

In a range of 14 towns spread across England that he studied for the
impact of plague, Paul Slack concluded that for the period after 1538
'plague crises occurred on average one year in every sixteen'[70] (Tables 5.2
and 5.3). Slack has also shown that 'plague was sufficiently common for
most communities, villages as well as towns, to expect one epidemic in the
course of a century and count themselves fortunate if they had no more.'
But 'the risks were greater and more real in the towns . . . Plague was thus
an inevitable hazard in urban centres . . . It was also in the largest centres of

Table 5.2 Epidemic years in fourteen English towns, 1485–1580

		P?	P+	P	P	P	P	P	P	P	P	P
London	(1485)	1498–1500 +1504	1513+ 1518	1521	(1535–6)	1543	(1548)	1558	1563	(1569–70)	(1574–5)	1578–9
Reading					1537	1543–4		1558	1564			
Salisbury						1546		1558	1563–4	(1570–1)		1579–80
Bristol					1535	1544–5	1551–2	1557–8	1565	1570	1575	
Exeter		1503–4			1537	1546–7		1557–8	(1563–5)	1570		
Worcester		1502		1528		1545	1553	1558	(1563–4)			
Shrewsbury					1536–7		(1551)				1575–6	
Chester		1506	1518				(1551)	1558			1574	
Norwich	(1485)	1500+ 1503–4	1513–14	1520		1544–5	1554–5	1557–9				1579–80
Leicester								1559	(1564)			
Lincoln						1546	(1550–1)	(1557–8)				
Hull					1537			1558–9				
York	(1485–6) +1493	1501+ 1505–6		(1521)	1538–41		1550–2				1575–6	
Newcastle						1544–5				1570–1	1576	1579

Notes:

P? = presumed plague

P+ = plague and other diseases

Source: From P. Slack, The Impact of Plague in Tudor and Stuart England, 1985.

Table 5.3 Epidemic years in fourteen English towns, 1581–1666

	p	p	p	p	p	p	p	p	p	p+	p	p
London	1582	1592–3	(1597)	1603+ (1606–10)		(1623–4)	1625	(1630)	1636	1641+ (1646–7)	(1661)	1665–6
Reading			1596–7	1606–8			(1625)	1638–40	1646–7			(1665)
Salisbury			1596–7	1604			1626–7			(1644)	(1661)	1666
Bristol			1597	1603					(1637–8)	1643+ 1645	(1650–1)	(1666)
Exeter	(1586–7)	1590–1	1596–7	(1603–5)			1625					
Worcester	1587	1593–4	1597–9	1609–10		1624			1637	1643		
Shrewsbury	1587		1597	1604–5		(1623)		1631		1644	1650	
Chester				1603–5+ 1608	(1613–14)			1631		1647–8	(1654)	
Norwich	1584–5	1589–92	(1597–9)	1603–4	(1618)	(1622–4)	1625–6	(1631)	1636–8			1665–6
Leicester		1593–4		1610–11	1615	(1623)	1625–6		1638–9			
Lincoln	1586–7	1590–1	(1597)	(1610–11)				1631		(1642)		
Hull	1582			1602–3					1637–8	1643–5	(1660)	
York			(1597–8)	1604				1631		(1645)		
Newcastle		1588–9	1596–7	1604–10			1625		1636	1642+ 1644–7	1651	(1665)

Notes:

P = presumed plague

P+ = plague and other diseases

Source: From P. Slack, The Impact of Plague in Tudor and Stuart England, 1985.

population that the impact of plague was most spectacular and disruptive, if only because the gross number of deaths was so much larger.'[71] As for its frequency, in the capital, London, 'there was scarcely a year in the sixteenth and early seventeenth century when the disease [i.e., plague] was absent . . . the intermissions between outbreaks . . . rarely lasted for as long as a decade and were often much shorter'.[72] The Bills of Mortality, which recorded the weekly deaths in London and their supposed causes, which were kept intermittently from 1519, and from 1563 regularly, 'show great surges of infection, in 1603, 1625, 1636 and 1665'. These followed on from two major epidemics in London in Elizabeth's reign: in 1563 and 1593.

In general, and this obtains throughout Europe, the larger the town the more frequent the outbreaks of plague. And, again in general, the larger the town the more prosperous it was, hence the more prosperous the town the more frequent the outbreaks of plague. Thus rich and growing towns were particularly unhealthy and unsafe places to live. The countryside was a much safer place to live in years of plague, though it could follow one even there, slowly working its way along trade routes to the most distant and isolated settlements.

Because such a high proportion of those who suffered the symptoms of plague died from it, and in a very short space of time, it was not a disease to which the people could ever become inured. Every outbreak appeared like a divine judgement. The medical men acknowledged this divine origin of plague. Ambroise Paré, surgeon to four French kings and the most celebrated surgical innovator of his day, devoted a chapter of his 1568 book on plague to 'the Divine causes of an extraordinarie Plague', claiming that

> It is confirmed, constant, and received opinion in all Ages amongst Christians, that the Plague and other Diseases which violently assail the life of Man, are often sent by the just anger of God punishing our offences. The Prophet Amos hath long since taught it, saying *Shall there be affliction, shall there be evil in a Citie, and the Lord hath not done it?* On which truly we ought always to meditate . . . For thus we shall learn to see in God, our selves, the Heaven and Earth, the true knowledge of the causes of the Plague, and by a certain Divine Philosophy to teach, God to be the beginning and cause of the second causes, which well without the first cause cannot go about, nor attempt, much less perform any thing. For from hence they borrow their force, order, and constancy of order; so that they serve as Instruments for God, who rules and governs us, and the whole World, to perform all his works, by that constant course of order, which he hath appointed unchangeable from the beginning. Wherefore all the cause of a Plague is not to be attributed to these near and inferior causes or beginnings, as the Epicures, and Lucianists commonly do.[73]

Thus only atheists and scoffers would claim that plague has only natural (secondary) causes. However, the first cause – God – customarily acts through secondary causes, so Paré as a medical man could then immediately turn to the natural causes of plague to discuss its causes, course and cure.

Paré's account of plague, which was written at the request of the French Queen-Mother, Catherine de Medici, after a widespread outbreak of the disease in France in 1565, is one of the classic descriptions of the disease, and indicates how painful and fearsome it was. In Paré's view, the 'first original' of plague was a corruption of the air, entering the body and reaching the heart, 'the Mansion, or as it were the Fortress or Castle of Life' (p. 33), where it acted like a poison, attacking the vital spirit. If the vital spirit is weak, it 'flies back into the Fortress of the Heart, by the like contagion infecting the Heart, and so [it infects] the whole Body, being spread into it by the passages of the Arteries' (p. 2). The pestiferous poison brought about a burning fever, whose effects drove sufferers to desperate measures. They had ulcerated jaws, unquenchable thirst, dryness and blackness of the tongue, 'and it causeth such a Phrensy by inflaming the Brain, that the Patients running naked out of their Beds, seek to throw themselves out of Windows into the Pits and Rivers that are at hand' (pp. 27–8).

Because he saw plague as a poison, a poison which acted on the heart and then on the blood, Paré's first concern in treatment was to provide an antidote, which by its specific property would defend the heart from the poison by opposing the specific power of the poison. It had to be quick-acting, since the poison itself was very swift. Paré's antidote of choice was a mixture of treacle and mithridatium, an ancient drug compounded of up to 60 different ingredients and thought to be a sovereign protection against poison. Taken inwardly or applied outwardly over the region of the heart and to the carbuncles, this antidote draws the poisons out 'as Amber does Chaff', and then digests the poison and robs it of its deadly force (p. 46). If the plague came with eruptions or little red spots all over the body (these are the famous 'tokens' of the plague), caused by the poison increasing the heat of the blood, Paré advocated that a 'drawing' medicine should be applied, such as pig's grease mixed with mercury and herbs, to draw the poison through the skin (Plate 5.9). Alternatively, he suggests, 'if any noble or gentleman refuse to be anointed with this unguent, let them be enclosed in the body of a Mule or Horse that is newly killed, and when that is cold let them be laid in another; until the pustules and eruptions do break forth, being drawn by the natural heat' of the animal's corpse (p. 64).

Die leſte tabule vander peſtilencie

Plate 5.9 Physician at the
bedside of a plague
victim. From *Fasciculo
medicine te Antwerpen*

Even worse than the fever or the red spots in plague were the distinctive and painful 'buboes' (or carbuncles), hard black tumours which appeared in the neck, armpits and groin. Following classical Greek medical teaching, Paré saw these buboes as 'emunctories', natural outlets for the infected matter draining from the three main organs of the body, the brain, heart and liver respectively (p. 50). The pain of the buboes was so intense that sufferers wanted to have them lanced by the surgeon, the pain increasing as the bubo hardened and ripened. Paré's remedy was to apply ointment, then a cupping-glass heated very hot; kept on for a quarter of an hour this would draw the poison from the bubo. Alternatively, 'when you see, feel and know, according to reason, that the Bubo is come to perfect suppuration, it must be opened with an incision knife, or an actual or potential cautery'. A 'potential cautery' is a corrosive of some kind which produces the same burning effect on the skin as a real cautery, such as a red-hot iron (p. 69). But sufferers would also take desperate measures for themselves in their agony:

> There are many that for fear of death have with their own hands pulled away the Bubo with a pair of Smith's pincers: others have digged the flesh round about it, and so gotten it fully out. And to conclude, others have become so mad, that they have thrust an hot iron into it with their own hand, that the venom might have a passage forth. (p. 68)

But if a bubo was so painful that the sufferer wanted to tear it out, yet worse was what Paré called 'a pestilent carbuncle':

> A Pestilent Carbuncle is a small tumour, or rather a malign pustule, hot and raging, consisting of blood vitiated by the corruption of the proper substance. . . . In the beginning it is scarce so big as a seed or grain of Millet or a Pease . . . but shortly after it encreaseth like unto a Bubo unto a round and sharp head, with great heat, pricking pain, as if it were with needles, burning and intolerable, especially a little before night, and while the meat is in concocting, more than when it is perfectly concocted. In the midst thereof appeareth a bladder puffed up and filled with sanious [= bloody] matter. If you cut this bladder you shall find the flesh under it parched, burned, and black, as if there had been a burning coal laid there, whereby it seemeth that it took the name of Carbuncle; but the flesh that is about the place is like a Rainbow, of divers colours, as red, dark green, purple, livid, and black; but yet always with a shining blackness, like unto stone pitch, or like unto the true precious stone which they call a Carbuncle, whereof some also say it took the name. Some call it a Nail, because it inferreth like pain as a nail driven into the flesh . . . a Bubo and Carbuncle are tumours of a near affinity, so that the one doth scarce come without the other. (pp. 83–4)

In his attempt to provide the best advice for treatment of plague, Paré had consulted widely amongst his fellow practitioners during the plague of

1565, asking all those that he came across as he travelled with Charles IX's court to Bayon, what their experience had taught them about the value of bleeding and purging in treatment for plague. They all agreed that those affected with the plague who were bled or purged all grew progressively weaker and died. So from this communal experience of medical men, Paré urged that bleeding and purging be discontinued in the plague.

The traditional remedy in plague was flight. Cito, longe, tarde: flee quickly, stay long, return slowly, as the old tag had it. This made eminent medical sense too. Since the infection came from corrupted air, moving to a place of pure air removed one from the action of the poison. Windy places were to be preferred, and well-ventilated rooms. It was a matter of experience that while one town or village was struck by plague, a neighbouring town or village was often spared, and this was attributed to the differing quality and condition of the air. The differing quality of the air was also the explanation for the different fates of neighbours within towns or villages.

But what might seem like the obviously sensible thing to do about plague – avoid it, and flee it if it breaks out – was not a straightforward matter for some Christians, especially those of the Reformed denominations, for many of whom the question of election was important. For if God has already decided who shall be saved and who shall be condemned, and if the plague is one of God's ways of acting to carry out His own decisions, then both the elect and the non-elect will be contravening God's will in seeking to flee or take medical measures in plague. There were certainly those Christians who stayed during outbreaks of plague, trusting their fate to God. But many afflicted Christians fled to safe areas, and they were subject to strong criticism from those who stayed. Several of the major Reformers faced the issue directly when they themselves witnessed the arrival of plague, or were consulted by those currently suffering an outbreak. When they tried to lay down the proper behaviour of believers who were confronted by plague, their rulings were always firm but ambiguous. This reflected the ambiguous roles of plague in the Bible. It was possible to point to instances in the Bible of God using the plague as punishment for sin, but it was equally possible to point to instances of God delivering His people from the plague. So it was certainly clear that God was speaking through the pestilence, but what was He saying? The problem was a recurrent one, and opinions were divided every time.

For instance, the Elector of Saxony ordered the religious Reformer Martin Luther and his colleagues to move from Wittenberg when plague struck it in 1527. But Luther and his friend pastor Bugenhagen refused to run away, and stayed and comforted the sick and dying. Luther believed that God was punishing the town by sending plague. Yet, he wrote to a colleague, Amsdorf, 'It is a comfort that we can confront Satan's fury with the word of God, which we have and which saves souls even if that one [i.e. Satan] should devour our bodies.'[74] A Dominican mocked the Reformers for running away, so Luther spelled out the Protestant position as he saw it in an open letter. In this Luther forbids the minister and holders of public offices to flee the plague: they are like the good shepherd who, if necessary, lays down his life for his sheep. Leaving a community without spiritual guidance or governance, hands it over to the Devil, and invites civil disorder. But for non-officeholders, 'If someone is sufficiently bold and strong in his faith, let him stay in God's name; that is certainly no sin. If someone is weak and fearful, let him flee in God's name as long as he does not neglect his duty to his neighbour but has made adequate provision for others to provide nursing care.'[75]

Luther argues both sides of the question. On the one hand, he claims that 'According to Holy Scripture God sent his four scourges: pestilence, famine, sword, and wild beasts [Ezekiel 14:21]. If it is permissible to flee from one or the other in clear conscience, why not from all four?' On the other, he writes: 'if a deadly epidemic strikes, we should stay where we are . . . we can be sure that God's punishment has come upon us, not only to chastise us for our sins but also to test our faith and love . . . I am of the opinion that all epidemics, like any plague, are spread among the people by evil spirits who poison the air or exhale a pestilential breath which puts a deadly poison into the flesh. Nevertheless, this is God's decree and punishment to which we must patiently submit and serve our neighbour'. Yet he also criticises those who stay during an epidemic and say that there is nothing one can do to alleviate it since it is God's punishment, accusing them of tempting God.[76] Should a believer use medicines? Luther's argument is that 'You ought to think this way: "Very well, by God's decree the enemy has sent us poison. Therefore I shall ask God mercifully to protect us. Then I shall fumigate, help purify the air, administer medicine, and take it. I shall avoid places and persons where my presence is not needed in order not to become contaminated . . . If God should wish to take me, he will surely find me".'[77]

Andreas Osiander, leading Reformer in Nuremberg, in 1537, in response to fears of the plague, made a sermon on the comforting Psalm 91:

Whoso sitteth under the defence of the highest, and abideth under the shadow of the Almighty.

He sayeth unto the LORD: My hope, and my stronghold: my God on whom I trust.

For he delivereth me from the snare of the hunter, and from the noisome pestilence.

He shall cover thee with his feathers, and thy trust shall be under his wings: his truth is spear and shield.

So that thou needest not to fear for the horribleness of the night, for the arrows that fly by daytime.

For the pestilence that cometh privily in the dark: for the sickness that destroyeth in the noonday.

Though a thousand fall at thy side, and ten thousand at thy right hand, yet shall it not come nigh thee.

Yea with thine eyes shalt thou see thy desire, and behold, how the ungodly shall be rewarded.

Like others of the Protestant persuasion, who put a greater stress on literal interpretations of the strict text of the Bible, Osiander's view was that natural explanations ought to take second place to supernatural ones: that explanations about why plague had struck should be in terms of sin and God's punishment rather than in terms of natural events. He wrote:

I will not enter against them, that speak naturally thereof, and say: Such plague cometh out of the influence of the stars, out of the working of the Comets, out of the unseasonable weather and altering of the air, out of the South winds, out of stinking waters, or out of foul mists of the ground: For such wisdom of theirs will we leave unto them undespised, and not fight there against: But (as Christian men) we will hold us unto the word of God, the same will we suffer to be our most high wisdom, and give credence unto it, and follow it: and so shall we find much better and surer instruction: Namely, that this horrible plague of the pestilence cometh out of God's wrath, because of the despising and transgressing of his godly commandments: For thus saith the holy prophet Moses in the fifth book [i.e. Deuteronomy], the xxviii Chapter:

If thou wilt not hearken unto the voice of the LORD thy God, to observe and keep all his commandments and ordinances which I command thee, then shall all these curses come upon thee &c

And it followeth: The LORD shall cause the pestilence to endure long with thee: the LORD shall smite thee with swelling, fever, heat, burning, blasting, drought, &c. and shall persecute thee till he utterly destroyeth, and bring ye to naught.

And certainly this is the plain truth and the very original of these plagues. No man ought to doubt thereon. For though the forsaid natural causes do somewhat also thereto, yet is it sure and undoubted, that the same causes be sent and stirred up out of God's wrath for our sin and unthankfulness. And truly that it is even so, the holy scripture declareth, not with bare words only, but showeth it also with notable examples. . . . Seeing then that out of the word of God we know the very cause of this horrible plague: Namely, that it is the default of our sins, as unbelief, disobedience & unthankfulness. Therefore before all things it shall be necessary, that we refrain from the same, repent, and amend our lives. If we will else be preserved and delivered from this horrible plague . . . But if we acknowledge our sin, refrain from it, repent and ask grace, then shall he also take away his wrath. And this horrible wrath (with other heavy burthens as war & dearth that lie upon our neck) shall be mercifully taken away from us again.

Theodore Beza, Calvin's fellow worker in the Reformation of Geneva, and later his successor and also professor of theology at the Academy there, found the dispute amongst Reformed Christians as to whether to flee or stay in plague so strong in the late 1570s that he too took up his pen to resolve it in his *Treatise of the Plague* (1580). The dispute raised questions about whether or not Christians should accept that the plague was infectious.[78]

As God sent the plague as a punishment and did not deliver His people from it, what did He expect Christians to do at an outbreak? Should they flee or should they stay? Which decision was the greater provocation of God (who was of course the first cause of this sickness)? On one side were those who deplored that flight at the outbreak of plague destroyed the Christian bonds of society and duty. People only took to flight because they believed plague to be infectious. But (it was claimed) this was false: plague was not infectious, and there was no evidence that a Christian should credit, which showed that it was so. Beza himself found this claim paradoxical, it was 'a strange opinion' that 'can no more be proved by good reason than if a man with *Anaxagoras* would hold the snow to be black, or out of the Hypothesis of *Copernicus* labour to prove that the earth doth indeed move, and the Sun to stand still, as the centre of the world' (A1v–A2r). The advocates of this opinion supported themselves on the Word of God, rejecting the opinions of physicians. The plague, they claimed, is sent direct from God. It is the Hand of God, they said (citing 2 Samuel 24, 1 Chronicles 21 and Psalms 31 and 90), and it is His arrows which He sends direct, and sometimes, they said (citing Revelation), He sends it via His angels: therefore it does not come from infection or from other natural secondary causes. Beza countered this claim by saying that 'in the same book 6, verse 8 [of Revelations] the pale horse, on whom death the rider sitteth, receiveth power to kill with the sword, famine and pestilence, and with sending of wild beasts': here then is an angel, Beza claims, using second causes, so there is no reason why God should not be acting out His anger through a natural secondary cause such as infection. Well, they countered, 'if infection be reckoned among second causes appointed by God, how can we avoid that which is ordained by God?' Running away will not save us from the fate ordained for us by God; indeed it is impious to try and avoid our just punishment, so we should stay.

On the other side of this passionate life and death dispute in Geneva were those who held that the true Christian owed it to God to take the sensible precaution of flight: the arrival of plague was for them like 'the setting up of a sign to run away' (B8r). Beza's sympathies were more with this point of view, for he believed that just as God 'by his everlasting and unchangeable degree hath appointed the course of our life, so hath he also ordained middle causes, which we should use to preserve our life withal' (c8r). However, indiscriminate resort to flight was not to be encouraged, in Beza's view, for it did indeed go against the Christian's duty to care for other members of society and it threatened the stability of the Christian commonwealth. In resolving the dispute Beza turned, as he did in other matters of Reformed religion, to the pivotal duty of the Christian magistrate, in alliance with the physician and the pastor, to take every precaution to cope with plague:

> it shall be the duty of the Christian Magistrate to provide that those things which either breed or nourish the plague, so far as may be, be taken away, and that regard may be had of those that be visited with this sickness, that all be not driven to be careful for all. But how they that serve in any public Civil office may leave their charge in the time of plague, I do not see: and for faithful Pastors to forsake but one poor sheep at that time when as he most of all needeth heavenly comfort, it were shameful, nay too wicked a part. (D2v)

The community leaders also had an obligation, while carrying out these duties, not to put themselves unnecessarily at risk. This had, mercifully, been the case when Beza himself had suffered from plague in 1551 in Lausanne. Then his fellow ministers, including Peter Viret and John Calvin, were prepared to visit him, but Beza forbade them to do so 'lest I might have been thought to have provided for myself with the loss of the Christian commonwealth, which was manifest would have been very great by the death of so worthy men' (D4r). And above all, the pastor had a duty to bring his flock to repentance since 'as our sins are the chief and the true cause of plague, so this is the only proper remedy against the same'. In 1588 Beza's own wife was to die of plague: perhaps taking flight, rather than staying with her pastor and magistrate husband, might have saved her.[79]

This debate about whether Christians had a duty to flee the plague or not went on for a long time also in the Dutch Republic amongst the Calvinists there, and along much the same lines. Similarly amongst the Calvinists in sixteenth-century France, and also among the Puritans in England, the question was repeatedly raised about whether one could escape God's justice, and whether it was even legitimate to try to do so.[80]

The presence of plague of course incited the people everywhere to seek heavenly forgiveness. The language of sin as disease and affliction as medicine purging that sin, had a long history, dating back at least to the time of St Augustine. 'Sin, the sickness of the soul, is the real and radical cause of all bodily sickness', John King preached in a sermon of thanksgiving in London in 1619.[81] Not only was repentance seen as a way of diverting plague, God's punishment, but plague and medicine were often simultaneously used as models for spiritual sin and healing, with Christ often referred to as the heavenly physician, healing both our sins and our bodies. For Christians the visitation of disease has always been an ambiguous matter, since their God is a benign god, and nothing happens without His will and knowledge. Obviously God must send disease, and obviously it must be as punishment, like a kindly father, for our sins. But it was not always clear, even to men of religion, quite which sins were being punished by a particular visitation of a pestilence, nor why the good died under God's justice as well as the wicked. Though unable to answer these questions in a final way, the Church, whether Catholic or Protestant, still remained the centre for seeking divine intervention against this divine punishment.

In our period, this religious response to plague was accompanied by a flood of printed matter in every large town with an active printing trade. There were sermons calling for fasts and communal repentance; there were rules and recipes to help avoid or cure the plague issued by individuals, or the magistracies of towns, or the local College of Physicians if there was one;[82] there were pamphlets which claimed to identify the particular great sin that brought on the plague as punishment. There were accounts of how God was responding to the people's prayers and repentance. And after the passing of the plague there were printed thanksgivings, with warnings about avoiding sin for the future.

Regimes against the plague were printed from the earliest days of printing, usually related to a local outbreak of disease (Plate 5.10). One from 1495, published at Rouen, written by a doctor and directed to the poor, promised that, by its use, 'each and anyone of any complexion whatever will be able to recognise and become familiar with the things which are requisite, useful and profitable, to use them to preserve his health.

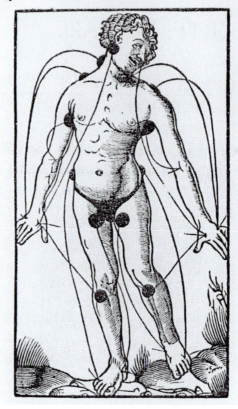

Plate 5.10 Regimen
against the pox, drawn
up by the physicians of
Basel, 1519. *Regime contre
la pestilence faict et compose
par messieurs les medecins de
la cite de Balle en allemagne*
(c. 1519)

Similarly, he will be able to hear about and clearly recognise the things
which are unhealthy and causing the said pestilence, so that he can flee,
avoid and forsake them.' The author of this regimen, Dr Thomas le
Forestier, gave thanks to 'God our Saviour and Redeemer, to His most
sacred Virgin and mother Mary, Queen of Heaven and Earth, and to all the
blessed heavenly court of Paradise', for having been able to complete this
little work.[83] Another such work, drawn up by the physicians of Basel and
published in 1519 in Lyons, put its advice into rhyme with a repeated chorus
line, of which this is one verse:

> Qui veult son corps sante maintenir
> Et resister contre l'epydimie
> Doit ioye avoir et tristesse fouyr

En frequentant ioyeuse compaignie
D'infection totalement bannie
Boyre bon vin nettes viandes user
Ay bon odeur contre la punaisie
N'aille point hors si ne fait bel ou cler [84]

If you want to keep your body healthy
And to put up resistance to the epidemy
You must be joyful and flee misery
By frequenting happy company
Completely clear of infection
You should drink good wine, eat good food
Have a good pomander against the pong
Nor go outside unless the weather's clear or good.

London offers a good example of ways in which people responded to plague outbreaks. In the first place, there was usually a call for prayers and contrition. Since the early years of the reign of Elizabeth I, the Bishop of London put forth forms of prayers in time of pestilence. In times of affliction the godly have been stirred up to crave God's pardon:

> Now therefore calling to mind, that God has been provoked by us to visit us at this present with the plague and other grievous diseases, and partly also with trouble of wars, it hath been thought meet to excite and stir up all goodly people within this Realm, to pray earnestly and heartily to God, to turn away his deserved wrath from us, and to restore us as well to the health of our bodies by the wholesomeness of the air, as also to godly and profitable peace and quiet-ness . . . First, that all Curates and Pastors shall exhort their Parishioners to endeavour themselves to come unto the Church, with so many of their families as may be spared from their necessary business (having yet a prudent respect in such assemblies to keep the sick from the whole, in places where the plague reigneth) and they to resort not only on Sundays and holy days, but also on Wednesdays and Fridays, during the time of these present afflictions, exhorting them, there reverently and godly to behave themselves, and with penitent hearts to pray unto God to turn these plagues from us, which we through our unthank-fulness and sinful life, have deserved.[85]

After an outbreak had passed, the Church called for thanks to be given to a merciful God. In 1563, for instance, the Bishop of London had printed *A short form of thanksgiving to God for ceasing the contagious sickness of the plague*, with a *mélange* of psalms to be added to the weekday service, and a modified version of the Collect. God is good to us, the Collect ran,

> but forasmuch as we have dishonoured thee, by, and with the abusing of thy good gifts, thou doest even in this like a father correcting his children whom he loveth, when they offend, no less mercifully punish us, for the said abuse of thy gifts, than thou didst bounteously before give them unto us, scourging us

sometime with wars and troubles, sometimes with famine and scarcity, sometime with sickness and diseases, and sundry other kinds of plagues, for the abusing of peace, quietness, plenty, health, and such other thy good gifts, against thy holy Word and will, and against thy honour and our own health, to thy great displeasure and high indignation. As thou now of late terribly but most justly and deservedly plagued us with contagious, dreadful and deadly sickness, from the which yet thou hast most mercifully, and without all deservings on our part, even of thy own goodness, now again delivered us, and saved us . . . [and thou didst also] deliver our most gracious Queen and governor from all perils and dangers, yea even from the gates of death.

It was quite clear to contemporaries that prayer worked, and its efficiency could even be calculated. Toward the end of the long plague outbreak of 1636, John Squier, preaching in St Paul's church in London, was able to compute God's response to the community's fasting and prayer.[86] The Lord calls upon us to turn to him in time of trouble: 'Call upon Me in the time of trouble: I will hear thee, and thou shalt praise Me'.

> In the time of trouble! [Squier writes] Surely our Time of Plague, was a Time of trouble; When there died each week in this City and Suburbs above a Thousand, and in particular Parishes above an Hundred: then was a Time of trouble: When the Able fled citò, longè, tardè; and the Multitude must tarry, notwithstanding a multitude of Dangers to themselves, to their servants, but especially to their poor Children, then was a Time of trouble. When Tradesmen became poor: when the Poor became Beggars: and when the Beggars were ready to starve: then was a Time of Trouble. (pp. 10–11)

But God had looked after them in this time of trouble, since they called upon God by prayer and fasting: 'Upon our Prayer and Fasting, God doth make the Plague his instrument; to work in his Children, Innocence, penitence, patience, humiliation, sanctification, mortification. O felix culpa quae talem meruit Redemptorem! Happy is that plague which openeth the way to Heaven, to us miserable Sinners' (p. 24). God heard their prayers and rewarded their fasts. With the full rhetoric of the pulpit Squier showed how the Bills of Mortality (the weekly London listing of the numbers who had died of plague and other diseases) revealed God's mercy, week by week, from the first fast which was begun on October 26. 'Let us compute God's goodness towards us', Squier urged:

> The first week, We did call upon God, in the time of the Plague, by Prayer and Fasting; and God did hear us in that time of our trouble. So the Burials decreased 190.
> The second week, We did call upon God, in the time of the Plague, by Prayer and Fasting; and God did hear us in that time of our trouble. So the Burials decreased, 139.
> The third week, We did call upon God, in the time of the Plague, by Prayer and Fasting; and God did hear us in that time of our trouble; and the burials decreased, 80.
> The fourth week, We did call upon God, in the time of the Plague, by Prayer and

Fasting; and God did hear us in that time of our trouble, and the burials decreased, 197.

The fifth week, *We did call upon God, in the time of the Plague, by Prayer and Fasting; and God did hear us in that time of our trouble, and the Burials Decreased, 165.*

The sixth week, *We did call upon God, in the time of the Plague, by Prayer and Fasting; and God did hear us in that time of our trouble, and the Burials Decreased, 61.*

The seventh week, *We did call upon God, in the time of the Plague, by Prayer and Fasting; and God did hear us in that time of our trouble, and the Burials Decreased likewise, 61.*

Here the *Fast ended:* would God I could say here the *Plague ended:* Or if *Authority* thought it meet, *that the Fast were continued and not ended,* before the Plague ended. (pp. 24–5)

The obvious implication is that if the fast had been continued, the plague would have ended: that God's mercy was poured out in strict accord with the people's repentance.

In terms of coping with the social dislocation and disturbance of plague, the north Italian city states led the rest of Europe in adopting measures for dealing with recurrent plague.[87] The measures they took indicate that the rulers of the cities regarded the plague as contagious, whatever medical theory might say. Florence kept Books of the Dead from 1385, which listed cause of death. Methods of quarantine, for persons and ships, were introduced in Italy from the early fifteenth century. The designating of a hospital to be a lazaretto, or pest house, for the course of a plague outbreak, and the creation of health boards to run emergency measures, had been adopted fully in Venice as early as 1423, in Ferrara in 1463, and in Florence in 1463. The Milan lazaretto was purpose-built, and was completed in 1488 (Plate 5.11). It consisted of a field with a line of huts around the sides, and tents in the field. The tents and huts isolated the sufferers from the community, while the open space allowed the fetid air to be blown away.

The measures Florence took while it was under threat of plague from 1493–8 are instructive in this regard. It first established an Eight of Watch and Ward, to watch out for the disease coming in from outside, and to take measures to prevent the arrival of the disease. An extraordinary committee was appointed in March 1494, a *balìa* of five citizens 'pro la cura della peste', controlling markets and travel. This was replaced in March 1496 by another committee, a group of plague officers (*Ufficiali del morbo*), whose duty again was to prevent plague coming to Florence. Watchmen were appointed to guard the property of those who fled the town to preserve their lives. The plague hospital at Florence, the *spedale del morbo*, was first used during the 1497 epidemic. A diarist lamented about the plague in 1498 that:

Plate 5.11 Mary Misericordia, with saints Sebastian and Roch, and the Lazaretto of Milan

The officers of the plague went into the hospitals and drove out the unfortunate sufferers; and wherever they found them in the city they sent them out of Florence. The were actually so cruel as to place hempen rope with a pulley outside the Armourers' Guild to torture those who tried to return. It was a brutal thing and a harsh remedy.[88]

Savonarola's mission in Florence was interrupted by this outbreak of plague. With up to a hundred people a day dying of plague, Savonarola sent his fellow friars out of town for their safety, though he chose to remain heroically in the city himself. 'Doubt not but that God will triumph', he wrote to his brother. 'Fear not that I remain here in Florence in the midst of the plague, for the Lord will help me. I stay to comfort the afflicted, friars and citizens alike . . . so that the living not only no longer fear death, but welcome it.'[89]

Other places adopted versions of the Italian ways of coping, but only decades later. In England the first steps were taken only with a proclamation issued by Cardinal Wolsey in 1518, saying that infected houses should be marked by a bundle of straw, and their inmates should carry a white rod when in the streets. During the next half century in England particular towns made regulations in time of plague and set up temporary pest-houses outside their town walls. In 1578 the Privy Council issued orders to be implemented throughout the kingdom whenever plague broke out, and these remained in force for the rest of our period. Justices of the peace were to receive reports from searchers of the dead in the parishes, raise taxes for the relief of the sick, dispose of infected bedding, close infected houses and incarcerate the relatives of the sick in them, certify deaths, control times of burial, appoint and control watchmen, and control travel in and out of infected areas.[90] But the creation of permanent pest-houses was not undertaken in England until after 1666.

CONTAGION OR CORRUPTION AS CAUSE OF EPIDEMIC DISEASE?

The period from 1490 to the mid-seventeenth century witnessed a 'renaissance' of medicine, as of many other fields of intellectual endeavour. The works of the great Ancients of medicine, Hippocrates, Galen and others, were recovered from the Greek, printed in Greek editions and Latin translations, commented on, and introduced into university medical faculties as improved texts on which the theory and practice of medicine should be built. The medical writings from the Arab tradition, which had themselves originally been built on the same Greek writings and then had been developed in particular ways, came to be despised and rejected by the advocates of returning to the 'true founts', Hippocrates and Galen. The arguments between the partisans of the Arab physicians and those of the Greek physicians raged in the medical faculties and in print for a hundred years. We have seen how physicians resorted to the works of Hippocrates and Galen when trying to resolve whether the French pox or typhus were new diseases or not, and how to treat diseases such as plague. Despite the very extensive discussion of disease they found in these ancient writings, even those who wholeheartedly sided with the ancient Greeks could not come to agreement among themselves about whether the Ancients had or had not known the pox, nor what Galen would have done in times of plague, for he hardly mentioned it. Moreover, the kind of medicine that Galen had taught and which the university medical student learnt, concentrated on treating the individual patient. For each patient was believed to be different, and the occurrence of a disease in a patient was unique. Thus each patient had to be treated with regard to his or her distinctive condition. The physicians learnt therefore to manage what were called the six 'non-naturals': the quality of the air around the patient, their food and drink, fullness or emptiness (especially of the four humours, in particular blood), their sleep and wake, their motion and rest, and the accidents of their mind. All of these could be modified to strengthen the patient against suffering from a particular disease, and to help him or her recover from a given disease. Hence bleeding, and giving advice about diet, air and rest, were part of the regular procedures that physicians adopted. But when faced with an *epidemic* disease, one which fell on many people at the same time, the physician's capacity to intervene was severely restricted. The physician could, and did, continue to give advice and treatment to individuals who could afford his fees, and continued to regard the incidence of the epidemic disease as being distinctive in the case of each particular patient. But as for people in the mass, the best that a physician or a College of Physicians could do when their advice was sought by civic authorities, as it often was, was to offer a generalised version of the treatment they gave to individuals.

But even though their medicine was inappropriate for treating people in the mass as they suffered from epidemic disease, some medical professionals were nevertheless very exercised about the sudden appearance of the new epidemic diseases, and particularly concerned with their mode of spread.

An eminent practioner of medicine in Verona, Fracastoro, whom we have had occasion to quote already on the French pox and on typhus, decided in the 1530s to investigate the phenomenon of 'contagious' diseases as a group, the diseases which are apparently catchable, whether by physical contact or without. The great epidemics of the age, old and new, all seemed to have this characteristic. Fracastoro had already written his celebrated poem on one such disease, the French pox ('Syphilis'). Now he was writing (as he says) not as a poet but as a doctor, investigating what it was that contagious diseases had in common – something (he claimed) which the ancients of medicine had not done. So he turned to asking 'what is the nature of contagions as a whole; by what principle they infect; how they are generated; why some of them leave *fomes* [literally 'tinder', i.e. inanimate objects, such as clothing, which harbour the infection], and some propagate themselves even at a distance; why some diseases are contagious, though they are milder and more gentle, while others, though much more acute and more virulent, are not at all contagious; how contagion differs from poisons, and many other questions of this sort'.[91] He was able to group together as contagious certain old and new diseases, including some fevers, smallpox and measles, typhus, rabies, the French pox, the English sweating sickness, elephantiasis, leprosy and scabies. He had wide practical experience of many of these diseases, but he did not use experiment to investigate them. His general conclusions were that contagion required the same disease to exist in the person infected as in the person from whom it was contracted, and that this could only be explained by assuming it was a phenomenon of 'imperceptible particles' (*insensibilia*) which were transmitted from the sufferer to the healthy. Amongst the conditions giving rise to such particles, in Fracastoro's view, were unfavourable conjunctions of the planets.

Contagion and contagious diseases had of course been widely discussed before the work of Fracastoro.[92] Contagion does not need to be explained in terms of 'seeds', whether visible or subvisible, or minute animals ('animalcula'). Galen and his modern followers believed it was performed primarily by putrid air turned bad by miasmata or vapours and fumes (and some sixteenth-century physicians outside the Galenic tradition talked also in terms of 'ferments' poisoning the air). This putrid air then acted like a poison on susceptible individuals, or upset their humoral balance. This is the kind of explanation that we have seen adopted by most physicians in the case of all the epidemic diseases of our period. The susceptibility of the patient could be regulated and strengthened by the physician's advice, especially by adjusting the so-called 'non-naturals'. Other measures which changed the immediate environment included isolating affected persons, or changing the quality of the air, by fumigation, burning fires, or pomanders, and all these measures were adopted, as we have seen. But to talk of seeds or animalcula, in the view of Galen in Antiquity and now of his sixteenth-century followers, was to go beyond the evidence of the senses. So Fracastoro's claim that contagion was effected by the transmission of 'imperceptible particles' was unusual for the time, and out of step with current thinking. It has been claimed that Fracastoro's concept of 'seeds of disease' was part of an ongoing debate amongst philosophers and physicians of the time to account for a range of kinds of natural action which seemed to be accomplished without contact, such as the magnet, poison, the evil eye, and the imagination. Such 'sympathy' and 'antipathy' were usually explained in terms of 'occult' (hidden, unknowable) causes: that is, they were explained in terms of the mysterious conveyance of a particular *quality* from one object or person to another. Fracastoro's 'seeds', by contrast, introduce a *material* cause for this purpose. He may have derived the concept from the atomism of the ancient Roman philosopher Lucretius, whose great poem 'On the nature of things' (*De natura rerum*) had been rediscovered in 1417 (printed 1473). If this was indeed the case, then Fracastoro had every reason not to acknowledge Lucretius as his inspiration, since in the early modern period Lucretius's atomistic theory, in which everything is explained as happening by the chance collision of minute particles, clearly showed that he was an atheist, whose opinions must not be followed by a good Christian. Although Fracastoro's book on contagion had four printings before 1554, in the long term it had very little influence on medicine, and it is only since the dominance of the germ theory of infectious disease in the late nineteenth century, that his view has been seen as prescient.[93]

The four major new epidemic diseases or groups of diseases we have dealt with, did not exhaust the number of diseases experienced as 'new' in this period. Scurvy, a deeply painful disease associated with long sea voyages, became feared amongst sailors. Rickets appeared, apparently from nowhere, in the early seventeenth century. And new fevers, or agues, appeared year after year.[94] It really was a period of many new diseases, and the Pale Horseman visited in many guises.

EPIDEMICS AS MORTALITY CRISES?

It is always tempting to use modern medical knowledge when discussing historical outbreaks of epidemic disease. If we were to do this here for the people of the period 1490–1648, we would be equating their 'French pox' with our syphilis, their 'camp' or 'hunger fever' with our typhus, their plague with our bubonic plague. For if their 'camp fever' or 'famine fever' was our typhus (for instance), then we can understand why it should have occurred among besieging soldiers and besieged citizenry from our scientific knowledge of the habits of the body-louse and the causative micro-organism of typhus that it hosts. Similarly if their plague was the same as our plague, then we can understand why it should have occurred in crowded urban living conditions from our scientific knowledge of the habits of the rat flea and the causative micro-organism of plague that it hosts. In other words, we could recognise that the incidence of new diseases in this period was the direct result of hygienic ignorance and sanitary defects on their part, and no more than that. We could conclude that these epidemics were simply social diseases, caused simply by a lack of hygienic practices. It seems obvious to a modern-day person, that *their* perception of these diseases was merely *mis*perception: the real truth is and was germ truth. We would be tempted to conclude that if they had had the scientific knowledge that we have, then they would have not needed to resort to explanations in terms of divine anger or the end of the world. Disease would have been seen as something wholly natural, not supernatural. Hence we could conclude that they misunderstood their own situation and predicament, and the view that epidemic disease was one of the Four Horsemen of the Apocalypse was simply a mighty social delusion, a case of mass hysteria.

Such an approach on our part would not only be deeply patronising about the intelligence of our predecessors, but would also be based on a misapprehension about disease identity. For the identity of an infectious disease, even today, does not consist solely of its causative micro-organism, its pathogen. A significant part of its identity is constituted by how it is experienced by those who suffer it: that is to say, by people's *perception* of it. Different diseases are perceived differently within different societies. Similarly, particular diseases are experienced differently – they have a different perceptual identity – at different periods or in different societies. Take for instance smallpox, which in the period 1490–1648, was a disease considered something reasonably benign, a rite of passage, something everyone had to go through, and while some died from it most survived it, and while many were scarred by it, most were not. Yet in later ages, such as the present, it is regarded as a most dangerous and fearsome disease, and its recurrence is greatly to be dreaded. Similarly, a disease such as plague, once regarded as most dangerous and fearsome, can in different circumstances or ages, such as today, be experienced as containable and manageable, because it is treatable. We may still be scared about outbreaks of plague, but we are not remotely as scared of plague as people were in the sixteenth century, because we think of it in a different way. Our experience of it is different, and to that extent the disease has a different identity at the psychological level. Again, we find that a disease such as consumption, the nineteenth-century predecessor of tuberculosis, had a popular image as a mark of the genius, the hypersensitive, the talented, and the disgusting nature of its symptoms was downplayed.[95] Today it is merely a physical disease and has no special aura about it. We can perhaps anticipate a period in the future when AIDS will also be seen as a merely physical disease, with no special social or moral subtext attached to it.[96]

But epidemic diseases of past and present also have different identities at the technical level. Until the advent of the medical laboratory in the latter part of the nineteenth century, infectious diseases were defined primarily by their symptoms and course. In the laboratory world of today, they are defined primarily by their causative micro-organisms. It is simply not logically possible to compare these two different ways of defining diseases and claim that a pre-laboratory and a post-laboratory disease were 'the same', since the criteria of sameness have been changed.[97] So we are unable legitimately to make identifications of their diseases with our diseases, even if the social and psychological dimensions of disease identity were to be put aside from our considerations.

What we have to conclude is that a disease's identity is made up of both natural elements (how it is in nature) and perceptual elements (how human beings think about it and about its causes and significance). This is true today, and was also true in the period under study here. This makes it possible for us to understand how an epidemic disease in the sixteenth century could be considered to be a divine punishment for communal or individual sin, yet also be amenable to physical treatment. The religious and the natural explanations went hand in hand, and if a doctor chose to limit himself to dealing with the natural element (as John Caius did with the English sweating sickness, for instance), this does not mean that epidemics were (or indeed are) *merely* natural events, or that interpreting them as events with divine causes and meanings was to misinterpret them.

But once we have put aside the modern temptation to look at the people of the early modern period as being the mere victims – the mere *ignorant* victims, at that – of germs and germ life, what we *can* say with respect to the epidemic diseases they suffered, is that the people of Europe of this period were indeed victims, but victims not of their ignorance but of their own success. They were victims of their *demographic* success. We saw with respect to famines in the previous chapter, that the frequent tragic visitations of the Black Horse did not lead to any long-term depression of the population, despite the thousands on thousands of deaths that the famines produced. On the contrary, the famines and food shortages were themselves side-effects of long-term uncontrolled population *increase*, but an increase occurring within a society with grossly uneven distribution of food and purchasing power. Here we see a parallel phenomenon with respect to epidemic diseases which, like famines, killed thousands on thousands of the population of Europe. For these visitations of the Pale Horse were side-effects of the great population increase, and particularly of new ways of living which resulted from it, especially re-urbanisation, new sexual freedoms, and the new conditions of warfare. In this light it may be timely to question the way in which this period, and especially its demographic history, is currently viewed as a period of successive demographic 'crises', a term with necessarily negative connotations.

The stories that historians tell about epidemic disease in the past usually take the form of 'disease-biographies': the subject and villain of the piece is the disease, while the role of human society is customarily portrayed not as active but as *reactive*. We tend to portray such societies as reacting in ignorance of the real nature of the disease, reacting with panic, desperately seeking scapegoats or hoping to see some pattern in divine action.[98] From this disease-biography tradition, it comes to look as though the germs are running us – that we are the playthings of the germs – that the development (or otherwise) of human societies is an epiphenomenal feature of germ history.[99] One of the origins of this approach is the work of the great 'disease-disaster-historians' (as one could call them) of the nineteenth century, who first called attention to the possibility and desirability of writing the history of epidemics, and who had a disposition to regard epidemics as crucial turning-points in human history, that is quite literally as 'crises', decisive moments. Prompted initially by the great outbreaks of cholera across Europe in 1832, the work of Justus Hecker (1830s), then of Heinrich Haeser (1880s), August Hirsch (1860–80s), and others, was based, at least in part, on a practical medical desire to map diseases in time and space in order to inform the medical practice of their own day.[100] These researchers also took it for granted that one could give (in Hirsch's words) 'a picture of the occurrence, the distribution, and the types of the diseases of mankind, in distinct epochs of time, and at various points of the earth's surface'.[101] They were interested, that is, not only in the history of the diseases, but also in 'the distinct epochs of time' which typified or governed their incidence. They believed that epidemic diseases had a history related to place, climate and population. But they believed that epidemic diseases also had a role in fulfilling the great drama of history and of human history, for this disease-history intersected with human history. Thus for Hecker, for instance, the great plague of 1348 played a crucial role in such history, and he gave it the new name 'the Black Death', marking it as a crucial moment when the twin histories of the development of the organism of the individual and of the organism of the earth came into collision.

This assumption about the crucial role of epidemic diseases as *crises*, and that those crises are more than just unpleasant episodes but also turning-points in some way, with the greatest of them marking 'epochs' in the history of the earth and of mankind, and the lesser ones as marking turning-points in the development of society at the local level, has been inherited by historical demographers today. Hence, with the appearance of so many epidemic diseases and with such frequency in the years under study here, historical demographers have taken to speaking about repeated 'mortality crises', though they have not yet agreed on quite what death-rate higher than normal should count as a 'major crisis' or a 'minor crisis'.[102] But this tendency to talk in terms of 'mortality crises' invokes an exclusively negative view of the population history of this period: it is presented as crisis after crisis, one setback followed by another. One would hardly guess from such treatments that the population of Europe was rising so spectacularly and inexorably. Of course at the level of the individual person and of local society, every outbreak of an epidemic disease was a crisis, a disaster, and was experienced as such, as we have been showing earlier. But at the level of European society *as a whole* the story is one of great demographic success, and the frequency of the outbreaks of epidemic disease and their resultant thousands of deaths was, curious as it may seem at first sight, one of the marks of this success.

For, in any given society there is a relationship between that society and the diseases it is subject to. This relation may be stable at a given moment, but it always changes over time. The change in the relationship depends on the way in which humans *change their own environment*, bringing themselves into contact with new sources of disease, introducing round themselves new circumstances, such as advancing into (or retreating from) certain geographical areas, or taking up (or abandoning) certain forms of cultivation. Arno Karlen has recently argued that in the second half of the twentieth century, we have encountered a host of new threatening infectious diseases of international significance: new 'plagues' he calls them. He counts over thirty major ones since 1951. Where have they come from – or, more accurately, why have they arisen? Karlen points out that in the last century, Western man has changed his environment more radically than in any previous period. He claims that, 'most human diseases were once new. They came to us because we changed our environment, our behaviour, or both. Sometimes, as is happening now, they came in waves.'[103] Karlen's argument about how the change of human environment brings new diseases into play is paralleled by more historically focused works of recent years, such as those of Alfred Crosby, Philip Curtin, Kenneth F. Kiple, William McNeil and Thomas MacKeon.[104] The arguments of all these writers are based on a germ-theory view of infectious disease: that is, they claim either that pre-existing germs are brought into first contact with man via man-made environmental changes, or that such man-made environmental changes lead to changes in the nature and virulence of microbes already present within human society. We do not need to follow them down this particular route in order to accept the main theses: (i) that changing environments mean changing disease incidence, and (ii) that rapidly changing environments mean rapidly changing disease incidence – visible most of all in the occurrence of 'new' epidemic diseases or of epidemics of old diseases but with new virulence.

In this sense the repeated outbreaks of epidemic diseases on a great scale can be seen not just as *negative causes* – causes, that is, of setbacks in the history of a society – but rather as *positive consequences* of the development of particular societies. To put it another way, every society gets the diseases and the epidemics it deserves. Or as Marcel Sendrail has expressed it, from a slightly different position, every society 'shapes its pathological destiny'.[105] A contracting and ageing society (a post-industrial one, for instance) will develop a particular disease profile, with its own epidemics. Our own society, for instance, has an 'epidemic' of cancer(s) on a scale never before experienced. Similarly, a society (whether present-day or historic) which is static in terms of reproductive pattern and in forms of agriculture, industry and commerce, will have its own pattern of disease.

So again, a society which is rapidly expanding, which has a great and continuing increase in population, which expands beyond its old line of agricultural exploitation, which is land-hungry and food-hungry, and which packs itself into growing industrial towns, such a society will have its own pattern of disease and especially of epidemic disease. Rapidly changing environments mean rapidly changing disease incidence.

Such a society was Europe in the period 1490 to 1648, when it had completed its demographic recovery from the so-called Black Death and as its population continued to increase dramatically. The epidemic disease moments that we have been discussing here were taking place in the context of a momentous change in population: nothing less than a doubling of the population of Europe in these 150 years. The inexorable population rise with its immediate social consequences – land pressure, the search abroad for new living space, the introduction of new crops, travel, urban living, new needs for warfare and new modes of warfare, new mores of sexual behaviour – meant that people were continually changing the environment in which they lived. New epidemic diseases were inevitably among the consequences.

DISASTER

The importance of astrology to explaining the arrival of epidemic diseases, particularly of the pox, has already been indicated. Doctors were trained in astrology in their university courses. As we have seen, they usually ascribed the outbreak of epidemics to a change in the air, itself brought on usually by a change in the heavens – that is, among the planets. The affected air was thought to act on the body like a poison, outside the normal course of diseases, which helped account for the non-normal course and impact of epidemic diseases. This kind of explanation, leaning on astrology, was given at every outbreak of the French pox, of the English sweat, of plague and of typhus.

As we have already seen in Chapter 1, on the White Horse, portents in the sky and natural disasters and supernatural events were all interpreted as signs of the End. A dis-aster is literally the effect of an unfavourable aspect of a star or planet: or an 'obnoxious' planet.[106] Right through our period the existence of some sort of important connection between celestial and terrestrial bodies, which eventuated in a *causal* connection between celestial and terrestrial events, was taken for granted by everyone. It was always controversial, but mostly believed in and practised. We need to remember that for most astrologers, an astrological explanation was not a *supernatural* one (as we would consider it today), but rather a *natural* one, pointing to a natural route of causation used by God, employing the stars as *secondary* causes, through eclipses, conjunctions of planets, and by the position of particular planets in the zodiac. Indeed, astrology shared the same concept of causality as did the dominant theory of physics of the time, as taught in the universities: that of Aristotle.[107] But when people believed, as they sometimes did, that the stars were *first* causes, then their astrology was heretical by Christian standards, since

God's agency was thus denied while active agency was ascribed to the planets themselves.

The primary astrological theory that was called on to predict and explain disasters on earth was the doctrine of the 'Great Conjunctions'. Based ultimately on an ancient Greek theory that 'the planets, returning to the same point of longitude and latitude which each occupied when first the universe arose, at fixed periods of time bring about a conflagration and destruction of things',[108] its theoretical underpinnings were taken from the Muslim philosopher Albumasar (ninth century AD). Within this theory special importance was given to certain historical periods, which supposedly correspond to the periods of the 'regular' (20 years), the 'major' (240 years) and the 'maximum' (960 years) conjunctions of Saturn, Jupiter and Mars. Moreover, it was a point of principle in this theory that the rarer the conjunction, the more potent its force on political and religious events on earth.[109] Hence the expectation that the 'major' conjunctions would bring with them disastrous events such as epidemic diseases and famines, and the rise and fall of dynasties and religions. Because the theory invoked regular periods between conjunctions, it was possible to predict disasters as well as explain them after they had happened. Some of the predictions turned out to be true, while the less successful ones could be explained away by special local circumstances. The theory of the Great Conjunctions was constantly called on throughout the sixteenth century, and was eminently respectable, being believed in by academics and church dignitaries, both Catholic and Protestant, and by the members of princely and papal courts. In itself, there was nothing inherently Christian about this theory of the Great Conjunctions, as it did not involve God's agency. But of course it was deployed by people who were Christian believers, so it was constantly related to Christian views of a providential God who was both loving and punitive. Hence God could be taken to be using secondary causes – the planets – to express His anger and call on Christians to cease their sinning. This ambiguity between the purely secular and the thoroughgoing Christian interpretations of the movements of the heavenly bodies accounts for the repeated arguments over whether astrology was or was not an appropriate study for a believing Christian.

Moreover, to this respectable Greek and Arab tradition of astrology in the Great Conjunctions, was conjoined something seemingly similar, but with a distinctively Christian and apocalyptic dimension. This was Joachimism: a Christian and popular movement predicting the imminent end of the world, and which called on the conjunctions of the planets in its support. Joachim of Fiore, an abbot and prophet of the twelfth century, had been very concerned with the Apocalypse, and with predicting when the Antichrist would come. His writings, and those of others writing prophetically in imitation of him, had been taken up very seriously by the Spiritual Franciscans, who saw St Francis himself as the initiator of the third and final period of world history, as the Angel of the Sixth Seal. This Joachimist view of the world and its history made a popular connection of astrology with concepts of a Messianic Age, a Millennium, the preachers of Antichrist, and the like. Thus disastrous events on earth were connected, via the planets and stars, to the imminence of the Apocalypse. Plagues were signs of the Second Coming. Thus we need to recognise that episodes of plague in this period did not of themselves bring on a religious *reaction*, leading to fears of the Apocalypse, but by contrast were frequently taken as *signs* of the Second Coming.[110]

Astrology was challenged from time to time. The greatest challenge on logical and intellectual grounds to astrological divination came from a work by Pico della Mirandola, which was prepared in 1493 though not published until later. But even though Pico shows himself critical of the astrologers' methods and results, he nevertheless readily accepted that the heavens influence terrestrial events. His attack on astrology did not prove its death-blow by any means. His nephew was embroiled in a debate on the same theme a few years later, when Agostino Nifo in 1504 supported astrology in a work on the causes of the calamities of the day. According to Lynn Thorndike, Nifo lists the recent calamities and misfortunes: 'various diseases, acts of violence, immoralities, the crimes of Caesar Borgia. Then he divides their causes into four books: the first on eclipses – there have been ten visible in Italy within a decade – the second on comets, the third on synods and annual conversions, the fourth on the 119 conjunctions'. Giovanni Francesco Pico della Mirandola eventually, in 1519, replied with a work on *The True Causes of the Calamities of our Times*, addressed to Pope Leo X. He denied all the astrological causes that had been proposed by Nifo, or that the ills were the work of chance and fortune. However, he found their causes in God, in the crimes of men, the discord and wars of kings and peoples.[111]

In addition to astrology being important for doctors at the time of epidemics, specifically astrological kinds of medicine were also practised.[112] William Lilly, for instance, publishing in 1647, thought he could promote a Christianised astrology.[113] He was not very precise about how to resolve the problems inherent in this position – that is, quite how or why God allowed the planets to fulfil, as instruments, His high decree or will, or why they could be used to foretell what God had ordained. He wrote to his reader that he should be fearful of God:

> My Friend . . . In the first place, consider and admire thy *Creator*, and be thankful unto him, be thou humble, and let no natural knowledge, how profound and transcendent soever it be, elate thy mind to neglect that *divine Providence*, by whose all-seeing order and appointment, all things heavenly and earthly, have their constant motion; but the more thy knowledge is enlarged, the more do thou magnify the power and wisdom of *Almighty God*, and strive to preserve thyself in his favour; being confident, the more holy thou art, and more near to God, the purer *Judgement* thou shalt give . . . How many *pre-eminences, privileges, advantages* hath God bestowed on thee? thou rangest about the heavens by *contemplation*, conceivest the *motion* and *magnitude* of the *stars*; thou talkest with *Angels*, yea with God himself . . . As thou daily conversest with the heavens [in performing astrology], so instruct and form thy mind according to the image of *Divinity*; learn all the ornaments of *virtue*, be sufficiently instructed therein; be humane, courteous, familiar to all, easy of access, afflict not the *miserable* with terror of a harsh *judgement*; in such cases, let them know their hard fate by degrees; direct them to call on *God* to divert his *judgements* impending over them . . . let no worldly wealth procure an *erroneous judgement* from thee, or such as may dishonour the *Art*, or this divine *Science*.

Lilly's Christianised astrology was very domestic: how to find things lost, how to predict conception and whether a child will be a boy or a girl, would someone become rich or not, would a messenger sent to collect a debt return successful or not. The whole of daily life was subject to astrological worry. Amongst these domestic cares Lilly also applied his astrology systematically to questions about illness, erecting his astrological figure on the time when the patient was so ill he had to take to his bed, or had to have his urine taken to a physician. This 'Christian Astrology' could answer questions such as what part of the body is affected, the identity of the disease, its duration and outcome, whether it would be fatal, what medicines to apply. But with medicine as with everything else, astrology at this level was exquisitely linked to the lives of individuals, not to people in the mass as they might undergo an epidemic disease.

Indeed the daily lives of people in Europe during this whole period were full of low-grade astrology and of belief in the role of the stars: the period did not witness a reduction in superstitious astrological belief but, if anything, an increase, even amongst the highly educated. Indeed, the production of almanacs and prognostications was one of the most basic uses of printing. Thus it is understandable how astrology on the grand scale – predicting or explaining disasters such as epidemics, famines or wars – was not out of place; it did not represent a different kind of explanation or belief to be appealed to only in times of grave crisis, but was very much of a piece with the rest.

In addition to these roles, astrology played a crucial part in an extremely important new kind of medicine which was itself apocalyptic in inspiration, and which spread throughout Europe, challenging the medical system inherited from the ancient Greeks which was taught in the universities. In the spring of 1527 a physician of a new kind, calling himself Paracelsus (Philippus Aureolus Theophrastus), arrived in Basel during the course of its religious reformation. He was appointed by the town council to a position in the university, as part of the strategies the council was using to bring the university round to the new religious confession. Here he first taught publicly his new medicine. This medicine was – unlike that of Galen and Hippocrates – Christian in inspiration, form, aims and content. Paracelsus was an extreme radical reformer, a Spiritualist. For him the true physician should be someone who was dedicated primarily to four things: to seeking the kingdom of God, to the knowledge of the stars, to alchemy and to living an upright Christian life. Man was a microcosm of the universe, and his health could only be maintained by understanding the interdependence of celestial and terrestial events, which were connected by a kind of magic.[114] One of the keys to understanding the correspondences, Paracelsus believed, lay in the book of Revelation.[115] Astrology was crucial since it taught one the power of the firmament, and one could predict the outcome of cases on this basis. In his own time Paracelsus was renowned for his predictions and prophecies in general, which had an eschatological framework, since Paracelsus 'believed that the Day of Judgement was near and might come at any time'.[116] Only the person inspired by the Holy Spirit could be a true physician, and thus carry out God's and Christ's work in caring for the sick. The true physician consulted the stars and the correspondences between the heavens and terrestrial things, seeking in plants and minerals 'signatures' which indicated their true uses for cure and bodily purification. Inspired by the Spirit, the physician prepared his medicines by use of the fire: successively separating the powerful part – the spiritual power – of plants and minerals from their material dross by chemical operations.

In 1529 Paracelsus published his book attacking the use of guaiacum wood in the pox. He had in 1525 apparently seen the use of the guaiac cure in the *Holzhaus* at the *Fuggerei*. He believed that the Fuggers were conspiring against the poor in their monopoly of the wood, and that they were acting hand in hand with Cardinal Lang and the Catholic Church.[117] Instead of the wood, Paracelsus advocated the use of mercury, recommending mercury ointment together with healthy diet, sexual restraint and isolation of the sick.[118] Paracelsian medicine had great appeal for the poor, the artisan, the person opposed to established authority and monopoly. In particular Paracelsian doctrines appealed to radical Protestants, and it was of great ideological importance for a century and a half, being developed and practised in the English Revolution of the mid-seventeenth century, especially in the form developed by Paracelsus's follower J. B. Van Helmont. Van Helmont was very aware of the appearance of new diseases in the sixteenth and early seventeenth centuries, and of fiercer forms of known diseases, and equally aware of their ultimate cause: 'as the Scurvy, Plague of *Hungary*, &c. unknown to our Ancestors: but our stripes increase daily, because impieties are multiplied. Truly diseases are changed, are masked, are increased, and do degenerate through their coupling'. As for the causes, Van Helmont referred to an apparition that several saints had seen, of an angry Saviour armed with three darts:

> For covetousness there was a dart of Wars . . . for pride, there was in the hand of the Almighty, a dart of want and famine . . . and at length against luxury, he bare a dart of contagion or infection in his hand . . . [and] under the fullness of days, under the maturity and completed number of sinners, the long-suffering God sent forth one of the three darts into the middle of the flesh, and forthwith the *Lues Venerea* [French pox] appeared, being plainly cruel, poisonous, and killing with a poisonous putrefaction.[119]

These were the darts sent by the infant Christ: the reformed, mystical, Christian, astrological, medicine of Paracelsus and Van Helmont had a strong eschatological message.

DEATH

The population rise of this period had led to many man-made changes in the human environment, and these in turn had led to epidemics, of great severity and frequency and of many kinds, on an unprecedented scale. Death – sudden death – was thus always threatening, and preparation for it had to be on the conscience of every Christian. God sent disease, but God wanted the soul of every person to be preserved for the after-life. Frequent episodes of mortal epidemic diseases meant that life as experienced across Europe was deeply unstable: health was fragile for everyone, plague and plagues could find everyone out. The Horseman on the Pale Horse, whose visits punished sin and promised apocalypse, was, appropriately, a skeleton, now intended as a death figure, and Hell followed with him.

Thus the Horseman on the Pale Horse signified Death. The diseases and disasters of this Apocalyptic Age, in all their profusion and unpredictability, meant that death was an ever-present feature of daily life. The sight of other people dying was familiar to everyone, and celebration or marking of their deaths was customary. For a Christian, his or her death, and what comes after it, is both the end of life, and thus to be feared, but also the beginning of the high-point of the journey of life, and thus to be anticipated with joy, for it means the end of the exile of the soul in this world. It will be no surprise to learn that images of death were everywhere in this period, reminding the Christian of the ubiquity of death, of the shortness of life, of the need to prepare for the after-life. Printing helped spread these visual and verbal messages to the semi-literate and completely illiterate. In the words of the great French historian of art, Emile Mâle, 'the image of death was everywhere' in the fifteenth century, while 'no century was more familiar with death than the sixteenth. Its generations seem to have made friends with death. They put its image everywhere.'[120] We will discuss three parallel, and virtually simultaneous, traditions of representation of death, whose impacts were mutually reinforcing.

The first of these traditions, that of the *ars moriendi*, the art of dying well, was represented in numerous books and woodcuts in many languages, from Catalan to Danish, from before the 1490s through to the mid-seventeenth century. It originated in the early fifteenth century, around 1418, and probably as an outcome of the Council of Constance which had wished to promote greater devotion in Christian living.[121] It continued to be popular during the sixteenth century. It was known in two forms: either as a plain text, the 'Treatise or Mirror of the Art of Dying Well', or as a series of illustrations with a shorter text. The version with illustrations was published as early as 1450 as a block-book. The purpose of the work, in both versions, was to prepare people for when they died, and also to instruct the bystanders to pray and counsel the dying person. It was a handbook for dying with dignity and in the Christian faith, used by both Catholics and Protestants. Erasmus, Thomas Lupset and other humanists produced versions of their own.[122] It appeared in literally dozens of editions, with almost a hundred versions being published before 1500 alone.

William Caxton, the London printer, translated one version from Latin and published it in London in 1490:

When it is so that what a man maketh or doeth, it is made to come to some end, and if the thing be good and well made, it must needs to come to good end, then by better and greater reason, every man ought to intend in some wise to live in this world, in keeping the commandments of God, that he may come to a good end. And that out of this world of wretchedness and tribulations, he may go to heaven unto God and his saints into joy perdurable. But now, in these days, few there be that advise them[-selves] of their end so much as they ought to do, though they be sick, ancient or old. And to them cometh that folly by a foolish hope, that every man, in what estate he be, hath an hope to live long. And therefore hath this present treatise been made, composed in short terms, for to teach every man well to die, whilst he hath understanding, health, and reason. To the end that it is needful to him to be the better warned, informed, and taught, the which treatise is divided into six parts, of which the first treateth the praising of death, and how one ought to die gladly. The second treateth of the temptations that they have which be or lie in the article of death. The third treatise is of the questions that ought to be made to them then. The fourth containeth a manner of instructions and of teaching that ought to be made to them. The fifth of the remembrance what God hath done and suffered for us. The sixth and last treateth of certain oraisons and devout prayers that they ought to say if they may, or else ought to be said for them by some that be assistant or present.[123]

The illustrated version of the *ars moriendi* takes the second book of 'The Art of Dying Well', and shows the dying man, 'Moriens', being put through five temptations 'which lie in the article of death', by the Devil, and receiving five inspirations from Scripture and the Church from an angel. He is tempted to (i) give up his faith, (ii) to despair, (iii) to not suffer patiently, (iv) to vainglory and (v) to avarice, that is to desire the things of this world rather than the next. He is inspired by Scripture and the Church to resist each of these temptations. If the advice was followed then the soul of the Christian was received into heaven and the devil and his demons were defeated (Plates 5.12 and 5.13). The third temptation is illustrated here, the temptation to impatience in the suffering of the dying man. The demon says 'How well I have deceived him'. The good inspiration of the angel toward patience is the next picture. God is shown with an arrow. The four saints represented here are all ones who had to be patient under suffering: St Barbara with her tower; St Catherine with her wheel; St Lawrence with his gridiron; St Stephen holding the stones with which he was stoned. The demons cry 'I have been taken captive' (Sum captivatus) and 'Lost labour' (labores amisi). It has been argued that the *ars moriendi* both represents, and encouraged, a tradition of public death-bed spectacle.[124]

The second widespread form of visual image reminding people of the imminence of death and the need to prepare for it, was the *memento mori*:

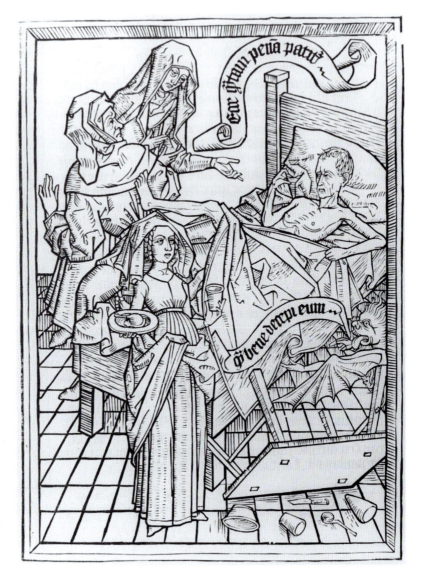

Plate 5.12 The third
temptation from The Art
of Dying, 1450. The Arts
Moriendi (Editio Princeps,
circa 1450). A Reproduction
of the Copy in the British
Museum, ed. W. Harry
Rylands (London, 1881)

Plate 5.13 (opposite)
The third inspiration
from The Art of Dying,
1450. The Ars Moriendi
(Editio Princeps, circa
1450), A Reproduction of the
Copy in the British Museum,
ed. W. Harry Rylands
(London, 1881)

the picture with the message 'remember your death'. This was a conceit,
often used throughout this period in portraits of the well-to-do. The live
sitter would be portrayed holding or looking at a skull, or looking into a
mirror where a skull reflects the live face. The message is 'I was once what
you [the viewer] are now: a living being. What I am now, you will also be: a
skeleton. The portrait shows my face as it was: a skull shows it as it is.'[125] In
this highly peopled age, life was ephemeral, human life was the vanity of
vanities.

A third tradition of portraying the ever-presentness of death, was that known as the 'Dance of Death'. This could be found painted on the walls of cemeteries and churches from Ferrara to Edinburgh, and in many printed books too. The Dance of Death, or Danse Macabre, was apparently first painted on the wall of the cemetery of the Church of the Holy Innocents in Paris in 1424–5. The Paris painting became a celebrated sight, and was copied across most of Europe in various forms right through until 1635.[126]

At the Church of the Holy Innocents charnel houses were used to store and display the bones of those who had once been buried in the cemetery, but who had been dispossessed of their graves to make room for fresh corpses. As a contemporary remarked, 'these skulls, piled up in these charnel houses, they may have been magistrates . . . or else just street porters; I might as well say the one as the other. For all I know, they were either bishops or lamp-lighters . . . They are all jumbled together in a heap now.'[127] Taking its key from the presence of all these bones, the great painting on the cemetery wall used, for the first time, the image of the skeleton to represent Death as a character, and in a long cycle of images it showed Death leading men and women of all stations in life into the dance of death.

The Dance of Death is a procession in which both the living and the dead take part, with up to 40 characters portrayed in the printed versions, from the pope and emperor to the hallbardier and the sot, each being addressed in verse by Death and responding in verse to Death. The orders of the Church are represented including the cardinal, patriarch, archbishop, bishop, abbot, priest, monk and friar. So too are the degrees of lay society: the king, constable, baron, knight, bourgeois, merchant, teacher, physician, lawyer, minstrel, jailer, pilgrim and labourer.

The Danse Macabre was first printed in Paris in 1485 by Guy Marchant, reproducing the verses from the wall of the Holy Innocents cemetery, and its images too may possibly be copies of those painted on its walls.[128] Its moral purpose is described in its title: 'A saving mirror for every person, and of all estates. And it is of great utility and consolation, for the many lessons both in Latin and French that it contains. Composed thus for those who desire and seek their salvation, and who want to possess it.'[129] The astrologer and bourgeois, the prebend and the merchant, are all led into Death's dance, their work in this world all of no avail (Plates 5.14 and 5.15). The Danse Macabre was a great success, being followed by frequent subsequent printings, and being given a parallel 'Danse Macabre des Femmes'.

The painted versions of the Dance second in fame to that of Paris, were the two in Basel: the Grossbasel Totentanz and the Kleinbasel Totentanz. The

Plate 5.14 (opposite)
The Dance of Death,
1486. La Danse Macabre,
Reproduction en Fac-Similé
de l'Edition de Guy
Marchant, Paris, 1486
(Paris, 1925)

Mors facit exosū: res auffert: atz coloꝛe. Vermib⁹ exponit: fetecia coꝛpoꝛa reddit,
Vado moꝛi ſapiens. ſed quid
ſapiencia nouit: Moꝛtis cau
telas fallere: vado moꝛi.

Vado moꝛi ſperans per longum
viuere tempus. Foꝛte dies hec
eſt vltima. vado moꝛi.

Le moꝛt

Maiſtre: pour voſtre regarder
En hault: ne pour voſtre clergie:
Ne pouez la moꝛt retarder.
Cy ne vault rien aſtrologie.
Toute la genealogie
Dadam qui fut le premier homme
Moꝛt pꝛent: ce dit theologie.
Tous fault mouꝛir pour vne pōme

Laſtrologien

Pour ſcience ne pour degrez:
Ne puis auoir pꝛouiſion.
Car maintenant tous mes regrez
Sont: moꝛir a confuſion.
Pour finable concluſion.
Je ne ſcay rien que plus deſcriue.
Je pers cy toute aduiſion.
Qui vouldꝛa bien moꝛir bien viue

Le moꝛt

Bourgoiſ haſtez vouſ ſans tarder.
Vous nauez auoir ne richeſſe
Qui vous puiſſe de moꝛt garder.
Se des biens dont euſtes largeſſe:
Aues bien vſe: ceſt ſageſſe.
Dautruy viét tout: a atruy paſſe
Fol eſt qui damaſſer ſe bleſſe.
On ne ſcet pour qui on amaſſe.

Le bourgois

Grant mal me fait ſi toſt laiſſier
Rentes: maiſōs: cens: noꝛꝛitures
Mais pouures: riches abaiſſier
Tu faiz moꝛt: telle eſt ta nature
Sage neſt pas la creature.
Damer trop les biens q̄ demeurét
Au monde: et ſont ſien de dꝛoiture.
Ceulx q̄ plus ont: plus éuiz meurét

Es sapiens: marcet sapiencia morte. redundans Diuiciis: lapsu mobiliore fluūt
Dado mori non me tenetorna   Dado mori magnus mundi
tus: neꝗ vestis: ꝉ inea: nec   moriturus amator. Hunc
mollis culcitra vado mori.   spernens possū dicere vado mori

Le mort   *Le mort*
Sire chanoine prebendez: Marchant: regardez par deca.
Plus ne aures distribucion: Pleuseurs pays auez cerchie
Ne gros: ne vous il acttendez: A pie: et a cheual de pieca:
Prenez cy consolacion.   Vous nen seres plus empeschie.
Pour toute retribucion   Decy vostre dernier marchie.
Mourir voꝰ conuient sãs demeure   Il conuient que par cy passez.
Ia ny aurez dilation.   De tout soing seres despeschie.
La mort vient quon ne garde leure   Tel couuoite qui a assez.
        Le chanoine   *Le marchant*
Cecy guere ne me conforte: Jay este amont et aual:
Prebende fus en mainte eglise.   Pour marchander ou ie pouoye.
Or est la mort plus que moy forte: Par long temps a pie: a cheual:
Que tot en mainne: cest sa guise.   Mais maintenant pers toute ioye
Blanc surpelis et amusse grise   De tout mon pouoir acqueroye:
Me fault laissier: et a mort rendre. Or ay ie assez. mort me contraint.
Que vault gloire sy tost bas mise.   Bon fait aller moyenne voye.
A bien morir doit chascun tendre.   Qui trop embrasse peu estraint.

Plate 5.15 The Dance of
Death, 1486. *La Danse
Macabre. Reproduction en
Fac-Similé de l'Edition de
Guy Marchant, Paris,
1486* (Paris, 1925)

Grossbasel version, painted on the wall of a Dominican churchyard, is
probably a copy from about 1480 of the earlier Kleinbasel one, which had
been in an Augustinian nunnery and dated from about 1450. The Basel
Totentanzen was one of the inspirations for Hans Holbein. In the 1520s
Holbein produced two series of exquisite woodcuts of the Dance of Death,
the second of which has continued to be celebrated since it was first printed
in 1538 in Lyons under the title 'Les simulachres et historiees faces de la

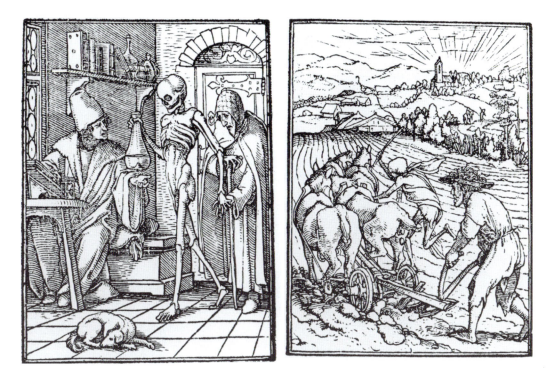

Plate 5.16 'Physician cure thyself', from the Dance of Death, 1538. *The Dance of Death. 41 Woodcuts by Hans Holbein the Younger. Complete Facsimile of the Original 1538 French Edition*

Plate 5.17 'In the sweat of thy face shalt thou eat bread', from The Dance of Death, 1538. *The Dance of Death. 41 Woodcuts by Hans Holbein the Younger. Complete Facsimile of the Original 1538 French Edition*

mort', that is, 'Images and storied aspects of Death'. The artistic inspiration of Holbein is matched by the astonishing skill of the block-cutter Lützelburger. Of the 41 illustrations showing a wide range of occupations, from emperor to pedlar, Plates 5.16 and 5.17 show the physician and the ploughman. The physician is advised to 'heal thyself' (Luke 4:23): although he knows how to heal his patient, he does not know the illness from which he himself will die. The ploughman fulfils God's curse in Genesis: 'in the sweat of thy face shalt thou eat bread, till thou return unto the ground' (Genesis 3:19). But after all the ploughman's work, death will come to take him away. This work went through many editions, thus spreading the images of the Dance of Death very widely. Death awaits everyone, no matter their station in life.[130]

The point of combining the sombreness of Death and the joyfulness of the dance is not self-evident to us today. But to contemporaries it had a twofold meaning. One (of course), to remind everyone that no matter what their status or what they achieve in life, death nevertheless awaits them, when their wealth and wisdom shall be of no avail; and two, since the skeletons are represented as joyous, the painting combines the twin, contradictory, Christian attitudes to death: it is to be feared, and it is to be welcomed.

This of course corresponds to the Day of Judgement, which was also to be feared and welcomed simultaneously. And in an apocalyptic context, death means more than the death of the individual. It means also the death of mankind at the Day of Judgement, something which obsessed the people of this age. Part of the vision of John in the Book of Revelation was of the Day of Judgement, the resurrection of the dead, and the everlasting life which all Christians desired:

> And I saw a great white throne, and him that sat on it, from whose face the earth and the heaven fled away; and there was found no place for them. And I saw the dead, small and great, stand before God: and the books were opened: and another book was opened, which is the book of life: and the dead were judged out of those things that were written in the books, according to their works . . . And I saw a new heaven and a new earth. (Revelation 20:11–12; 21:1)

6 Epilogue

In the four parts of this book we have respectively dealt with the crises or scourges associated with the White, Red, Black, and Pale Horsemen from the Book of Revelation. We have argued that these were images which contemporaries used, not only to understand, but also to decode and give meaning to the troubles and disasters which they found themselves exposed to in the increasingly unstable and changing world of the sixteenth and early seventeenth centuries. For early modern European society witnessed dramatic changes in social, religious and political terms, due in particular to the demographic expansion which saw Europe's population grow continuously from the late fifteenth century until the mid-seventeenth century, following upon more than a century of stagnation after the Black Death in 1348.

The Bible, printed for the first time in the vernacular in mass-produced and relatively cheap editions, provided an interpretative 'looking-glass' for lay Christians who could read. They in turn would read it aloud to their family and friends. They used the Bible to try to comprehend the many changes and disasters they were experiencing. Reading the Bible, it became evident to many of them that Luther's appearance and religious message was a prophetic, indeed apocalyptic event, which had served to save the Gospel from total corruption by the Devil and Antichrist.

Thus to contemporaries the increase and growing intensity of warfare, new epidemics and diseases, not to mention the higher incidence of famine, and the perceived increase in celestial signs, such as comets, new stars and great conjunctions, plus natural and supernatural portents such as monstrous births and witchcraft, were all evidence that the Day of Judgement, as foretold in the Bible, was rapidly approaching. Obviously, these scourges often appeared separately, but the truly remarkable aspect of these 150 years of European history, is the fact that they were increasingly seen to appear together, to an extent, and with a magnitude and intensity, which had never before happened in history. It was exactly as Dürer had portrayed them in his woodcut of 1498: galloping together across the sky and bringing upon early modern man all possible eschatological punishments and trials.

These afflictions were also seen to strike mankind with much greater frequency, and also in conjunction – as prophesyed in the Bible – and this served to heighten anxiety within Western Christianity, and gave rise to a growing and sustained apocalypticism during our period. This sense of apocalyptic affliction brought on by all the scourges of the Four Horsemen of the Apocalypse was repeatedly felt within every locality, while occasionally it engulfed nearly the whole of Europe.

A good example of simultaneous affliction by all the Horsemen can be seen in the events in Germany during the Peasants' Wars of the mid-1520s. Rumours and news of this conflict affected the whole of Europe, and its eschatological significance was immediately recognised. The southern and central areas of Germany where the peasants rebelled had seen a wave of failed harvests from the 1490s to 1519 causing severe shortages, while the great and destructive hailstorm in July 1524, which passed through many of these parts of Germany, caused further suffering. The unwillingness of the local feudal landlords to take these disasters into account in their demands for rent and tithes added to the peasants' grievances at a time when the peasants were beginning to question both political and religious authority.[1] The evangelical movement in general, and Luther in particular, had unwittingly provided a religious, apocalyptic matrix for the peasants by identifying the pope with Antichrist and shaping their own theological arguments in strongly eschatological terms. The peasants themselves could find confirmation for such views and for their own anxiety in Luther's own newly published translation of the New Testament. The millenarian and apocalyptic dimensions of the Peasants' Wars were amplified when evangelical and millenarian preachers such as Thomas Müntzer joined the peasants' struggle.

In the 1520s this feeling that the Day of Judgement was imminent, was of course not confined to the peasants who had taken up arms against their feudal masters, for it also affected law-abiding citizens across Europe who found proof of it in the breakdown of the traditional social order caused by the peasants' rebellion. Their anxiety was fed by what they saw as the ever growing threat to Western Christianity from the Ottoman Turks. The fall of the impregnable fortress of Rhodes to the Moslems in 1522 had caused a great stir across Europe, and when by the middle of the 1520s the Moslem forces of Suleiman the Magnificent were conquering most of the Balkans and Hungary, many ordinary Christians felt a deep sense of despair.

The epidemics of the 1520s, which affected most of Europe, added further fuel to people's eschatological expectations. The pox, still being seen as a new disease or punishment from God, was spreading rapidly in a highly virulent form in the decade leading up to 1520. By 1522 plague had returned with a vengeance. The English sweating sickness, another 'new' disease, affected most of the coastal areas around the North Sea in the 1520s, causing considerable distress. Writing in the mid-1550s the Danish Lutheran church leader, Peder Palladius, emphasised how this disease had arrived 30 years ago 'through the wrath of God' and had 'rushed through the country like a consuming fire, killing many, including those who had never been to England'. Like the other new diseases, this disease, according to Palladius, was a punishment from God for new sins in an age of decaying morals, all signifying that the world was rapidly coming to its End.[2]

The planetary conjunction in 1524 confirmed the eschatological expectations of contemporaries. By the beginning of the sixteenth century, the growing popular preoccupation with apocalyptic astrology was being nourished by the publication of a growing number of cheap printed *practica* and *prognostica*, as well as sermons which drew attention to signs in the sky. There was ample support for the idea that the End was, indeed, imminent. Thus the conjunction of planets in Pisces in February 1524 generated a virtual explosion of eschatological speculation. Around 160 pamphlets dealing with this subject were published, and it caused mass hysteria and collective panic across Europe, especially because of the forecast of a Second Deluge, a biblical eschatological event linked to the Second Coming of Christ. Despite the failure of the expected deluge to appear, such astrological prophecies continued to affect the popular imagination, especially since a fair number of the pamphlets or *practica* had correctly forecast uprisings by the common man, seeking to institute a regime of social justice and equality, i.e. the Peasants' Wars.

Just as this whole set of eschatological events had occurred in quick succession in the 1520s, each reinforcing the apocalyptic message of the other, so similar widespread apocalyptic scares affected most of Europe a hundred years later, on the eve of the Thirty Years War. The appearance of 'Halley's' Comet in 1618 was followed by failed harvests in the early 1620s and by the return of major plague epidemics, especially in Northern Protestant Europe. By then these areas were already deeply preoccupied with the inability of the Protestant powers to stop the victorious armies of the Catholic Counter-Reformation and Antichrist in Germany, causing deep apocalyptic anxiety among Lutherans and Calvinists.

Yet by the end of the Thirty Years War in 1648, the apocalyptic age was pretty much over, except in England and Scotland where it had a somewhat longer life during the Civil Wars and Republic. The incidence of war, famine and epidemic disease decreased, while the interpretations of their arrival no longer insisted so strongly on their apocalyptic message. Why did this change happen? What underlay the transition from an apocalyptic age to a post-apocalyptic age?

We have been arguing in the course of the book that there really was an exceptional number of wars, of outbreaks of epidemic disease and of famines in the period 1490 to 1648, and that the spontaneous interpretation of these events in apocalyptic terms was natural in a period of great religious fervour and friction. Further, we have argued that what underlay these disasters was the constant pressure of population increase. The impulse of population growth was so great that the population of Western Europe as a whole at least doubled during this period, despite all the hundreds of thousands of premature deaths that war, epidemic disease and famine caused. It seems probable that this population increase in turn was prompted and propelled by the climatic changes – the 'global warming' – of these same 150 years.

The relation between climate and long-term population increase or decrease is not sufficiently proven for us to speak of a direct causal connection between the two. However, it is striking how closely the two cycles, climate and population, seem to have run together at this time: the warming period of c.1470 to c.1590 was followed by a cold period, what has been called a 'little ice age'. In turn, the great population increase of our apocalyptic age was followed by a period of population stagnation from around 1650 in most areas of Europe, lasting for a century or more.

At all events, whatever its cause, it is a matter of consensus amongst historians that the dynamic population growth typical of Western Europe in the sixteenth century stopped early in the seventeenth century. According to the demographic historian Michael Flinn, for instance, population growth in Spain had stopped by 1590; in England by 1640; in France by the 1650s; in Germany he says, due to the effects of the Thirty Years War (which ended in 1648), 'there can hardly have been any secular growth of German population during the seventeenth century'. Only in Holland and Scandinavia was there growth in the second half of the seventeenth century, and even that was very modest.[3]

The great epidemics of infectious disease seem to have pretty much followed this same pattern, which indicates that just as their arrival and incidence were directly related to the population growth of the period 1490 to 1648, so the diminution in their incidence was directly related to the population stabilisation. The great pandemics of plague were receding from Western Europe. There were very serious outbreaks in the 1630s, 1640s and 1650s. But apart from a localised outbreak in Marseilles in 1720, the great plague of 1665 was the last such event in Western Europe until the nineteenth century. The drama of the great pox was also over, as the disease seems to have stabilised and become endemic rather than epidemic. Siege disease effectively disappeared as sieges became less frequently employed as a military tactic – and indeed major wars themselves became less frequent for a period, as the so-called 'military revolution' came to an end.

With respect to famines, there was a diminution of subsistence crises in peace-time after the mid-seventeenth century. Flinn has written that 'sheer famine was less obvious . . . though severe, often prolonged hunger remained the lot of many of the poorer Europeans'.[4] Thus the incidence of famine also followed the curve of population. Possibly the famine relief measures of the Poor Laws made a substantial difference in preventing unnecessary deaths in times of dearth and famine.

Altogether, as the population stabilised, so the people of Western Europe were able to break out of the cycle of crises of war, famine and disease which had characterised the period from 1490 to 1648. As the crises themselves retreated, so there was less need for them to be interpreted as divine messages, and in particular there was less occasion for them to be treated as signs of the imminence of the Apocalypse. As the Apocalypse receded into the future, so the importance of its herald, Antichrist, also diminished. With the exception of England until the 1660s, Antichrist was less frequently detected either on the papal throne or elsewhere. While Antichrist did not disappear completely, he did not again become so important until the end of the eighteenth century. With the Peace of Westphalia in 1648, ending the Thirty Years War, the period of religious confrontation between different forms of Christianity within the Holy Roman Empire came to an end.[5] The Peace created a framework for the peaceful co-existence of the major Christian denominations: Catholicism, Lutheranism and Calvinism. Thus the Four Horsemen of the Apocalypse were no longer constantly seen riding across the sky signalling that the end of the world was nigh.

Notes

1 INTRODUCTION: AN APOCALYPTIC AGE

1 For surveys, see Bob Scribner, '1525 – Revolutionary Crisis?', in *Krisenbewußtsein und Krisenbewältigung in der Frühen Neuzeit – Crisis in Early Modern Europe*, ed. Monika Hagenmaier and Sabine Holt, Frankfurt am Main 1992, 25–45; Ferdinand Seibt and Winfried Eberhard, eds., *Europa 1400: Die Krise des Spätmittelalters*, Stuttgart 1984; Ferdinand Seibt and Winfried Eberhard, eds., *Europa 1500: Integrationsprozesse im Widerstreit: Staaten, Regionen. Personenverbände, Christenheit*, Stuttgart 1987.

2 See Robert Scribner, 'Oral Culture and the Diffusion of Reformation Ideas', *History of European Ideas*, 5, 1984, 237–56.

3 On this aspect, see Jean Delumeau, *La Peur en Occident (xIVe–xVIIIe siècles): une Cité Assiégée*, Paris 1978.

4 R. W. Scribner, *For the Sake of Simple Folk: Popular Propaganda for the German Reformation*, Oxford 1994, 148–63.

5 Joseph Wittreich, 'The Apocalypse: A Bibliography', in *The Apocalypse in English Renaissance Thought and Literature*, ed. C. A. Patrides and Joseph Wittreich, Manchester 1984, 369–440.

6 Alexander Perrig, *Albrecht Dürer oder die Heimlichkeit der deutschen Ketzerei: Die Apokalypse Dürers und anderer Werke 1495 bis 1513*, Würzburg 1987, 1.

7 For these pre-1498 illustrations, see F. van der Meer, *Apocalypse: Visions from the Book of Revelation in Western Art*, London 1978.

8 For the dating of the Dutch block-books, see E. Purpus, 'Die Blockbücher der Apokalypse', in *Blockbücher des Mittelalters*, Mainz 1991, 81–97. We would like to thank Dr Kristian Jensen of the British Library for drawing this work to our attention.

9 Jane Campbell Hutchison, *Albrecht Dürer, A Biography*, Princeton, New Jersey 1990, 61. See also the essays in D. Eichberger and C. Zika, eds., *Dürer and his Culture*, Cambridge 1998.

10 It has been argued that Cranach only drew superficially on Dürer for his illustrations: see P. Martin, *Martin Luther und die Bilde zur Apokalypse*, Hamburg, 1983, 88–90, 115 ff., and Robin Bruce Barnes, *Prophecy and Gnosis. Apocalypticism in the Wake of the Lutheran Reformation*, Stanford, 1988. This may hold true for a number of the twenty-one illustrations (six more than Dürer) which Cranach cut for the 1522 New Testament, where the identification of Antichrist – beast of the Apocalypse – with the papacy is made for the first time. But it certainly does not hold true for the image of the Four Horsemen, something which Martin acknowledges (36–42).

11 P. Schmidt, *Illustrierte Lutherbibel 1522–1700*, Basle 1962, 304–6.

12 Merian's elaboration of the theme may have something to do with the limited number of illustrations he used (only nine); see Schmidt, *Illustrierte Lutherbibel 1522–1700*, 328.

13 Hutchison, *Albrecht Dürer*, 62.

14 Robert Lerner, 'Medieval Prophecy and Religious Dissent', *Past and Present*, 72, 1976, 3–29; Robert Lerner, 'The Black Death and Western European Eschatological Mentalities', *American Historical Review*, 86, 1981, 533–52.

15 Katherine Firth, *The Apocalyptic Tradition in Reformation Britain, 1530–1645*, Oxford 1975; B. W. Ball, *A Great Expectation. Eschatalogical Thought In English Protestantism to 1660*, Leiden 1975; Paul Christianson, *Reformers and Babylon: English Apocalyptic Visions from the Reformation to the Eve of the Civil War*, Toronto 1978; Charles Webster, *The Great Instauration: Science, Medicine and Reform, 1626–1660*, London 1975.

16 Robin Bruce Barnes, *Prophecy and Gnosis. Apocalypticism in the Wake of the Lutheran Reformation*, Stanford 1988.

17 Jean Delumeau, *Sin and Fear. The Emergence of a Western Guilt Culture 13th–18th Centuries*, originally published in French in 1983; translated by Eric Nicholson, New York 1990; Delumeau, *La Peur en Occident*.

18 See the survey by Stuart Clark, *Thinking with Demons: The Idea of Witchcraft in Early Modern Europe*, Oxford 1997, 335–45.

19 For a somewhat different approach, concentrating on one country and only on disasters, but putting them into a religious interpretation, see Jean Delumeau and Yves Lequin, *Malheurs des Temps: Histoire des Fléaux et des Calamités en France*, Paris 1987; the chapters on the period 1450–1660 are by H. Neveux and J. Céard.

20 This identification with Christ the Conqueror is possibly through conflation with the horseman on another white horse which appears in Revelation 19, who is clearly Christ, who has 'a sharp sword, that with it he should smite the nations'.

21 R. W. Scribner, *The German Reformation*, London 1986, 4.

22 Excellent treatments of this issue can be found in Jan de Vries, 'Population', in *Handbook of European History 1400–1600. Late Middle Ages, Renaissance and Reformation. Volume 1: Structures and Assertions*, ed. Thomas A. Brady, Heiko A. Oberman, and James D. Tracy, Leiden 1994, 1–50; David Grigg, *Population Growth and Agrarian Change. An Historical Perspective*, Cambridge 1980; Karl Helleiner 'The Population of Europe from the Black Death to the Eve of the Vital Revolution', in *The Cambridge Economic History of Europe, Volume IV, The Economy of Expanding Europe in the Sixteenth and Seventeenth Centuries*, ed. E. E. Rich and C. H. Wilson, Cambridge 1966, 1–95; Massimo Livi-Bacci, *A Concise History of World Population*, translated by Carl Ipsen, Oxford 1997; E. A. Wrigley and R. S. Schofield, *The Population History of England, 1541–1871. A Reconstruction*, London 1981.

23 As quoted from the *Zimmerische Chronik* in Wilhelm Abel, *Agricultural Fluctuations in Europe from the*

Thirteenth to the Twentieth Centuries, first published in German in 1935; translated by Olive Ordish, London 1980, 101; also quoted in Helleiner, 'The Population of Europe from the Black Death to the Eve of the Vital Revolution', 25. For the situation in Germany see Werner Rösener, 'The Agrarian Economy', in *Germany, A New Social and Economic History, Volume 1: 1450–1630*, ed. Bob Scribner, London 1996, 63–84.

24 See Thomas Robisheaux, *Rural Society and the Search for Order in Early Modern Germany*, Cambridge 1989, 43–8.

25 Peter Blickle, *The Revolution of 1525*, translated by Thomas A. Brady and H. C. Erik Midelfort, Baltimore 1981, passim; F. Braudel, *Capitalism and Material Life 1400–1800*, London, 1973, 39.

26 Elizabeth Eisenstein, *The Printing Press as an Agent of Change. Communications and Cultural Transformations in Early Modern Europe*, 2 vols., Cambridge 1979, vol. 1, 303.

27 Quoted in Latin in Ottavia Niccoli, *Prophecy and People in Renaissance Italy*, translated by Lydia G. Cochrane, Princeton, New Jersey 1990, 150, our translation.

28 See Eisenstein, *The Printing Press as an Agent of Change*, vol. 1, chapter 4, and Hans-Joachim Köhler, ed., *Flugschriften als Massenmedium der Reformationszeit. Beiträge zum Tübinger Symposien 1980*, Stuttgart 1981.

29 As cited in M. H. Black, 'The Printed Bible', in *The Cambridge History of the Bible, The West from the Reformation to the Present Day*, ed. S. L. Greenslade, Cambridge 1963, 408–75.

30 Eisenstein, *The Printing Press as an Agent of Change*, vol. 1, 311.

31 R. W. Scribner, *For the Sake of Simple Folk: Popular Propaganda for the German Reformation*, Oxford 1994, 2.

32 Scribner, *For the Sake of Simple Folk*, xxvii.

33 Cited in Scribner, *For the Sake of Simple Folk*, 244.

34 Scribner, *For the Sake of Simple Folk*, 5.

2 THE WHITE HORSE: RELIGION, REVELATION AND REFORMATION

1 For the significance of white, see Isa. 1:16, Dan. 1:35, Matt. 17:2 and 28:3, and Rev. 19:14; for divine judgement, see among other places Ps. 38:2 and 64:7; for the bow as a symbol of the covenant, see Gen. 9:12–13.

2 Cited in J. Campbell Hutchison, *Albrecht Dürer. A Biography*, Princeton 1990, 124–5.

3 Albrecht Dürer, *Dürer's Record of Journeys to Venice and the Low Countries*, ed. Roger Fry, New York 1995, 83–7, especially 86–8. Dürer here cites Rev. 6:9, concerning the opening of the fifth seal, which follows the opening of the four seals revealing the Four Horsemen!

4 A. Osiander, *Sant Hildegardten weissagung vber die Papisten vnd genanten geistlichen, wilcher erfüllung zu unsern zeiten hat angefangen, vnd volzogen sol werden*, Nuremberg 1527; see also R. B. Barnes, *Prophecy and Gnosis. Apocalypticism in the Wake of the Lutheran Reformation*, Stanford 1988, 56.

5 K. R. Firth, *The Apocalyptic Tradition in Reformation Britain 1530–1645*, Oxford 1979, 14–17.

6 H.-U. Hofmann, *Luther und die Johannes-Apokalypse*, Tübingen 1982, 662–72; see also Barnes, *Prophecy and Gnosis*, 47 and 98.

7 For this work, see Johann Eberlin Günzburg, *Sämtliche*

Werke, ed. L. Enders, 3 vols., Halle 1896; for Günzburg see also B. Riggenbach, *Johann Eberlin von Günzburg und sein Reform Program*, 1874, reprint Nieuwkoop 1967.

8 For Joachim and his followers, see M. Reeves, *The Influence of Prophecy in the Later Middle Ages: A Study of Joachimism*, Oxford 1969; see also D. West, *Joachim of Fiore in Christian Thought: Essays on the Influence of the Calabrian Prophet*, 2 vols., New York 1975.

9 R. L. Petersen, *Preaching in the Last Days. The Theme of 'Two Witnessess' in the 16th & 17th Centuries*, Oxford 1993, 130 and 151–5; for Sebastian Meyer and Matthias Gerung's woodcuts, see P. Roettig, *Reformation als Apokalypse. Die Holzschnitte von Matthias Gerung im Codex germanicus 6592 der Bayerischen Staatsbibliothek in München*, Bern 1991.

10 Hofmann, *Luther und die Johannes-Apokalypse*, 530–51, especially 530–3.

11 See the works cited in R. W. Scribner, *For the Sake of Simple Folk. Popular Propaganda for the German Reformation*, Oxford 1994, 20 and 277–8, notes 20–1.

12 Ibid., 19–20.

13 Petersen, *Preaching in the Last Days*, 103.

14 For Mathesius, see H. Volz, *Die Lutherpredigten des Johannes Mathesius. Kritische Untersuchungen zur Geschichtsschreibung im Zeitalter der Reformation*, Leipzig 1930, 63–8; see also Petersen, *Preaching in the Last Days*, 103.

15 Petersen, *Preaching in the Last Days*, 103.

16 P. A. Russell, *Lay Theology in the Reformation. Popular Pamphleteers in Southwest Germany 1521–1525*, Cambridge 1986, 159–72

17 H. Marschalck, *Von dem weyt erschollen Namen Luther: Was er bedeutet und wie er wirt missbraucht*, Augsburg 1523 and Scribner, *Simple Folk*, 20–1; for Marschalck see also Russell, *Lay Theology*, 127–43; see also 212.

18 There has been a considerable scholarly debate about whether or not Luther considered himself to be a prophetic figure. Hans Preuss was the first to emphasise Luther's view of himself as having prophetic significance; see H. Preuss, *Martin Luther. Der Prophet*, Gütersloh 1933, 51–2. This view has since been rejected by scholars such as J. M. Headley, *Luther's View of Church History*, New Haven 1963, 232. Luther's own emphasis on his prophetic role has, however, been convincingly demonstrated by M. Edwards, *Luther's Last Battles: Politics and Polemics 1531–46*, Ithaca 1983, 103.

19 For the construction of this saying see R. W. Scribner, 'Incombustible Luther: The Image of the Reformer in Early Modern Germany', *Past and Present*, 10, 1986, 41–2. The quotation from Luther is cited in H. A.

Oberman, *Luther. Man between God and the Devil*, New Haven 1989, 55. For Luther's increasing identification with Hus, see Petersen, *Preaching in the Last Days*, 98.

20 For this, see O. Niccoli, *Prophecy and People in Renaissance Italy*, Princeton, New Jersey 1990, 131–6.

21 Barnes, *Prophecy and Gnosis*, 25–6 and 47.

22 Paracelsus, *Chronica und Ursprung dieses Landes Kärntner*, 1564, and G. Moro, 'Die Kärntner Chronic des Paracelsus', in K. Goldammer (ed.), *Paracelsus: Die Kärntner Schriften*, Klagenfurt 1955, 21 and 327–47; see also Scribner, 'Incombustible Luther', 62–3.

23 Scribner, *Simple Folk*, 15–19 and his 'Incombustible Luther', 38–68.

24 Oberman, *Between God and the Devil*, passim.

25 Quoted in ibid., 70–1.

26 Cited in B. W. Ball, *A Great Expectation. Eschatological Thought in English Protestantism to 1660*, Leiden 1975, 15; see Luther, *The Signs of Christ's coming, and Of the last Day*, London 1661, 4 and 28; probably a translation of *Antichrictliche und vast wolgegründe beweysung von dem Jüngsten Tag*, Augsburg 1522.

27 Cited in Petersen, *Preaching in the Last Days*, 100; see also Headley, *Luther's View of Church History*, 256.

28 Barnes, *Prophecy and Gnosis*, 39–41.

29 J. Calvin, *Sermons . . . on the Epistles of S. Paule to Timothie and Titus* (published in French 1563), London 1579, 994–6; cited in Ball, *Great Expectation*, 16.

30 Peter Martin, *Luther und die Bilder zur Apokalypse*, Hamburg 1983, especially 100–14; for Zwingli's reservations towards the Book of Revelation, see G. Locher, 'Zwingli and Erasmus', in his *Zwingli's Thought: New Perspectives*, Leiden 1981, see also Petersen, *Preaching in the Last Days*, 150; for Calvin's reservations, see Barnes, *Prophecy and Gnosis*, 32–3.

31 See Barnes, *Prophecy and Gnosis*, 42–3; for the historical background see Scribner, *Simple Folk*, 42–3.

32 W. Harms, *Deutsche Illustrierte Flugblätter des 16. und 17. Jahrhundert in der Wolfenbüttel Sammlung*, 2 vols., Munich/Tübingen 1980/85, vol. II, no. 7. See also Scribner, *Simple Folk*, 84–8.

33 Harms, *Deutsche Illustrierte Flugblätter*, vol. II, no. 61.

34 Scribner, *Simple Folk*, 148–89; see also P. Martin, *Martin Luther und die Bolder zur Apokalypse. Die Ikonographie der Illustrationen zur Offenbarung des Johannes in der Lutherbibel 1522 bis 1546*, Hamburg 1983.

35 Hofmann, *Luther und die Johannes-Apokalypse*, 395–413.

36 P. Blickle, *The Revolution of 1525. The German Peasants' War from a New Perspective*, Baltimore 1981; see also G. Franz, *Der deutsche Bauernkrieg* (first published 1933), Darmstadt 1975.

37 For this see C. Hinrichs, *Luther und Müntzer. Ihre auseinandersetzung über Obrigkeit und Widerstandsrecht*, Berlin 1962, 5–76.

38 Thomas Müntzer, *Schriften und Briefe: Kritische Gesamtausgabe*, ed. G. Franz, Gütersloh 1968, 463–4; see also R. Schwarz, *Die apokalyptische Theologie Thomas Müntzers und der Taboriten*, Tübingen 1977 and Petersen, *Preaching in the Last Days*, 60–71.

39 See H.-J. Goertz, *The Anabaptists*, London 1996, 16–18.

40 Russell, *Lay Theology*, 48 and 215.

41 See the excellent work by K. Deppermann, *Melchior Hoffman, Social Unrest and Apocalyptic Visions in the Age of the Reformation*, Edinburgh 1987, 162–203; for Capito's role in the tolerance towards the Spiritualists, see J. M. Kittelson, *Wolfgang Capito. From Humanist to Reformer*, Leiden 1975, 171–206.

42 Deppermann, *Melchior Hoffman*, 96–9.

43 See M. Hoffman, *Van der waren hochprachtlichen eynigen magestadt gottes*, Deventer 1532, A1v–A2r; quoted in Deppermann, *Melchior Hoffman*, 203–4.

44 Deppermann, *Melchior Hoffman*, 203–11.

45 Ibid., 137 and M. Hoffman, *Auslegung der heimlichen Offenbarung Joannis des heyligen Apostels vnnd Euangelisten*, Strassburg 1530.

46 Ibid., 261–2.

47 For these crop failures and famines, see W. Abel, *Massenarmut und Hungerkrisen im vorindustriellen Europa*, Göttingen 1974, 47–54.

48 Ibid., 206–7 and 268.

49 See C.-P. Clasen, 'Executions of Anabaptists 1527–1618', *Mennonite Quarterly Review*, 47, 1973, 115–52.

50 For these events, see Deppermann, *Melchior Hoffman*, 268–311.

51 See A. F. Mellink, *De wederdopers in de Noordelijke Nederlanden 1531–44*, Groningen 1953, 25–38.

52 Goertz, *The Anabaptists*, 29–31; see also J. M. Stayer, 'Christianity in One City: Anabaptist Münster, 1534–1535', in H. J. Hillerbrand (ed.), *Radical Tendencies in the Reformation: Divergent Perspectives*, Kirkville, Mo., 1988, 117–34.

53 *Lektor Povl Helgesens Historiske Optegnelsesbog sædvanligvis kaldet Skibykrøniken*, ed. A. Heise, Copenhagen 1967, 175–6.

54 See J. I. Israel, *The Dutch Republic. Its Rise, Greatness, and Fall 1477–1806*, Oxford 1995, 88–9.

55 Barnes, *Prophecy and Gnosis*, 49.

56 H. Loewen, *Luther and the Radicals*, Ontario 1974, 101.

57 Barnes, *Prophecy and Gnosis*, 60–71.

58 For Peder Palladius, see M. Schwarz Lausten, *Biskop Peder Palladius og Kirken 1537–1560*, Copenhagen 1987, especially 17–30.

59 *Peder Palladius' Danske Skrifter*, ed. L. Jacobsen, 5 vols., Copenhagen 1916–18, vol. III, 1–134, especially 17 and 26.

60 Harms, *Deutsche Illustrierte Flugblätter*, vol. II, no. 62; for an earlier and different version of the same engraving, see Scribner, *Simple Folk*, 106–15, especially 112–14.

61 Harms, *Deutsche Illustrierte Flugblätter*, vol. III, 32.

62 Ibid., vol. IV, 51.

63 Ibid., vol. IV, 52–3.

64 Ibid., vol. IV, 62–7.

65 See H. Sandblad, *De Eskatologiska Förestälningarna i Sverige under Reformation och Modreformation*, Uppsala 1942, 62–3.

66 Ibid., 66–9.

67 See O. Petri, *En predican emoot the gruffueliga eedher och gudz försmädelse, som nu almenneliga brukas*, 1539, in B. Hesselman (ed.), *Samlade Skrifter af Olaus Petri*, 4 vols., Uppsala 1914–17, vol. I, 313–29; see also Sandblad, *Eskatologiske Förestälningarna*, 69–71.

68 See O. Petri, *Om werldennes största Förwandlingar och Ålder*, 1548 and 1558 in Hesselman (ed.), *Samlade Skrifter af Olaus Petri*, vol. IV, 535–9 and Sandblad, *Eskatologiske Förestälningarna*, 72–84.

69 Sandblad, *Eskatologiske Förestälningarna*, 87–114 and S. Lindroth, *Svensk Lärdomshistoria. Medeltiden. Reformationstiden*, Stockholm 1975, 258–63.

70 On the significance of printing, see E. L. Eisenstein, *The Printing Press as an Agent of Change: Communications and Cultural Transformations in Early-Modern Europe*, Cambridge 1979; see also Barnes, *Prophecy and Gnosis*, 60–76.

71 Barnes, *Prophecy and Gnosis*, 100–15.

72 Ibid., 115–40.

73 See ibid., 112 and 133.

74 Thus Barnes argues that apocalyptic expectations and calculations were characteristic of the Lutheran Reformation in Germany in particular; see Barnes, *Prophecy and Gnosis*, 1–12 in particular; while Firth and a number of other Anglo-Saxon scholars have emphasised that Reformation apocalypticism blossomed in late Tudor and Stuart England: Firth, *Apocalyptic Tradition*, 1–23 in particular; see also P. Christianson, *Reformers and Babylon. English Apocalyptic Visions from the Reformation to the Eve of the Civil War*, Toronto 1978, 3–12.

75 H. Bullinger, *A Hundred Sermons Upon the Apocalypse*, London 1561, fol. Bvr, and M. Flacius Illyricus, *Catalogus Testium Veritatis*, Basle 1556.

76 Bullinger, *Sermons Opon the Apocalypse*, fol. BVv.

77 For Bullinger's significance, see Petersen, *Preaching in the Last Days*, 120–48.

78 Bullinger, *Sermons Opon the Apocalypse*, fol. NIv.

79 J. Brocard, *The Revelation of S. Ihon reueuled*, London 1582, fol. 79r; see also Petersen, *Preaching in the Last Days*,162–5.

80 For the Earl of Leicester, see Israel, *The Dutch Republic*, 220–30.

81 Brocard, *The Revelation of S. Ihon reueuled*, fol. 5r.

82 Harms, *Deutsche Illustrierte Flugblätter*, vol. II, no. 8.

83 See Christianson, *Reformers and Babylon*, 36–9.

84 See H. Robinson (ed.), *The Zurich Letters . . . the Correspondence of Several English Bishops and Others with Some of the Helvetian Reformers*, Cambridge 1842, 98–9.

85 For Bale's significance, see Firth, *The Apocalyptic Tradition*, 38, Christianson, *Reformers and Babylon*, 21, and R. Bauckham, *Tudor Apocalypse*, Oxford 1978, 49.

86 For the apocalyptic significance and influence of John Foxe, see V. N. Olsen, *John Foxe and the Elizabethan Church*, Berkeley 1973.

87 See Christianson, *Reformers and Babylon*, 13–46.

88 Sandblad, *Eskatologiske Förestälningarna*, 90–107.

89 See A. Andersen (ed.), *Quattuor Centuriæ Epistolarum. Provst Johannes Pistorius' Brevsamling 1541–1605 (1614)*, Historisk Samfund for Sønderjylland 1971, 299–301.

90 N. Mikkelsen Aalborg, *En kaart oc Nyttig Forklaring Offuer S. Johannis Obenbaring*, Copenhagen 1611 and J. Foxe, *Eicasmi seu Meditationes in Apocalypsin S. Johannis*, London 1587.

91 J. Foxe, *Eicasmi seu Meditationes in Apocalypsin S. Johannis*, Geneva 1596 in the Royal Library in Copenhagen (84–2508).

92 N. Mikkelsen Aalborg, *Chronologia Sacra. Det Ny Testamentis Tid-Register om Verdens Ende*, Copenhagen 1628 and *Chronologia Sacra. Gog, Magog, Abaddon, Apollyon, Prophetie aff den Hellige Skrifft om Verdens Tilstand I det geistlige oc verdslige Regimente*, Copenhagen 1629; for Philipp Nicolai, see Barnes, *Prophecy and Gnosis*, 123–4 and 134–5.

93 See B. Kornerup, *Biskop Hans Poulsen Resen*, vol. II (ed. V. Helk), Copenhagen 1968, 227–9; for Luther's prophecies, see Barnes, *Prophecy and Gnosis*, 44–6.

94 T. Watt, *Cheap Print and Popular Piety, 1550–1640*, Cambridge 1991, 97.

95 J. Arrowsmith, *The Covenant avenging Sword brandished in a Sermon*, London 1643, 15.

96 Quoted in H. Trevor-Roper, *Catholics, Anglicans and Puritans. Seventeenth Century Essays*, London 1987, 120–65, especially 135.

97 Christianson, *Reformers and Babylon*, 93–131; see also K. Thomas, *Religion and the Decline of Magic*, Harmondsworth 1985, 106.

98 Thomas, *Decline of Magic*, 480–1 and B. T. Whitehead, *Brags & Boasts. Propaganda in the Year of the Armada*, Dover 1994, 17–32.

99 For Samuel Ward, see *Dictionary of National Biography*.

100 W. Bergsma, *De wereld volgens Abel Eppens een ommelander boer uit de zestiende eeuw*, Groningen 1988, 140.

101 A. TH. van Deursen, *Plain Lives in a Golden Age. Popular Culture, Religion and Society in Seventeenth-Century Holland*, Cambridge 1991, 207; for Alva, see Israel, *The Dutch Republic*, 155–68.

102 See J. Tanis and D. Horst, *Images of Discord. A Graphic Interpretation of the Opening Decades of the Eighty Years War*, Bryn Mawr, Pennsylvania 1993, 42–3.

103 Harms, *Deutsche Illustrierte Flugblätter*, vol. II, no. 105. For the Jülich-Cleves crisis, see G. Parker, *The Thirty Years' War*, London 1984, 26–37.

104 See Scribner, *Simple Folk*, 180–1.

105 See J. J. Woltjer, 'Introduction', 1–20, especially 4 and 14, and H. J. de Jonge, 'The Study of the New Testament', 65–109, especially 72 and 87 in Th. H. Lunsingh Scheurleer and G. H. M. Posthumus Meyjes (eds.), *Leiden University in the Seventeenth Century. An Exchange of Learning*, Leiden 1975.

106 See J. van den Berg, 'Eschatological Expectations Concerning the Conversion of the Jews in the Netherlands During the Seventeenth Century', in P. Toon (ed.), *Puritans, the Millennium and the Future of Israel: Puritan Eschatology 1600 to 1660*, Cambridge 1970, 137–53; for Petrus Serrarius, see E. van der Wall, *De mystieke chiliast Petrus Serrarius (1600–1669) en zijn wereld*, Leiden 1987.

107 For Brightman's work, see K. L. Sprunger, *Trumpets from the Tower. English Puritan Printing in the Netherlands 1600–1640*, Leiden 1994, 34, 69; for Hugh Broughton, see K. L. Sprunger, *Dutch Puritanism. A History of English and Scottish Churches of the Netherlands in the Sixteenth and Seventeenth Centuries*, Leiden 1982, 23–4 and 331 and Christianson, *Reformers and Babylon*, 107–9.

108 T. Goodwin, *A Glimpse of Sions Glory: or the Churches Beautie Specified*, London 1641 and Sprunger, *Dutch Puritanism*, 229–31 and 331–2.

109 See W. J. op't Hof, *Engelse Pietistische Geschriften in het Nederlands, 1598–1622*, Rotterdam 1987, 466–8.

110 Sprunger, *Trumpets from the Tower*, 74–83.

111 Hof, *Engelse Pietistische Geschriften*, 441–55, especially 452.

112 For Alsted, see R. G. Clouse, 'The Rebirth of Millenarianism', in Toon (ed.), *Puritans, the Millennium*, 42–56, and H. Hotson, 'Johann Heinrich

Alsted: Encyclopaedism, Millenarianism, and the Second Reformation in Germany', Oxford D.Phil. thesis 1991.

113 See H. Trevor-Roper, 'The Paracelsian Movement', in his *Renaissance Essays*, London 1985, 149–99 and O. P. Grell, 'The Enigma of Paracelsus', in O. P. Grell (ed.), *Paracelsus. The Man and his Reputation. His Ideas and Their Transformation*, Leiden 1998, 3.

114 See Matthew 10:26.

115 H. Trevor-Roper, 'Paracelsianism made Political 1600–1650', in Grell (ed.), *Paracelsus*, 119–33.

116 Harms, *Deutsche Illustrierte Flugblätter*, vol. II, no. 51.

117 See Barnes, *Prophecy and Gnosis*, 216–27; for the emphasis on the political importance of Rosicrucianism, see F. Yates, *The Rosicrucian Enlightenment*, London 1972.

118 See S. Åkerman, *Rose Cross over the Baltic. The Spread of Rosicrucianism in Northern Europe*, Leiden 1998, 125–66.

119 T. Brahe, *De Nova et Nullius Ævi Memoria prius Visa Stella, iam pridem Anno a nato Christo 1572*, Copenhagen 1573.

120 T. Brahe, *De Mundi Ætherei Recentioribus Phænomenis*, Copenhagen 1588; for this work, see V. E. Thoren, *The Lord of Uraniborg. A Biography of Tycho Brahe*, Cambridge 1990, 123–7; for the Sabbath conjunction, see Barnes, *Prophecy and Gnosis*, 156.

121 For Copernicus, see R. J. Ravetz, 'The Copernican Revolution', in R. C. Olby et al. (eds.), *Companion to the History of Modern Science*, London 1990, 201–16.

122 On the development of sixteenth-century research into comets, see W. Kokott, *Die Kometen der Jahre 1531 bis 1539 und ihre Bedeutung fuur die spätere Entwicklung der Kometenforschung*, Stuttgart 1994.

123 See the excellent chapter on apocalyptic astrology in Barnes, *Prophecy and Gnosis*, 141–81.

124 Cited from its first English edition of 1661 in Ball, *Great Expectation*, 114.

125 See Barnes, *Prophecy and Gnosis*, 176–81.

126 Ibid., 141–81, especially 175. That this was not only the case in Germany can be seen from Sandblad, *Eskatologiske Förestälningarna*, 267–8.

127 See Niccoli, *Prophecy and People*, 135 and 185–7; see also Barnes, *Prophecy and Gnosis*, 162 and 175.

128 For suns over Münster, see Deppermann, *Melchior Hoffman*, 340; for suns over Mecklenburg and Christian IV, see Åkerman, *Rose Cross over the Baltic*, 160.

129 See the review of Barnes, *Prophecy and Gnosis* by Gerald Strauss in *The Journal of Interdisciplinary History*, 20, 1990, 473f.

130 For the role and apocalyptic significance of almanacs and *practica*, see R. B. Barnes, 'Hope and Despair in Sixteenth-Century German Almanacs', in H. Guggisberg and G. Krodel (eds.), *The Reformation in Germany and Europe: Interpretations and Issues*, Göttingen 1993, 440–61 and B. Capp, *Astrology and the Popular Press. English Almanacs 1500–1800*, London 1979; for Paracelsus and his *practica*, see C. Webster, 'Paracelsus: Medicine as Popular Protest', in O. P. Grell and A. Cunningham (eds.), *Medicine and the Reformation*, London 1993, 57–77, especially 59 and 61.

131 For the predicted deluge of 1524, see Niccoli, *Prophecy and People*, 140–52 and Kokott, *Die Kometen*, 25–8; see also D. Kurze, 'Popular Astrology and Prophecy in the Fifteenth and Sixteenth Centuries: Johannes Lichtenberger', in P. Zambelli (ed.), '*Astrologi hallucinati*'. *Stars and the End of the World in Luther's Time*, Berlin 1986, 177–8, Russell, *Lay Theology*, 215, and H. Talkenberg, *Sinflut. Prophetie und Zeitgeschehen in Texten und Holzschnitten astrologischer Flugschriften 1488–1528*, Tübingen 1990, 154–316.

132 Barnes, *Prophecy and Gnosis*, 143; for Dürer's dream, see Hutchison, *Albrecht Dürer*, 182.

133 See Capp, *Astrology and the Popular Press*, 166 and 149–50.

134 J. Wittaker, *Eirenopoios, Christ the Settlement of Unsettled Times*, London 1643, 24.

135 See B. McGinn, *Visions of the End. Apocalyptic Traditions in the Middle Ages*, New York 1979, 284–5; see also Barnes, *Prophecy and Gnosis*, 29.

136 Barnes, *Prophecy and Gnosis*, 86.

137 Sandblad, *Eskatologiske Förestälningarna*, 203–30.

138 Harms, *Deutsche Illustrierte Flugblätter*, vol. I, 182.

139 Sandblad, *Eskatologiske Förestälningarna*, 203–37.

140 Harms, *Deutsche Illustrierte Flugblätter*, vol. I, no. 190.

141 Barnes, *Prophecy and Gnosis*, 92–3. Luther cited in Ball, *Great Expectation*, 114.

142 See Sandblad, *Eskatologiske Förestälningarna*, 265 and 269.

143 J. Beyer, 'Lutheran Lay Prophets (ca.1550–1700)', *Copenhagen Folklore Notes*, 2, 1996, 1–4.

144 For Frese, see J. Beyer, 'A Lübeck Prophet in Local and Lutheran Context', in B. Scribner and T. Johnson (eds.), *Popular Religion in Germany and Central Europe, 1400–1800*, London 1996, 166–82 and 264–72.

145 See D. W. Sabean, 'A Prophet in the Thirty Years' War: Penance as a Social Metaphor' in his *Power in the Blood. Popular Culture & Village Discourse in Early Modern Germany*, Cambridge 1984, 61–93, especially 65.

146 Ibid., 88–90.

147 For this, see J. Beyer, 'Lutherische Propheten in Deutschland und Skandinavien im 16. und 17.

Jahrhundert. Entstehung und Ausbreitung eines
Kulturmusters', in R. Bohn (ed.), Europa in
Scandinavia. Kulturelle und soziale Dialoge in der frühen
Neuzeit, Berlin 1994, 35–55.

148 See H. F. Rørdam, 'Mestermanden i Viborg som
Profet', in Ny Kirkehistoriske Samlinger, 4, 1867–8,
181–90, especially 184.

149 Ambroise Paré, On Monsters and Marvels, ed. J. L.
Pallister, Chicago 1982, 3–7. For this see also J.
Delumeau, Sin and Fear. The Emergence of a Western Guilt
Culture 13th–18th Centuries, New York 1990, 137–41.

150 Erasmus Lætus' skrift om Christian IVs fødsel og dåb (1577),
ed. K. Skovgaard-Petersen and P. Zeeberg,
Copenhagen 1992, 97–117.

151 Sandblad, Eskatologiske Förestälningarna, 219–21.

152 Ibid., 223–4; for the 1615 fish, see chapter 3 below,
'The experience of war'.

153 See S. Schama, The Embarrassment of Riches. An
Interpretation of Dutch Culture in the Golden Age, New York
1987, 133.

154 See Barnes, Prophecy and Gnosis, 87–94 and S. Clark,
Thinking with Demons. The Idea of Witchcraft in Early
Modern Europe, Oxford 1997, 364–7.

155 For witchcraft, see B. P. Levack, 'The Great Witch-

Hunt', 607–40 in T. A. Brady, H. A. Oberman and J. D.
Tracy (eds.), Handbook of European History 1400–1600.
Late Middle Ages, Renaissance and Reformation, vol. II:
Visions, Programs and Outcomes, Leiden 1995.

156 Cited in Clark, Thinking with Demons, 369.

157 This connection was originally noted in E. Peuckert,
Die grosse Wende: das apokalyptische Saeculum und Luther,
Hamburg 1948, 119–30; cited in Clark, Thinking with
Demons, 321.

158 Cited in Clark, Thinking with Demons, 325.

159 Deursen, Plain Lives in a Golden Age, 250 and Clark,
Thinking with Demons, 243.

160 See T. Cooper, The mystery of witch-craft, London 1617,
194; cited in Clark, Thinking with Demons, 361, see in
general 346–62.

161 See R. Gualther, Antichrist, that is to saye: a true reporte,
that Antichriste is come, London 1556, 29; cited in Clark,
Thinking with Demons, 355.

162 Clark, Thinking with Demons, 333.

163 Harms, Deutsche Illustrierte Flugblätter, vol. I, no. 154.

164 G. Wither, Fragmenta Prophetica; or, the remains of George
Wither Esq., being a Collection of the Predictions dispers'd
troughout his works, London 1669, in 'Campo-Musae'
(1644), 56; cited in Ball, Great Expectation, 90.

3 THE RED HORSE: WAR, WEAPONS AND WOUNDS

1 In spite of the influence of Dürer's image on
contemporary and later artists the specific
association of the Ottoman threat with the second
horseman seems to have been unique to Dürer,
whereas the first horseman, whom Dürer also
represents in Ottoman clothes, retained his Turkish
appearance when portrayed by contemporary and
later artists such as Lucas Cranach and Matthew
Merian.

2 For the Ottoman empire, see P. Coles, The Ottoman
Impact on Europe, New York 1968; see also H. Inalcik,
The Ottoman Empire. The Classical Age 1300–1600, rep.
New York 1989.

3 M. Geisberger, The German Single-Leaf Woodcut:
1500–1550, ed. W. L. Strauss, 4 vols., New York 1974,
vol. III, 1046.

4 See A. Perrig, Albrecht Dürer oder die Heimlichkeit der
deutschen Ketzerei: Die Apokalypse Dürers und andere Werke
1495 bis 1513, Würtzburg 1987; Perrig emphasises the
extraordinary popularity of Dürer's illustrated version
of the Book of Revelation, see 1.

5 See H. Thurston, The Holy Year of Jubilee, London
1900.

6 For Protestantism and the 'Turkish threat', see

S. Fisher-Galati, Ottoman Imperialism and German
Protestantism, 1521–1555, rep. New York 1972.

7 The Complete Woodcuts of Albrecht Dürer, no. 210; for the
engraving, see The Life and Times of Dürer, London 1970,
22–3.

8 See Geisberger, The German Single-Leaf Woodcut:
1500–1550, vol. IV, 1528.

9 G. Parker, The Military Revolution. Military Innovation
and the Rise of the West, 1500–1800, Cambridge 1988,
1.

10 See C. Kafadar, 'The Ottomans and Europe', in T. A.
Brady et al. (eds.), Handbook of European History
1400–1600. Late Middle Ages, Renaissance and
Reformation, 2 vols., Leiden 1994–5, vol. I, 589–635,
especially 616.

11 C. Read (ed.), William Lambarde and Local Government.
His Ephemeris and Twenty-nine Charges to Juries and
Commissions, New York 1962, 183–4.

12 See J. R. Hale, War and Society in Renaissance Europe
1450–1620, London 1985, 13–45 and 75–99 and
Parker, Military Revolution, 1–5.

13 See F. Tallett, War and Society in Early-Modern Europe,
1495–1715, London 1992, 16 and Hale, War and Society,
26–7.

14 P. A. Russell, *Lay Theology in the Reformation. Popular Pamphleteers in Southwest Germany 1521–1525*, Cambridge 1986, 172.

15 See H. A. Oberman, *Luther. Man Between God and the Devil*, New Haven 1989, 70 and P. Christianson, *Reformers and Babylon. English Apocalyptic Visions from the Reformation to the Eve of the Civil War*, Toronto 1978, 95 and 104.

16 J. Arrowsmith, *The Covenant avenging Sword brandished in a Sermon*, London 1643, 16.

17 Read (ed.), *William Lambarde and Local Government*, 83–4.

18 See Parker, *Military Revolution*, 24, Hale, *War and Society*, 24–5, and Tallett, *War and Society*, 7–9.

19 Tallett, *War and Society*, 69–76; for Wallenstein's murder, see R. Bireley, *Religion and Politics in the Age of the Counterreformation. Emperor Ferdinand II, William Lamormaini, S.J., and the Formation of Imperial Policy*, Chapel Hill 1981, 200–4.

20 For Hans de Witte, see A. Ernstberger, *Hans de Witte – Finanzmann Wallensteins*, Wiesbaden 1954; for Calandrini-Burlamachi, see O. P. Grell, *Dutch Calvinists in Early Stuart London*, Leiden 1989, 177–8.

21 O. P. Grell, *Calvinist Exiles in Tudor and Stuart England*, Aldershot 1996, 133–4 and A. T. S. Goodrick (ed.), *The Relation of Sydenham Poyntz, 1624–1636*, Camden Society, 3rd ser. 14, London 1908.

22 Tallett, *War and Society*, 85–7.

23 G. Parker (ed.), *The Thirty Years' War*, London 1984, 194.

24 Tallett, *War and Society*, 89.

25 For the bodily experience of early modern soldiers, see M. Dinges, 'Soldatenkörper in der Frühen Neuzeit. Erfahrungen mit einem unzureichend geschützten, formierten und verletzten Körper in Selbstzeugnissen', in R. van Dülmen (ed.), *Körper-Geschichten. Studien zur historischen Kulturforschung V*, Frankfurt am Main 1996, 71–98 and 233–9.

26 See G. Parker, *The Army of Flanders and the Spanish Road 1567–1659*, reprint Cambridge 1990, 288–9 and Parker, *The Thirty Years' War*, 199.

27 For these prints, see Geisberger, *The German Single-Leaf Woodcut: 1500–1550*, vol. I, 246 and 249.

28 See M. van Crevelt, *Supplying War: Logistics from Wallenstein to Patton*, Cambridge 1977, 34–40, Parker, *Military Revolution*, 75–7, and Tallett, *War and Society*, 54–5.

29 Cited by Parker, *The Thirty Years' War*, 200.

30 W. Harms, *Deutsche Illustrierte Flugblätter des 16. und 17. Jahrhundert in der Wolfenbüttel Sammlung*, 2 vols., Munich/Tübingen 1980/85, vol. I, no. 175. For Jacques Callot, see T. Schröder (ed.), *Jacques Callot*, 2 vols., Munich 1971.

31 See Geisberger, *The German Single-Leaf Woodcut: 1500–1550*, vol. IV, 1187.

32 For a recent reproduction of Fronsperger's print, see Parker, *Military Revolution*, 66; for Schoen's woodcut, see Geisberger, *The German Single-Leaf Woodcut: 1500–1550*, vol. III, 1162.

33 See C. R. Friedrichs, *Urban Society in an Age of War: Nördlingen, 1580–1720*, Princeton 1979, 28–34, 152–5 and 214–21.

34 *Lawes and Ordinances of Warre by the Earl of Essex*, n.p. 1642, B4r, C2v–3r; see also Tallett, *War and Society*, 123–6.

35 Parker, *The Army of Flanders*, 185–206.

36 J. I. Israel *The Dutch Republic: Its Rise, Greatness and Fall 1477–1806*, Oxford, 1995, 184–6.

37 For the Elizabethan legislation, see P. Slack, *Poverty & Policy in Tudor & Stuart England*, London 1988, 126–7; for Rye, see Tallett, *War and Society*, 140. See also R. Jütte, *Poverty and Deviance in Early Modern Europe*, Cambridge 1994, 26–7 and 188.

38 Read (ed.), *William Lambarde and Local Government*, 183.

39 For the number of English/Scottish soldiers serving in the Netherlands, see K. L. Sprunger, *Dutch Puritanism. A History of English and Scottish Churches of the Netherlands in the Sixteenth and Seventeenth Centuries*, Leiden 1982, 5 and C. Wilson, *Queen Elizabeth and the Revolt of the Netherlands*, Berkeley 1970, 86. For the number of demobilised soldiers arrested in the Netherlands, see F. Egmond, *Underworlds. Organized Crime in the Netherlands 1650–1800*, Cambridge 1993, 47–51.

40 Hale, *War and Society*, 87.

41 G. Keynes (ed.), *The Apologie and Treatise of Ambroise Paré, containing the voyages made into divers places with many of his writings upon surgery*, New York 1968, 33.

42 H. Hexham, *A Iournall of the taking in of Venlo, Roermont, Strale, the memorable Siege of Maastricht, the Towne and Castle of Limburch vnder the able and wise Conduct of his Exellencie the Prince of Orange, Anno 1632*, The Hague 1633, 33.

43 C. Carlton, *Going to the Wars. The Experience of the British Civil Wars, 1638–1651*, London 1992, 294–5; see also J. Morrill, *Revolt in the Provinces. The People of England and the Tragedies of War 1630–1648*, London 1999, 132–51 and 200–4, and C. Carlton, 'Civilians', in J. Kenyon and J. Ohlmeyer (eds.), *The Civil Wars. A Military History of England, Scotland and Ireland 1638–1660*, Oxford 1998, 272–305, especially 303–4.

44 Cited in B. W. Ball, *A Great Expectation. Eschatological Thought in English Protestantism*, Leiden 1975, 100.

45 Jacob de Gheyn, *Wapenhandlinghe van Roers, Musquetten ende Spiessen . . . Figuirlyck vutgebeelt door J. de Gheijn*, The Hague 1607, 3rd section, no. 25.

46 Keynes (ed.), *The Apologie and Treatise of Ambroise Paré*, 21–2.

47 Jacob de Gheyn, *Wapenhandlinghe van Roers*, 2nd section, no. 36.

48 For this episode and its military significance, see J. I. Israel, *The Dutch Republic. Its Rise, Greatness, and Fall 1477–1806*, Oxford 1995, 259. See also J. P. Puype, 'Victory at Nieuwpoort, 2 July 1600', in M. van der Hoeven (ed.), *Exercise of Arms. Warfare in the Netherlands, 1568–1648*, Leiden 1997, 69–112.

49 See Parker, *Military Revolution*, 23.

50 Hale, *War and Society*, 49.

51 For Schoen's broadsheet, see Geisberger, *The German Single-Leaf Woodcut: 1500–1550*, vol. III, 1168.

52 See Hale, *War and Society*, 46–50, Parker, *Military Revolution*, 7–16, Tallett, *War and Society*, 34–9 and C. Duffy, *Siege Warfare. The Fortress in the Early Modern World 1494–1660*, rep. London 1996, passim.

53 M. Merian, *Topographia Bavariae*, Frankfurt am Main 1648, 70–1 (view of Regensburg inserted beween these pages) and 78.

54 For this siege, see C. Paludan-Müller, *Grevens Fejde*, 2 vols., Copenhagen 1853 and 1854, vol. II, 349–60.

55 See F. Yates, 'Elizabethan Chivalry: The Romance of the Accession Day Tilts', *Journal of the Warburg and Courtauld Institutes*, no. 19, 1956, 86–103, and no. 20, 1957, 4–25.

56 *Erasmus Lætus' Skrift om Christian IVs Fødsel og Dåb* (1577), ed. and trans. K. Skovgaard-Petersen and P. Zeeberg, Copenhagen 1992, 239–40.

57 J. Cruso, *The Art of Warre*, Cambridge 1639, 155.

58 *Diaria di bello Carolino* by Alessandro Benedetti, ed. D. M. Schullian, New York 1967, 109.

59 Keynes (ed.), *The Apologie and Treatise of Ambroise Paré*, 132–3.

60 See R. A. Gabriel and K. S. Metz, *A History of Military Medicine*, 2 vols., New York 1992, vol. II, 52–6, and Tallett, *War and Society*, 108–9. For Paré, see also L. I. Conrad et al., *The Western Medical Tradition 800 BC to AD 1800*, Cambridge 1995, 297–8 and L. Brockliss and C. Jones, *The Medical World of Early Modern France*, Oxford 1997, 104–6.

61 Keynes (ed.), *The Apologie and Treatise of Ambroise Paré*, 23–4 and 137–40; see also Gabriel and Metz, *A History of Military Medicine*, vol. II, 52–60.

62 See Tallett, *War and Society*, 109.

63 Keynes (ed.), *The Apologie and Treatise of Ambroise Paré*, 148.

64 H. Hexham, *A True and Briefe Relation of the Famous Siege of Breda*, The Hague 1637, 21.

65 C. G. Cruickshank, *Elizabeth's Army*, Oxford 1966, 184–8.

66 See *Kancelliets Brevbøger, 1609–1615*, ed. L. Laursen, Copenhagen 1916, 9 March 1610, 21 November 1610 and 13 February 1611, and *Kancelliets Brevbøger, 1644–1645*, ed. J. Jørgensen, Copenhagen 1968, 4 April 1645.

67 W. Clowes, *A Prooved Practice for All Young Chirurgians*, London 1588, 25–7.

68 *Kancelliets Brevbøger, 1644–1645*, 25 June 1644 and 30 September 1644.

69 Cruickshank, *Elizabeth's Army*, 178 and J. Cruso, *Militarie Instructions for the Cavall'rie*, Cambridge 1632, 24.

70 For this, see Gabriel and Metz, *A History of Military Medicine*, vol. II, 50–2.

71 Keynes (ed.), *The Apologie and Treatise of Ambroise Paré*, 51.

72 Cruickshank, *Elizabeth's Army*, 302 (pgr. 44 & 45) and John Cruso, *Castrametation or the Measuring ovt of the Qvarters for the Encamping of an Army*, London 1642, 3–4.

73 See Parker, *The Thirty Years' War*, 203.

74 See Tallett, *War and Society*, 111; and T. Digges, *An Arithmeticall Militare Treatise Named Stratiocos*, London 1579.

75 Parker, *Military Revolution*, 72 and Parker, *The Army of Flanders*, 167–9.

76 For Vadstena, see E. I. Kouri, 'Health Care and Poor Relief in Sweden and Finland', in O. P. Grell and A. Cunningham (eds.), *Health Care and Poor Relief in Protestant Europe 1500–1700*, London 1997, 187 and Parker, *The Army of Flanders*, 168.

77 H. Hexham, *A Iovrnall . . .*, 42

78 Ibid., 23.

79 For Paracelsus, see W. Pagel, *Paracelsus. An Introduction to Philosophical Medicine in the Era of the Renaissance*, 2nd edn, Basle 1982, in particular 14, 23 and 148; for Clowes and Paracelsianism, see A. G. Debus, *The English Paracelsians*, New York 1965, 70. See also O. P. Grell (ed.), *Paracelsus. The Man and His Reputation, His Ideas and Their Transformation*, Leiden 1998.

80 Cited in R. P. Adams, *The Better Part of Valor. More, Erasmus, Colet, and Vives, on Humanism, War, and Peace, 1496–1535*, Seattle 1962, 23. For the Christian humanists' attitude to war see Q. Skinner, *The Foundations of Modern Political Thought*, vol. I, *The Renaissance*, Cambridge 1978, 243–8.

81 Erasmus, *The Lives of Vitier . . . and John Colet*, trans. J. H. Lupton, London 1883, 43–4, cited in Adams, *The Better Part of Valor*, 69.

82 J. M. Mackail (ed.), *Erasmus against War*, Boston 1907, 10. Cited in Adams, *The Better Part of Valor*, 97.

83 Mackail, *Erasmus against War*, 57–60. Like the Christian humanists the utopians in Thomas More's *Utopia* are pacifists. When forced to they would employ mercenaries, the Venalians, who were remarkably similar to the Swiss, whom they despised and were quite happy to see destroyed *en masse*, because their destruction might help to 'wipe the filthy scum off the face of the earth completely', thus 'doing the human race a very good turn', see Thomas More, *Utopia*, Penguin Classics 1972, 109 and 113; see also H. Trevor-Roper, 'Sir Thomas More and Utopia', in H. Trevor-Roper, *Renaissance Essays*, London 1985, 46–7.

84 *Lektor Povl Helgesens Historiske Optegnelsesbog sædvanligvis kaldet Skibbykrøniken*, ed. & trans. A. Heise, Copenhagen 1967, 103.

85 Adams, *The Better Part of Valor*, 209.

86 For battle of Pavia, see J. Black, *Warfare. Renaissance to Revolution 1492–1792*, Cambridge Illustrated Atlas, Cambridge 1996, 51–2 and R. J. Knecht, *Renaissance Warrior and Patron. The Reign of Francis I*, Cambridge 1994, 216–27.

87 H. T. Lehmann (ed.), *Luther's Works*, vol. XLVI, Philadelphia 1967, 'Whether soldiers, too, can be saved', 94–5 and 98. See also G. Wolf (ed.) *Luther und die Obrigkeit*, Darmstadt 1972 and M. Schwarz Lausten, 'Luther and the Princes' in P. Newman Brooks (ed.), *Seven-Headed-Luther. Esssays in Commemoration of a Quincentenary 1483–1983*, Oxford 1983, 52–76.

88 *Ibid.*, 131.

89 *Ibid.*, 134.

90 *Ibid.*, 136.

91 Lehmann (ed.), *Luther's Works*, vol. XXXI, Philadelphia 1961, 91–2.

92 Cited in Adams, *The Better Part of Valor*, 209.

93 *Dialogue Concerning Tyndale* (1528), cited in Adams, *The Better Part of Valor*, 275.

94 Cited in Hale, *War and Society*, 72. Many Catholics, however, considered the sack of Rome to be God's punishment. Cardinal Giles of Viterbo added a somewhat apocalyptic flavour to his description: 'You must understand just how wicked are these days and how angry is Heaven at the rabble now admitted everywhere to the exalted office of the priesthood (lazy, untrained, disorganised, and immoral, mere youths, bankers, merchants, and soldiers, not to mention usurers and pimps) . . . The Emperor's army, rearing to pieces, the barbaric filth, have overthrown and burnt everything in this dunghill. They have triumphed over pride, wealth and power. The ungodly say "If God cares for sacred things, why does he allow this?" I reply that it is because God cares that he not only allows this thing, but even carries it out himself.' See J. W. O'Malley, *Giles of Viterbo on Church and Reform: A Study in Renaissance Thought*, Leiden 1968, 133.

95 Lehmann (ed.), *Luther's Works*, vol. XLVI, 157–205.

96 *Ibid.*, 164 and 171.

97 *Ibid.*, 181.

98 *Ibid.*, 205.

99 J. Calvin, *Institutes of the Christian Religion*, trans. H. Beveridge, Michigan 1989 (Book IV, pgr. 12), 661–2.

100 J. Calvin, *Sermons on 2 Samuel. Chapters 1–13*, trans. D. Kelly, Edinburgh 1992, 85. Cited by B. Gordon, 'Toleration in the Early Swiss Reformation: The Art and Politics of Niklaus Manuel of Berne' in O. P. Grell and B. Scribner (eds.), *Tolerance and Intolerance in the European Reformation*, Cambridge 1996, 128.

101 T. Harding (ed.), *The Decades of H. Bullinger*, Parker Society, Cambridge 1849–52, 370–1.

102 *Ibid.*, 373–4.

103 *Ibid.*, 376–7.

104 *Ibid.*, 380–1.

105 J. Turner Johnson, *Ideology, Reason, and the Limitation of War. Religious and Secular Concepts 1200–1740*, Princeton 1975, 110.

106 Francis Bacon, *Certaine Miscellany Works of the Right Honourable Francis Lord Verulam, Viscount S. Alban*, London 1629, 32 (*Touching a Warre with Spaine*).

107 Stephen Gossen, *The Trumphet of Warre*, London 1598.

108 William Gouge, *Gods Three Arrowes: Plagve, famine, Sword, in three Treatises*, London 1631, 214–15.

109 Gouge, *Gods Three Arrowes*, A6v.

110 Gouge, *Gods Three Arrowes*, 217 and 290. See also Johnson, *Ideology, Reason*, 123–5.

111 William Gouge, *The Dignitie of Chivalry, Set forth in a Sermon preached before the Artillery Company of London 13 June 1626*, London 1626, 431–2.

112 Alexander Leighton, *Speculum Belli Sacri: or the Looking Glasse of the Holy War*, London 1624, 6; see also Johnson, *Ideology, Reason*, 125–7.

113 It should be emphasised that not all Puritans of this period supported the notion of holy war. Thus the influential divines William Perkins and his pupil William Ames opposed this drift towards Protestant crusades with a strong apocalyptic flavour. See William Perkins's attack on popular apocalypticism in his pamphlets *A Godlie and Learned Exposition upon the*

Whole Epistle of Jude and *A Fruitfull Dialogue Concerning the Ende of the World* in *The Works of William Perkins*, vol. III, London 1616 and William Ames's arguments for just war based on natural justice, which are much closer to Luther and Calvin than Bullinger and his many English followers, *Conscience, with the Power and Causes Thereof*, n.p. 1639. See also Johnson, *Ideology, Reason*, 95, 118 and 171–4.

114 See H. Trevor-Roper, 'Paracelsianism made Political 1600–1650', in Grell (ed.), *Paracelsus. The Man and His Reputation*, 119–33, especially 125.

115 Bireley, *Religion and Politics*, 115 and 130–1.

116 For the Wars of Religion, see M. P. Holt, *The French Wars of Religion, 1562–1629*, Cambridge 1995. For the eschatological fear and motivation of Catholics, see D. Crouzet, *Les Guerriers de Dieu. La Violence au Temps des Troubles de Religion, vers 1525 – vers 1610*, 2 vols., Seyssel 1990; see also B. B. Diefendorf, *Beneath the Cross. Catholics and Huguenots in Sixteenth-Century Paris*, Oxford 1991, especially 91 and 154–5.

117 See Crouzet, *Les Guerriers de Dieu*, vol. II, 362–462.

118 M. Newcomen, *The Craft and Cruelty of the Churches Adversaries*, London 1643, 19.

119 Israel, *The Dutch Republic*, 178. See also W. S. Maltby, *Alba: A Biography of Fernando Alvarez de Toledo Third Duke of Alba, 1507–82*, Berkeley 1983, 241–5.

120 O. P. Grell, *Dutch Calvinists*, passim.

121 J. H. Hessels (ed.), *Ecclesiae Londino-Batavae Archivum*, 3 vols., Cambridge 1887–97, vol. III, no. 242.

122 For siege of Haarlem, see Israel, *Dutch Republic*, 178–80.

123 G. Parker, *The Dutch Revolt*, London 1981, 162.

124 Hessels, *Londino-Batavae*, vol. III, no. 259.

125 Ibid., vol. III, no. 269.

126 Ibid., vol. III, no. 315.

127 Ibid., vol. III, no. 638.

128 Israel, *Dutch Republic*, 184–5; for the letter from Zierikzee, see Hessels, *Londino-Batavae*, vol. II, 152. For the siege of Zierikzee, see J. Pot, *Het beleg van Zierikzee*, Leiden 1925, passim.

129 'Mater' in *Bustorum aliquot Reliquiae* by B. Hamey. MS in Royal College of Physicians. Cited in J. J. Keevil, *Hamey the Stranger*, London 1952, 27.

130 L. Voet, *Antwerp: The Golden Age*, Antwerp 1973, 202–3; for the higher figure of 8,000 killed, see Parker, *Dutch Revolt*, 178. See also Israel, *Dutch Republic*, 185.

131 Hessels, *Londino-Batavae*, vol. III, no. 824; for the Malcontents, see Israel, *Dutch Republic*, 198. For Daniel de Dieu, see Grell, *Dutch Calvinists*, 55–6.

132 Hessels, *Londino-Batavae*, vol. III, no. 876; for siege of Brussels 1584/85, Parker, *Dutch Revolt*, 214.

133 Hessels, *Londino-Batavae*, vol. III, no. 879.

134 According to a letter from Antwerp also written in July 1584 more than 20,000 people from the countryside had fled to Ghent, Hessels, *Londino-Batavae*, vol. III, no. 919; for Jacob Regius's letter see no. 924; for siege and surrender of Ghent, see Parker, *Dutch Revolt*, 214. For Jacob Regius, see Grell, *Dutch Calvinists*, 126–7 and 136.

135 Hessels, *Londino-Batavae*, vol. III, no. 963.

136 Ibid., vol. III, no. 967.

137 Ibid., vol. III, nos. 977, 995 and 996.

138 Ibid., vol. III, no. 1052.

139 Ibid., vol. III, nos. 1218, 1221 and 1222; between 1568 and 1576 the Dutch Reformed communities in England had supported William of Orange and the rebel cause with both men and money, see Grell, *Dutch Calvinists*, 28 and Parker, *Dutch Revolt*, 148.

140 Hessels, *Londino-Batavae*, vol. III, no. 1195.

141 Ibid., vol. III, no. 1404.

142 See Israel, *Dutch Republic*, 260.

143 Duffy, *Siege Warfare*, 85–8 and J. Cruso, *The Art of Warre*, Cambridge 1639, 78–9.

144 Hessels, *Londino-Batavae*, vol. III, no. 1546.

145 Ibid., vol. III, nos. 1614, 1622, 1636 and 1639.

146 Ibid., vol. III, no. 1678.

147 For Geoffrey Gates, see P. Collinson, *The Elizabethan Puritan Movement*, rep. Oxford 1990, 278 and 283.

148 G. Gates, *The Defence of Militarie Profession*, London 1579.

149 Gates, *Militarie Profession*, 6.

150 Ibid., 17.

151 Ibid., 21–2.

152 Ibid., 24–5.

153 See O. P. Grell, 'Godly Charity or Political Aid? Irish Protestants and International Calvinism, 1641–1645', *Historical Journal*, 39, 3 (1996), 743–53, especially 743–6.

154 See H. L. Zwitzer, 'The Eighty Years War', in Hoeven (ed.), *Exercise of Arms*, 33–55.

155 See Tallett, *War and Society*, 40 and Carlton, *Going to the Wars*, 72.

156 Carlton, *Going to the Wars*, 72.

157 For Hexham, see C. W. Schoneveld, *Intertraffic of the Mind*, Leiden 1983, 122 and K. L. Sprunger, *Dutch Puritanism. A History of English and Scottish Churches of the Netherlands in the Sixteenth and Seventeenth Centuries*, Leiden 1982, 158, 159 and 161.

158 John Polyander, *The Refutation of an Epistle written by a Doctor of the Augustins Order*, trans. Henry Hexham, Dort 1610, introductory letter by John Burgess; for Burgess, see Sprunger, *Dutch Puritanism*, 143–4.

159 John Polyander, *A Disputation against the Adoration of the Reliques of Saints Departed*, trans. from French by Henry Hexham, Dort 1611, f.A3v.

160 H. Hexham, *A Journall . . .*

161 *Ibid.*, f. 3v.

162 *Ibid.*, 13.

163 *Ibid.*, 32–4; see also H. Duits, *Van Bartholomeusnacht tot Bataafse opstand*, Hilversum 1990, 172–5 and Israel, *Dutch Republic*, 516.

164 For the psychological impact of the war, see B. Roeck, 'Der Dreissigjährige Krieg und die Menschen im Reich. Überlegungen zu den Formen psychischer Krisenbewältigung in der ersten Hälfte des 17. Jahrhundrets'; for the impact on civilians, see also M. Kaiser, 'Inmitten des Kriegtheaters: Die Bevölkerung als militärischer Faktor und Kriegsteilnemer im Dreissigjährigen Krieg', both in B. R. Kroener and R. Pröve (eds.), *Krieg und Frieden. Militär und Gesellschaft in der Frühen Neuzeit*, Munich 1996, 265–79 and 281–303. A number of articles, especially in section IV, 'Life in Times of War and Peace', and W. Schmidt-Biggermann, 'The Apocalypse and Millenarianism in the Thirty Years War', 259–64 in K. Bussmann and H. Schilling (eds.), *1648. War and Peace in Europe, I. Politics, Religion, Law and Society*, Münster 1999, offer further insight.

165 E. Calamy, *Englands looking-glasse*, London 1642, 33–44.

166 See C. A. Campan (ed.), *Bergues sur le Soom Assiégée le 18 de juillet 1622 & deassiégée le 3 d'octobre ensuivant, selon la description faite par les trois pasteurs de l'église d'icelle*, 2nd edition, Brussels 1867, 247; cited in Parker, *The Thirty Years' War*, 199.

167 See G. Parker, *The Army of Flanders and the Spanish Road 1567–1659*, revised edition, Cambridge 1990, 176–7.

168 Parker, *Army of Flanders*, 211; Israel, *The Dutch Republic and the Hispanic World 1601–1661*, Oxford 1986, 101–2 gives the somewhat lower figure of 1,900 deserters who sought asylum in Bergen-op-Zoom.

169 For this, see Grell, *Dutch Calvinists*, 176–91.

170 Hessels, *Londino-Batavae*, vol. III, no. 2000.

171 *Ibid.*, vol. III, no. 2003.

172 Christian IV had a painting made of his vision, in the frame of which he had his own description of the event inserted, see S. Heiberg (ed.), *Christian IV and Europe*, Copenhagen 1988, 65. See also H. Rasmussen, 'Chr. 4.s syn', *Fynske Minder*, 1957, 60–75.

173 For the significance of fish, and whales in particular, as portents and warnings, see S. Schama, *The Embarrassment of Riches. An Interpretation of Dutch Culture in the Golden Age*, London 1987, 130–50.

174 Harms, *Deutsche Illustrierte Flugblätter*, vol. I, no. 216. The Dutch chronicler G. Baudart had no doubt that this fish signified God's great wrath, even if he applied it to humanity at large, see A. Th. van Deursen, *Plain Lives in a Golden Age. Popular Culture, Religion and Society in Seventeenth-century Holland*, Cambridge 1991, 253–4.

175 See E. Ladewig Petersen, 'The Wrath of God. Christian IV and Poor Relief in the Wake of the Danish Intervention in the Thirty Years' War', in Grell and Cunningham, *Health Care and Poor Relief*, 147–8.

176 See J. Nordström, 'Lejonet från Nörden', in *De Yverbornes . . . Sextonhundratalsstudier*, Stockholm 1934, 9–51 and 157–80, especially 30 and 169.

177 V. Petersen, 'Fremmede Tropper i Jylland i det syttende Aarhundrede', *Historisk Archiv*, 1871, II, 482–3.

178 Cited in V. Mollerup, 'Bidrag til Jyllands Historie i Krigsaatene 1627–1629', *Danske Samlinger*, 2, vol. VI', 294 and 295.

179 Harms, *Deutsche Illustrierte Flugblätter*, vol. I, no. 173.

180 For Swedish propaganda, see S. Arnoldsson, *Krigspropagandan i Sverige före tretioåriga kriget*, Göteborg 1941 and G. Rystad, *Kriegsnachrichten und Propaganda während des dreissigjährigen Krieges*, Berlin 1960. For Gustavus Adolphus and Magdeburg, see M. Roberts, *Gustavus Adolphus*, 2nd edition, London 1992, 130 and 136.

181 See Harms, *Deutsche Illustrierte Flugblätter*, vol. II, no. 228.

182 For this unique description of the siege and sack of Magdeburg, see J. Peters (ed.), *Ein Söldnerleben im Dreissigjährigen Krieg*, Berlin 1993, 46–50.

183 See B. von Krusenstjern (ed.), *Selbstzeugnisse der Zeit des Dreissigjährigen Krieges*, Berlin 1997, 89–90 and E. Neubauer (ed.), *Magdeburgs Zerstörung 1631. Sammlung zeitgenössischer Berichte*, Magdeburg 1931 (Daniel Friese, *Vom magdeburgischen Unglück*), Magdeburg 1931, 27–37.

184 See Krusenstjern, *Selbstzeugnisse*, 186–7 and Neubauer, *Magdeburgs Zerstörung* (Simon Printz, *Die Erzählung von einem Bürger, der mit in der Eroberung gewesen*), 47–52.

185 See Krusenstjern, *Selbstzeugnisse*, 223–4 and Neubauer, *Magdeburgs Zerstörung* (Christopher Thodaenus) 55–63.

186 Krusenstjern, *Selbstzeugnisse*, 107–8 and H. Schimank, 'Otto von Guericke', in *Magdeburger Kultur- und Wirtschafsleben*, 6, 1936, 71–6.

187 Cited in W. Lahne, *Magdeburgs Zerstörung in der zeitgenössischen Publizistik*, Magdeburg 1931, 25–30, especially 28.

188 *Ibid.*, 36.

189 *Ibid.*, 67.

190 *Ibid.*, 96–7.

191 Cited ibid., 104–5.

192 See ibid., 147–55.

193 *Die Jämmerlich, betrübte Prophetin, Frau Sybilla Magdeburg*, n.p. 1631, fol. BIIv.

194 *Die jämmerliche Prophetin, Frau Sybilla Magdeburg. Das ist: Historische Auszführung, Was die erbärmliche Verderbung der Stadt Magdeburg . . . mit sich bringen werd durch Mein Anbringen Bestehet Mit der vorigen Geschichte, Klarheit, Warheit, vnd Gleichheit*, n.p. 1631; cited in Lahne, *Magdeburg Zerstörung*, 157–9.

195 See W. Strauss, *The German Single-Leaf Woodcut 1600–1700*, vol. II, 2 vols., New York 1977, 574 and 586.

196 Cited in B. Roeck, *Eine Stadt in Krieg und Frieden. Studien zur Geschichte der Reichsstadt Augsburg zwischen Kalenderstreit und Parität*, 2 vols., Göttingen 1989, vol. II, 522–3.

197 Parker, *Thirty Years' War*, 97–9.

198 Roeck, *Krieg und Frieden*, vol. II, 656–68.

199 For the role and significance of this chiliastic Protestant vision of the lion from the north, see above, chapter 2, 'The White Horse: Religion, Revelation and Reformation'.

200 See F. A. Yates, *The Rosicrucian Enlightenment*, London 1986, 172 and Roeck, *Krieg und Frieden*, vol. II, 680–1.

201 *The Swedish Intelligencer*, 2nd part, London 1632, To the Favovrable and Ivdiciovs Reader.

202 See *The Swedish Intelligencer*, 3rd part, London 1633, 186; see also M. Roberts, *Gustavus Adolphus. A History of Sweden, 1611–1632*, vol. II, London 1958, 735, and Bireley, *Religion and Politics*, 187.

203 Roeck, *Krieg und Frieden*, vol. II, 681.

204 See E. Seaton, *Literary Relations of England and Scandinavia in the Seventeenth Century*, Oxford 1935, 80.

205 Harms, *Deutsche Illustrierte Flugblätter*, vol. II, no. 263.

206 Cited Roeck, *Krieg und Frieden*, vol. II, 686; see also 682–5.

207 Roberts, *Gustavus Adolphus*, vol. II, 168.

208 Hessels, *Londino-Batavae*, vol. III, no. 2134.

209 Ibid., vol. III, no. 2155; see also no. 2169.

210 Ibid., vol. III, no. 2193; see also no. 2170.

211 For these broadsheets, see E. A. Beller, *Propaganda in Germany during the Thirty Years War*, London 1940, Plates XIX and XX and 42–3; Roeck, *Krieg und Frieden*, vol. II, 698–701; Harms, *Deutsche Illustrierte Flugblätter*, vol. II, nos. 265 and 266. See also M. Schilling, 'Das Flugblatt als Instrument gesellschaftlicher Anpassung', in W. Brückner, P. Blickle and D. Boener (eds.), *Literatur und Volk. Probleme populärer Kultur in Deutschland*, 2 vols., Wiesbaden 1985, vol. I, 601–26.

212 Roeck, *Krieg und Frieden*, vol. II, 731–66; see also Duffy, *Siege Warfare*, 182–3.

213 See E. A. Beller, *Propaganda in Germany during the Thirty Years War*, 28 and plate IX.

214 Roberts, *Gustavus Adolphus*, vol. II, 170–2.

215 Hessels, *Londino-Batavae*, vol. III, no. 2207.

216 Ibid., vol. III, no. 2214.

217 R. Grossner and B. Frhr. v. Haller, ' "Zu kurzem Bericht umb der Nachkommen willen". Zeitgenössische Aufzeichnungen aus dem Dreissigjährigen Krieg in Kirchenbüchern des Erlanger Raumes' in *Erlanger Bausteine zur fränkischen Heimatsforschung*, 40, 1992, 9–107, especially 20, 25 and 26.

218 Ibid., 27 and 33.

219 Hessels, *Londino-Batavae*, vol. III, nos. 2223 and 2225.

220 Bireley, *Religion and Politics*, 188.

221 For the Heilbronn League, see Parker, *Thirty Years' War*, 135–6.

222 Hessels, *Londino-Batavae*, vol. III, no. 2228.

223 Ibid., vol. III, no. 2236; for the lack of action and hesitation in Germany in the wake of Gustavus Adolphus's death, see also Parker, *Thirty Years' War*, 132–3.

224 Hessels, *Londino-Batavae*, vol. III, no. 2326. For the battle of Nördlingen, see Parker, *Thirty Years' War*, 140–1.

225 Hessels, *Londino-Batavae*, vol. III, no. 2314.

226 Ibid., vol. III, no. 2386.

227 Ibid., vol. III, no. 2426.

228 Harms, *Deutsche Illustrierte Flugblätter*, vol. I, no. 176.

229 Hessels, *Londino-Batavae*, vol. III, no. 2617.

230 See 'A Declaration of the English Army in Scotland 1st Aug. 1650', in A. S. P. Woodhouse (ed.), *Puritanism and Liberty*, reprint London 1974, 474–8.

4 THE BLACK HORSE: FOOD, F(E)AST AND FAMINE

1 Pitirim Aleksandrovich Sorokin, *Man and Society in Calamity. The Effects of War, Revolution, Famine, Pestilence upon Human Mind, Behavior, Social Organization and Cultural Life*, New York 1943, 14.

2 The history of famine is a very recent discipline. As pointed out in Catherina Lis and Hugo Soly, *Poverty and Capitalism in Pre-Industrial Europe*, translated by James Coonan, Hassocks, Sussex 1979, xi, historians have been guided in their research topics in these areas by the problems current in their own society. Thus the Depression of the 1930s prompted historical work on prices, wages and incomes, while concerns

with social tensions in the 1970s prompted work on the history of poverty. Similarly, the recent development of historical demography, which has brought to light the occurrence of death by famine, together with the present-day concern with famine in the Third World, have prompted work on the history of famine.

3 J. P. W. Rivers, 'The Nutritional Biology of Famine', in G. A. Harrison (ed.), *Famine*, Oxford 1988, 57–106, 58.

4 W. A. Dando, 'Man-Made Famines. Some Geographical Insights from an Exploratory Study of a Millennium of Russian Famines', in John R. K. Robson (ed.), *Famine: Its Causes, Effects and Management*, New York 1981, 139–61, 141, 140.

5 François Vincent, *Histoire des Famines à Paris*, Paris 1946, chapter 4.

6 B. H. Slicher von Bath, 'Agriculture in the Vital Revolution', in E. E. Rich and C. H. Wilson, (eds.), *The Cambridge Economic History of Europe. Volume V: The Economic Organization of Early Modern Europe*. Cambridge 1977, 42–132, 60. For a summary listing of periods of dearth and famine, see Bob Scribner, '1525 – Revolutionary Crisis?' in Monika Hagenmaier and Sabine Holt (eds.), *Krisenbewußtstein und Krisenbewältigung in der Frühen Neuzeit – Crisis in Early Modern Europe*, Frankfurt am Main 1992, 25–45, see 28–30. For an attempt to list all famines that had ever happened and of which there was some written trace, see Cornelius Walford, *The Famines of the World: Past and Present. Being Two Papers read before the Statistical Society of London in 1878 and 1879 respectively, and Reprinted from its Journal*, London, 1897, rep. 1970.

7 Peter Laslett, *The World We Have Lost*, first published London 1965; edition of London 1971, the title of chapter 5.

8 David Arnold, *Famine: Social Crisis and Historical Change*, Oxford 1988, 29.

9 Ronald E. Seavoy, *Famine in Peasant Societies*, New York 1986. For an alternative radical, and in this case non-Malthusian, interpretation of the relation of population growth to agricultural changes, see Ester Boserup, *The Conditions of Agricultural Growth. The Economics of Agrarian Change under Population Pressure*, London 1965, who claims that 'population growth is the independent variable which in its turn is a major factor determining agricultural developments' (p. 11). Her argument is a very broad one which applies to all forms of cultivation across the world, to which the Western European case is the only exception, because of the particular form of expanding land use that it adopted, viz. the expansion of production at the so-called extensive margin, by the creation of new fields, compared to the expansion of production by more intensive cultivation of existing fields, which she claims is the case in all other forms of agricultural production in the world; see 12. One territory in Western Europe may be said to have followed this larger pattern in our period, and that is the Netherlands, where the option of the creation of new fields could only be adopted by reclaiming land from the sea.

10 Seavoy, *Famine in Peasant Societies*, 29–30.

11 A similar case could be made for the Netherlands, as we shall see below, but this is not a case considered by Seavoy.

12 Seavoy, *Famine in Peasant Societies*, 76.

13 *Ibid.*

14 Jan de Vries, *The Dutch Rural Economy in the Golden Age*, 1500–1700, New Haven 1974, 5.

15 Andrew Appleby, 'Diet in Sixteenth Century England. Sources, Problems, Possibilities', in Charles Webster, (ed.), *Health, Medicine and Mortality in the Sixteenth Century*, Cambridge 1979, 97–116, see 105–7; the quotation is from page 107.

16 Amartya Sen, *Poverty and Famines: An Essay on Entitlement and Deprivation*, first published 1981; see edition of Oxford 1987, 5.

17 In the early twentieth century, before the Revolution, 'the peasant, even when harvests were below average or even if there was a crop failure, would still sell grain for he was dependent on the cash earned from the sale of grain to pay his redemption payments and taxes, and to buy salt, cloth, some tools, etc. Famine catastrophes were greater in this crude form of commercial agriculture than in the previous subsistent agricultural system.' Dando, 'Man-Made Famines', 141.

18 We follow here the valuable summary of recent work offered by P. R. Galloway, 'Long-term Fluctuations in the Climate and Population in the Pre-Industrial Era', *Population and Development Review* 12, 1986, 1–24, 7.

19 Emmanuel Le Roy Ladurie, *Times of Feast, Times of Famine. A History of Climate since the Year 1000*, trans. Barbara Bray, first pub. 1967; see edition of New York 1988.

20 Galloway, 'Long-term Fluctuations', 3, 12. On p. 12 Galloway is at this point speaking specifically of the period of warming from 1670 to 1800, for which there is an adequate amount of information, but it is reasonable to extend this general claim for the earlier period with which we are concerned.

21 Galloway, 'Long-term Fluctuations', 9.

22 Galloway, 'Long-term Fluctuations', 10–11.

23 Karl Helleiner, 'The Population of Europe from the Black Death to the Eve of the Vital Revolution', in E. E. Rich and C. H. Wilson, (eds.), *The Cambridge Economic History of Europe. Volume IV, The Economy of Expanding Europe in the Sixteenth and Seventeenth Centuries*, Cambridge 1966, 1–95; see 41.

24 For an attempt to perform retrospective diagnosis on diseases associated with some nineteenth- and twentieth-century famines, see Frederik B Bang, 'The Role of Disease in the Ecology of Famine', in *Famine: Its Causes, Effects and Management*, 61–75.

25 On these plant diseases see chapters 1 and 2 of Garnet Lindsay Carefoot and Edgar R. Sprott, *Famine on the Wind. Plant Diseases and Human History*, London, 1969.

26 Ulf Dirlmeier and Gerhard Fouquet, 'Diet and Consumption', in Bob Scribner, (ed.), *Germany. A New Social and Economic History. Volume 1: 1450–1630*, London 1996, 85–111, 86.

27 For England see Appleby, 'Diet in Sixteenth Century England'.

28 William Harrison, *The Description of England (1587)*, ed. Georges Edelen, Ithaca, New York 1968, 264. See also Margaret Pelling, 'Food, Status and Knowledge: Attitudes to Diet in Early Modern England', in her *The Common Lot: Sickness, Medical Occupations and the Urban Poor in Early Modern England*, London 1998, 38–62, 46–7.

29 On the history of fish and fishing, see A. R. Mitchell, 'The European Fisheries in Early Modern History', in E. E. Rich and C. H. Wilson, (eds.), *The Cambridge Economic History of Europe. Volume V: The Economic Organization of Early Modern Europe*, Cambridge 1977, 133–84.

30 Françoise Hildesheimer, *Fléaux et Société de la Grande Peste au Choléra, XIV–XX Siècle*, Paris 1993, 35–6.

31 Wilhelm Abel, *Agricultural Fluctuations in Europe from the Thirteenth to the Twentieth Centuries*, trans. Olive Ordish, first published in German in 1935; edition of London 1980, 142, analysing work by Etienne Scholliers.

32 More recently it has been claimed that if people spent more than 44 per cent of their income on bread then they fell below the subsistence level and became paupers. See A. T. van Deursen, *Plain Lives in a Golden Age. Popular Culture, Religion and Society in Seventeenth-century Holland [1572–1648]*, trans. Maarten Ultee, first published in Dutch in four volumes, 1978–81; edition of Cambridge 1991, 6, citing the work of W. P. Blockmans and W. Prevenier, 'Armoede in de Nederlanden van de 14e tot het midden van de 16e

eeuw: Bronnen en problemen', *Tijdschrift voor Geschiedenis* 8, 1975, 502.

33 We use 'wheat' rather than 'corn' since 'corn' is a generic term, in practice used to refer to the local cereal crop. Hence in America corn = maize, in England corn = wheat, while in Scotland corn = oats.

34 For the history of bread we depend on Sir William Ashley, *The Bread of our Forefathers [in England]. An Inquiry in Economic History*, Oxford 1928.

35 Daphne A. Roe, *A Plague of Corn. The Social History of Pellagra*, Ithaca 1973; see also Alfred W. Crosby, 'The Demographic Effects of American Crops in Europe', in his *Germs, Seeds and Animals. Studies in Ecological History*, New York 1994, 148–66.

36 A. De Maddalena, *Rural Europe 1500–1750*, Glasgow 1978, 342, as quoted in Michael North, *From the North Sea to the Baltic. Essays in Commercial, Monetary and Agrarian History, 1500–1800*, Aldershot 1996, chapter VII, 313.

37 Ashley, *The Bread of our Forefathers*, quoting Charles Best Robinson (ed.), *Rural Economy in Yorkshire in 1641, being the Farming and Account Books of Henry Best, of Elmswell, in the East Riding of the County of York*, Durham 1857.

38 Quoted in E. M. Leonard, *The Early History of English Poor Relief*, Cambridge, 1900, 145.

39 Harrison, *The Description of England*, 133.

40 For a diet sheet of 1569 for farm servants on the royal estates of Saxony, which clearly shows the presence of grain products in every meal, see Abel, *Agricultural Fluctuations*, 143.

41 Slicher von Bath, 'Agriculture in the Vital Revolution', 67–9; David Grigg, *Population Growth and Agrarian Change. An Historical Perspective*, Cambridge 1980, 31–9; De Vries, *The Dutch Rural Economy in the Golden Age*.

42 Norman J. G. Pounds, *Hearth and Home. A History of Material Culture*, orig. pub. 1989; edition of Bloomington, Indiana 1993, 152.

43 Andrew Appleby, *Famine in Tudor and Stuart England*, Liverpool 1978, 7.

44 Ashley, *The Bread of our Forefathers*, 145.

45 See Dirlmeier and Fouquet, 'Diet and Consumption', 87, for changes in grain choice in Germany.

46 Deursen, *Plain Lives in a Golden Age*, 14.

47 On these changes see Michael North, *From the North Sea to the Baltic*, passim, and David Kirby, *Northern Europe in the Early Modern Period. The Baltic World 1492–1772*, London 1990.

48 Slicher von Bath, 'Agriculture in the Vital Revolution', 53.

49 W. Harms, *Deutsche Illustrierte Flugblätter des 16. und 17.*

Jahrhundert in der Wolfenbüttel Sammlung, 2 vols., Munich/Tübingen 1980/85, vol. 1, no. 162.

50 Abel, Agricultural Fluctuations, 133.

51 Caroline Walker Bynum, Holy Feast and Holy Fast. The Religious Significance of Food to Medieval Women, Berkeley 1987, 73.

52 Robert Sauzet, 'Discours Cléricaux sur la Nourriture', in Pratiques et Discours Alimentaires à la Renaissance. Actes du colloque de Tours de mars 1979 Centre d'études supérieures de la Renaissance, ed. Jean-Claude Margolin and Robert Sauzet, Paris 1982, 247–55.

53 Abel, Agricultural Fluctuations, 144.

54 Dirlmeier and Fouquet, 'Diet and Consumption', 91.

55 John Taylor, 'Jacke a Lent his Beginning and Entertainment: with the Mad Pranks of his Gentleman-Usher Shrove-Tuesday that goes before him, and his Footman Hunger attending', in All the Works of John Taylor the Water-Poet. Being Sixty and three in Number. Collected into one Volume by the Author: With sundry new Additions, corrected, revised, and newly Imprinted, London 1630, 112–20, 114, composed in 1617, spelling modernised; as quoted in part also in Bridget Ann Henisch, Food and Fast. Food in Medieval Society, 1976, 38.

56 Taylor, 'Jacke a Lent', 115.

57 Steven Ozment, Protestants. The Birth of a Revolution, London 1992, 102.

58 L. Jacobson (ed.), Peder Palladius' Danske Skrifter, Copenhagen, 1925, vol. v, 117–18, our translation.

59 Kristof Glamann, 'The Changing Patterns of Trade', in The Cambridge Economic History of Europe. Volume v, 185–289, see 196.

60 J. Walter and K. Wrightson, 'Dearth and the Social Order in Early Modern England', Past and Present 71, 1976, 22–42, see 41. 'If the effects of famine be duly considered, it will appear that it is a most sore and fearful judgement', William Gouge, God's three Arrowes: Plague, Famine, Sword, in three treatises. I. A Plaister for the Plague. II. Dearth's Death. III. The Churche's Conquest over the Sword. (The Extent of God's Providence set out in a Sermon [on Matt. x. 29, etc.]. The Dignitie of Chivalry, set forth in a sermon [on 2 Chron. viii. 9] . . . Second edition, London 1631, 135.

61 Jean Delumeau, Sin and Fear. The Emergence of a Western Guilt Culture 13th–18th Centuries, originally published in French in 1983; trans. Eric Nicholson, edition of New York 1990, 3.

62 From the full title of John Udall, The true remedie against Famine and warres. Five Sermons upon the first chapter of the prophecie of Joel, wherein the Councell that the holy Ghoste

gave the Israelites to redress the famine which they felt and prevent the warres that were threatened to come upon them; is applied in particular unto our present time: Preached in the time of the dearth. 1586. By John Udall, preacher of the worde of God at Kingston upon Thames, London 1586.

63 Udall, The true remedie against Famine and warres, 2v–3r, spelling modernised.

64 See Ludwig Lavatere, Three Christian Sermons, made by Lodovike Lavatere, Minister of Zuricke in Helvetia, of Famine and Dearth of Victuals: and translated into English, as being verie fit for this time of our Dearth: By W. Barlow, Bachelar in Divinite, London 1596. These sermons were first published in 1571 in German, in Zurich.

65 The translator adds here: 'as it happened this year 1596 in England'.

66 Lavatere, Three Christian Sermons, 11, 12, 19, 21–2, 29, 31, 33 (all pagination after 30 is incorrect).

67 Lavatere, Three Christian Sermons, 49–54.

68 Gouge, God's three Arrowes, 171–2.

69 i.e. the worst of the trio of war, famine and disease. Martin Parker, A briefe dissection of Germaines Affliction: with Warre, Pestilence, and Famine; and other deducable miseries, Lachrimable to speak of; more lamentable to partake of. Sent as a (friendly) monitor to England, warning her to beware of (Generally) Ingratitude, and Security; as also (Particularly) Other greevous sinnes, the weight whereof Germany hath a long time felt, and at this present doth (and England may feare to) feele. Written from approv'd intelligence, by M. Parker. [In verse.], London 1638, verses 32–4.

70 Parker, A briefe dissection of Germaines Affliction, Postscript. For examples of English broadsheets of 1558–1615, embroidering the account of mothers eating children during famine that can be found in Josephus's Jewish War, see Tessa Watt, Cheap Print and Popular Piety, Cambridge 1991, 97–8.

71 Adel P. Den Hartog, 'Adjustment of Food Behaviour During Famine', in Famine: Its Causes, Effects and Management, 155–6, drawing on modern experience of famines in Africa and South America.

72 Sorokin, Man and Society in Calamity, 51.

73 Ibid., 177–8.

74 Appleby, Famine in Tudor and Stuart England, 7–8.

75 Jean de Léry, Histoire Memorable de la Ville de Sancerre. Contenant les Entreprinses, Siege, Approches, Bateries, Assaux & autres efforts des Assiegeans: les Resistances, faits Magnanimes, la Famine Extreme & Delivrance Notable des Assiegez Le tout fidelement recueilli sur le lieu, par Jean de Lery, n.p., n.p., 1574. The famine section (chapters 10–14) has been reprinted as Jean de Léry, 'Discours de la Famine de Sancerre. Discours de l'Extreme

Famine, Cherté de Vivres, Chairs, et autres Choses non Acoustumées pour la Nourriture de l'Homme, dont les Assiégez dans la Ville de Sancerre ont été Affligez, et ont Usé environ Trois Mois', in L. Cimber and F. Danjou (eds.), *Archives Curieuses de l'Histoire de France Depuis Louis XI jusqu'à Louis XVIII*, 1st series, vol. VIII, 19–82, Paris 1835. The edition we have used is Géralde Nakam (ed.), *Au Lendemain de la Saint-Barthélmy: Guerre Civile et Famine. Histoire Mémorable du Siège de Sancerre (1573) de Jean de Léry*. Paris 1975. Translations are our own.

76 Louis-Raymond Lefèvre (ed.), *Journal de L'Estoile pour le Règne de Henri IV. Vol.* 1, 1589–1600, Paris 1948; where she has rendered the relevant passages we use the translation in Nancy Lyman Roelker, ed., *The Paris of Henry of Navarre as seen by Pierre de l'Estoile. Selections from his Mémoires-Journaux*, Cambridge, Mass. 1958; otherwise the translations are our own.

77 Mark Greengrass, 'The Later Wars of Religion in the French Midi', in Peter Clark (ed.), *The European Crisis of the 1590s. Essays in Comparative History*, London 1985, 106–34, 117.

78 Quoted from Gustaf Utterström, 'Climatic Fluctuations and Population Problems in Early Modern History', *The Scandinavian Economic History Review*, 3, 1955, 27–8, in Appleby, *Famine in Tudor and Stuart England*, 133.

79 See David Souden, 'Demographic Crisis and Europe in the 1590s', in Clark (ed.), *The European Crisis of the 1590s*, 231–43, 232; see also Clark's introduction to this volume, especially 7–14. The essays in this volume cover the incidence of famine across Europe in this decade.

80 Appleby, *Famine in Tudor and Stuart England*, 54, quoting a report by Edmund Hall and William Homberston on properties in Cockermouth.

81 As quoted in Appleby, *Famine in Tudor and Stuart England*, 141. 'Cleanness of teeth' is a quotation from Amos 4:6, where God is promising this as a result of famine.

82 As quoted in Appleby, *Famine in Tudor and Stuart England*, 143.

83 Sir Hugh Platt, *Sundrie new and Artificiall Remedies against Famine. Written by H[ugh] P[latt] Esq., uppon the occasion of the present Dearth*, London 1596, A2r.

84 See H. Hauser, 'Une Famine il y a 400 Ans: Organisation Communale de la Défense contre la Disette', in his *Travailleurs et Marchands dans l'ancienne France*, Paris 1920, 114–29, 114 (where the French is given), which is good for local government responses.

85 As quoted (without further reference) in Yves-Marie Bercé, *History of Peasant Revolts. The Social Origins of Rebellion in Early Modern France*, published in French in 1986; English translation by Amanda Whitmore, Cambridge 1990, 176.

86 Ashley, *The Bread of our Forefathers*, 43.

87 Lis and Soly, *Poverty and Capitalism in Pre-Industrial Europe*, 84; and on these issues see also 82–96.

88 As quoted in Brian Pullan, 'The Famine in Venice and the New Poor Law, 1527–1529', *Bolletino dell' Istituto di Storia della Società e dello Stato Veneziano* 5/6, 1964, 141–202, see 153.

89 Pullan 'The Famine in Venice and the New Poor Law, 1527–1529', 172–3; Brian Pullan, *Rich and Poor in Renaissance Venice: The Social Institutions of a Catholic State, to 1620*, Oxford 1971, chapter 3.

90 Lis and Soly, *Poverty and Capitalism in Pre-Industrial Europe*, 92–3.

91 On these issues see the chapters in Ole Peter Grell and Andrew Cunningham (eds.), *Health Care and Poor Relief in Protestant Europe, 1500–1700*, London 1997, and Ole Peter Grell, Andrew Cunningham and Jon Arrizabalaga (eds.), *Health Care and Poor Relief in Counter-Reformation Europe*, London 1999.

92 Brian Pullan, '"Support and Redeem": Charity and Poor Relief in Italian Cities from the 14th to the 17th Century', *Continuity and Change* 3, 1988, 177–208, 181.

93 William C. Innes, *Social Concern in Calvin's Geneva*, Allison Park, Pennsylvania 1983.

94 See Paul Slack, *Poverty and Policy in Tudor and Stuart England*, London 1988; for the relation of the poor law to famines, see 117.

95 Seavoy dates the stabilisation of the English population at about 1650: Seavoy, *Famine in Peasant Societies*, 76. This is supported by Roger Schofield, 'The Impact of Scarcity and Plenty on Population Change in England, 1541–1871', in Robert I. Rotberg and Theodore K. Rabb (eds.), *Hunger and History. The Impact of Changing Food Production and Consumption Patterns on Society*, Cambridge 1985, 67–93, see esp. 70–1. De Vries charts the stabilisation moment somewhere between 1650 and 1670. When talking about the five greatest cities of the Netherlands, he writes, 'Before the 1570s the cities grew slowly . . . After the Revolution [i.e. after 1579], the urban population veritably exploded. This growth, centered in the largest cities, continued, at gradually falling rates until the third quarter of the seventeenth century, when it was replaced by a downward movement that reached its nadir in the 1740s'; De Vries, *The Dutch Rural Economy in the Golden*

Age, 88; see also the graph on 89. When speaking just about Holland, he dates the stabilisation at 1650, writing 'By the mid-seventeenth century, when population growth in most areas ceased, Holland could claim to be the most highly urbanized and most densely populated province in western Europe' (96, see also 107–18). It should be noted that De Vries and Seavoy interpret the cessation of population increase in the Netherlands and England in opposite ways: De Vries sees it as 'stagnation', whereas Seavoy regards it as 'stabilisation'. Schofield, writing about England, also sees it as a 'population decline . . . due in almost equal measure to a fall in fertility and to an increase in mortality' (81). We obviously follow Seavoy in our interpretation. For further exploration of why England now escaped peace-time famine, see John Walter, 'The Social Economy of Dearth in Early Modern England', in Peter Laslett, Roger Schofield and E.A. Wrigley (eds.), *Famine, Disease and the Social Order in Early Modern Society*, Cambridge 1989, 75–128.

96 Glamann, 'The Changing Patterns of Trade', 221.

97 Joan Thirsk, 'Enclosing and Engrossing', in Joan Thirsk (ed.), *The Agrarian History of England and Wales. Volume IV*, 1500–1640, Cambridge 1967, 200–55, gives an excellent account of these phenomena and of perceptions and misperceptions of them in Tudor England.

98 Harrison, *The Description of England*, 216–17.

99 *Ibid.*, 217–18.

100 J. Walter, 'The Economy of Famine in Early Modern England', *Society for the Social History of Medicine Bulletin* 40, 1987, 7–10, 8. That the population was increasing still at this period, not decreasing as one might assume from Harrison's complaints about depopulation of town and countryside, can be seen from the work of the nineteenth-century statistician J. Rickman, as discussed in Helleiner, 'The Population of Europe from the Black Death to the Eve of the Vital Revolution', 31–2.

101 E. Kerridge, *The Agricultural Revolution*, New York 1967, has made the case very forcibly, and with much evidence, that England's agricultural revolution

occurred in the sixteenth and seventeenth centuries, not (as hitherto thought by historians) in the eighteenth and nineteenth. On the advantages of up-and-down husbandry, see esp. 206–13.

102 Kerridge, *The Agricultural Revolution*, 332.

103 *Ibid.*, 344.

104 In general see Sir William Ashley, 'The English [Agricultural] Improvers [of the 1620s]', in *Mélanges d'Histoire Offerts à Henri Pirenne par ses Anciens Élèves et ses Amis à l'Occasion de sa Quarantième Année d'Enseignement à Université de Gand 1886–1926*, Brussels 1926, 1–6; in particular see Arthur Standish, *The Commons Complaint. Wherein is Contained Two Special Grievances: The first, the generall destruction and waste of Woods in this Kingdome, with a remedy for the same . . . The Second Grievance is, the Extreame Derth of Victuals. Foure Remedies for the Same: 1. By a generall planting of Fruit-trees . . . 2. By an extraordinary breeding of Fowle and Pullen . . . 3. By a general destroying of all kinde of Vermine . . . 4. Proving the abundance of Corne that is yearely devoured and destroyed by the infinite number of Pigeons, kept and maintayned in this Kingdome*, London 1611; Gervase Markham, *Markhams farewell to Husbandry or, The inriching of all sorts of Barren and Sterile grounds in our Kingdome, to be as fruitfull in all manner of Graine, Pulse, and Grasse, as the best grounds whatsoever: Together with the annoyances, and preservation of all Graine an Seede, from one yeare to many yeares*, London 1625; and Walter Blith, *The English Improover [sic], or a new Survey of Husbandry. Discovering the Kingdome, That some Land, both Arrable and Pasture, may be Advanced Double or Treeble . . . Clearly demonstrated from Principles of sound Reason, Ingenuity and late, but most certaine Reall Experiences . . . By Walter Blith a Lover of Ingenuity*, London 1649.

105 De Vries, *The Dutch Rural Economy in the Golden Age*, 242.

106 Jonathan Israel, *The Dutch Republic. Its Rise, Greatness and Fall 1477–1806*, Oxford 1995, 106.

107 Israel, *The Dutch Republic*, 111.

108 *Ibid.*, 330–2.

109 Deursen, *Plain Lives in a Golden Age*, 58–9.

110 Charles Webster, *The Great Instauration: Science, Medicine and Reform, 1626–1660*, London 1975.

5 THE PALE HORSE: DISEASE, DISASTER AND DEATH

1 We have used the edition: Girolamo Savonarola, *Compendium Revelationum*, Ulme 1496; the English version is as translated in Bernard McGinn, ed. and trans., *Apocalyptic Spirituality: Treatises and Letters of . . . Savonarola*, New York, 1979, 192–275, see 195–6. In

fact Savonarola misremembered both the date and the place of his first preaching (it was San Gimignano in 1486), though he remembered the topic correctly; his first apocalyptic teaching in Florence was in 1490: see Donald Weinstein, *Savonarola and Florence: Prophecy and*

Patriotism in the Renaissance, Princeton, New Jersey 1970, 74–5. On the fate of Savonarola's movement, see L. Polizzotto, *The Elect Nation: The Savonarolan Movement in Florence 1494–1545*, Oxford 1994.

2 Savonarola in McGinn, *Apocalyptic Spirituality*, 197–8.

3 Savonarola in McGinn, *Apocalyptic Spirituality*, 199–200.

4 Savonarola in McGinn, *Apocalyptic Spirituality*, 201.

5 Today the term is usually limited to *infectious* diseases, except when it is used in a metaphorical way. As will be seen below, whether epidemic diseases were infectious or not was a disputed point in early-modern Europe. It is not helpful to apply modern concepts of disease infectivity to the early-modern period.

6 On the royal and imperial sufferers, see Owsei Temkin, 'On the History of "Morality and Syphilis",' in his *The Double Face of Janus*, Baltimore, Maryland 1977 (orig. pub. in German in 1927), 472–84, see 475. On the early literature see Claude Quétel, *History of Syphilis*, original French edition 1986; English edition trans. Judith Braddock and Brian Pike, Cambridge 1990, chapter 1; and P. A. Russell, 'Syphilis: God's Scourge or Nature's Vengeance? The German Printed Response to a Public Problem in the Early Sixteenth Century', *Archiv für Reformationsgeschichte* 80, 1989, 286–307.

7 Quétel, *History of Syphilis*, chapter 1, passim.

8 Roger Fry (ed.), *Dürer's Record of Journeys to Venice and the Low Countries*, New York 1945; Dürer was writing to Wilibald Pirkheimer, 18 August 1506.

9 Ulrich von Hutten, *Of the Wood Called Guaiacum, that Healeth the Frenche Pockes, and also Helpeth the Goute in the Feete, the Stone, Palsie, Lepre, Dropsy, Fallynge Evyll, and Other Diseases. Made in Latyn by Ulrich Hutten Knyght, and Translated in to Englysh by Thomas Paynel*, London 1540 (first published in Latin in 1519), f. 2r. We have modernised the spelling and punctuation in the quotations.

10 Quétel, *History of Syphilis*, 10, citing a report of 1495. A hundred years later the English surgeon William Clowes was still reporting cases of pox with no genital lesions: William Clowes, *A Profitable and Necessarie Booke of Observations, for all those that are burned with the flame of Gun powder, &c . . . Last of all is adjoined a short Treatise, for the cure of Lues Venerea . . .*, 1596; reprinted New York 1945, 150.

11 Von Hutten, *Of the Wood Called Guaiacum*, f. 49v.

12 Cited in Karl Sudhoff, *The Earliest Printed Literature on Syphilis, Being Ten Tractates from the Years 1495–1498. In*

Complete Facsimile With an Introduction and Other Accessory Material, trans. Charles Singer, Florence 1925, xix, our translation from the Latin version of the edict. It was drafted at the Imperial Diet in Lindau, and predated to 1495: see Russell, 'Syphilis: God's Scourge or Nature's Vengeance?', 292.

13 Von Hutten, *Of the Wood Called Guaiacum*, 1.

14 As cited and translated in Jon Arrizabalaga, John Henderson and Roger French, *The Great Pox. The French Disease in Renaissance Europe*, London 1997, 50, from Coradino Gilino, *De Morbo Quem Gallicum Nuncupant*, Ferrara 1497, f. 1 verso.

15 Francisco Lopez de Villalobos, *El Sumario de la Medicina con un Tratado de las Pestiferas Bubas*, Salamanca 1498, verse viii; as translated into English from the French edition of 1890, in Ralph Major, *Classic Descriptions of Disease*, London 1932, 35.

16 On the hierarchy of causes of diseases, see Jon Arrizabalaga, 'Facing the Black Death: Perceptions and Reactions of University Medical Practitioners,' in Luis García-Ballester, Roger French, Jon Arrizabalaga and Andrew Cunningham (eds.), *Practical Medicine from Salerno to the Black Death*, Cambridge 1994, 237–88.

17 Von Hutten, *Of the Wood Called Guaiacum*, ff. 2v–3r.

18 Sudhoff, *Earliest Printed Literature*, xxvi.

19 As quoted and translated in John (Jean) Astruc, *A Treatise of the Venereal Disease, in Six Books*, translated by William Barrowby, M.B., 2 vols., London 1737, vol. II, 229.

20 See Leonard Schmaus, *Lucubratincula de Morbo Gallico, et Cura ejus Noviter Reperta cum Ligno Indico*, Augsberg 1517.

21 Von Hutten, *Of the Wood Called Guaiacum*, f. 3v. On the later history of this concept of impure blood, see Ludwig Fleck, *Genesis and Development of a Scientific Fact*, first published in German in 1935; trans. Fred Bradley and Thaddeus Trenn, Chicago 1979, chapter 1, 'How the modern concept of syphilis originated'.

22 Von Hutten, *Of the Wood Called Guaiacum*, f. 4r–v.

23 Johannes Vigo, *The Most Excellent Workes of Chirurgerye, Made and Set Forth by Maister John Vigon, Heed Chirurgien of our Tyme in Italie, Translated into English*, first published in 1543; edition of Amsterdam 1968, f. CLX.

24 Winfried Schleiner, 'Moral Attitudes toward Syphilis and its Prevention in the Renaissance', *Bulletin of the History of Medicine* 68, 1994, 389–410, 395, quoting William Clowes, an English surgeon writing in the 1580s.

25 Winfried Schleiner, 'Infection and Cure through Women: Renaissance Constructions of Syphilis',

Journal of Medieval and Renaissance Studies 24, 1994, 499–517, 507–8.

26 Arrizabalaga, Henderson and French, *The Great Pox*, 49.

27 Arrizabalaga, Henderson and French, *The Great Pox*, 49.

28 Von Hutten, *Of the Wood Called Guaiacum*, f. 5v.

29 Von Hutten, *Of the Wood Called Guaiacum*, f. 8r.

30 Von Hutten, *Of the Wood Called Guaiacum*, f. 18r.

31 Von Hutten, *Of the Wood Called Guaiacum*, ff. 46r–47r.

32 Temkin, 'Morality and Syphilis', 475–8.

33 This information comes from the editor's introduction to Girolamo Fracastoro, *Fracastor: Syphilis or the French Disease. A Poem in Latin Hexameters*, trans. Heneage Wynne-Finch, London 1935, 28; but the origin of the story is Andreas Vesalius, *Epistola, Rationem Modumque Propinandi Radicis Chynae Decocti, Quo Nuper Invictissimus Carolus V Imperator Usus Est, Pertractans . . .*, Basle 1546.

34 For the story of the Bolognese surgeon Leonardo Fioravanti (1517–88), and his claims about cannibalism in his book of 1561, see William Eamon, 'Cannibalism and Contagion. Framing Syphilis in Counter-Reformation Italy', *Early Science and Medicine* 3, 1998, 1–31.

35 The original title was *Ain Recept von ainem Holtz zu brauchen füdie Krackheit der Franzosen und ander flüssig offen schäden aus hispanischer Sprach zu Teutsch gemacht . . .* For details of this issue see Max H. Fisch, *Nicolaus Pol Doctor 1494. With a Critical Text of his Guaiac Tract. Edited with a Translation by Dorothy M. Schullian*, New York 1947, esp. 43.

36 Schmaus, *Lucubratincula de Morbo Gallico*. We have used the version as reprinted in Aloysius Luisinus, *De Morbo Gallico Omnia Quae Extant apud Omnes Medicos cuiuscunque Nationis*, 2 vols., Venice 1566, vol. 1, 331–6, under the title of 'De Morbo Gallico Tractatus', and with the Preface dated Salzburg 1518. Schmaus does not say that the disease was brought to Europe from the Indians; he speaks only about proximate causes. But he does say that the disease is in fact an old one, as witnessed by the fact that the western Indians have suffered grievously from the disease for very many years, and they have even sold to our merchants the medicine they have always used against this disease. As for the arrival of this disease in Europe, there are various opinions, Schmaus says. He follows the physicians, limiting himself to proximate causes. Thus it arose from the terrible wet weather of 1494; see 332, col. 1.

37 This was not published until 1535. The tract is printed and translated in Fisch, *Nicolaus Pol Doctor 1494*.

38 As cited and translated in Fisch, *Nicolaus Pol Doctor 1494*, 44–5. See also Robert S. Munger, 'Guaiacum, The Holy Wood from the New World', *Journal of the History of Medicine and Allied Sciences* 4, 1949, 196–229, esp. 226–9.

39 Anna Foa, 'The New and the Old: The Spread of Syphilis (1494–1530)', in Edward Muir and Guido Ruggiero (eds.), *Sex and Gender in Historical Perspective*, Baltimore 1990, 26–45.

40 See William Allen Pusey, *The History and Epidemiology of Syphilis*, Springfield, Illinois 1933. From a modern perspective the apparent cures from the pox were not cures at all, but coincided with the latent period after the secondary stage of the disease as it ran its course, a period which can vary from one to twenty years before the third 'stage' arrives. However, such 'stages' of syphilis were only recognised in the nineteenth century.

41 See Greg W. Bentley, *Shakespeare and the New Disease: The Dramatic Function of Syphilis in Troilus and Cressida, Measure for Measure and Timon of Athens*, New York 1989.

42 'A marriage in name only, or the unequal match', in Desiderius Erasmus, *The Colloquies*, trans. Craig R. Thompson, Chicago 1965, 410.

43 Schleiner, 'Renaissance Moralizing'.

44 For the Latin text and an English prose translation see *Fracastor: Syphilis or the French Disease. A Poem in Latin Hexameters*, trans. Wynne-Finch. For the English verse translation we have used here, see *Syphilis: or, A Poetical History of the French Disease. Written in Latin by Fracastorius. And now attempted in English by N. Tate*, London 1686. Tate translates into iambic pentameters, giving a very free rendering into very inferior verse.

45 On its merits as Latin verse, see 'Fracastor and Virgil' in *Fracastor: Syphilis or the French Disease. A Poem in Latin Hexameters*, trans. Wynne-Finch, 172–8. For the many editions of the Latin version (there were 15 by 1648), see Leona Baumgartner and John F. Fulton, *A Bibliography of the Poem Syphilis sive Morbus Gallicus by Girolamo Fracastoro of Verona*, New Haven 1935.

46 The first medical writer after Fracastoro to use the name for the disease seems to have been Daniel Turner in England in 1717 in his *Syphilis. A Practical Dissertation on the Venereal Disease. In which, after an Account of its Nature and Original, the Diagnostick and Prognostick Signs, with the best Ways of Curing that Distemper, together with many Histories relating to the same, are candidly, and without Reserve, communicated*, first edition 1717, second edition 1724. It did not begin to

be adopted generally as the name for the disease until the1820s in France and Germany, and then presumably as a euphemism.

47 According to Wynne-Finch, it was preceded by the *Vaticinium in Epidemicam Scabiem*, published in Nurnberg in 1496, and the Spanish poem *El sumario de la medicina, con un tratado sobre las pestiferas bubas*, by Francisco Lopez de Villalobos, published in Salamanca in 1498 (*Fracastor: Syphilis or the French Disease. A Poem in Latin Hexameters*, trans. Wynne-Finch, 41n.). To these can be added one in French by Jean le Maire, published in 1525, *Les Trois Comptes, intitulez de Cupido et d'Atropos*, which gives a mythical origin of the disease; on which see Astruc, *A Treatise of the Venereal Disease*, vol. II, 261–4.

48 See Hieronymus Fracastorius, *De Contagione et Contagiosis Morbis et Eorum Curatione, Libri III* (first published 1546), trans. William Cave Wright, New York 1930, 217 et seq.

49 Astruc, *A Treatise of the Venereal Disease*, vol. I, 124, 128, 133, 134.

50 For this information we rely on Robert Jütte, 'Syphilis and Confinement. Hospitals in Early Modern Germany', in N. Finzsch and Robert Jütte (eds.), *Institutions of Confinement. Hospitals, Asylums, and Prisons in Western Europe and North America, 1500–1950*, Cambridge 1996.

51 Fisch, *Nicolaus Pol Doctor 1494*, 46.

52 We rely here on Arrizabalaga, Henderson and French, *The Great Pox*, chapters 7 and 8.

53 Arrizabalaga, Henderson and French, *The Great Pox*, 22. For information on special hospitals throughout southern Europe in this period, see the chapters in Ole Peter Grell, Andrew Cunningham and Jon Arrizabalaga, (eds.), *Health Care and Poor Relief in Counter-Reformation Europe*, London 1999.

54 Arrizabalaga, Henderson and French, *The Great Pox*, 155.

55 The basic authority on these is still Friedrich Prinzing, *Epidemics Resulting from Wars*, Oxford 1916, chapters 2 and 3. See also Ralph Major, *War and Disease*, London 1943. Neither work is very satisfactory.

56 Fracastorius, *De Contagione et Contagiosis Morbis et Eorum Curatione, Libri III*, trans. Wright, 103 (translation modified).

57 Tobias Corberus, *Observationum Medicarum Castrensium Hungaricarum Decades Tres. In Usum Publicum Hoc Tempore Recusae cum Indice et Praefatiione Henrici Meibomii*, Helmstadt 1685, 32, our translation.

58 See Hans Zinsser, *Rats, Lice and History. Being a Study in Biography, Which Deals with the Life History of Typhus Fever*, London 1935, 241–3.

59 I. F. C. Hecker, *The Epidemics of the Middle Ages. No. II, The Dancing Mania*, trans. B. G. Babington, London 1835, 229–34.

60 Zinsser, *Rats, Lice and History*, 159.

61 Marchmont Nedham, *Medela Medicinae. A Plea for the Free Profession, and a Renovation of the Art of Physick, out of the Noblest and most Authentick Writers. Shewing The Publick Advantage of its Liberty; The Disadvantage that comes to the Publick by any sort of Physicians, imposing upon the Studies and Practise of others; The Alteration of Diseases from their old State and Condition; The Causes of that Alteration; The Insufficiency and Uselessness of meer Scholastick Methods and Medicines, with a necessity of new. Tending to the Rescue of Mankind from the Tyranny of Diseases; and of Physicians themselves, from the Pedantism of old Authors and present Dictators. The Author, M.N. Med. Londinens*, London 1665, 162.

62 As quoted in Klaus Deppermann, *Melchior Hoffman. Social Unrest and Apocalyptic Visions in the Age of Reformation*, trans. Malcolm Wren, Edinburgh 1987, 326.

63 Medics have, however, continued to try and identify the sweating sickness with some modern disease. The latest candidates put forward have been an arbovirus (Christopher Dyer, 'English Diet in the Late Middle Ages', in T. H. Aston, P. R. Coss, Christopher Dyer and Joan Thirsk (eds.), *Social Relations and Ideas: Essays in Honour of R. H. Hilton*, Cambridge 1983, 191–216), and a 'viral infectious agent with a rodent reservoir' (Mark Taviner, Guy Thwaites and Vanya Gant, 'The English Sweating Sickness, 1485–1551: A Viral Pulmonary Disease?', *Medical History* 42, 1998, 96–8). The value of such retrospective diagnoses is extremely dubious; see Andrew Cunningham, 'Transforming Plague: The Laboratory and the Identity of Infectious Disease', in Andrew Cunningham and Perry Williams (eds.), *The Laboratory Revolution in Medicine*, Cambridge 1992, 209–44.

64 The edition and pagination we have used is John Caius, *A Boke or Counseill against the Disease commonly called the Sweate or Sweatyng Sicknesse Very Necessary for Everye Personne and much Requisite to be had in the Handes of al Sortes, for their Better Instruction, Preparation and Defence, against the Soubdein Comyng, and Fearful Assaultyng of the same Disease*, 1552, as reprinted in John Venn, *The Works of John Caius, M.D.*, Cambridge 1912; spelling and punctuation have been modernised.

65 *Holinshed's Chronicle of England, Scotland and Ireland*, 6 vols., London 1808, vol. III, 482, as cited in 'The

Sweating Sickness', in Hecker, *Epidemics*, pp. 181–350; quotation from p. 181 note c, spelling modernised.

66 'La peste s'évira chaque année en Europe, tantôt sur de vastes territoires, tantôt seulement dans quelques localités, mais sans sauter un seul maillon annuel de cette longue et douloureuse chaîne', Jean-Noël Biraben, *Les Hommes et la Peste en France et dans les Pays Européens et Méditerranéens*, 2 vols., Paris 1975, 1976, vol. 1, p. 105, our translation. The following paragraphs are highly dependent on this work, which includes a most extensive and valuable bibliography.

67 We are not concerned here whether all epidemics which were attributed to plague by contemporaries were the same disease, or whether they can be identified as the same as modern plague. 'Plague' probably covered a multitude of diseases.

68 Biraben, *Les Hommes et la Peste*, vol. 1, 125. Of these seventeen outbreaks, the next most severe ones across Europe occurred in 1502, 1506, 1545 and 1645, with the relatively lesser outbreaks in 1494, 1537, 1557 and 1592.

69 These figures are from Leo Noordegraaf and Gerrit Valk, *De Gave Gods: De Pest in Holland vanaf de late Middeleeuwen*, first published 1988, 2nd edition Amsterdam 1996, 231–4.

70 Paul Slack, *The Impact of Plague in Tudor and Stuart England*, London 1985, 64.

71 Slack, *The Impact of Plague*, 109–10.

72 Slack, *The Impact of Plague*, 145.

73 Ambroise Paré, *A Treatise of the Plague, contayning the causes, signes, symptoms, prognosticks, and cure thereof. Together with sundry other remarkable passages (for the prevention of, and preservation from the Pestilence) never yet published by anie man. Collected out of the Workes of the no lesse learned than experimented and renowned Chirurgian Ambrose Parey*, trans. Thomas Johnson, London 1630, 3. 'Epicures' are followers of the ancient Greek philosopher Epicurus, and the term means atheists; 'Lucianists' are followers of the Greek dialogue writer Lucian, and the term meant those who scoff at God and religion.

74 Martin Luther, 'Whether one may Flee from a Deadly Plague' (1527) in Gustav K. Wiencke (ed.), *Luther's Works Volume 43. Devotional Writings II*, 113–38. Philadelphia 1968, 113–38, see 116. This pamphlet was republished nineteen times, usually in times of pestilence.

75 Ibid., 123.

76 Ibid., 126, 127, 131.

77 Ibid., 132.

78 Theodore Beza, *A shorte learned and pithie Treatize of the Plague, wherin are handled these two questions: The one, whether the Plague be infectious, or no: The other, whether and howe farre it may of Christians be shunned by going aside. A discourse very necessary for this our tyme, and country; to satisfie the doubtful consciences of a great number: Written in Latin by the famous and worthy divine Theodore Beza Vezelian; and newly turned into English by John Stockwood, Schoolemaister of Tunbridge*, London 1580.

79 Henry Martyn Baird, *Theodore Beza, the Counsellor of the French Reformation, 1519–1605*, New York 1899, 332. On these issues in general, see Ole Peter Grell, 'Conflicting Duties: Plague and the Obligations of Early Modern Physicians Towards Patients and Commonwealth in England and the Netherlands', in Andrew Wear, Johanna Geyer-Kordesch and Roger French (eds.), *Doctors and Ethics: The Earlier Historical Settings of Professional Ethics*, Amsterdam 1993, 131–52.

80 See Leo Nordegraaf, 'Calvinism and the Plague in the Seventeenth Century Dutch Republic', in Hans Binneveld and Rudolf Dekker (eds.), *Curing and Insuring. Essays in Illness in Past Times*, Hilversum 1993, 21–31; and Alison Klairmont, 'The Problem of the Plague: New Challenges to Healing in Sixteenth-Century France', *Proceedings of the Annual Meeting of the Western Society for French History* 5, 1977, 119–27.

81 As quoted in Winfried Schliener, *The Imagery of John Donne's Sermons*, Providence, Rhode Island 1970, 72.

82 For London, see for instance that of 1604: *The King's Medicine for the Plague prescribed for the Year 1604, by the whole College of Physicians, both Spirituall and Temporall . . .*; other editions in 1630 and 1636.

83 Thomas Le Forestier, *Le Regime contre Epidemie*, Rouen 1495, our translation from the French original as reproduced in Arnold C. Klebs and E. Droz, *Remedies against the Plague. The Earliest French Tracts Printed in the Fifteenth Century. Facsimiles, Notes, and List of All the Incunabula on Plague*, Paris 1925, 47–8.

84 *Regime Contre la Pestilence faict et compose par Messieurs les medicins de la Cite de Basse en Allemaigne*, Lyons, 1519, as reproduced in Klebs and Droz, *Remedies against the Plague*, 49–50, our translation.

85 *Certaine Praiers Collected out of a Fourme of Godly Meditations, set forth by her Majesties authoritie in the great Mortalitie, in the fift yeere of her Highnesse raigne, and most necessarie to be used at this time in the like present visitation of Gods heavie hand four our manifold sinnes, and commended unto the Ministers and people of London, by the Reverend Father in God, John Bishop of London, July 1593*, London 1593, A2r–v.

86 John Squier (Squire), *A Thankesgiving, for the decreasing,*

and the hope of the removing of the Plague. Being a sermon preached at St Pauls in London, upon the 1 of January, 1636. by John Squier Priest, Vicar of St Leonards Shordich, sometime Fellow of Jesus Colledge in Cambridge, London 1637.

87 This information is taken from Ann Carmichael, *Plague and the Poor in Renaissance Florence*, Cambridge 1986. For the circumstances of plague in other Italian towns in this period, see the following works by Carlo M. Cipolla: *Cristofano and the Plague. A Study in the History of Public Health in the Age of Galileo*, London 1973; *Public Health and the Medical Profession in the Renaissance*, Cambridge 1976; *Faith, Reason and the Plague. A Tuscan Story of the Seventeenth Century*, trans. Muriel Kittel, Brighton 1979; *Fighting the Plague in Seventeenth Century Italy*, Wisconsin, Madison 1981; and Richard John Palmer, 'The Control of Plague in Venice and Northern Italy, 1348–1600', Ph.D. thesis, University of Kent at Canterbury, 1978.

88 Quoted from Del Badia, *A Florentine Diary*, transcribed by Alice Jarvis, New York 1927, by Carmichael, *Plague and the Poor in Renaissance Florence*, 106.

89 Quoted in R. Ridolfi, *The Life of Savonarola*, London 1959, 208. Savonarola also gave written advice to the city of Ferrara about what to do about plague. See Michele Savonarola, *I Trattati in Volgare della Peste e dell'Acqua Ardente*, ed. Luigi Belloni, Milan 1953. This ends with an invocation to 'the praise of God omnipotent, the glorious Virgin Mary, Saint Jerome, and the confessors James, Paul, Nicolas, Anthony of Padua and St Francis' (our translation from the Latin original).

90 Paul Slack, 'The Response to Plague in Early Modern England: Public Policies and their Consequences', in John Walter and Roger Schofield (eds.), *Famine, Disease and the Social Order in Early Modern Society*, Cambridge 1989, 167–87, see 168–71. See also Paul Slack's major book, *The Impact of Plague in Tudor and Stuart England*, London 1985, 20.

91 Fracastorius, *De Contagione et Contagiosis Morbis et Eorum Curatione, Libri III*, trans. Wright, Dedication. We follow Wright's translation, with modifications.

92 The information in this paragraph comes from Vivian Nutton, 'The Seeds of Disease. An Explanation of Contagion and Infection from the Greeks to the Renaissance', *Medical History* 27, 1983, 1–34.

93 See for instance the view of Jean Astruc, French medical teacher and practitioner, in 1737, which takes a Galenic position and opposes the Fracastorian one (though using the metaphor of 'seeds'): 'the *Venereal Disease in Europe* is propagated solely by Contagion. There are therefore convey'd from the diseas'd into the sound, certain seeds of morbifick matter, which being introduc'd into a sound body in the smallest quantity and by indiscernable ways, and by degrees increasing in bulk, form and efficacy, sooner or later are able to infect and corrupt the whole mass of humours. And these seeds of the Disease are usually and not improperly nam'd the *Venereal Ferment, Venom, or Poison*' (vol. 1, 145). 'The Venereal poison if left to itself by little and little corrodes, exulcerates, and feeds upon the parts, which it has once inflamed . . . There are some however, whom I care not now to spend time in confuting, that think the Venereal poison is nothing else but a numerous brood of little, nimble, brisk *animalcula*, of a very prolifick nature, which when once admitted increase and multiply in abundance; which lead frequent colonies to different parts of the Body; and inflame, erode, and exulcerate the parts they seize on by vellicating, stinging and biting 'em; in short, which, without any regard had to the energy of any humour, occasion all the symptoms, which occur in the *Venereal Disease*. But as these are mere visionary imaginations, unsupported by any authority, they do not stand in need of any argument to set 'em aside.' Astruc, *A Treatise of the Venereal Disease*, vol. 1, 145, 146, 149.

94 Lloyd G. Stevenson, ' "New Diseases" in the Seventeenth Century', *Bulletin of the History of Medicine* 39, 1965, 1–21.

95 Susan Sontag, *Illness as Metaphor*, New York 1978.

96 Susan Sontag, *Aids as Metaphor*, London 1988.

97 On this see Cunningham, 'Transforming Plague'.

98 A recent example of this genre which deals with our period is Edward A. Eckart, *The Structure of Plagues and Pestilences in Early Modern Europe. Central Europe, 1560–1640*, Basle 1996. While going beyond the usual form of studying of individual episodes of plague in the past, Eckart's book nevertheless has plague and its career as its subject-matter: it is a form of biography of a disease, in which mankind is helpless against the machinations of the disease.

99 For instance: 'In the centuries-long struggle between the parasites, causing these diseases, and their human hosts, man was too often the loser . . . In the centuries before the 1850s, the microbes . . . really had the advantage, progressively determining the fate of armies, monarchies, cities, family-life and, as it turned out, even life-expectancy itself . . . For nearly five hundred years before this pivotal [nineteenth] century, harmful pathogens had been dampening

down Europe's population growth . . .', Vincent J. Knapp, *Disease and its Impact on Modern European History,* Lampeter 1989, 5, 7.

100 I. F. C. Hecker, *The Black Death in the Fourteenth Century,* trans. B. G. Babington, London 1833; Heinrich Haeser, *Historisch-pathologische Untersuchungen. Als Beiträge zur Geschichte der Volkskrankheit,* Dresden 1839; August Hirsch, *Handbook of Geographical and Historical Pathology,* trans. Charles Creighton from the second German edition, 3 vols., London 1883–6. For an earlier argument that all epidemics come from extraordinary climatic and cosmic events, see Noah Webster, *A Brief History of Epidemic or Pestilential Diseases,* 2 vols., Hartford, Connecticut 1799.

101 Hirsch, *Handbook of Geographical and Historical Pathology,* vol. I, 1.

102 Roger Schofield, '"Crisis" mortality', In Michael Drake (ed.) *Population Studies from Parish Registers. A Selection of Readings from 'Local Population Studies',* Matlock, Derbyshire 1982, 97–10; E. A. Wrigley and R. S. Schofield, *The Population History of England, 1541–1871. A Reconstruction,* London 1981; Paul Slack, 'Mortality Crises and Epidemic Disease in England, 1485–1610', in Charles Webster (ed.) *Health, Medicine and Mortality in the Sixteenth Century,* Cambridge 1979, 9–59. Wrigley and Schofield, 332, say that 'Any discussion of crisis mortality entails an arbitrary decision as to what constitutes a crisis'.

103 Arno Karlen, *Plague's Progress. A Social History of Man and Disease,* London 1995, 10–11.

104 Alfred W. Crosby, *The Columbian Exchange: Biological and Cultural Consequences of 1492,* Westport, Connecticut 1972; Alfred W. Crosby, *Ecological Imperialism. The Biological Expansion of Europe, 900–1900,* Cambridge 1986; Philip Curtin, 'Disease Exchange Across the Tropical Atlantic', *Pubblicazioni della Stazione Zoologica di Napoli* 15, 1992, 329–56; Kenneth F. Kiple, 'The Ecology of Disease', In W. F. Bynum and Roy Porter (eds.), *Companion Encyclopedia of the History of Medicine,* London 1993; William H. McNeill, *Plagues and Peoples,* Oxford 1977; William H. McNeill, *The Human Condition. An Ecological and Historical View,* Princeton, New Jersey 1980; Thomas McKeown, *The Origins of Human Disease,* Oxford 1988. These historians of disease also claim that communities acquire a 'natural immunity' to particular epidemic diseases. This, they claim, is what leads to the stabilising of epidemic disease – enabling societies to live at peace with their microbes – and thus explains the big initial impact of new epidemics in a 'virgin soil' and the

much lesser impact thereafter, unless a germ of new virulence is brought in afresh.

105 Marcel Sendrail wrote: 'Each civilization, by its customs, its laws, its principles of thought, creates for itself a pathology appropriate to itself . . . a society chooses its diseases, shapes its pathological destiny'. See Marcel Sendrail, *Le Serpent et le Miroir,* Paris 1954, chapter 10, 'Civilisations et Styles Pathologiques', 211–37, see 212, our translation. See also his *L' Histoire Culturelle de la Maladie,* Toulouse 1980.

106 These are the primary meanings in this period as recorded by the *Oxford English Dictionary.*

107 See Tullio Gregory, 'Temps Astrologique et Temps Chrétien', in *Le Temps Chrétien de la Fin de l'Antiquité au Moyen âge III–XIII Siècles,* Paris 1984.

108 Nemesius (fourth century AD Neoplatonist), quoted in John D. North, 'Astrology and the Fortunes of Churches', *Centaurus* 24, 1980, 181–211, see 188.

109 Ibid., 185 et seqq.

110 Robert E. Lerner, 'The Black Death and Western European Eschatological Mentalities', *American Historical Review* 86, 1981, 533–52.

111 See Lynn Thorndike, *A History of Magic and Experimental Science: Volumes III and IV, Fourteenth and Fifteenth Centuries,* New York 1934, vol. V, 163–4.

112 For one kind, see Michael MacDonald, *Mystical Bedlam. Madness, Anxiety, and Healing in Seventeenth-Century England,* Cambridge 1981.

113 On Lilly see Ann Geneva, *Astrology and the Seventeenth Century Mind. William Lilly and the Language of the Stars,* Manchester 1995.

114 See Walter Pagel, *Paracelsus. An Introduction to Philosophical Medicine in the Era of the Renaissance,* Basle 1982; for some of the texts of Paracelsus, see Arthur Edward Waite (ed.), *The Hermetic and Alchemical Writings of Aureolus Philippus Theophrastus Bombast, of Hohenheim, called Paracelsus the Great, Now for the First Time Faithfully Translated into English,* 2 vols., London 1894. For other recent studies, see Ole Peter Grell (ed.), *Paracelsus. The Man and his Reputation. His Ideas and their Transformation,* Leiden 1998.

115 Charles Webster, 'Paracelsus: Medicine as Popular Protest', in Ole Peter Grell and Andrew Cunningham (eds.), *Medicine and the Reformation,* London 1993, 57–77, see 69.

116 Webster, 'Paracelsus: Medicine as Popular Protest', 61.

117 According to Max Fisch, in many passages of his works Paracelsus 'links the Fuggers with Lang and his mission. He repeatedly inveighs against the doctors for taking refuge under the Cardinal's hat and for running to the Fuggers' store to help them unload

their wood. "The spiritual and worldly traders (odd as
it is to make wood an article of trade) have brought
you doctors a wood and you have taken your medical
theory and practice from them". "The red hat and the
Fuggers' wagons have brought the wood but not its
virtue". "Didn't you learn anything at school, that you
must now learn your art from the Fuggers and let the
Cardinal play the schoolmaster to you?".' See Fisch,
Nicolaus Pol Doctor 1494, 46, citing Sudhoff's edition of
Paracelsus's *Works*, vols. VI, 312, 327, 420, and VII,
418.

118 Russell, 'Syphilis: God's Scourge or Nature's
Vengeance?', 301.

119 Cited from Van Helmont (1648), by Stevenson, '"New
Diseases" in the Seventeenth Century', 4.

120 Emile Mâle, 'L'Art Français de la Fin du Moyen Age.
L'Idée de la Mort et la Danse Macabre', *Revue des Deux-
Mondes* 32, 1906, 647–79, 649, 650, our translation.
Generally on the topic of attitudes to death see
Philippe Ariès, *Western Attitudes toward Death from the
Middle Ages to the Present*, trans. Patricia M. Ranum,
London 1976; this is amplified in his *The Hour of our
Death*, trans. Helen Weaver, New York 1981; and also
his *Images of Man and Death*, trans. Janet Lloyd, Harvard
1985.

121 See Sister Mary Catherine O'Connor, *The Art of Dying
Well: The Ars Moriendi*, New York 1942, and N. L. Beaty,
*The Craft of Dying. A Study in the Literary Tradition of the
Ars Moriendi in England*, New Haven 1970, chapter 1.
For a Catalan version of 1493 by D. Pedro Bohigas see
*Art de be Morir. Edición catalana, 1493 (?). Edición facsimil
con la traducción al castellano moderna*, Barcelona 1951,
and for a Danish one of 1510 see Poul Lindegård
Hjorth, ed., *Sjaelens og Kroppens Traette og Ars Moriendi.
Med Faksimileudgave af Ghemen-trykket*, Copenhagen
1971.

122 See Roger Chartier, 'Texts and Images. The Arts of

Dying, 1450–1600', in his *The Cultural Uses of Print in
Early Modern France*, Princeton, New Jersey 1987,
32–70.

123 Caxton, 'The Arte and Crafte to Know Well to Dye',
reprinted in David Wiliam Atkinson (ed.), *The English
Ars Moriendi*, New York 1992, 21–35, see 21 (spelling
modernised by us). Atkinson reprints fourteen
English versions in this book, dating from 1490 to
1689.

124 Chartier, 'Texts and Images. The Arts of Dying,
1450–1600', 68.

125 Roy Strong, *The English Icon*, London 1969, 37–41; as
cited in William Schupbach, *The Paradox of Rembrandt's
'Anatomy of Dr Tulp'*, London 1982, 42.

126 For a listing of the chief examples of paintings and
sculptures on the theme, see Appendix A to James M.
Clark, *The Dance of Death in the Middle Ages and the
Renaissance*, Glasgow 1950, 23. Clark is our main
source for our information on the Dance of Death.
For the English tradition see Florence Warren (ed.),
The Dance of Death. Edited from MSS. *Ellesmere 26/A.13 and
B.M. Lansdowne 699, Collated with the Other Extant* MSS.,
London 1931. For the Spanish tradition see Anónimo,
*Dança general de la muerte (siglo XV–1520). Edición y Nota
de Victor Infantes*, Madrid 1982.

127 François Villon, in his *Testament*, written from 1461, as
quoted and translated in Clark, *The Dance of Death*.

128 Mâle, 'L'Art Français de la Fin du Moyen Age. L'Idée de
la Mort et la Danse Macabre', 661–2.

129 *Miroer salutaire pour toutes gens: Et de tous estatz. Et est de
grant utilite: et recreacion, pour pleuseurs ensengnemens tant
en latin comme en francoys lesquelx il contient. Ainsi compose
pour ceulx qui desirent ac querir leur salut: et qui le voudront
avoir*, Paris 1486.

130 See Hans Holbein, *The Dance of Death. 41 Woodcuts by
Hans Holbein the Younger. Complete Facsimile of the Original
1538 French Edition*, New York 1538.

6 EPILOGUE

1 See B. Scribner, '1525 – Revolutionary Crisis?', in M.
Hagenmaier and S. Holtz (eds.), *Krisenbewusstsein und
Krisenbewältigung in der Frühen Neuzeit – Crisis in Early
Modern Europe*, Bern 1992, 25–45.

2 Peter Palladius's introduction to his Danish edition
(1556) of Andreas Musculus, *About the Stocking Devil*
(1555) in Peter Palladius, *Danske Skrifter*, vol. IV,
Copenhagen 1919–22, 48–50.

3 Michael W. Flinn, *The European Demographic System,
1500–1820*, Brighton 1981, 76–80. See also Stephen J.

Kunitz, 'Diseases and the European Mortality
Decline, 1700–1900', in Kenneth F. Kiple (ed.) *The
Cambridge World History of Human Disease*, Cambridge
1993, 287–93.

4 Flinn, *The European Demographic System*, 63.

5 H. Schilling, 'Confessionalisation in Europe: Causes
and Effects for Church, State, Society, and Culture', in
K. Bussmann and H. Schilling (eds.), *1648. War and
Peace in Europe, I. Politics, Religion, Law and Society*,
Münster 1999, 219-28, especially 223-4.

Index